Purchasing and Supply Management

D1612762

Chapman & Hall
Materials Management/Logistics Series
Eugene L. Magad, Series Editor
William Rainey Harper College

Total Materials Management: Achieving Maximum Profits through Materials/Logistics Operations, Second Edition by Eugene L. Magad and John M. Amos

International Logistics, by Donald Wood, Anthony Barone, Paul Murphy and Daniel Wardlow

Global Purchasing: Reaching for the World, by Victor Pooler

MRP II, by John W. Toomey

Distribution: Planning and Control, by David F. Ross

Purchasing and Supply Management: Creating the Vision, by Victor Pooler and David Pooler

Competing through Supply Chain Management by David F. Ross

Purchasing and Supply Management

Creating the Vision

Victor H. Pooler, C.P.M., P.E.,
President, Pooler & Associates,
DeWitt, NY

David J. Pooler
Vice President,
Global Business Development for Tachtech, Inc,
Yorba Linda, CA

CHAPMAN & HALL

I(T)P® International Thomson Publishing
New York • Albany • Bonn • Boston • Cincinnati • Detroit • London • Madrid • Melbourne
Mexico City • Pacific Grove • Paris • San Francisco • Singapore • Tokyo • Toronto • Washington

JOIN US ON THE INTERNET   WWW: http://www.thomson.com
EMAIL: findit@kiosk.thomson.com

thomson.com is the on-line portal for the products, services and resources available from International Thomson Publishing (ITP).

This Internet kiosk gives users immediate access to more than 34 ITP publishers and over 20,000 products. Through *thomson.com* Internet users can search catalogs, examine subject-specific resource centers and subscribe to electronic discussion lists. You can purchase ITP products from your local bookseller, or directly through *thomson.com*.

Visit Chapman & Hall's Internet Resource Center for information on our new publications, links to useful sites on the World Wide Web and an opportunity to join our e-mail mailing list. Point your browser to: **http://www.chaphall.com**

A service of   I(T)P®

Cover Design: Saïd Sayrafiezadeh, *Emdash, Inc.*

Copyright © 1997 by Chapman & Hall

Printed in the United States of America

For more information, contact:

Chapman & Hall
115 Fifth Avenue
New York, NY 10003

Chapman & Hall
2-6 Boundary Row
London SE1 8HN
England

Thomas Nelson Australia
102 Dodds Street
South Melbourne, 3205
Victoria, Australia

Chapman & Hall GmbH
Postfach 100 263
D-69442 Weinheim
Germany

International Thomson Editores
Campos Eliseos 385, Piso 7
Col. Polanco
11560 Mexico D.F.
Mexico

International Thomson Publishing-Japan
Hirakawacho-cho Kyowa Building, 3F
1-2-1 Hirakawacho-cho
Chiyoda-ku, 102 Tokyo
Japan

International Thomson Publishing Asia
221 Henderson Road #05-10
Henderson Building
Singapore 0315

All rights reserved. No part of this work covered by the copyright hereon may be reproduced or used in any form or by any means—graphic, electronic, or mechanical, including photocopying, recording, taping, or information storage and retrieval systems—without the written permission of the publisher.

1 2 3 4 5 6 7 8 9 10 XXX 01 00 99 98 97

Library of Congress Cataloging-in-Publication Data

Pooler, Victor H.
    Purchasing and supply management : creating the vision / by Victor H. Pooler and David J. Pooler.
        p.   cm.
    Includes bibliographical references and index.
    ISBN 0-412-10601-9 (alk. paper)
    1. Industrial procurement—Management. 2. Materials management. 3. Business logistics. I. Pooler, David J.   II. Title.
HD39.5.P659 1997
658.7'2—dc21   96-46666
                                                    CIP

British Library Cataloguing in Publication Data available

LEEDS METROPOLITAN
UNIVERSITY LIBRARY
1701757639
70-KU
607211 31797
2.10 97
658.72 POO

To order this or any other Chapman & Hall book, please contact **International Thomson Publishing, 7625 Empire Drive, Florence, KY 41042.** Phone: (606) 525-6600 or 1-800-842-3636. Fax: (606) 525-7778, e-mail: order@chaphall.com.

For a complete listing of Chapman & Hall's titles, send your requests to **Chapman & Hall, Dept. BC, 115 Fifth Avenue, New York, NY 10003.**

This book is dedicated to Michael, Amanda, Christian, Danielle, and Richard Pooler

Contents

Preface

This book is unique! Until now, purchasing and materials management books have had a primarily domestic outlook. This book has global vision tied into management principles based on an understanding of the basic job of purchasing and supply management, as both authors have held high level positions directing the effort.

This book is also unique because management philosophy, ideas, and opinions are expressed in an attempt to reengineer and shape a progressive vision of the purchasing and supply management concepts. *Purchasing and Supply Management: Creating the Vision!* will be of interest to professional managers and buyers charged with the responsibility of integrating outside supply with a company's needs. It is the only management book that the newly appointed manager from another business function can read that applies to the disciplines of purchasing and supply.

Practitioners can use this book as a buyer's handbook—a reference and "How-to" manual. On the job, the book's outline allows easy access to specific topics. Because it is written for the professional by practitioners, all students of purchasing will find meaty material from this technically detailed text. Some educators have called for such a book from which teachers can gain experience and material to teach their students. This book fills that need as well, and can be used as a textbook for colleges that offer purchasing and supply management subjects in a business curriculum.

Much survey data were collected from seminars conducted by Pooler and Associates for numerous corporations, including the following:

World Trade Institute at the World Trade Center

National Association of Purchasing Management

American Management Association

The American Supply Education Foundation

As with any major undertaking, success can be achieved only with much coordinated collaboration to create a comprehensive and quality result. This book is no exception, as a number of individuals were especially helpful and supportive in the completion of this work.

The authors acknowledge Professor Eugene L. Magad of William Rainey Harper College who persistently encouraged the writing of this book. It is part of the publisher's *Materials Management/Logistics* series that he has developed as the Series Editor. Professor Magad is an author, teacher, and consultant with wide experience.

The authors also acknowledge the efforts and enthusiastic support of the following who served as an authoritative body of experts to review this work:

Samuel Farney, Senior Manager of Corporate Purchasing, United Technologies Corporation, Corporate Purchasing. He was the publisher's official reviewer, and has been in charge of Career Development and Training, and participated in many NAPM activities. Sam was especially helpful in the management and measurement areas because of his experience in purchasing engineering and purchasing techniques.

John Burlew, President, Hemstreet Tool & Die Co., Syracuse, NY. Mr. Burlew is a pioneer in the application of engineering techniques to purchasing. He has held positions as Commodity Purchasing Manager, Planning Manager, Material Control Manager, Materials Manager, Director of Quality Assurance, and Corporate Director of Productivity and Advanced Manufacturing Process. John has lectured with Pooler & Associates in seminars about purchasing engineering and quality.

Thanks to Allen Elliott of Carlyle Compressor Company, Division of Carrier Corporation, Syracuse, NY, for his insightful and helpful charting and critiques for Chapter 8. Al, a Quality Control Manager, teaches quality courses, and helped assure the quality issues are well and accurately covered. He created the innovative statistical process control and bell curve charts in cooperation with the authors.

Steven M. Pooler, Business Unit Manager, former Supervisor of Operations Planning and Procurement, and former Manager of Production Scheduling, and Manager of Manufacturing, Crouse Hinds Division of Cooper Industries, Syracuse, NY. A strong supporter of the buyer/planner concept, Steve is well versed in both the positive aspects as well as the shortcomings of controlling inventory. He largely shaped Chapter 9 about modern inventory management thinking. Furthermore, the authors thank him for his insightful suggestion for the subtitle of this book—"Creating the Vision!"

Tomas R. Serrano of ATServices, as with our past works, has transformed our sketches into fine graphics. Herbert P. Mehlhorn, who specializes in researching data, secured accurate updated statistical information on GDP and trade data that was provided by DRI/McGraw-Hill.

All the above generously gave of their talents to make this book what it is. While we've used many, though not all, of their suggestions, the authors are solely responsible for the material.

We believe this book will speak for itself. Hopefully, you will agree with several reviewers' comments that this is the most advanced, technically detailed, management book about purchasing and supply management written to date!

Purchasing and Supply Management

1

The Role of the Purchasing and Supply Functions

Purchasing is indeed an unusual and multifaceted job. It operates at the vital intersection between buyer and seller, where supply and demand forces meet. As such, its scope is broad, encompassing both internal and external elements of supply interaction.

Purchasing is an exciting and challenging profession that is evolving rapidly. In small and newer businesses, historically the owners have almost always controlled the buying activity to keep control of the company's vital cash flow. As the businesses grew, one of the last duties that was delegated was buying— precisely because of its importance to the company's success. Delegation has accordingly become a necessary and inevitable result as management functions become more complex with positive business growth. With increasing size, it becomes necessary to have someone pick up this responsibility.

The terminology used in the purchasing profession has witnessed a similar evolution. The term *buyer* has taken on a generic connotation today, but in fact many types of buyers exist. For example, a buyer can be a wholesaler, a contractor or distribution buyer, an industrial buyer, a technical buyer, a commodity specialist for metals or electronics, and so on. Whether purchases are solely for individuals, for a small family operation, or for a large corporation, the underlying principles are the same. However, while the buying process can be viewed as quite simple from a perfunctory "paperwork" standpoint, quite the opposite is true with respect to the complexities of controlling the expenditure process itself. We will explore both of these aspects in detail in this book.

Another term that has undergone some revision is *vendor*. While some conjure up images of "vendors" tossing peanuts in the ballpark, others are quite comfortable in retaining the term. Some prefer the term *supplier*. Although the words *vendor* and *supplier* are essentially synonymous, in this book the word *supplier* is used more often, in keeping with the supply management theme. Also, the terms "purchasing" and "procurement" have become essentially synonomous in the profession, so these terms are used interchangeably in this book. In addition, we have generally denoted the person who heads up the purchasing department as the purchasing manager (PM) while the chief procurement officer (CPO) designates the top level executive.

Irrespective of the terminology used, it takes a seller and a buyer to reach an agreement. It has been said that "Nothing happens until someone makes a sale." So true! But, consider that "No sale was ever made until a buying *decision* was reached!" Many top sales managers have repeatedly stressed, "Know your customers and *how* they buy!" Going further, Peter Drucker, noted management spokesperson, has said, "The key to efficient and effective industrial marketing is not the supplier but the buyer."[1]

The job of purchasing continues to receive increased recognition as a vital management function. Profit, basically the difference between a company's income and outgo, is obviously dependent on either of these factors. Although traditionally more emphasis has been given to the incoming money, that is changing as markets have saturated or become global. Because competitive conditions make it difficult to increase prices automatically to cover costs, management interest has focused increasingly on the cost aspect. Since purchases represent the largest single element of cost to a company (typically between 50% and 60% of incoming sales dollars), this is where more attention and effort will be directed.

In addition to the above, a number of historic factors have created renewed interest in purchasing and supply management. Purchasing evolved from a part of manufacturing or management, and gained its independence as an expanded financial contributor to a company's success. Progressive CEOs and owners of businesses came to realize that management of the supply base is critical. To manage supply, the manager and buyers must know and use the full range of techniques and procedures available to the true professional.

Among the historic factors that generated awakened interest in purchasing and supply management are the following:

- World War II, and the postwar booms that brought serious material shortages, government requirements, and priorities

- The cyclical swings of surpluses and shortages, with attendant fast-rising material costs

- The continual "profit-squeeze" necessitating use of the full resources of the company to ensure survival

- The brutal foreign competition encountered by U.S. products, and trade alliances such as NAFTA and ECC

---

[1] Peter F. Drucker, "The Economy's Dark Continent," *Fortune Magazine,* April, 1962, p. 265.

- The increased complexity of newer technologically driven products, of which computers are the most notable example
- The emergence of truly global markets, with reduced tariffs and a freer flow of components between foreign and domestic companies
- Growth of government oversight and control with respect to company procedures and reporting in areas such as minority subcontracting, environmental issues, and various other sociological demands
- Evolution of a business philosophy of manufacturing only "core" requirements, and buying virtually all else

Although all of the above factors have played a part in purchasing's becoming a key area of management focus, probably the most significant issue relates to the last of these, that is, the effect on purchasing of the recent trend of much of corporate America to "downsize" (or as some prefer to say, "rightsize") as a means to reengineer the organization to improve competitive position.

This effect can be viewed from two perspectives. First, consider that an organization that cuts its manpower usually suffers some reduction in workload capacity—unless, of course, the reduction is based on the achievement of a breakthrough that entirely removed the need for the human resources affected by the reduction. As the reduction is made, purchasing is often called upon to buy certain goods and/or services that were previously manufactured or performed in-house. Examples include:

- Payroll and benefits
- Cafeteria and food services
- Certain manufacturing functions
- Facilities maintenance and janitorial services
- Customer and field service and repair
- Information technologies

In this case, increased outsourcing has put additional demands on the purchasing function. However, sometimes the paradoxical result has been a net reduction in overall procurement activity. As an example, let's consider the decision to henceforth outsource the cafeteria operations to a third-party vendor. Now the cafeteria services supplier buys the plates, the silverware, the mustard, and the coffee! So the single (albeit relatively more complex) procurement award to the new supplier has eliminated perhaps hundreds of tedious procurement requirements from the buyer's direct responsibility.

Purchasing Objectives

For any function to be successful, it must establish clear measurable objectives and work diligently to achieve them. Purchasing, as the caretaker of the largest share of the company's revenue inflow, is no exception. To maximize its contribution to the company's overall performance, purchasing must establish the following two overarching objectives:

1. To ensure economic supply by the procurement of goods, supplies, and services to keep the company in operation
2. To contribute to profits by efficiently controlling the flow of money passing through the operation

While many business people think of the first function only, it is through the smart handling of point 2 (after point 1 is assured) that defines the difference between an average and a world-class purchasing organization.

In addition to the above general goals, some specific purchasing objectives include:

- To get the *best* buy—suitable quality at minimum cost
- To pay reasonably low prices, negotiating and executing all company commitments
- To develop satisfactory sources of supply and maintain good relation ships with them
- To secure optimal supplier performance
- To locate new and better materials and products
- To keep inventories as low as is consistent with company needs
- To carry out programs to continually reduce costs of purchases
- To develop effective controls and procedures
- To keep acquisition costs at the minimum compatible with optimal performance

This list is far from all-inclusive; other objectives will become evident to the alert purchasing manager based on the specific nature of the procurement activity involved. Furthermore, although the above list is largely conceptual, it is important in practice that specific objectives be quantified to the maximum practical extent.

A company will have stated objectives, but the individual manager must interpret what company officials actually say and do. For example, chief executive officers (CEOs), backed by the law of the land, will usually stress their responsibility to the stockholders. But the company's objectives are usually composites of many decisions, resulting in various cross-functional compromises. So in actual practice the CEO's goal is to balance the objectives of a fair return on investment to stockholders, stable and satisfying employment for employees, satisfaction of customers and the community, and so forth. In setting its functional objectives, the PM must be aware of the CEO's (and accordingly, the company's) objectives, and ensure consistency in developing the specific objectives for the purchasing department.

Impact on Profitability

It is clear that since purchasing is responsible for controlling a dominant share of the company's revenue dollars, it directly impacts profitability and the financial success of the overall business enterprise. As a buyer, simply maintaining adequate sources of supply is not enough. Making sure that suppliers are the "right" suppliers, selling at the "right" price—and then seeing that they keep serving well—are important activities.

Let's look at purchasing's impact on profitability. The purchasing profit ratio shown in Figure 1-1 is based on an average company with a 7% profit before tax. A $1 reduction in the cost of purchased goods produces a profit of $1, or a 1-to-1 ratio, whereas it takes $14 of sales to produce the same amount! A dollar saved in purchasing equals the profit from $14 of sales: so, the profit leverage of the material cost reduction dollar is 14 times that of the sales dollar. The purchasing profit ratio can be computed for any company by dividing its annual sales volume by profit before tax.

Purchasing claims to be a profit-producing profession. Fine! But, where's the profit? As an example, an $8 broom is bought for $7.00. A dollar is saved. We can agree on that, but where does that saved dollar show up? It's not itemized on the profit and loss statement, balance sheet, or "where-got–where-gone" cash flow comparison. Unfortunately, traditional accounting systems don't take into account purchasing's contribution.

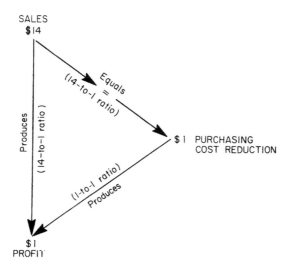

Figure 1-1   Purchasing profit ratio.

So where is the dollar savings? We know the savings for buying brooms has to be in the using department's budget! However, the issue isn't solely about buying brooms. As of 1995, the gross domestic product (GDP) for the U.S. was $7.418 trillion. In 1997, the collective spending of about $4 trillion by American buyers means that during any working day over $16 billion will be spent throughout the U.S! But, "How well will that money be spent?" is the question.

Let's look at purchasing's impact on profit in further detail. The profit ratio shown in Figure 1-2 depicts a typical performance for a healthy $20 million sales company. Purchases, in this case 53% of sales, are equal to $10.6 million, and are part of company costs. The figures within the boxes are company results without purchasing's contribution. Starting at the lower right box, a 2½% savings reduces purchases to $10.3 million, which causes a chain reaction all the way back; first, by reducing total cost that increases profit, and of course, profit margin, and ultimately return-on-investment (ROI).

The return on invested capital for the company has increased from 10.5 to 13.6, which is a 28% improvement because of purchasing profit contributions. Also, lower material prices will reduce inventory value, or assets. So, the final result is a higher investment turnover than shown. This is a measure of purchasing's effect on the total company results. Such results are of significant interest to the management of successful companies.

Here is an interesting exercise. To prove the strong impact of good or bad buying on any specific company, fill in a blank ROI chart using the company's performance as stated in its annual report. In the case of smaller or privately held companies, estimate as best you can. Then simply add 2% (or a figure you judge appropriate) to the cost of purchases and change the original numbers. Also, drop the purchases by 2% and watch those changes. A 2% change in

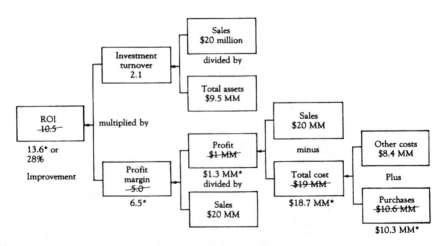

Figure 1-2   ROI productivity impact.

purchasing expenditures swings the return on invested capital dramatically! This is a clear example of purchasing's leverage on profitability.

Although the impact of purchasing on a company's profit is great, it is not easily achieved! It takes a skillful team of buyers under a competent manager who understands scientific purchasing techniques and methods. In marginal companies, the difference between operating at a profit or a loss may lie in the efficiency of the purchasing function.

If this purchasing function can make money, it can also lose money by poor performance that can reduce profits; so, purchasing is an heir to a profit-producing responsibility. The purchasing manager is key in the ability to influence company profit and thereby affect ROI.

Controlling the Process

Procurement is a process with many components that can influence the result. Figure 1-3 shows the typical procurement process. It is doubtful that any other operating group is involved in more functional interrelationships than is purchasing, not only within its own company but also within the suppliers' organizations.

Materials disputes must often be settled between requesting departments and suppliers. Rejected purchases must be adjusted, costs controlled, and replacements made. Many operating functions often represent a very narrow interest to the supplier. If purchasing is to settle disputes wisely, it must find a common ground for settlement; then it must balance the interest of its own company with that of the supplier, to protect long-range material availability and service.[2]

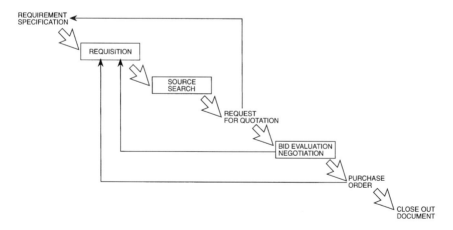

Figure 1-3   The procurement process.

[2]Victor H. Pooler and David J. Pooler, "Purchasing's Elusive Conceptual Home," *Journal of Purchasing and Materials Management,* Summer 1981, pp. 13–18.

To operate effectively, the purchasing executive must become a coordinator representing total company interests, and not solely those of purchasing. Often the buyer must be the arbitrator between the supplier's engineers and the buyer's own technical people. Sometimes under fire from many conflicting sources, buyers must get the most value in goods purchased at minimum cost. At the same time, the manager and buyers must keep inventories low to maintain or achieve high turnover ratios, yet always have material ready for production use. It takes a balancing of these often conflicting requirements to achieve optimum performance.

A matrix that breaks down the functions and relationships is given in Table 1-1, showing who is responsible and who is a contributor in any given buying situation.

The Buying Job

Some say, "Anyone can buy!" Sure they can, provided they know: *where* to get goods; *how* and *why* the things they buy are used in their own company; *how* to judge value, get along with people, and *how* to control and follow through on purchases. Further, they must be willing and able to use available purchasing techniques.

Today's purchasing chief must be one of the most knowledgeable managers in the company. Unless the CPO understands the design, engineering, manufacturing, marketing, and related functions in sufficient detail, the buyers can't possibly do their jobs effectively.

Purchasing managers often see themselves as managers of materials and expenditures. But how do others see them? Professor Renato Tagiuri at the Harvard Graduate School of Business analyzed the role of a purchasing manager, comparing it to that of a production manager. The production manager works within the center of the sphere defined as manufacturing. The purchasing man or woman is at the border of this production sphere, but also on the border of a sphere of many suppliers. The PM is in "conflict between two worlds!" It takes a high degree of statesmanship to operate in such an environment.

While progressive managements today accept purchasing as a vital management function, there is still little understanding of purchasing's role among many non-purchasing executives. One reason has been the inability of those in purchasing to clearly explain their own roles.

What about the buying job itself? We need a bigger vision or "mental picture." The buying job is indeed unusual and one of the least understood in industry. Because conflicts and disputes have to be settled with suppliers and contractors, friction is often an aspect of this job.

It is easy for any buyer to let details drift and become a "paper pusher," but he or she will not survive in a highly competitive organization. Two buyers may be given identical purchase requisitions for $1 million dollars. One might buy the

Table 1-1   Supplier purchasing interface matrix

Function/department	Plant purch.	Central purch.	Matrl. contr.	Qual. contr.	Engr.	Mktg.	Mgmt.	Mfg. engr.	Mfg.
1. Specification	C/R	R/C		C	R	C		C	
* 2. Source search—critical/routine	C	R			C	C			
* 3. Source selection study	R	C	C	C	C			C	
* 4. Supplier survey		C	C	C	C			C	C
* 5. Component qualification				C	R			C	C
6. Release specs.				C	R				
7. Establish production req.			R			C			C
* 8. Select sources	R or C	R or C	R	C	C				
* 9. Negotiate final unit prices	R	C							
*10. Negotiate PED** (if applicable)	C	R							
*11. Issue blanket P.O.	R		C						
*12. Establish split of business	R	C	C	C	C				
*13. Exp. delivery—routine/special	C/R	R/C	R/C						
14. Inspect				R	C			C	
*15. Process rejected materials	R		C	C	C			C	C
*16. Review invoice exceptions	R		C					C	
*17. Set standard and LIFO cost	R/C	R/C							
*18. Resolve quality problems	R	C		C	C	C	C	C	C
*19. Supplier stock programs	R	C	C		C				C
*20. Strike protection	R	C	C				C		R
*21. Initiate cost savings	R	C	C	C	C				
22. Allot short material	C	R or C	C						
*23. Obsolescence (disposal)	R or C	C	R or C	C	C		C	C	R
*24. Pool buying strategy	C	R	C						C
*25. Interface with engineering	R or C	R or C	C	C	C			C	
*26. Procurement planning	C	R	C	C	C		C	C	
*27. Make versus buy	C	C	C	C	C	C	C	C	R

*Primary responsibility of purchasing function.

**Purchase earned discounts for high-volume pooled buys.

R, responsible; C, contributes.

desired goods without sacrifice in quality for $950,000, and the other might spend the full $1 million. Strangely, the first buyer may not be as well liked as the second, who is a real "good Joe." In the office, "Joe" will seldom question a requirement, and will buy it. Standardization to save money is of little importance. Which of these two, from a buying viewpoint, is doing the better job for his employer?

Buyers must often raise questions about a purchase. Why is a "special" needed? How about a different, standardized, and more readily available model? The ideal situation would be if the buyer who can buy for less also has good interpersonal skills.

The Accountability Concept

In many specific purchases, the buyer must control and coordinate two or more requirements dictated by other functions such as engineering, quality control, and manufacturing. Yet, in no instance does the buyer have any direct authority over a single one of the people or other departments involved! Numerous other jobs require coordination, but they usually have more direct authority.

"If only the boss would give me the authority, I'd sure straighten out this mess. I won't be responsible unless I'm given complete authority to control this buy." What buyer or manager hasn't heard such a statement about occasional job frustrations? In the past, authority and responsibility supposedly went hand in hand. That seems a reasonable assertion—no authority, no responsibility— but it is a management myth that "dies hard." Who in any company has all the authority he or she needs? It may be more accurate to say that almost no one has enough authority to control completely any facet of the business. How many times do presidents state what they want done, yet it doesn't seem to happen?

The threat of being fired or losing a job is a business reality, yet it is happening so often these days that it has lost much of the negative stigma. Authoritarianism has given way to what might be termed "situation authority." Consider an analogy: when people drive by a serious traffic accident, they normally obey a citizen signaling traffic. That person has no authority over traffic, yet the situation demands compliance. So too, in buying, the situation often demands a similar response.

A high degree of interdependence among people in the company is a fact of life. The buyer is the shock trooper on the line, holding prices steady, keeping increases reasonable or rolling them back. Supply and demand still affects prices and this action often takes place at the buyer's desk. Buyers are often the only force combating the seller's natural drive for higher prices.

Buying Influences

Much of the confusion in communication about the buying job stems from failure to understand the true buying influences. Buyers should answer the question, "Who buys at this company?" Let's list the major factors and influences on them.

Decision factor	Influences
Source and price	Buyer Design engineer Purchasing engineer
Quality	Design engineer Manufacturing engineer Quality assurance/control Buyer/purchasing engineer
Quantity	Materials control Buyer Industry shortages, strikes, etc.
Time	Sales projection Scheduling Production control Availability

Knowledgeable buyers know they have many items over which they have absolute authority. They also know of other buys for which they have practically no control. Of course, they recognize that most buys are between those two extremes. Buying decisions reflect composite judgment. Depending on the situation, the buy can range from a one-person to a group or committee decision where no one individual dominates. Many buying decisions may be shared, delegated, or coordinated.

Despite delegating authority to others, buyers must keep responsibility to get results, even in those cases when they have little say in what is bought. This is important even though a good argument can be made that the buyer controls little of what has been defined as "purchasing." Production tells the buyer how much to buy and when it's needed. Quality is determined by engineering specifications and quality standards. Price may be non-negotiable and controlled by supply and demand. Not too much "authority" here; yet, have a supplier deliver two weeks late, and who's responsible and to blame—manufacturing, engineering, quality control? Not usually. Though it may be the supplier's fault for missed production, it is the buyer who hasn't performed.

What makes a successful buyer? Two qualities are especially important—the ability to motivate and encourage others to perform, and the drive to work harder and smarter when under pressure. Flexibility—the ability to shift mental gears quickly, is key, as purchasing often demands a hectic pace beset by a variety of problems. Examples are: cost studies, supplier negotiations, and "fire-fighting" to overcome inferior quality or failure to deliver on time.

Buying is a demanding job, requiring a dedication and commitment to serving the company's best interests over the long run. How do you measure up? The competent buyer will:

1. Handle his or her share of the departmental workload.
2. Perform work quickly yet accurately.
3. Let the manager know when workload can be increased.
4. Pitch in to help other buyers during times where workloads become strained.
5. Accept some overtime work, with or without pay.
6. Accept that periodic assignment changes are sometimes required in a dynamic business environment.
7. Offer workable ideas for improving purchasing systems.
8. Know supplier capabilities and limitations.
9. Recognize that the suppliers' success reflects on his or her own performance.
10. Keep up with market and technology developments.
11. Become and remain familiar with his or her company's product.
12. Continue to add to personal knowledge of the job.
13. Work within procedures and guidelines of the department.
14. Maintain the highest personal ethical standards.
15. Justify sourcing decisions based on best interest of the company.
16. Know how to challenge specifications and delivery dates tactfully.
17. Accept constructive criticism without excessive defensive excuses.
18. Keep long-term supplier relationships in mind.
19. Reasonably enjoy his or her work.
20. Remain loyal to the manager, the department, and the company!

When PMs are asked to give their opinions as to what qualities are required in a buyer, they often describe someone who has a background and characteristics similar to their own. For example, the PM who is an industrial engineer often says that industrial engineering is the finest background for buying; the business school graduate may insist that an educational background in business administration offers the type of background required; and so on. Actually, all types of backgrounds, including liberal arts, have produced and are still producing good PMs; and despite speculation in the literature, probably no one has human qualities that are indispensable in any field (unless it's honesty!).

Buyers without a college degree can be highly successful, though a degree is almost mandatory to get the job. The true test is that PMs and buyers must have backgrounds that allow them to meet, on an equal footing, people of the caliber of those with whom they must negotiate and associate. Whatever the background, buyers as well as managers can pursue development through certification.

The buyer should be firm and decisive, yet, when necessary, eloquent in pleading a case for special treatment. It's all in the daily job; the individual who can't make swift transitions will be unhappy as a buyer. Purchasing's role will continually shift as supply and demand forces change. Scarcity of materials will cycle again. Higher prices are needed at times, to reduce consumption as the world's resources are being depleted. The buyer will need to be knowledgeable about global supply!

Of course, the buyer can't, like the chameleon, change colors as every market changes. However, the buyer has to moderate away from extreme positions and be flexible enough to understand his or her cross-cultural environment.

Buyers can change many aspects of a purchase, while allowing others in the organization a say representing their sphere of interest and influence. Being knowledgeable about *what* is bought and *why* it is bought, plus this right to question, can affect profitable operation. Logically, purchasing personnel should: (1) understand buying influence and what *does* happen, (2) be able to explain it to others, and (3) understand and accept that buyers do not make all buying decisions.

Does this influence detract from purchasing authority? Not at all; rather it emphasizes it! Who in any company other than the buyer can correlate the facts in an organization interested in a vital purchase? The more important the purchase, and the larger the number of participants, the more urgent is the coordination role, requiring the highest of competence. Purchasing must be of sufficient stature and position to handle these important situations.

Buying influence is a way of life. With absolute authority, the buyer would be solely a decision-maker. As it is, decisions must be made with the involvement of others in the purchasing process. An understanding of buying influence emphasizes the *true managerial role* of the buyer.

Let us explore the buyer's interpersonal communication role, which is quite unusual. The buyer has the challenge of communication within the company, and with suppliers as shown in Figure 1-4.

The upper diagram shows that a supplier wishing to sell to a prospective customer sends out a salesperson. That person will probably come into contact with engineering, expediting, quality control, receiving, and even management. Lines of communication with the supplier's salesperson allow direct communication between sales and the buying company's personnel. Suggestions or conflicting instructions might be given to the salesperson, making it difficult for the supplier to know who speaks for this buying company. Conflicts can arise between various plant departments. Quality control may want extra inspection which will slow down delivery, causing the expediting group to complain to the buyer about the supplier. Under this setup, the salesperson handles the complete coordination job for the supplier, but the buying company is left uncoordinated in its approach to purchasing.

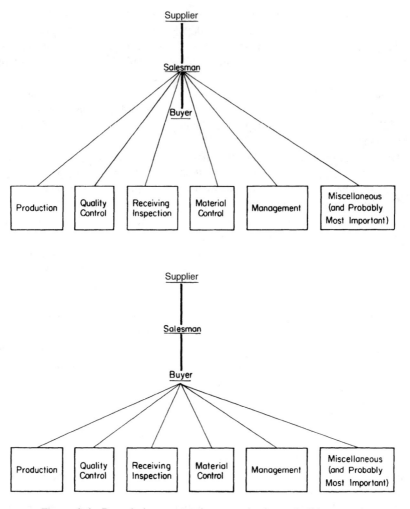

Figure 1-4 Buyer's interpersonal communication to build a screen.

In the lower diagram, under an ideal communication system, the buyer is in a position to coordinate the various functions within the buying company to present a united front to the salesperson. While this second method seems logical, there is simply too much communication needed for everything to be processed through the buyer. It simply won't work. A buyer must work through others to get answers, guidance, and a coordinated decision to present to suppliers. There is a need to lead, but not funnel, the communication exchange.

The buyer needs to *maintain a screen and not build a wall*. Other communication lines may exist between the supplier and the buyer's interested departments, as long as the buyer is kept informed. This setup does not impose a block between the selling and buying companies. Here purchasing is in a position to maintain cost control over expenditures as the buyer remains accountable for results.

Changing Demands on the Job

As purchasing has evolved over the past few decades, increasing demands have been placed on the profession. One study concluded that "several activity areas were indicated as ones in which purchasing has assumed an increased role or responsibility since 1980: strategic planning (43% of the firms), providing economic forecasts/indicators (41%), capital equipment buys (37%), product development (31%), new product evaluation (26%), traffic/transportation (23%), personal travel (16%), countertrade/offset planning/execution (15%), and cash-flow planning (13%). Obviously, the purchasing function has assumed many increased responsibilities in the past decade, requiring more-talented, better-trained personnel to perform the function."[3]

Socioeconomic Programs

In the areas noted above, purchasing managers have to be alert to recognizing shifts in not only the economic areas, but also in the total work environment comprising organizational, people, legal, systems, and government-driven factors. The expansion of the buying job also concerns new domestic requirements as companies bear some accountability to societal needs. Placing demands on purchasing are programs mandated by law. As an example, Public Law 95-507 mandates goals for minority purchases. It requires any prime contractor hoping to get government contracts over $1 million to establish minority sourcing programs. The Defense Department itself has set percentage minority participation goals for its defense procurements, and these in some cases allow premium prices to be paid to meet the legislation's objectives.

Other legislation has been put into place covering ecological issues. Ecological regulations affect procurement on issues such as PCB contamination and purity of water effluent, for example.

Still other examples of regulations include the Toxic Substance Control Act of 1977, which addresses disposal of hazardous substances, the radioactive materials and reactors regulations, the Narcotics and Drug Control Act, the Consumer Product Safety Act as well as the Flammable Fabrics Act, and finally, the household appliance regulations which must comply with the Energy Policy and Conservation Act.

Of course, these are all important regulations which require compliance. They all lead to increased demands on the supplier, which *must be enforced through*

---

[3]Harold E. Fearon, William A. Ruch, and C. David Wieters, *Fundamentals of Production/Operations Management,* 4th ed., West Publishing Co., 1989, p. 126.

the buyer. The challenge lies in balancing these requirements, while striving to meet other important cost and supply goals.

Purchasing managers as well as buyers need to understand their expanded management and social value roles. For centuries astronomers made little headway in understanding the universe with the planets moving in odd gyrations, until they finally accepted the fact that the earth is not the center of our solar system. So, buyers must see themselves as part of the whole company, contributing to its cost effectiveness and profitability.

Purchasing Redefined

Purchasing has long been defined as "Getting the right item, at the right price, at the right quality and quantity, and at the right time, from the right source." Although all this is true, that old definition doesn't cover today's more demanding world, and the multifaceted buying job. We first need to develop some theory to give us more vision and scope when we think creatively of purchasing.

We have great imagery for space launches from Earth. Our spaceships fly upside down after taking off, solely because the astronauts want to *see* the Earth while orbiting! What image pops into your mind when you think of Earth? Some see their hometown, the state—or map of the country. One thing is certain: we can't *think* of anything without creating a vision in our mind's eye.

To help us gain perspective on the buying job, let's mentally go way out into the solar system and look back at the *Earth.* When our astronauts reached the moon, through TV's eye we shared the experience of looking back to see an "Earthrise." What a vision! Our solar system, so vast we're just beginning to explore it, much less our galaxy beyond. The point is that the Earth itself never changed, but our outlook about it certainly has.

Now think about the buying job. Ask yourself, "What are the roles to play?" "Where is the script?" The buyer and manager need to create the vision!

Consider this definition as an indication of the job's scope:

> "Purchasing represents internal and end-use consumers in the global buyer/seller supply relationship. Through authority to commit and control expenditures to suppliers, assurance of supply and profitable operation is secured."

The essence of buying is to create competition among sellers, just as selling legitimately seeks to eliminate it. The ability to reward or punish a supplier by using economic leverage in purchasing is a powerful responsibility.

Leading sales training sessions have made it clear that *buyers have enormous inherent power*—if they know how to use it! But sometimes that leverage isn't used because the buying role is not understood. To create and use competition among sellers, a company must put into the hands of its buyers as much leverage as is possible. And the buyer must use it!

As we redefine purchasing in today's complex and dynamic global environment, we will need to proceed with flexibility and creativity. When Martin Luther King, Jr. said, "I have a dream . . . ," this was a great example of creative leadership. He was providing the vision and the script. So too, the purchasing manager *must create the vision.* As the future is conceived, so it shall be channeled.

2

Evolution of Purchasing and Supply Management

Today's focus on empowerment and team-based structures is not always consistent with older, traditional organization principles. To better grasp the evolution of current thought or practice, let's trace the development of purchasing's organizational status.

An organizational challenge first emerges when a business expands beyond a single manufacturing location. Establishment of a second plant location does not necessarily affect the marketing operation; after all, it is possible to keep up sales and related activities just as though the company still had a single production operation. However, buying isn't quite the same. Management has several organizational choices to consider with respect to optimizing the purchasing function.

Various organizational arrangements accompany business growth. Buying can be done (1) from the original plant with existing people; (2) by new buyers at the second plant reporting to the new plant manager, or (3) back to the purchasing manager at the original plant, or (4) to other top management personnel.

There are four basic types of organization: (1) line, (2) line-and-staff, (3) functional, and (4) committee. In practice, purchasing departments are combinations of these four types. Though they seldom appear in pure form, it helps to distinguish them for analytical purposes.

These organizational setups are usually depicted by a box chart, but others such as a concentric or circular graph are occasionally useful. The concentric type has the advantage that no one is represented as inferior or of "lower rank" than anyone else. It is employed by at least one of the country's largest businesses and serves its purpose well.

Charts can be a useful management tool to the head of purchasing. They help in setting lines of authority and responsibility for both buyers and managers, and also in depicting formal communication lines. They show who has the right to hire, to promote and discharge, and to establish an orderly allocation of "jobs to be done." Deficiencies in an organization can often be detected through the use of well-prepared charts. In cases where a chart has never before been attempted, channels of reporting, for instance, may be more clearly recognized.

Responsibilities should be spelled out as clearly as possible; so should limits of authority. This is where use of job descriptions and a purchasing manual come into play. The chief purchasing officer (CPO), like most leaders, is constrained by tradition, practicality, requirements of teamwork, and other demands of the organization.

Authority derives from one's place in the organization, but it relies heavily upon the respect of others for the manager's competence. When that competence produces the trust of others, true authority will exist. Authority depends on the ability to enforce a reward or punishment. Two early outstanding examples of organization were the church and the military. The church used excommunication, while the military Articles of War read, ". . . or punishable by death."

The four major types of organization are shown below, and are defined as follows.

1. *Line.* The concept of the line organization is, of course, borrowed from the military. The captain commands the lieutenant; who in turn commands the sergeant; and so on. This, in its pure form, may be practical in smaller and medium-size companies. (See Figure 2-1.)

2. *Line-and-staff.* The line-and-staff organization is the most prevalent in business and industry. A good example is the purchasing department of the typical large manufacturing concern. The "line" consists of those in command—the vice president, manager, senior buyers, and buyers. The "staff" is composed of vital specialists who collect and analyze data, recommend policy, work with the line to solve problems, and so relieve line management of much detail. Examples of staff functions in Figure 2-2 are those of purchase analyst, price/cost analyst, and purchasing engineer. Staff functions and personnel become involved when line managers cannot personally handle all their responsibilities. They cannot delegate management duties; so, a staff assistant is added to help extend the management function by overseeing specific areas of responsibility. Currently, there is a tendency in business practice to combine the line and staff into a "fused" organization. Under this setup, staff analysts, for example, because of their knowledge of a particular study, may give instructions to the buyer as needed, whereas that would not normally be expected.

3. *Functional.* Some companies—for example, those that manufacture a broadly diversified array of products or have important functions other than buying—feel that organization by function is better suited to their particular needs than the ordinary line-and-staff setup. A Functional Commodity Buying Organization is quite common, as it makes no sense

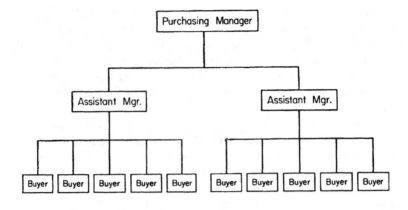

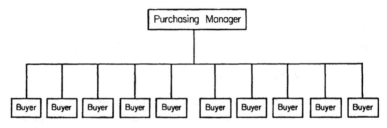

Figure 2-1   Types of line organizations.

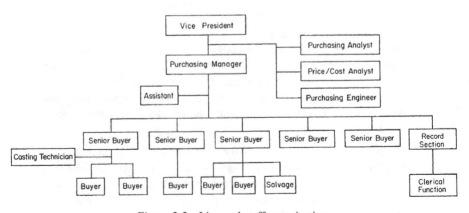

Figure 2-2   Line-and-staff organization.

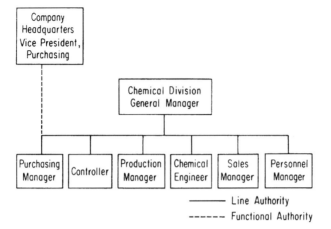

Figure 2-3 Centralized functional control with decentralized buying.

to have two or three buyers all talking to say, motor manufacturers. Channeling buys for motors through one individual gives that buyer greater "economic voice" in dealings with suppliers. However, to do this in multiplant operations is not simple.

A highly efficient organizational hybrid is the commodity manager arrangement (not shown). In this example, the central purchasing department does the buying, while the various plants are free to control their inventory, and release directly against the blanket orders. Each plant performs its own expediting, calling on the buyers only when they can't get the required delivery. Figure 2-3 shows centralized functional control with decentralized buying.

4. *Committee*. A committee is usually grafted into an existing organization where a special function or project requires that the skills and efforts of several company areas be coordinated. In purchasing, such a function might be value analysis, which draws its members from purchasing, engineering, manufacturing, finance, and other areas as needed.

Span of Control

In a one-person department there is little or no need for supervision, since the person in charge handles all the duties and bears all the responsibility. However, adding a subordinate changes the situation. Duties must be assigned, and some delegation of responsibility must take place, thereby creating the need for control. This in turn has an effect on the organization structure.

Span of control is determined by the number of buyers or other personnel reporting directly to the purchasing manager. In a department of ten buyers, all reporting to the PM, the span of control is obviously broad; whereas, if this same department had two assistant managers and several senior buyers, the span would be quite narrow and have greater depth (as shown in Figure 2-1).

Whether the PM has a wide or narrow span of control depends on his or her (or the company's) theory of management. The advantages of wide-span control include better morale, shorter lines of communication, and the likelihood that promising young buyers will be identified and rewarded sooner. On the other hand, there may be so many people under supervision, PMs are unable to devote much time to training each individual. Moreover, a successor may not be developed who has had direct supervisory responsibility.

The span of control should not be so great that it prevents giving adequate attention to each subordinate, yet it should be broad enough that the department operates well without long communication lines. Under some current theories of management, PMs may be assigned an organization much broader than they can properly control. The idea is that the buyers will have to develop initiative and grow in skill and competence. This is an effective plan if management wants to loosen the reins of a capable but overzealous manager who can't avoid interfering in subordinates' work.

The organization chart is a highly useful management planning tool that all purchasing managers should be able to use in their quest for smoother operations. However, it has definite limitations. None has yet been devised to show completely the complex communication lines of the buying function. A chart is only a snapshot of the existing structure. Moreover, charts are unable to show the organization's most important dimension—the personalities and talents of those individuals represented by the boxes on the charts.

Centralized Versus Decentralized Department

Centralized as applied to purchasing has two connotations. The first concerns the concentration of buying authority for a single plant within the purchasing department. There are situations where a vital item may be bought by a company official, even by the president, because of the serious leverage it could have on the survival of the business. Examples might be hides for a tannery, wood for a paper mill, or lumber for a furniture plant. There are fewer such exceptions today than in past years. In general, most single-plant companies have centralized control of the buying function.

The second, more common connotation of the term implies central purchasing control, usually at headquarters, even when there are several plants in different locations, run by division managers. Conversely, a department is said to be *decentralized* if there are several independent purchasing groups reporting to the individual plant managers and not to one purchasing head. Either form of organization can, and does, operate in similar industries; sometimes strong management personalities will influence the choices. There are, however, situations that usually will make one of them more appropriate.

Advantages of Centralization

Why is centralization desirable? Under this form of organization it is possible to maintain greater control over the total commitment of purchasing dollars. A buyer can offer the largest buy-package to the seller, resulting in better buying agreements that take full advantage of company-wide usage.

Whether a department is centralized or decentralized may depend in the last analysis on such factors as top management preference, the availability of the data-processing equipment necessary to facilitate centralization, the physical layout and location of the company's plants, and the types of products manufactured, or the processes utilized.

Uniform procedures, and better control over them, are more readily attained by centralized purchasing. It is easier to bring new people into the larger department and train them properly before they are put on the important buying job. Individuals can be assigned the tasks for which they are best suited. Those who have exceptional negotiation skills may be designated to handle the large-value items; those with the most ingratiating personalities may be designated to the touchier areas of trade relations; and those who are especially aggressive may become excellent expediters and troubleshooters.

There is probably a point beyond which the purchasing operation cannot be centralized with a further increase in profitability. The fact remains, however, that some of the finest and strongest purchasing departments are centralized.

Advantages of Decentralization

Compare a decentralized company whose three plants require a salesman to call on three buyers with the one in which centralized purchasing enables the salesman to service the three plants in one call. This saves buying as well as selling time.

Usually the decentralized purchasing department can react more quickly in emergencies than the centralized group. Also, central buyers who are physically distant from the point of use may be less in touch with materials problems and specifications.

The loss of a key person is not as serious as it might be in the strongly centralized group. And it is possible to keep responsibility and authority closer to the firing line to permit greater flexibility where decisions do not have to be referred to a remote head office.

Like centralization, decentralization can be overdone. Small, scattered buying groups may have little opportunity to be heard by top management and be so weak that they have little voice in company affairs. Buying decisions may then be dominated by other, more powerful departments that are not aware of purchasing's role in profitability.

Generally most companies start with centralized purchasing, frequently converting to a decentralized function as the company expands and grows into separate divisions. There are no strict rules to follow. Some large companies remain centralized even with many plants in different parts of the country; others are decentralized, having several departments in the same plant area.

In practice there are numerous variations on the organizational theme; however, they are usually combinations of the line and staff and functional types. They may be either centralized or decentralized. It is possible, for instance, to have centralized functional control along with decentralized buying as seen in Figure 2-3. This sort of structure allows the divisional manager to retain authority over buying, but it permits procedural and policy control to be retained by the central purchasing authority.

Many large corporations find it completely impractical to centralize many buying organizations throughout the world. The global corporation presents an organizational challenge about how to bring together buying actions. How can buying be centralized despite confusing organizational channels? In organizing to do the job, the classic question is, "Do we buy centralized or decentralized?" We can do both! In dealing with suppliers, a specific item can be bought solely by a plant, or centrally. To enhance productivity, the challenge is to get over organizational barriers and form cross-functional teams.

Without question, the most popular organization is the central/decentralized organization. Purchasing is one area of materials management that a company can centralize, regardless of the organizational structure that exists. Whereas centralizing inventory may be difficult in a multiplant environment, the buying activity can be controlled for maximum economic leverage, regardless of location of the buyers and suppliers.

Titles Used in Purchasing

Purchasing uses a variety of titles, the most common today being purchasing manager, which replaced the title of purchasing agent almost universally used before 1960. If a company has several PMs, the person over them may be assigned the title general purchasing manager, manager of purchasing, director of procurement, or sometimes materials manager or director of material or supply, the latter titles usually implying added materials responsibilities.

According to a 1988 study by the Center for Advanced Purchasing Studies, "The chief purchasing officer in 297 major corporations carries the title of Director of Purchasing (38%), Vice President of Purchasing (23%), Manager of Purchasing (18%), or Vice President of Materials Management (9%)."[1]

The person doing the buying is, logically enough, referred to as the buyer. At

---

[1]Harold E. Fearon, William A. Ruch, and C. David Wieters, *Fundamentals of Production/Operations Management,* 4th ed., West Publishing Co., 1989, p. 113.

one time the title procurer was strongly favored by the National Association of Purchasing Managers (NAPM), but it hasn't found popular acceptance. Senior buyers handle vital items of high dollar value, or are in charge of several buyers and assistant buyers; sometimes the term supervising buyer is used.

The title buyer/planner has gained favor by those plants who prefer to tie buying, expediting, releasing, and inventory responsibilities to the same person. Sometimes referred to as the "cell concept," this relationship works well for some, though managers wanting concentration of attention on costs of acquisition might question placing more detailed routine with those doing the purchasing.

The expediter is, as the title implies, an individual who follows up the material bought to ensure delivery as required. In common usage are such additional titles as purchasing engineer and research analyst. These are the specialists who have proved valuable in ferreting out costs through special concentrated study.

Other titles used include: purchasing engineering, analyst, and group coordinator. The "purchasing and supply manager" title may become more popular. Titles in purchasing are no different from other business titles; it is almost impossible to determine a person's responsibilities from the title alone. In some companies a purchasing agent has more authority and responsibility than a vice president of purchasing elsewhere, while others may apply the PA title almost to the buying level.

Where Should Purchasing Report?

There is no universal agreement about where the function of purchasing belongs. It can be performed from almost any level, and can range from a purely clerical activity to that of a professional group reporting to the chief executive officer. *Purchasing Today* stated that CPOs report to senior executive vice presidents in 34% of all companies surveyed. That included 16% to presidents and CEOs and the balance to a VP. And, 66% changed who they reported to since 1988.[2]

The Materials Management Organization

The materials management (MM) and logistics management concepts have evolved in recent years to gain popularity among many in the profession. Several interpretations of "materials management" exist, but the central point is that purchasing is a subsystem of the larger materials management process. Basically, the concept places all functions having to do with materials—including production scheduling, material control, inventory management, purchasing, traffic, and materials handling—under a materials manager.

Materials management came into being during World War II and was employed

---

[2]CAPS Research Summary, June, 1996.

by large aircraft manufacturers who were operating under government contracts. With mostly cost-plus-fixed-fee contracts, the total overall cost was not the driving concern. The prime objective was to get the planes and the guns out the door.

Originally this MM position was envisioned to be on the same level as the production manager; both reporting to a vice president, or to the president. Various other attached functions such as traffic, receiving, and inspection may or may not be included within the MM jurisdiction, depending on the particular operation or company. The main idea was to make one individual accountable for inventories and materials.

A typical MM organization chart, designed to provide the widest possible control over materials, is shown in Figure 2-4. Several variations of this concept are found in practice today, some placing purchasing on a par with "materials." So, we witness a tendency to use the terms "purchasing" and "materials management" interchangeably, though they are not technically equivalent.

Some prefer "logistics management," viewing the supply function primarily from a systems standpoint. In many companies, finished goods inventory, which is not manufacturing's concern, is larger in value than the in-process inventory. Also, the distribution of the products to customers engages transportation personnel. So, logistics management, or physical distribution, envisions control under a manager detached from manufacturing, who concentrates on activities such as handling product, warehousing, moving product to customers, and the like.

In most companies in-process inventory is handled by manufacturing (material control) or by purchasing, so conflicts may arise when this responsibility is split. A prime advantage of placing all materials functions under one executive, the materials manager, is that much friction is eliminated and accountability is clear. For example, when a buyer tries to increase order quantities to reduce the unit prices paid, inventory will be affected. If those responsible for inventory have no responsibility for product costs, they can easily override price advantages to keep their stocks low. Further, inventory can be cut by depleting stocks and forcing shorter-than-normal supplier lead-times on purchasing, causing loss of negotiating time, supplier ill-will and irritation, and extra expediting expense.

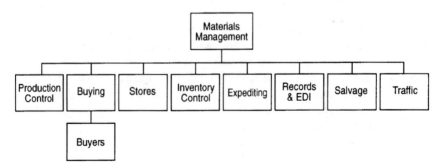

Figure 2-4   Typical materials management organization.

Some practitioners have touted MM as a means to allow purchasing to better carry out its materials coordinating duties. This organization concept often produces a bigger job for some, and others have seen it as an answer to the almost universal cry for recognition and understanding.

The MM concept is quite effective in putting out day-to-day fires, especially for smaller companies. The old alibi game is done away with. Purchasing can't blame material control for not requisitioning on time, and material control can't blame purchasing for taking too much time to shop. There is one impartial referee to blow the whistle who is responsible for the whole show. In numerous ways, MM is a reasonable approach to eliminating many friction areas of production and supply problems that constantly face purchasing, manufacturing, and plant management.

There is potentially more danger in the materials concept when it includes production scheduling, which is integrally allied to manufacturing. Some proponents of the concept draw a sharp and abrupt halt, claiming that when it attempts to interfere or take over a shop's production scheduling, MM is in danger of overstepping the purpose for which it was designed. And, they've learned that probably an eventual conflict with manufacturing is to be expected. The less radical form of organization that they favor is to leave production scheduling under manufacturing. Otherwise it is identical to the arrangement shown. These advocates define MM as the grouping under one manager of functions responsible for the flow of materials, including requisitioning, purchasing, expediting, and stores up to the point of introduction to the production line.

Yet some companies with a materials manager place only purchasing and inventory control under his or her direction. Not to confuse the issue but to show the real need to define the concept, some have a materials manager who is a "super" purchasing person (presumably with a higher grade title); others have a "purchasing" department that encompasses all the functions in a full materials setup; and, finally, several large companies have divisions with a materials management organization and other divisions with a traditional purchasing group.

Why Do Some PMs Not Embrace MM?

Some purchasing executives believe that materials or logistics management is their ultimate destiny, while others have been vehement in denouncing it. The concept has been rejected by many top people in the field. Some have tried MM and found it inadequate; many purchasing practitioners persist in believing that purchasing itself is where profit is made. This viewpoint has largely been muted— for how can a part be greater than the whole? Obviously, it can't be, so this seemingly reactionary, largely silent school persists. They believe the "part" that is purchasing is simply too important, too diverse, too externally oriented, and too allied with management and other functions outside the MM area itself to be subjugated within any such functional grouping. These are compelling arguments that should be considered.

One cannot refute the claim that there is need for a coordinating activity. Some assume that this coordination can best be effected through MM whereas advocates of modern purchasing believe it can be achieved by an upgraded, aggressive, and intelligent purchasing department. Dr. Howard T. Lewis, author of the first purchasing book published by NAPM, recognized the need for coordination of materials, and termed it materials management. Yet, he later admitted that "control of the purchasing function itself is justification enough for the purchasing manager's existence, without the need to encompass other activities."[3]

To hold that MM *must control* all facets of inventory and materials processed is questionable. Here it appears that some proponents are being guided by the old concept of "responsibility and authority." But who controls the effect of engineering design on prices, sales forecasts and production requirements on inventories, production scheduling, and machine loading on availability of stock, financial management on inventory values, or supplier lead-time on purchase commitments? All these factors and more have bearing on the functions included in MM, yet materials managers actually have little to say about them.

For instance, so the case goes, material managers do not usually run the independent material entity envisioned by original advocates who saw MM on a par with the manufacturing unit. In a complex corporation this may mean that the individual empowered to commit large purchase expenditures is located on the middle or low rungs of the management ladder. The direct head of the buying activity, in this case, may not even be a member of the plant manager's staff. This situation is seen by many as an unsatisfactory informational power base for individuals expected to exercise strong profit responsibility.

Discussion of MM is further confused by failure to distinguish between the headquarters and the plant organizations. MM at headquarters often entails perhaps 85% or more "purchasing" activity, and 15% functional inventory surveillance; at the plant level, it may involve 85% inventory control—delivery and quality oriented—with 15% of the effort devoted to "purchasing." MM can be quite effective at the plant level. Yet it may not be possible to centralize the MM function, since primary inventory responsibility must remain with each specific plant.

To embrace the MM theme, with purchasing as a subsystem of materials, may indeed serve only to further confuse the long range issue. Keeping purchasing at a lower level are poor performance, lack of recognition, and the allegiance of purchasing to the production line. A good case can be made for the argument that MM's "home" should be in manufacturing. Some purchasing chiefs view it as a threat to return purchasing to the production cocoon from which it emerged in the 1950s.

Production needs must be met, but some argue that PMs could become so

---

[3]Discussion about MM between Dr. Lewis and senior author Victor H. Pooler, Clarkson College, 1960.

engrossed with a highly complex scheduling system that they might not be as interested with materials costs as with "getting the goods on time." It is precisely why purchasing was divorced from manufacturing—so that it might be just free enough to concentrate on controlling purchasing essentials. Purchasing wouldn't be an evolving function if this issue were finally settled.

An external force on purchasing and supply is that there has not been, and may well never be, one proper organization for this function within its own company structure. Many opinions exist, and may be settled within a given company. New managements, or new people with a different way of thinking, move to set the function up as they see things. And, conflicting forces are a reality.

Tending to push purchasing to the top of the management level is its vital impact on profitability through pooled buying. So, the advantages claimed for MM are identical to those that should result when good purchasing people work in conjunction with a sound overall organization. Gaining an understanding of sales and manufacturing requirements, keeping an eye on suppliers' innovations, and watching the needs of the engineering department as it works to ready new products for manufacturing and marketing is expected. This job of modern purchasing as a profit enhancer encompasses far more than just those functions that are generally considered to fall within MM.

Because buying decisions require conflict resolution and lateral negotiations within the company, an effective setup is when the CPO is on a par organizationally with the general managers of the operations for which they have purchasing responsibility. These managers report to a senior vice president or CEO. This arrangement provides an umbrella under which purchasing cannot be coerced or dominated by powerful nonpurchasing influences.

Reconsidering Organization Concepts

Centralization does bring strength to externally oriented functions. Yet, at the same time, there is a significant need for freedom to act at specific locations where the activity occurs.

Purchasing is not alone in its identity crises. Engineering, for example, has problems stemming from its splintered disciplines, but engineering stands on its own intrinsic value, as does accounting, marketing and sales, manufacturing, and management itself. If purchasing is to succeed professionally, it must identify its "raison d'etre," then claim its rightful role to satisfy its technical, economic, and legal heritage.

Recycling efforts have been termed demanufacturing. Can depurchasing be far behind? Demanufacturing can recycle and redirect about 95% of electronic product parts away from landfills. An operation by Laidlaw Waste Systems accepts discarded electronic equipment. Plastic casings are ground up and used for lower tolerance applications. Memory chips are reused, and circuit boards give up refined precious metals. Aluminum and copper cables are also recycled.

Reengineering is fundamentally changing the way people do their work to achieve superior results. Process reengineering has resulted in eliminating duplication, avoiding suboptimization, and gaining continuous improvement by taking advantage of technology. Theory invites questions without which there is no learning.

To be highly practical, a manager first has to be aware of the theoretical aspects of creative management. To take a fresh look at the area of technical buying and design techniques, let's give free range to a creative approach. Many people have what might be called "functional fixation." For example, pass them a broom and they figure, logically, it's for sweeping the floor. However, put a broom in the hands of imaginative youngsters. Perhaps they'll sweep the floor, but likely they'll pretend to shoot someone across the room, or ride it like a witch. Their instincts are not programmed to limit a broom's usefulness.

The degree of organizational confusion about purchasing is indicative of a function still evolving. So, let's depart from traditional organization ideas and creatively explore another perspective. Regardless of the type of organization, the basic functions must still be performed. It is doubtful whether any organization ever existed without an occasional healthy argument or disagreement. There is never any one, and only one, system that will work, although there is usually one that will work more efficiently when adapted to the specific need.

People try to "see" a corporation as a picture or symbol. Early management literature depicted the corporation as a pyramid. At the top is the president, down through the upper and middle management is where our purchasing chief resides, and finally the workers make up the base. This viewpoint spawned expressions such as the "pinnacle-of-success," "reached the top," "head-of-the-firm," and the like.

As people achieve they want to share the pinnacle. You don't like to be seen as inferior or below anyone, do you? Neither do others; so, circular organization charts have been developed, with the president as the hub and workers as the rim. And, these images change. Some management planners describe a corporation as "energy exchange systems." Reflecting systems theorists, a corporation is seen as an open system engaged in constant transactions with its environment, which is seen as a system of systems. The transactions are said to take place in a field of force operating in space/time and made up of all the patterned but individual desires and aspirations of all the people who make up both internal and external environmental systems.

Organizational Structure and Relationships

We may hear, "It isn't my job; someone else has that responsibility." There has probably been more success in breaking purchasing job responsibility into component areas than in fitting the pieces together as a cohesive working unit. But organization is not simply a matter of breaking a function down into its components and depicting them in a chart. Rather, it is a means of bringing together people working in different spheres of interest and coordinating their abilities to achieve the common goals of the department and company.

Company A   Company B

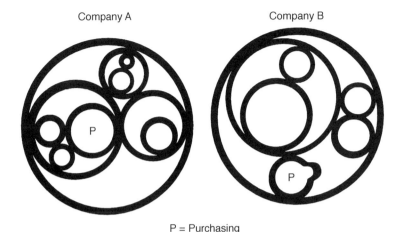

P = Purchasing

Figure 2-5   Circles representing spheres of influence.

More recent attempts have shown an organization as spheres of influence, with a variety of circles representing functions or people. The organization as seen in Figure 2-5 is not the oblong box chart of authority. The purchasing sphere will be larger in company A, and smaller in B, depending on capabilities to do the job.

Use of multitask teams calls for more flexible horizontal type organizations. Cross-functional teams working on projects or key commodities require innovators. As seen from this figure, supplying the in-between areas that do not neatly fit into any manager's job scope will have to be done by the purchasing or supply chief of the future.

If we look at these spheres of influence as eggshells within eggshells, if we punch through our shell, we either crack the one next to us, or we move into a void. In any company there are always those vacuums or voids that no one else appears interested in or knowledgeable enough to fill. The purchasing and supply chief needs to take the lead more often to fill these voids. The important thing, as far as the good of the total organization, is to get the job done.

Authority to Commit Independent of the Organization?

Companies operate under the laws of the state, which provide each specific company with authority to conduct business. Statutory "powers" are conferred through incorporation; one of these is "to purchase as required." The owners, stockholders in a public corporation, technically have that authority and, in turn, invest the Board of Directors with authority to act in behalf of their corporation.

Figure 2-6 traces a complex chain of command to "commit the corporation," depicting the derivation of authority of the buyer who legally is an "agent" of the company. While agency can exist verbally, most corporate charters require

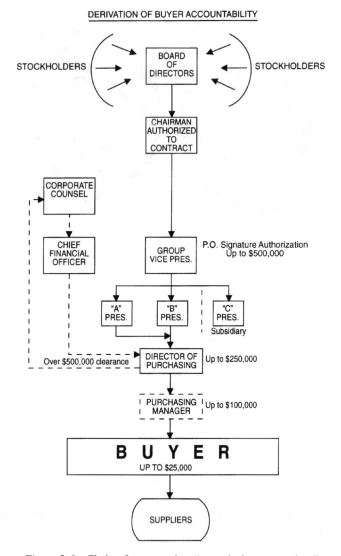

DERIVATION OF BUYER ACCOUNTABILITY

Figure 2-6 Chain of command to "commit the corporation."

these authorizations to be in writing. Since the corporation is basically a "mental creation," individuals must be empowered to act for it. This legally delegated authority explains the historic "purchasing agent" title.

Purchasing derives its authority within the law of agency. Purchasing alone has the formal authority to commit the corporation to expenditures. The concept of agency defines the manner in which an agent may bind the principal. An agent is "one who acts for and under the contract of a principal." So, the agent/principal relationship is a fiduciary one. Acts of the agent result in the principal being bound to a third party. Both individual and principal agree to the arrangement which results in conditions binding on both.

The buyer as a fiduciary agent accepts duties to the principal: to give loyalty, to obey instructions, to give notice of material facts, to use care and skill, and to account for property and money. In return, the principal has duties to its agents: to adhere to the terms of agency, to pay for services rendered, and to reimburse the agent for expenditures incurred on the principal's behalf.

As seen in Figure 2-6, delegation of expressed "authority to commit" is passed down from the stockholders to the presidents. From the need to execute the responsibility, additional implied authority accrues. Regardless of how simple or complex an organization may be, the commitment chain must be traceable so that ultimately this authority arrives at the buyer's desk. Within the limitations placed on the buyer, he or she is formally empowered to commit and make binding arrangements with other corporations or individuals.

Confusion often arises concerning purchasing authority because of the normal tendency of people within any organization to think and act in terms of organization structure. A general lack of understanding of the authority/responsibility role of purchasing has affected it as a profession. The important point is that the "authority to commit" channel that defines purchasing's responsibility may be, and usually is, quite independent of organization structure itself. So, it is not surprising that research has documented that "professional purchasing managers do not appear to use the organization as their reference source."[4]

PMs can make use of a "commitment channel" diagram in lieu of the organization chart. For example, a manufacturing cost center reporting to president A in Figure 2-6 does not have its own purchasing department. People within such a center may wish to work directly with suppliers, independently of buyers. However, the commitment channel shows that president A has delegated buying authority to the director of purchasing. Conversely, subsidiary president C has not delegated this authority since he operates with a separate buying organization overseas. While an organization chart may emphasize multidivisional complexity and independence with no clear organizational relationship to purchasing, the commitment channel diagram is explicit. By using the commitment channel concept in lieu of the organizational structure concept, purchasing managers determine when responsibility is clearly theirs, and, using implied authority, then discharge the responsibility to act! There is no need to debate or call meetings to determine "who buys?"

Before dismissing the above as too abstract, the figure shown and operating mode was the role that the senior author's position required for many years. The same purchasing department reported to a variety of executives as reorganizations altered the corporation, without affecting how the department itself worked.

Much confusion about purchasing could be dispelled if we recognize that

---

[4]R. M. Barth and P. S. Hagstad. "The Effects of Professionalism on Purchasing Managers," *Journal of Purchasing and Materials Management,* Spring 1979, p. 30.

purchasing operates in two different ways: (1) day-to-day, and (2) long-range planning. By thinking in this way, it can be seen that the more decentralized day-to-day activities (logistics) can be undertaken within the plant operations while the centralized management control can exist independently at headquarters. Long-range aspects of source of supply, pricing negotiation, in-depth market studies, long-term contracts, and the higher management objectives must remain centralized unless a corporation wishes to be merely an accumulation of smaller companies.

Day-to-Day Versus Long-Range Buying

To gain background about strategic "long-range" versus "day-to-day" buying, we might compare management to building a two-story building. The lower floor plan will contain the functions of the business; that is engineering, sales, manufacturing, finance, and purchasing. The second story will mirror the first, and contain the same functions as shown in Figure 2-7 which depicts how we'll build our functional view.

Multilevel buying activities can be classified into two classes:

1. strategic long range buying, or the "planning loop," versus

2. tactical day-to-day buying, or the "doing loop"

Multiple-level buying occurs when the "high and low" of buying approaches problems in the same way. The doing loop hits low and the planning loop high. This results in a multiple attack on the same job, but at different levels. An analogy would be a team of surgeons performing an important operation, where all are consulted, voice opinions, and perform tests, but when it's time for action, only the doctor holding the scalpel makes the incision. While the surgeon has

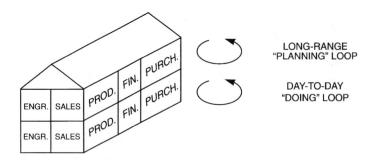

LONG-RANGE
"PLANNING" LOOP

DAY-TO-DAY
"DOING" LOOP

THE FIRST AND SECOND FLOOR PLANS ARE SIMILAR

Figure 2-7   Two-story overview of multilevel management "planning" and "doing" loop.

the "line" responsibility, the others share a part of the planning; but that surgeon alone must be charged with the success or failure of the operation.

Day-to-day buying and strategic long-range buying can be compared as follows:

Factor	Day-to-day	Strategic approach
Time	Short run	One to three years
Channels of buying	No control	Choice exercised, direct when warranted
Resources	Minimal	Best personnel available
Objective	Get goods	Lowest total landed costs to support goals
New product development	Usual sources	Long-range source advice to engineers
Outlook	Local	Global

How does a practical manager use this philosophy? Here is an example. A manager explains to the planning loop that they are responsible to see that inventory in the plants is at an agreed upon level, and is maintained properly. At the same time, the top manager reminds the doing loop that *they* are directly responsible for inventory. The top manager tells all plant purchasing managers they must keep their inventory under control. If inventory is too high or out of balance, both loops are responsible. So, we have a team effort. The planners monitor and help the doers, while the doers get the job done day-to-day. How this works is one of the strategies described in Chapter 4 that explains the down-to-earth way buying teams operate.

The long-range strategic buying is the "upper" or planning loop and is led by the division, headquarters, or corporate operation. The day-to-day, doing-loop is located at the plant or decentralized buying site(s). Whether a company has two or 52 plants doesn't matter—it's just more complex.

By thinking of multiple-level buying operations in this conceptual way, it is seen why the more day-to-day activities are done within each plant, or buying section. The longer ranged aspects of source of supply, pricing negotiations, and the higher goals may be centralized. Both loops cooperate and focus on the same area of operation, but in different ways. The planning loop decides *how* to do the job and makes plans. The doing loop carries out those plans.

Today, with divisions stacked on top of, or grouped with, other divisions often having little relationship to one another, purchasing finds itself structured quite differently in different companies. Figure 2-8 is the suggested vision we propose for a conglomerate, or skyscraper management. Divisions are acquired, sold, merged, or are closed. Like a stack of trays, they are rearranged. Can such groupings possibly control their purchasing activity? Of course they can!

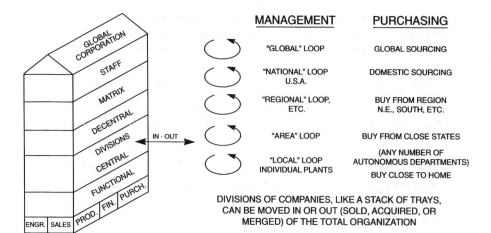

Figure 2-8. Suggested vision of a conglomerate, or "skyscraper" management.

Movement seems to be toward two distinct roles (1) strategic analysis, planning, and relationship building; and (2) tactical orders, execution, expediting, and so on. If both roles are foreseen, but not assigned to separate people, the tactical will always displace the strategic because the short-range tactical will always be more urgent.

Where Does This Leave Us Organizationally?

The preceding discussion paints a picture of an evolving, often meandering, profession in search of its conceptual home. We can summarize the evolution of organizational concepts we have discussed to this point in the following matrix:

Title Applied	Emphasis Placed on	Result
Purchasing	Buying, act of acquisition	Three quotes to lowest price and narrow scope
Materials management	Broadening scope to all aspects of material flow	Less organization conflict, less emphasis on purchasing activity.
Logistics management	Support from military and academics; emphasis on physical distribution and transportation	Not widely accepted

| Supply management | Control of the supply chain | Term long used by Europeans; stresses management |
| Purchasing *and* supply management | Linkage of acquisition and supply economics as complementary and global in scope | Consistent with rising importance of supplier base management of the entire supply chain |

"Purchasing and Supply Management" Comes of Age

It appears the term "purchasing" is too restrictive to those who advocate a total materials or logistics approach. To those who see the act of acquisition and the allegiance to the financial and management goals, the function commonly called "purchasing" is not broad enough to encompass its profit impact. To many PMs, the term materials management relates to decentralized, plant-level activities.

The term "supply management" is gaining favor, as it conceptually implies control of the entire *supply* chain.

By combining the two terms, can we perhaps maintain the focus on purchasing's importance, yet include expansion into a globally oriented management of the total supply chain? The concept of "purchasing *and* supply management" (P&SM) emphasizes buying while recognizing the expansion of the ancillary supply functions which are often difficult to separate. Focus is on managing the supplier base. P&SM seeks to shift from a tactical to a strategic-based outlook. Strategic emphasis is placed on value-added activities and total cost savings.

The NAPM is endorsing the supply concept and recently has established a new Advanced Technology Center (ATC) that is dedicated to developing and executing computer-based education and training applications in *"purchasing and supply management"* functions. So, it appears sound to join the act of buying with the control of supply in all that these activities entail. Figure 2-9 shows how such an organization might be structured.

Debate among managers about the *one* best form of organization may be fruitless. Like most any organizational setup, they all can work; the question is, how well will it work and how effectively will it add to the overall operation of the company? We believe that purchasing will contribute most when it is an independent, interdependent major company department. Improvement of the buying function will provide a more cost-conscious approach, and in the final analysis, this is more important to company survival than elimination of any so-called "friction" areas, though strong purchasing will minimize them in any event. In the final analysis, management should place purchasing where it believes it can perform best. Each company must evaluate its own situation.

In the ensuing chapters, we will discuss strategies to optimize the process of

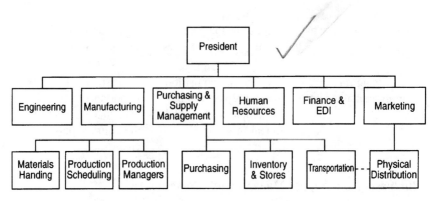

Figure 2-9 Company organization chart with Purchasing and Supply Management.

purchasing and supply management. Perhaps the single most important strategy is "going global," because in *not* pursuing worldwide opportunities, buyers can't know if they've got the best buy! And that's what purchasing is all about. However, before reviewing this and other strategies let's refresh ourselves on purchasing fundamentals.

3

Developing Purchase Order Procedures

Before getting into specific strategic supply initiatives that will ultimately improve the job, we will first review purchasing basics. This will serve as both a refresher for experienced purchasing managers and a source of essential information for nonpurchasing personnel seeking insights into the profession.

In this chapter we will briefly outline the basic steps in making a purchase, and overview some of the more common clauses used in purchase contracts. (A more detailed discussion of purchase order clauses will be covered in Chapter 14.) We will conclude with a review of some of the data processing aids available to the buyer, as a prelude to the discussion of strategic purchasing supply initiatives in Chapter 4.

The buying process begins with a requisition, which the buyer will analyze and ultimately fill in with pertinent purchase data. To edit the requisition, buyers will also need their company's forms and records, supplier catalogue file, past-buy records, and purchase order number file (unless forms are prenumbered). Of course, if the department has achieved the ideal of the "paperless" office, this information will relate to computerized forms.

Much has been written about the basic records needed by the buyer. Buyers are urged to use as a desk reference the *Purchasing Handbook*, published by McGraw-Hill. For our purpose, the key items listed below need to be available to the buyer:

1. Address books

2. Supplier profiles for major suppliers that list key people contacts, phone numbers, and the like

3. Price history records, which are essential, and which should include alternate suppliers and all their latest prices

Fundamental Steps to Complete a Purchase

In the process of completing a buy, editing the requisition is among the first administrative steps taken by a buyer. The fundamental administrative steps to the purchase are:

1. Editing the requisition
2. Making purchase decisions
3. Issuing the purchase order (PO)
4. Issuing change notices (as required)
5. Receiving acknowledgments
6. Follow up and expediting
7. Receiving (bar coding)
8. Price checking
9. Invoice approval
10. Corrections if needed
11. Recording data and closing the PO

Editing the Requisition

The first step in buying is always recognition of a need. It may be a request to replenish stock on a repetitive item, or it could be a special one-time buy of a frequently ordered item. It may be for commodities, components, or services. It is best to be in written form. Usually a requisition ("req") represents an unfulfilled need. Increasingly, this data is FAX'd or transmitted electronically over intercompany computer networks.

A "traveling req" for repetitive purchases is sent to the buyer by the person providing internal authorization for the purchase. A smaller firm may have the buyer order by review of the inventory records directly, eliminating the req. Information typically identified on the req includes: approval, account number, description of what is needed, quantity, date wanted, ship-to information, and so on. The form may also contain supplier information, prices, and part order history.

While buyers get lots of incoming mail, these reqs are actually "action orders," and hence take top priority. The buyer must first identify those items that must be acted on quickly. Upon making the purchase, buyers must add this information to the requisition, which ultimately becomes the basis for the purchase order: unit price, order dollar value, supplier's name, agreed delivery date, FOB shipping terms, shipment method, and terms and conditions including payment.

Issuing the Purchase Order (PO)

What determines the type of contract to be negotiated? Some buyers continually use one type; however, it's important to realize there are variations to suit special situations. Buyers should ask themselves the following questions:

- Is more than one supplier willing or able to make the product?
- How much money is involved, and how "rush" are the deliveries?
- What risks are involved—has a similar item ever been built?
- What is the financial status of the supplier?
- Have any cost data been developed?

There are about 20 known types of contracts which can be divided into three major categories: fixed price, cost-plus, and blanket orders.

Fixed price. This is the most common type of contract, and can be used to buy anything. It has many variations.

Cost-plus. For most work, a cost-plus contract is not the most desirable type of contractual instrument as there is generally no cost limit, so cost is difficult to control. But sometimes it is the only way to get a contractor to handle the job where significant or unknown risks abound. These contracts are usually reserved for construction, complex defense contracting needs, service or special contracts—where the buyer is uncertain what will be required until the work is in progress. Naturally, suppliers are not going to tackle this type of work on a fixed price basis unless they get a high price to cover any eventuality.

Normal practice is to get detailed analyses on hours worked and expenses. With cost-reimbursement arrangements, always include the right of audit—including the rates of labor! The supplier's profit is either a percentage of the costs or a fixed fee that is set during negotiation. That amount is paid regardless of other costs. Be wary of agreeing to profit as a percentage of cost, as there will be absolutely no economic incentive to contain costs; to the contrary, in such a case the incentive is to raise costs to get a better return.

Another variation on the cost-plus theme is the cost-plus incentive fee (CPIF) arrangement which has been increasingly utilized by the Department of Defense. These arrangements can include a value engineering clause that allows any supplier to keep a portion of savings achieved. The idea is to reward superior performance and penalize substandard work. An excellent recent example was the rebuilding of highways after the California earthquake a few years ago. The contractor worked night and day, completing the job months ahead of the experts' best estimate. The incentive was large—but well worth it to stop the traffic tie-ups.

Blanket orders. Blanket orders are generally based on fixed pricing, but because they cover a period of time over which pricing is applicable, may also include price adjustment features. The blanket order will be reviewed in more detail, but first let's identify the types of contracts used to make an acquisition. Below are some different formats:

- Purchase Order
- Blanket Order
- Systems Contract
- Letter of Intent

- Letter Order, or Letter Contract
- Memorandum of Agreement (MOA)
- Cost/Price Agreement
- Corporate Purchase Agreement
- Legal Agreement document

Buyers may use a Letter of Intent to arrange early parts buys and plan their production schedule. This is a binding arrangement which obligates the buyer to complete a purchase if it causes the seller to start action.

A contract is usually more complex and detailed than a purchase order (PO), although a PO is actually a contract itself. Handshakes may still work for some purchases, but for most buys a written agreement is needed to give proper documentation and avoid misunderstandings. For all but the most unusual circumstances, use a purchase order, and spell out anything that is important.

Purchase orders are issued based on suppliers' quoted prices and lead-time, and other specifics relevant to the purchase requirement. The forms in use vary greatly, and an example is shown in Figure 3-1. An occasional review of the format and terms and conditions versus other available formats is helpful. Larger firms generally have good models based on the availability of legal guidance to draft their order forms carefully.

The purchase order is the legal document by which buyers commit their company to pay for desired purchases. Problems are minimal if buyers plan and prepare a well documented purchase order. Specific prices should always be defined in the fixed price purchase order.

Buyers have to think defensively when preparing the purchase order. Although difficult to do, the objective is to try to consider all possible events that could go wrong. A buyer's PO checklist of terms and conditions may be useful to ensure that the basics get covered:

1. If order confirmed, to whom
2. Exact quantity, and unit of purchase—keg, bale, bag, etc.
3. Accurate and complete description, or specification of goods or services ordered
4. Unit price (identified by currency if other than U.S. dollars)
5. Date delivery is needed
6. Invoice instructions. Invoice to be sent to: (name and address)
7. Ship to information: (name and address)
8. Type of packing and container to be specified
9. Method of shipment, "FOB" INCOTERMS (denotes ownership transfer point)

Tactech

Transition Analysis of Component Technology, Inc.
22700 Savi Ranch Parkway
Yorba Linda, California 92687

PURCHASE
ORDER

The following number must appear on all related correspondence, shipping documents, and invoices:

P.O. NUMBER:

To: _____   Ship To: _____
      _____   _____
      _____   _____
      _____   _____

P.O. DATE	REQUISITIONER	SHIP VIA	F.O.B. POINT	TERMS
				See Reverse

QTY	UNIT	DESCRIPTION	UNIT PRICE	TOTAL
			SHIPPING	
			TAX	
			OTHER	
			TOTAL	

Tactech, Inc.
Giving You the Ability to Manage Technology

_____
Authorized by   Date

Figure 3-1 Example of purchase order form.

10. Routing instructions

11. Method of payment (i.e., prepaid, paid on delivery, cash discounts, and the like)

12. Insurance details—extent of coverage and whether to be paid by buyer or seller

13. Any general or special conditions

14. Any special documents required, such as:

    a. Packing List

      b. Commercial Invoice

      c. Airway Bill or Bill-of-Lading

    Also, for offshore buys:

      d. Letter of credit

      e. Certificates of origin

      f. Insurance Certificates

      g. Special Instructions, or other documents required, such as special inspection, and condition

15. Various technical clauses that should be included (a few are reviewed later in this chapter, though the detailed discussion is in Chapter 14.)

16. Signature(s) of authorized person committing the company.

Any special transportation, insurance, marking, or packaging requirements should be spelled out in separate clauses. Specific documents used break down into credit documents, commercial invoice, transport, and insurance documents.

Use of Blanket Orders for Repetitive Purchases

A one-time buy means that a new purchase order is issued each time an item is bought. That can be costly. When an item is bought frequently (four or five times per year), it will pay to consider an open, or blanket PO. Releases are made— sometimes by telephone—and this keeps the ordering costs down. Each buyer decides when to blanket order, based on knowledge of the costs. By grouping items into larger packages that can be purchased more economically, there is the added bonus that administrative costs are greatly reduced as well.

A buyer can use a blanket order for these types of items (as examples):

- Low dollar value items
- High-volume items
- Repetitively purchased items
- Maintenance, repair, and operating items (MRO)

Blanket POs are ideal for mill supplies, small tools, and office supplies, among other things. The objective is to combine small, relatively unattractive quantities into reasonably large packages to gain price and service advantages. So the result is that time and expense to buy are reduced. Also, the burden of stocking inventory is largely shifted to the supplier. The advantages in using blanket orders can be summarized as follows:

- Saves repetition and time
- Simplifies paperwork by eliminating many reqs

- Allows expediting by using department
- Assures continuity and uniformity
- Decreases lead-time for buyer and seller
- Usually provides price advantage

Terms and Conditions of Purchase

In addition to the "nuts and bolt" issues covered by the purchase order document, such as prices, delivery dates, and quality requirements, there will almost always be other terms and conditions that will need to be clearly worked out between buyer and seller. One fairly common term covers cash discounts.

Payment Terms

Cash discounts are part of the terms of purchase and should not be confused with a quantity discount, a package discount, or a trade discount which are reflected in the price of the items purchased. Cash discounts are an allowance extended to the buyer to encourage prompt payment of the seller's invoice before a stated time interval. Suppliers usually have standard discounts used for this purpose. Sometimes, these discounts can be negotiated higher as one of the considerations when buying. Usual discounts range from 1/2, 1, and 2%, while a 3% discount is usually tops. Any larger discount is a signal that something may be wrong. The seller may be desperate for cash, or in financial trouble.

As an example, a typical discount will be expressed as "2 percent 10/Net 30," which means 2% of the value of the purchase may be deducted if the invoice is paid within 10 days after receipt. Otherwise, the invoice is to be paid "net" within 30 days. "Net" terms require that payment be upon receipt of invoice, while "Net 10" implies a 10 day grace period, and so on.

"Net 10 prox." means payment of entire invoice by the 10th of the month following the month of invoice. "1% e.o.m." means that a 1% discount can be deducted if paid before the end of the month. While the term "or Net 30" is usually added, even if omitted it is customary that the invoice be paid 30 days after receipt. Although ethically questionable the truth is that many companies delay when they can get away with it.

Use a Payment Terms Clause such as:

"Payment terms shall be Net 30 (or as negotiated), per this P.O. covering this purchase."

If an international buy add:

"Payment shall be in U.S. dollar funds (or a foreign currency, if so negotiated). Documents to accompany shipment shall include items as spelled out herein below, or in the Letter of Credit" (or other type of collection).

Shipment Terms

An "FOB" term spells out the division of responsibilities for transportation and passage of title. The goods are deemed to be delivered by seller to buyer at a point spelled out in this clause.

Based on identifying the transfer point for possession of goods, the term determines who will pay the costs and who assumes the risks. Called "INCOTERMS" (an acronym for International Commercial Terms), these spell out "What the buyer must do" and "What the seller must do." Lacking mention to the contrary, a PO is assumed to be a "shipping point contract," which means that the buyer is responsible when the seller has delivered the goods to the carrier.

Because these INCOTERMS are fully spelled out in detail in Chapter 17, they will not be repeated here. As previously noted, many additional specific clauses also will be found in Chapter 14.

Change Notices

If important conditions of purchase change following the issuance of a purchase order, a formally numbered *Change Notice* should be issued to confirm the action being taken. Failure to formally document and issue a Change Notice can be cause for later dispute.

Acknowledgments

Although formal purchase order acknowledgments are still used by some, many companies have dropped these as useless paperwork. Most suppliers insist on using their own acknowledgment forms anyway. But the acknowledgment is mandatory for major purchases such as construction and equipment. A case is often made for their legal necessity. Although it may be said there is no contract without an acknowledgment, it is also true that *shipment* is an acceptable form of acknowledgment. Companies may prefer to use formal acknowledgments, but don't get caught up in an elaborate system of control for this document. Probably 50% of the major companies don't use one, and, of those that do, few insist on them in all circumstances.

Follow-Up and Expediting

Even when the job of expediting is delegated, buyers are ultimately responsible for deliveries. Sometimes referred to as "follow-up," it's still one of the most important parts of the buying process to get the goods into the plant or office as needed. Expediting is a problem-solving function, and in fact, the term derives from Latin, meaning literally, "to free one caught by the foot."

Most PO forms have a page devoted to follow-up notations. Routine follow up can be a postcard, or special form that is readily checked off for information requested. Boxes to be checked for such information as "Will Ship," "Freight car No.," "Pro-bill No.," and so on. Still, most information will be by telephone.

Today, the attempt to keep minimum inventories with a just-in-time (JIT) outlook can badly hurt the customer if anything goes wrong. Just-in-time requires that goods be delivered on time. Routine expediting can be handled by stores or someone watching over the inventory. Even then, when difficulties arise, the problem comes back to the buyer's desk.

Common delivery problems that occur include:

- Late shipments
- Delivery promises not made, or given and not reliable
- Shipments seldom complete; with many backorders
- Lost or delayed shipments due to incomplete or late shipping documents
- Delayed shipments due to insufficient or wrong information in the bill-of-lading
- Shipment by more expensive method than requested

What forms are used for the routing tasks? There should be some ground rules for your clerical people to follow. Some companies still prefer manual card type systems, such as an open tub with all POs filed by date or supplier. Colored tabs may signal those POs requiring action. Tickler or follow-up files that are computerized can remind what action to take. Using the World Wide Web can also sometimes provide valued assistance. As an example, Federal Express maintains a web site that can be accessed to track any of its shipments. Go to http://www.fedex.com, and click on "Tracking," and this will bring up a form to enter the airbill number. Upon entering the number, and clicking the "Request Tracking Info" button, finally the information about delivery is given.

When routine expediting fails, buyers must back up the activity by contacting whatever supplier management level is needed to get results. They must phone and take action to apply pressure for results. This may include field expediting or buyer visits to the supplier. Having expediters report to buyers clearly says, "They speak for me." Moreover, some companies do not segregate the expediting function, opting instead to leave it as a part of the buyer's job. The underlying philosophy in this regard is that buyers are accountable well beyond the initial placement of the purchase order.

Buyers have more muscle to get the goods than clerical people because sellers try to convince them how well they serve. When the buyer calls attention to poor service, action soon follows, as salespeople are always looking for the next order.

Receiving

Packing lists are used to inventory the merchandise received. These are documents prepared by the seller for use in receiving, to verify that what is received conforms to what was ordered. Information typically includes purchase order number, part number, quantity shipped, and any other data the buyer requests. Receiving reports are matched against invoices before payment.

If an import, the packing list is required by customs officials at both export and import ports to check the cargo. A bill of lading is a receipt for the cargo and contract for transportation between a shipper and the carrier.

In recent years, bar coding has speeded up the receiving stores process. Industry's Code 39, as an example, provides a common language, allowing fast on-line receiving and inventory control. When receiving goods, they are checked in by bar coding, which immediately updates the status of stock on hand. Likewise, as an item is withdrawn for shipment, a sweep of the scanner deducts the item from the inventory. Used widely by major retail stores, bar coding is commonly used by manufacturers and distributors.

Price Checking

Payment is normally handled by accounts payable, with exceptions routed to buyers for approval or correction. The buyer verifies price and terms that do not agree, and adjusts any discrepancies.

As previously noted, some companies play games by seeing how long they can delay payment and get away with it. Buyers on occasion are called upon to press their own accounts payable function to pay on time. Most buyers want their company to pay promptly, in the interest of maintaining supplier relationships.

Buying Documents to Complete an International Purchase

The foreign purchase contract can be the normal PO, but buyers must spell out lots of detail that they wouldn't normally use for a domestic purchase. If specific wording and added information is needed, refer to the *Purchasing Handbook,* or a reference book on international buying such as *Global Purchasing: Reaching for the World.*

Documents break down into credit documents, commercial invoice, transport and insurance documents. Export documents, obtained by the seller and shipper, that move as a packet, along with the shipment, are shown in Figure 3-2. How many do buyer's know and influence?

- Certificate of Insurance assures the buyer that the seller has insured the goods, to cover loss or damage while en route.

- Commercial Invoice is a must! It itemizes the items shipped and/or the services rendered, quantity, terms, and other data. Prepared by the seller, it is the bill from the seller and states the amount of money and the

PRIMARY DOCUMENTS REQUIRED IN INTERNATIONAL TRADE

PRODUCT DESCRIPTION AND IDENTIFICATION ON ALL DOCUMENTS		USED BY: ✔ = YES				
DOCUMENT	PURPOSE	EXPORTER'S GOVERNMENT	EXPORTER	IMPORTER'S GOVERNMENT	IMPORTER	COMMON CARRIER
BILL OF LADING	RECEIPT FOR SHIPMENT BY SPECIFIED DATE, LINE OR SHIP		✔	✔	✔	✔
INSURANCE POLICY OR CERTIFICATE	COVER RISKS OF DAMAGE OR LOSS		✔		✔	✔
COMMERCIAL INVOICE	QUANTITY, PRICE, CURRENCY, PAYMENT DUE, CREDIT TERMS	✔	✔	TO DETERMINE APPLICABLE DUTY	✔	
SHIPPER'S EXPORT DECLARATION	SOURCE OF EXPORT STATISTICS IDENTITY OF EXPORTER, IMPORTER DESTINATION PORT, METHOD OF SHIPMENT, WEIGHT AND CLASSIFICATION	✔	✔			✔
EXPORT LICENSE	PERMISSION TO EXPORT	✔	✔			✔
IMPORT ENTRY	SOURCE OF IMPORT STATISTICS SAME AS SHIPPER'S DATA, BUT ADDS LOADING PORT AND COUNTRY OF ORIGIN			IMPORT STATISTICS	✔	
CERTIFICATES OF WEIGHT, CONDITION, MANUFACTURE, ETC.	PROOF PRODUCT MEETS SPECIFIED CHARACTERISTICS		✔	IF AFFECTS HEALTH OR SANITARY LAW	✔	
CERTIFICATE OF ORIGIN (FORM A)	ALLOWS IMPORT CONTROL, AND DETERMINES PROPER DUTY		✔	DETERMINE DUTY RATE & IMPORT CONTROL	✔	

Figure 3-2 Documents to complete an international buy.

currency in which the seller expects the buyer to pay. This invoice is used by the importer to clear merchandise through U.S. Customs.

- Shipper's Export Declaration lists quantity, weight, value, identity of goods, exporter, consignee, manner of transport, port of export and carrier, port of unloading, and ultimate destination. It provides the local government with export statistical information.

- Letter of Credit is a commonly used form to make payment for an offshore buy. It is a financial document, issued by the bank, guaranteeing payment to the seller when proper documents are received. Contains a description of goods and how payment is to be made.

- Import Declaration shows basically the same information as on Shipper's Declaration.

- Certificate of (various, special items, such as . . .) Weight, Inspection, Manufacture, Sanitary Condition, and others. Various certificates may be required or requested by the buyer to ensure satisfaction that what is bought, is received. An inspection certificate is normally prepared by an independent party. It attests to condition, quality, or quantity of goods shipped.

With respect to the Certification Clause, consider something like the following:

> "Seller will submit products for approval, to (either UL, or other agency, such as German TUV, and Canadian CAL approval, depending on where your purchases are to be sold.) Seller must submit proper certificates that its products comply with DOE/FTC, OSHA, ASHRE, ASME, and other requirements and will meet published rated capacity and efficiency per Seller's submitted specifications."

A Certificate of Origin assures buyers and the government of the country in which the products or goods were manufactured. The Certificate may show origin of any materials and labor used to produce goods. It may specify percent of local content to secure reduced tariffs for goods, produced in certain favored countries.

To ensure you get proper documentation, include a certification clause both in the Purchase order, and in any Letter of Credit, such as:

> "Seller must submit a Certificate of Origin Form A (or Insurance, etc.) stating the percentage of Seller's product that is made or produced in their country. Submittal must be made on Form A."

The above is a brief overview of the documentation requirements for an international buy. Any buyer actually buying offshore will want to read the much greater detailed material in *Global Purchasing: Reaching for the World.*

Use of the Computer in Buying

Computers help rid buyers of burdensome paperwork. Computations that used to take days are now possible in milliseconds. The impact of data processing on purchasing is difficult to measure. Although some purchasing people in the past have resisted using the computer, managements generally viewed the computer as aiding communications between customers, distributors, suppliers, carriers, manufacturers, and its financial operations.

Historically, in-house inventory and accounting systems were first to be auto-mated, as these areas have traditionally had heavy clerical workloads. Of course, purchasing issued the purchase order, which triggered much of this paperwork system, so purchasing was always viewed with potential for automation. Now, purchasing is automated in most companies. According to NAPM's 1995 member-ship needs survey, not only is this the case, but 20.9% stated they had a personal computer with a CD-ROM at work.[1]

Other reported advantages have been the availability of better statistical mea-surements not feasible if done manually. It is difficult to prove potential savings to justify more equipment in terms of economy. The big savings come from compressing clerical time to a minimum, thereby letting buyers spend more creative buying time.

While the electronic brain is very fast, it is still a fast "idiot." A machine can only differentiate between the numbers zero and one (the basis of the so-called binary system). However, huge capacity now allows a program to defeat a master chess champion (on at least one occasion). A danger in the ability to churn out huge volumes of data lies in the buyers being swamped with information that has to be digested.

Computers can't think, they can only evaluate what is programmed, and the hackneyed expression about the quality of data, "Garbage In—Garbage out" still rings true. The computer is an information retrieval system, based on what it is fed. It can crank out information, print forms, POs, and the like. However, the buyer must determine the prices to be paid, and the sources to be used. A computer is simply a tool that amplifies the buyer's ability to make sound decisions.

Use of the computer was often forced on the buyer, by those trying to control inventory data or accounts payable. Some buyers perceived extra workloads that were of little value to their buying functions. A major fear, and reason for early resistance, was that the decision-making itself would be computerized. But this is seldom the case, as buying decisions are still a vital human responsibility.

Today, computers are everywhere. Buyers long ago learned of the advantages in data manipulation which make routine the administrative drudgeries of the job. Having routine small-dollar value "call" orders issued via computer—without

---

[1]*Purchasing Today,* NAPM Tempe, AZ, May, 1996, p. 17.

buyer review—allows greater attention to high-value items. About 70% of all purchase orders could now be issued without buyer change, and not affect total material costs.

A bare bones system not only writes purchase orders, but also keeps track of them, their deliveries, invoices, and payments. It also makes available many details of the purchasing process for study. Follow-up can be handled by exception review of orders, acknowledgments, and inspection records.

Modems enable machines to "talk" to each other by sending data over phone lines. The supplier's computer can send back quotations and other availability information in a few minutes. By tying a supplier's data system into the buyer's, computers are able to determine when stock is low and automatically produce an order in the supplier plant, without need for requisitions or a purchase order.

Although computers may serve as a valuable tool to link company to company, scan the needs list, make the quotes, and so on, the buying decision will remain a vital human responsibility.

Buyer Information on Networks

PMs should consider getting their buyers a stand-alone PC to speed handling of routine paperwork. The computer located at the buyer's desk helps in sending inquiries, follow-up letters, and so on. It can by used to analyze and calculate purchases made, and it is used to file facts that can be arranged to produce reports for the buyer's analyses. The computer will improve accuracy and can be a great time saver in making better buying decisions.

In large or multibranch companies, each buying station can be connected with others into a network. A network allows communications with others, and provides inputs and reports from a central "server" computer.

Those companies wanting to prevent unauthorized access to price files will install various types of identification or blocking codes. Within the system, all users are identified by name and a number. Anyone not having the combination, or password, cannot get data. Some are allowed access to information, but can't make any data changes. Dollar limits before approval of a higher authority are often programmed in as well.

Before considering what equipment and software is available, it is wise to consider what we want to accomplish. Establishing an automated purchasing system can be considered in three steps: (1) define the things to be done, (2) design the structure of the data files to be maintained, and (3) put the existing data into the system.

Designing the Files

Files maintained most commonly are: (1) commodity information, (2) buyer user information, (3) standard phrases and forms, and (4) location index and information. Let's look at each of these files.

Any purchasing system needs a method to link information about the items bought and various suppliers. To do this, a commodity code is almost universally used, rather than a part number. For example, by calling up a two-, four-, or six-number code, all bolts used or bought would be listed. A control number is assigned each location for statistics and price comparisons. The greatest advantage is when multiple buying operations want to put the total buying package together.

With multiple buying operations, a central database can provide items to supplier linkage. Buyers, looking for a source for a new item, can scan the code numbers and study suppliers currently selling them a similar item. With each code number, a description and a name should be listed. Codes can also be used in setting up lead-time listings, a price index, and quality standards.

Many personal computers can be purchased for $1500 or less. Software will add another $500 to $600 cost, so for about a $2000 investment, the necessary equipment is available. Today, in all but the one person company it is almost inexcusable if a computer is not employed in some facet of purchasing!

Considering all of the available equipment and software is beyond the scope of this work, but it may be useful to generalize on the minimum standard that a buyer should have available to perform routine analyses and administrative functions with minimal clerical intervention.

Although computers come in a variety of sizes ranging from large mainframes to small personal computers, the latter will suffice for most small purchasing operations. The first choice will revolve around selection from one of the two main standards in the market—Apples and IBM PC compatibles.

Advocates of the Apple standard point to the attractive graphical nature and "user friendliness" of its operating system. However, the most popular equipment is IBM PC compatible, which offers a much larger availability of software. The PC model typically operates using the Microsoft Windows® operating system— which has become the world's largest seller. Though once deemed inferior by many in the field, Microsoft's standard has made great strides in recent years. Windows® 95 now provides most of the features previously available only on Apple's machines.

Other attributes to consider are the microprocessor and storage space. The former decision will be dictated more by availability, as the technology is evolving so quickly that today's recommendation may not even be available next year— so shop according to your budget.

For storage, today a gigabyte hard drive is common for primary storage of data and programs. In addition, a secondary 3 1/2 inch floppy disk is virtually indispensable, as it is the standard for program loading, while CD-ROMs are coming on strong because of their convenience coupled with storage capacity. CD-ROMs are a good investment; they are typically sold for less than $100, and offer the benefits of one disk program loading coupled with multimedia features heretofore unavailable on 3.5 disks.

Software Available

For word processing, WordPerfect, WordStar, and Microsoft's Word are three of the most popular packages, but others are available. These word processors often are the cornerstone of software "suites" designed to perform many of the common activities in an office from within a single integrated application. Examples include Microsoft Office and Lotus Smart Suite, two of the best sellers.

Microsoft Excel and Lotus 1-2-3 are two of the more popular spreadsheets available; output can be formatted as the user wishes to do many types of analysis and computation. In addition, both products provide "templates" which are electronic "boilerplates" that guide the user to complete the necessary information along the format of a prescribed form. These tools can be very useful to buyers.

Many other purchasing-specific packages have been put together to save starting from scratch. Following the lead of Computer Aided Design, and Computer Aided Manufacturing (CADCAM) is Computer Aided Purchasing (CAP) and Purchasing Electronic Notebook (PEN). This starter package allows usage without much preliminary study or effort.

CAP includes basic functions and database, master lists of suppliers, items, and POs. The buyer may sort by items, PO, supplier, purchase summary, supplier addresses, and contacts. The system will print purchase orders on existing PO forms, if desired. If the buyer gets into trouble, HELP keys provide explanation. Demonstration software is available from Greentree Software, 122 E. 42nd St., Suite 2200, NY, NY 10168.

There is great advantage in computerizing much of the time consuming, manual work in purchasing. This is an investment that will pay dividends in productivity.

Tapping into the Internet

With the microcomputer in purchasing, it is possible for the purchasing database to tie into a supplier's database through use of a communications modem. This speeds the dissemination of timely and accurate information, as it lets buyers quickly and electronically get price quotes and availability of stock, send a PO, and follow through to completion. The best example of such a modem-based communication tool is the FAX system commonly used to transmit purchase orders, design prints, changes, and miscellaneous inquiries.

In recent months, interest in the Internet has taken off! Many are exploring this relatively new resource as they "cruise the superhighway," or "tap into the Net". Much information is available to those who reach for it. The World Wide Web gives buyers a quick, low-cost medium to get data on suppliers and their offerings. Most major manufacturers have web sites with information of value to today's buyer. As an example, the buyer in search of a special electrical connector can explore AMP's catalog at http://www.amp.com. This is only one example of thousands of similar company sites now accessible on the internet.

Also, it is noted that NAPM has a World Wide Web: http://www.napm.org that allows you to browse their offerings.

Electronic Data Interchange (EDI) Used by Customs

Electronic Data Interchange (EDI) is another area being implemented across much of American business today. EDI is the process by which buyers and sellers can exchange data in machine readable format, thereby bypassing much of the administrative analysis normally required of incoming message traffic. EDI, therefore, when properly implemented, eliminates much if not all of the double and triple key stroke entry which occurs when paper documents flow between buyer and seller; in essence, the buyer presses a send button and the order is entered directly into the sellers order entry system. Such systems offer considerable value to the purchasing profession as a means not only of order entry and communication, but further into the payment process as payments for goods and services are provided electronically.

Let's look at one area where EDI has had a profound positive impact on improving business efficiency. A paperwork glut developed in the early 1990s as Customs paperwork has more than doubled over the past decade. As a result, U.S. Customs is pushed to automate. EDI for Administration Commerce and Transportation (EDIFACT) is striving for standardization of trade terms on invoices.

An array of new computerized systems is being used from the experimental stage to a variety of operating applications including transferring bills of lading. The Port of New Orleans system tracks ships and containers, checks the movement of any hazardous cargo, sends the export declaration, and notifies the broker of the ship's arrival. Use of EDI allows shipments to pass through customs in hours rather than days.

Automation will perhaps allow 80% of the goods to be precleared before arriving in the port. U.S. Customs would like a paperless system eventually. Customs has decided that electronically documented shipments will be cleared through Customs first, thereby creating the incentive for companies to gear up and use modern documentation. Likewise, PMs and buyers should unite on the task of use of the latest technology to enhance their efforts.

4

Strategic Purchasing Supply Initiatives

Experienced CPOs have had days that they thought were going to be easy, only to see them turn into a hectic bind. Other times, they've walked into the office in the morning knowing they were going to be busy with interviews to hire a new buyer—only to lean back in their chair that afternoon with everything done. "What's next," they've wondered and discovered that their busy day had somehow become routine. Why? Because they planned it better than an average day, to start their tasks at once.

Before anyone can effectively implement strategic purchasing supply management, he or she must plan a program of broad personal development and success, in concordance with his or her company's plans and objectives. Here are a few suggestions to begin with:

- List the company's basic characteristics, its strengths and weaknesses.
- What is the future of the markets the company serves?
- How does the company rate when compared to its competitors?
- Identify the company's strategy, its plans, and goals.
- How can the personal and organization values be met, and how can buyers assist in their implementation?
- Can ways to improve on any of the above be found?

Purchasing managers should occasionally ask themselves if they are doing the things expected of a manager. "Am I managing or being managed by my work?" "Am I living up to the proper ethical standard?" "Am I keeping management and the buyers informed of facts they should know?" "Do I support other departments such as engineering and quality control?"

When the managers have an idea that might improve the company's performance, do they speak up? Above all, they should implement the improvement within their own department when they have the opportunity. Far better that managers face up to shortcomings than to have others find them lacking.

Managers should set their strategies based on their unique situations. Purchasing managers should have a strategic plan, and then use effective buying tactics to carry it out. A "strategy" is a plan to reach long-term goals that takes one year or longer to complete. Strategy gives direction. While tactics form the basis for handling the various battles of the day, "strategic planning" is *how* to win the war!

Strategic purchasing planning inherently contains few specific details. Some examples will include:

- Selecting and evaluating suppliers and *motivating* them to supply
- Tapping supplier technological innovation first
- The need for closer ties with suppliers' design capabilities with purchasing/engineering coordination
- Post purchase liaison—warranty and dispute settlements
- Negotiating consigned stock to decrease inventory and free funds for growth requirements

Strategic purchasing planning seeks to identify critical long-range supply issues, and to foresee sourcing changes. This reduces uncertainty by formalizing analytical and creative thinking in cost reduction.

Strategic purchasing planning is a necessity for purchasing to become predictive and *proactive*, rather than *reactive* with short-term problem-solving. Integrating market and supply strategies is a top management responsibility. The CEO should strive to strategically orient the company globally, not solely in marketing but in procurement as well.

Interpreting the strategic implications of global supply assurance for the company is a purchasing management responsibility. The chief purchasing officer (CPO) and the department should:

- Understand interlocking supply relationships such as joint ventures and licensees.
- Integrate with the company's other business strategies through better communications.
- Support company strategic purchasing supply objectives.
- Use cost control to achieve product price leadership.
- Coordinate efforts to achieve quality results from suppliers.

What can the purchasing department buy to support marketing's effort to sell both domestically and abroad? The PM needs to set up cooperative efforts with joint supplier/buyer goals from a supply management outlook to better compete in world markets.

A disturbing survey[1] reported that while some academic literature advocates that purchasing should be significantly involved in major corporate activities *beyond supply*, research data do not show that this actually is taking place. But perhaps this should be of little concern, for in the scope of purchasing and supply management there is more than enough in the job to make major contributions to the company's welfare.

The Role of the Purchasing Manager

The purchasing manager has many roles to play. While he or she is required to be a part-time engineer, lawyer, materials systems analyst, arbitrator, and negotiator, perhaps the role as planner most often needs improvement. The first evidence of professional management is planning, long-range strategic planning.

So logically, a key strategy should be to *improve the management of the purchasing job*. This book has chosen to present a managerial approach to improvement in purchasing. After all, the purchasing manager is first and foremost a *manager*, carrying out company objectives within a policy framework. Purchasing is in the best position to coordinate other functions in reaching sound materials supply decisions. But, while purchasing is in the "best position," it doesn't follow that purchasing is necessarily the "best qualified." When purchasing becomes the best qualified through improvement of the skills of its people, then the goal of higher status will be achieved.

How well PMs get things done through their people is a measure of effectiveness. A frequent failure of the PM is to delegate, to allow those in a buying specialty to make their own decisions, within limits, and to develop good judgment through practice. Some PMs will complain that their buyers won't make such decisions. Perhaps this is the result of constraints that do not allow decisions to be made without prior approval. While major buying problems should be referred to the manager, routine decisions should be referred *only* when necessary.

Few PMs deny the need to delegate. Why, then, do they so often fail in this aspect of their job? This subject has been studied thoroughly, and the American Management Association and others have reported the following observations with respect to the basis of this shortcoming:

- *Failure to delegate fully.* Some managers give the responsibilities, and then later retract part of them. In some cases, there may be a good reason, but generally, this should be avoided.

- *Tendency to bypass others.* This makes it difficult for buyers to make their decisions stick.

---

[1]NAPM's 1996 CAPS inquiry of 556 U.S. and 46 Canadian firms. Three hundred and eight responded for a 49.6% response.

- *Lack of confidence in subordinates.* This really means lack of development of subordinates' competence.
- *Lack of self-discipline.* Buyers must be given a reasonable chance to do the job without constant oversight. Buyers need elbowroom, and that means making a few mistakes as well. Everyone will not perform precisely as we would.
- *Resistance to change.* Failure to accept new methods or new suggestions. Managers cannot know all the innovative things about all the jobs over which they exercise supervision.
- *Fear of competition.* Some executives fear their subordinates may outshine them, especially those brought in from another department, or from the outside.

Every purchasing manager will recognize some of these symptoms from on-the-job experience. Evidence of their existence can be found in the fact that NAPM sponsored a workshop at the 1996 NAPM conference entitled "I Wish My Boss Would Let Me Do My Job!" As a practical matter, no one can do all the tasks or make all the decisions for which he or she is responsible, unless he or she operates as a one-person department.

People who don't make mistakes are people who don't take chances. And people who don't take chances seldom end up winners. Study of failure can bring success just as logically as medical research leads to improved health. Some people may be tired of hearing "how to succeed," so, there can be virtue in failure—if buyers learn and profit from their mistakes. Let's look at "ten commandments" of bad purchasing management that guarantee failure[2]:

1. Don't plan for the future.
2. Worry a lot, especially about things that probably will never happen.
3. Don't recruit ambitious hard chargers.
4. Don't delegate authority; even better, don't teach anyone to handle your job.
5. Don't worry about your subordinates' needs.
6. Whatever happens, stick to your schedules and do things the way they have always been done.
7. Keep 'em ignorant. Don't brief your subordinates on plans and goals.
8. Publicly criticize mistakes to show who's boss.
9. Don't broaden yourself outside of purchasing circles.
10. Develop tunnel vision. Do your own job, but don't try to contribute to the growth and direction of your company.

---

[2]Victor H. Pooler's *Management Perspective* column, "You Can Tell a Winner by the Way He Fails," *Purchasing Week.*

These "guidelines for losers" may inspire some changes in your own mode of operations. Once in a while, it's worth taking a look at how *not* to do things. Although most of us will tend to stay with our patterns developed from habit—the things that usually work—if we're to expand our job performance, we have to open our mind to new patterns to find solutions to problems.

A good leader must have humility (at least some) and courage. One measure of leadership is the number of good decisions made by people while the manager is absent. If the needs or wants of the buyers are satisfied, most of us can lead. Each individual also thinks he or she can buy better than the leader because this is his or her specialization. Is each member better than the manager at his or her specific function? The answer should be "yes." If the answer is "no," it will be difficult to build team spirit. An option to fire or transfer is not *always* optimal or acceptable. The manager's responsibility is to hire, then train and allow buyers to develop themselves.

A leader can't be a success until his or her people are also successful at their jobs. So, a constructive attitude to have is, "I'll do anything I can to help you be successful." In this light the true role of the manager is to serve his or her people, and *not* the reverse. An important point to remember is that buyers should be free to develop their own analytical ability, even if there is a temptation to tell others what to do if you can readily see the solution to the problem.

Football coaches are said to be as good as their recruits. If a manager has the ability to attract good buying candidates, and see that they have the chance to develop themselves, then he or she will succeed as a manager. Without adequate support, failure awaits. Success, as any failure will tell you, is just a matter of luck! Robert Louis Stevenson said it well:

> "What is called Luck is simply Pluck,
>   And doing things over and over,
> Courage and will, perseverance and skill
>   Are the four leaves of Luck's clover."

Selection of Strategies Leads to Action

There are many purchasing issues that can be developed by the manager of purchasing into overall strategies and specific implementations. Because there are so many possibilities, we have divided them into five major groupings: management, sources, prices, inventory, and methods. Some areas for a purchasing organization to contribute to a company's success might include:

Management

- Locate and develop competent people.
- Analyze the purchasing functions to be performed, and eliminate unnecessary costs.

- Manage cost reduction and materials profit improvement programs.
- Develop ways to identify possibilities.
- Interpret the strategic implications of global supply for the company.
- Search globally for new and alternative ideas, products, and materials to improve company profitability.
- Assist in the integration of materials policies.
- See that smooth relationships exist within the company itself, particularly with engineering, finance, and manufacturing.
- Evaluate and participate in decision-making and procedure planning of off-shore purchases.
- Promote work on special materials projects.

Sources

- Develop reliable alternative sources to ensure economic supply for vital materials and components.
- Initiate and maintain good supplier relationships.
- Assist suppliers with quality and process improvements.
- Focus on the buyer's intrinsic buying power—use leverage to improve the company's competitive market position.
- Analyze and report on long-range availability and costs of major sources.
- Upgrade product quality through quality and reliability initiatives.

Prices

- Procure materials at the lowest total landed cost, consistent with the quality and service required.
- Substitute less costly materials when possible.
- Monitor price trends of major purchased items to provide management with reasonable cost forecasts of long-range material availability.

Inventory

- Set material standards for special inventory planning.
- Monitor assets in inventory to keep the minimum investment in materials inventory consistent with avoiding outages of critical supply items.
- Keep inventory losses due to duplication, waste, and obsolescence of purchased materials to a minimum.

Methods

- Construct and implement key commodity plans.
- Track short- and long-range material supply availability.
- Search out new materials development and availability.
- Strive to source through the best buying channel.
- Use available purchasing cost reduction techniques.
- Integrate commodity productivity projects with new product development projects.
- Maintain a strong Total Quality Management (TQM) System to achieve and maintain quality requirements.
- Promote standardization and simplification of components and products.
- Maintain adequate, and accurate records, and develop use of computer information tools to maximize administrative efficiency.
- Create material systems studies about information systems and techniques.
- Conduct or take part in make-versus-buy studies.
- Evaluate consolidation of shipments, forms of transportation, and the like, in cooperation with the traffic function.
- Manage performance-related strategies including control of department expenses.
- Measure purchasing productivity and interpret results by implementing integrated materials measurements.
- Construct and implement minority/small business programs.
- Prioritize all program elements according to importance.

Often there will be substrategies. For example, a strategy to "maintain supply" may have contributing strategies such as (1) develop new source, (2) develop supplier partnering, (3) contract long range, and so on. As another example, a strategy to import more low cost components might need a substrategy to maintain a domestic backup source.

Effective management seeks to look at future occurrences by projecting and interpreting trends. A long-range strategic approach of between three and five years is appropriate, as predicting further out becomes more difficult. A pronounced trend toward global purchasing makes this a top priority. In addition, here are some other promising strategies for purchasing management to consider:

- Use procurement planning to control major commodities.
- Search for low-cost suppliers.
- Seek buying leverage through buying teams.

- Compute total landed cost of acquisition.
- Gain assurance of economic supply for future needs through more intensive selection, motivation, and evaluation of suppliers.
- Foster supplier/buyer partnering.
  1. Joint cooperation on new products or projects.
  2. Seek greater use of suppliers' knowledge and capabilities.
  3. Negotiate consigned stock to decrease inventory and free funds for growth requirements.
- Establish national agreements for multibranch purchasing.
- Urge use of cost reduction techniques such as value analysis, systems contracting, make versus buy, and the learning curve.
- Develop an effective purchasing manual.
- Protect prices by a strategy of hedging versus forward buy.
- Improve post-purchase liaison, and settlement of disputes.

Develop and Use a Purchasing Manual

Purchasing policies exist, whether or not they are in writing. (Purchasing Manuals are useful to document policy and procedures, and are used extensively by most companies; smaller companies should adopt a simplified manual.) A company Purchasing Manual can be as brief as 7 to 15 pages giving simple, straightforward statements on general policy, forms, and their use. Medium to larger-sized companies gradually build a detailed working manual. This section is for those wanting to begin a manual or improve an existing one. This is certainly a strategic undertaking as it allows the purchasing department's long-term policy and procedures to become institutionalized as a guideline for efficient operation.

What does a manual do for buyers? It defines purchasing scope and clarifies purchasing's role and methods for other company functions affected by its activities. It is an aid to avoiding potential conflicts between departments.

A large company's purchasing manual may contain several volumes. Few manuals are written from scratch, rather they evolve as the need arises. A simple start calls for drawing up an outline and gradually filling it with various memos, bulletins, and data. Later, these can be reduced to a compact manual for endorsement by top management as the company's official purchasing policy. The editing job can be delegated, say to several "comers" who operate as a committee. A review of the material with the PM provides an excellent chance to discuss what is presently being done in the department and what some of the people think about it.

Most manuals are kept in a loose-leaf ring binder, thereby making additions and deletions easier. Also, the manual can be placed "on line" via the company's internal computer network. As in a book, there should be headings covering various subjects. Each section under a major heading should have its own sequence of page numbers, perhaps combining section and page designation (for example A-1, A-2, and so on.). In this way, changes or additions affect only one particular section. A table of contents will provide easy reference; and—to keep the manual as concise as possible—an appendix can be used for forms and details not included earlier.

The large amount of paperwork required in an acquisition is a detriment to efficient buying. The challenge is to minimize the documentation while not losing control. A manual is a place to keep many pieces of needed information. It's especially important to keep a record of special procedures. For example, an import from Denmark may require special handling information that may be spelled out and kept available for later reference.

The subjects you include will depend on what you want the manual to do and how your department operates. Below are some of the topics that may be covered:

1. Scope and responsibilities of purchasing
2. Various policies defined
3. Supplier relationships spelled out
4. Source selection criteria
5. Standards used when contracting for materials, subcontracts, equipment, or construction
6. Gift and entertainment policy
7. Any miscellaneous procedures needing to be explained

Many buyers have found a supplier card information file of value. The card will list the company's name, address, and zip code. The phone number and person to phone are helpful. The terms of sale, FOB point, local representative, his or her phone number, and so on are also noted. The supplier is identified as manufacturer, distributor, and the type of items normally stocked or manufactured. Obviously, this is best accomplished electronically with a personal computer.

Below is a sample outline that may be useful in creating a purchasing manual:

Part 1. Responsibilities and objectives of purchasing

    A. *Major responsibilities* (Outline the broad functions of purchasing. Avoid descriptions of specific duties.)

        1. Formulate buying policies, plans, procedures.

        2. Gather material and market information.

        3. Handle procurement and expediting.

        4. Other (e.g., surplus disposal, receiving, traffic).

        5. Exceptions (e.g., buying advertising, insurance).

B. *Primary objectives* (These should be the general goals of purchasing; a bit philosophical, perhaps, from which departmental policies are derived.)

1. Serve the company economically and contribute to profits.
2. Procure materials at the lowest cost consistent with quality and service.
3. Maintain adequate sources.
4. Keep inventories at minimum essential levels.
5. Keep management informed of market conditions and procurement problems.
6. Cooperate with other company units.
7. Search for new and improved materials.
8. Explore standardization.
9. Keep abreast of purchasing methods and techniques.

Part II. Policies. (Don't let procedures creep in. Define attitudes only.)

A. *General policies*

1. Determination of need; specifications, quantities. (Who is responsible? Does purchasing have any influence?)
2. Purchase commitments. (Who makes them? What are the restrictions?)
3. Supplier contacts. (By purchasing only? Any limits?)

B. *Buying policies*

1. Central or local procurement (Multiplant companies should state what headquarters buys, and what will be done by the branch locations, and so on.)
2. Selecting sources of supply (Discuss criteria used.)
3. Multiple versus single sources (What are the advantages of each for your company?)
4. Trade relationships (Do you favor them? When are they practiced?)
5. Buying from stockholders (You may want to avoid this one.)
6. Consideration of small business (A "must" if you have government contracts.)
7. Negotiation (When should it be used? When is it optional?)
8. Competitive bids (When required? How many?)
9. Trial orders and samples (State the obligations.)
10. Classified purchases (Again, for government orders.)

11. Speculative purchases (You'll be against them unless you're in a commodity business.)

12. Foreign purchases (When should they be considered?

13. Interplant buying (For multiplant companies.)

14. Employee purchases (For or against?)

C. *Pricing and payment* (Clearly state your position on each practice: when it may be used, when preferred, and special conditions.)

   1. Unpriced orders

   2. Estimated prices

   3. Escalation

   4. Liquidated damages

   5. Deferred payments

   6. Progress payments

   7. Cash discounts

   8. Use of forward buy or hedging action

D. *Relationships with other departments*

   1. Cooperation with requisitioners. (You will cooperate, of course; the point is to impress it on others.)

   2. Delegated authority (Any circumstances when others may assume purchasing prerogatives?)

   3. Emergency orders (You are prepared for them, but don't encourage them.)

   4. Dissemination of price information (Who may get it?)

   5. Inspection

   6. Receiving and traffic

   7. Legal assistance

   8. Credit assistance

   9. Make-or-buy (Who decides? Purchasing's role?)

E. *Supplier relationships*

   1. Receiving and interviewing sales people (Whom will you see? When? For how long?)

   2. Evaluating suppliers' prospects (Are you prepared to tell them their chances, or do you prefer to hedge?)

   3. Advising unsuccessful bidders (How much will you tell them? Will they have to ask?)

    4. Accepting suggestions from suppliers (Do you encourage them? What will you do with them?)

    5. Visiting suppliers' plants (Who arranges? Who pays?)

    6. Backdoor selling (You're against it; what are the penalties?)

    7. Handling complaints and rejections (Who handles them? What do you expect from the supplier as relief?)

    8. Dealing with cancellations (Do you try to limit them? Will you pay the costs?)

F. *Ethics*

    1. Courtesy and fairness (Of course, you're against sin, but how you say it counts.)

    2. Confidential information (What do you do to safeguard supplier confidences?)

    3. Entertainment (How much is acceptable? Do your buyers have expense accounts?)

    4. Gifts and gratuities (Where do you draw the line?)

    5. Conflict of interest (How is "interest" defined? If you have a code, to whom does it apply?)

Part III. Duties and organization

A. *Specific duties of the purchasing department* (Make a detailed list, but if you think it's too obvious, this section may be omitted altogether.)

    1. Select suppliers.

    2. Place purchase orders.

    3. Expedite.

    4. Audit invoices.

    5. Maintain order files.

    6. Maintain catalog files.

    7. Maintain price information.

    8. Disseminate product information.

    9. Report to management.

    10. Prepare statistics.

B. *Organization*

    1. Position of the purchasing department in the company.

    2. Organization chart

C. *Position guides*

    1. Guide for each key position: director of purchasing, purchasing manager, buyers or buyer/planners, expediters (if applicable), administrators, analysts, and so on.

        a. To whom does the manager report?

        b. Whom does the CPO supervise?

        c. Specific duties of position

        d. Authority: its limits and extent

Part IV. Procedures (This can be a large section if each detail is included. Many purchasing managers, however, believe it has no place in a manual. If desired, it may be made a separate document. Moreover, if your methods are relatively simple, there is probably no need for it all.)

A. *Buying procedures* (Reproductions or sample forms may be included.)

    1. Requisitions

    2. Inquiries

    3. Purchase orders

    4. Cash orders

    5. Blanket orders

    6. Invoices

    7. Receiving reports

    8. Change orders

    9. Credits

    10. Cancellations

B. *Filing practice*

    1. Order files

    2. Inquiry files

    3. Catalog files

    4. Price files

    5. Part history files

C. *Contracts* (This section should describe the various kinds of contracts: when they should be used; how they should be prepared.)

    1. Subcontracts

    2. Service contracts

    3. Construction contracts

D. *Special procedures* (Those that require unusual attention, involve special trade practices, or are performed so infrequently that reminders are needed.)

   1. Buying raw materials

   2. Commodity buying

   3. Buying capital equipment

   4. Disposing of scrap and surplus

E. *Reports* (Define each report: who gets it, what it contains, when it is due.)

F. *Statistics* (Explain where to get them, how to organize them, what to do with them.)[3]

Any manual, to be effective, must be tailored to meet the needs of the individual company. While it may be helpful to find out how other companies have worded theirs and what is included in them, it is a mistake to believe that any existing manual can be found that will fit every department's requirements. In fact, much of the benefit you can expect to derive from your manual lies in the thought and care that goes into the process of putting existing purchasing policies into writing.

Supply Plans to Control Major Commodities

A buyer in a smaller company can use planning as well as one in a huge conglomerate, even though they may have little need to cooperate with other buyers. In that case the planning is still valid, but the buyer can ignore the interplay of others. However, the following section will clarify the difficult role of pooling volumes of purchases from several independent departments or divisions.

With knowledge of the needs and interests of the operating divisions, planning is made possible by a document in the form of a *Commodity Supply Plan* that is the basis for action. Each manager should decide how to approach the tasks by using the combined inputs of top management, finance, marketing, engineering, manufacturing, and purchasing. At a minimum, the plan should include (1) targets for the number of new buying or value analysis teams to add, (2) savings targets for each, (3) steps to take to coordinate with engineering, (4) efforts to manage suppliers, and (5) steps to improve make-versus-buy approaches.

Commodity supply plans maintain focus. They should be adjusted to the supply market and production systems, as well as marketing strategies and company

---

[3]Originally developed by John Van de Water and Harold Barnett, in senior author's "Purchasing Man and His Job," *1964 AMA*, pp. 212–216, and now updated.

objectives. Each manufacturing location can use the plan in the sourcing of its requirements.

The commodity supply plan is a written strategy, and is controlled by the lead buyer as agreed to by the team. The task of planning and nurturing teams is the job of the central headquarters commodity manager, or PM. Depending on organization, the "captain" who puts the plan into action, most logically, but not always, is the largest user. Some of the most successful teams have been led by that buyer who has the enthusiasm and talent to get the job done. When located in a remote plant, there is no way the team captain can do the job of the central manager, or the reverse. They are separate responsibilities.

The roles of planning and team activities need to be defined enough for each participant to get good results. There shouldn't be shackling red tape! There is sometimes friction when a buyer from headquarters tries to coordinate buying with many decentralized buying operations, so the central buyer must have enough "statesmanship" to allow the team captains to perform their job. The team captain, who is to negotiate for all, still has to respect the headquarters manager's central interests.

Commodity supply plans are a means of putting together combined usages. Figure 4-1 shows the three parts of procurement planning for a commodity: History, Commodity Overview, and the Strategic Plan itself. The brief history is the volume by using location, suppliers and splits of business, prices over the last three years, and source evaluation. The latter includes supply issues, labor contract dates, delivery performance, quality, and cost performance.

The plan should include the manner of implementing strategic goals into tactical actions to achieve desired results and controlling progress. The objective is to foresee and eliminate supply problems before they occur. The important team members are identified. The documented plan becomes the blueprint used by each buying location as it sources its requirements.

To execute the plans, teams need to be formed. Once in place, this team is quickly activated by phone, under stress of impending price increase, product trouble or deliveries, or whatever the need. However, teams will not be built without management support and direction. First we need to answer, "How do these teams work?"

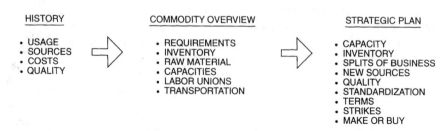

Figure 4-1   Three parts of a procurement commodity plan.

Seek Leverage with Buying Teams

To ensure that company buyers have leverage to exercise they must have options of where to buy. The best of both worlds is to strengthen the autonomy of the decentralized buying unit while using combined "economic voice" as leverage in negotiations. Most companies achieve the former go-it-alone approach. The latter requires teamwork and more strategic planning, and a good "climate" is needed to achieve results.

A PM needs to build teamwork. Using a sports analogy, assume you're on a football team that is playing in the Super Bowl on national TV. Which would a person prefer?: Your team wins by four touchdowns, but you dropped four of five passes thrown to you. Compare that to the team losing by two touchdowns, despite your catching a record 20 passes for 300 yards. Which do you choose? So, if to a degree everyone is out for himself, it's obviously not easy for a manager to build a team.

Teams are useful when buyers seek to have a say in controlling their market-place. If a company consists of a single plant, or performs decentralized buying, the seller often can determine the marketplace. That is, the suppliers may decide to sell to them as a house account, off the street, or by special arrangement. The supplier may decide to be highly competitive in the east, but get higher prices out west where they have little competition. In short, buyers buy in the market that *they* define. And, sellers will negotiate with each buyer in a company who buys from them, that is, unless *the buyer* defines his or her marketplace.

It's often a stated management objective that the corporation is going to use its combined volume leverage in making its purchases. There is no debate about the results required, but the question is, "How do you do it?" One way is to mobilize buyers into task force teams to present a united front to suppliers. These teams often do not follow organization structure. A variety of goals is set by the team. This way, the buyer and not solely the supplier is defining the marketing arena and deciding when to negotiate. Whoever can define the global marketplace often can command the pricing situation. By redefining the marketplace to the buyer's advantage by breaking local, or regional selling, a much better deal often results.

Of course everybody is for teamwork. However, if one believes teamwork means, "Others have to cooperate with me," but not the reverse, then it's not going to work! The roles of planning and teams need to be defined.

PMs should foster commitment from the team members, manage team conflicts, and help keep teams focused on reachable goals. They can help solve obstacles in the team's way, and make sure team members know their role. Giving support and feedback helps the team know where it stands. Experience has shown that:

- Teams have been highly successful.
- They are fragile.

- Communication suffers if leadership is not shared.
- Team leaders normally are the largest buyers of the item.
- Team members who endorse a plan will follow it.

There is strength in consensus in carrying out what the team decides should be done. When a team endorses a plan, each member has a commitment to carry out a specific negotiation with the objective of obtaining company-wide contracts. The result is the lowest possible cost material acquisition.

Many examples of successful teams are known to the authors for buying items such as motors, valves, capacitors, fans—and numerous other commodities common to multiple plant organizations. Only about 25 teams are needed for most companies to control more than 90% of their production purchases.

Purchasing councils are formed by having a representative from each purchasing location that meets to plot strategy and check results. Usually, the PM will fill this function.

Table 4-1 shows how an actual team today controls its major motor purchases. This chart depicts combining purchase volume for a typical buying team. At the top the using plants Nos. 1, 2, and so on, are listed. The suppliers are A, B, and so on. Analysis shows that 30 million dollars are spent on motors purchased from supplier A by buyers in all the plants. Negotiations of this magnitude should produce greater savings than each buyer could achieve alone.

If plant No. 1 centralized its motor buys, it could negotiate 65 million dollars. Plant No. 2 could negotiate 35 million, and so on. Smaller plants may buy under $1 million. However, what would be the result if all 145 million dollars were collectively negotiated?

If 25 buyers are all buying from the same suppliers, usually three or four buyers will spend the most dollars. The remaining buyers all need to have the same story and approach with the suppliers. The smaller slices of the purchase pie have much to gain so they usually will go along with those with greater leverage, *if their input is requested and valued.* The combination central/decentral-

Table 4-1. Team combines purchase volume

"Multi-level" approach to buying. Millions of U.S. dollars.

| Supplier | Plants | | | | |
	#1	#2	#3	Others	Total
A	15	0	10	5	30
B	35	5	5	3	48
C	0	20	5	1	26
D	10	8	2	1	21
All others	5	2	3	10	20
Total	65	35	25	20	$145 million

ized approach has proven effective, but takes a high degree of cooperation. Requirements can be combined for a central negotiation.

Here is another example of a successful purchasing team with purchases of $5.5 million of fans. In this example, 14 individual buyers throughout the company buy these type fans. Five major buying team members, with concurrence from the others, met before the supplier was invited to negotiate an announced price increase. Exercising leverage, the price increase was cut in half. This amounted to a $250,000 cost savings through use of combined buying power. Prices stayed firm for several months while under negotiations.

If each buyer buys at the lowest price he or she can get, what more can be expected with a decentralized organization? What kind of negotiation leverage or power has the buying company got? How does anyone speak for a company in a decentralized setup? The answer is in the use of buying teams and councils that focus on the highly repetitive purchases where every company has potential high volume leverage, and many common items from major suppliers. Let's summarize how buying teams operate:

- All plant (or decentralized) buyers buy each item to the best unit price, using normal "day-to-day" purchasing practices.

- The commodity team, under guidance of its "captain," uses a purchasing strategic supply plan to gather information, and form the negotiation team.

- All buyers carry out the negotiation strategy of the plan because they take part in setting it, realizing how their buying is strengthened.

- The result is lower total purchase material costs and/or improved service because of the buyer's individual negotiations that are enhanced by total volume leverage, which in turn reduces unit price and/or improves service at each plant location.

We have seen how consolidated buying can pay big dividends to participating locations in the multiplant organization. A logical implementation vehicle for such arrangements is a National Purchasing Agreement (NPA), which may be issued from the headquarters or a designated major branch. Many major companies like to sell by such agreements. They can be used for most materials and components, provided the volume warrants it. All buyers may draw upon the volume negotiated prices.

National Purchasing Agreements can cover about 80% of most companies' purchases. They are most commonly used for metals, motors, hardware, copper products, chemicals, and the like. They can have specific prices, but often have purchased earned discounts (PED) that grant reductions by a percentage of volume over set target amounts. For example: 1% reduction in price for volume over $1 million, 3% over $3 million, and so on. Recall there must be some justification for lower prices in the suppliers' costs. Benefits are a mutual win–win for the partners, with higher volume sales for lower priced purchases.

Tactics to Carry Out Strategic Plans

Tactical initiatives are short-range, day-to-day actions concluded usually in less than 1 year. Tactics are how to *win the battle*! Many experienced managers each morning write down at least three tactical things to be done during the day, regardless of any interruptions.

Tactical planning has two key components, one that is quantifiable, the other not. The quantifiable part might be in a budgetary form that equates money or quantity with time. The nonquantifiable portion balances such factors as the economics, operating assumptions, objectives, and means of doing the job.

Tactics are the actions buyers will take to carry out the strategic plans. Buyers should set their tactics based on *their* strategic plans. Some tactics the buyer might use include:

- Develop an effective purchasing manual.

- Buy materials, components, and services at lowest total cost, consistent with maintaining both quality and service.

- Spread purchases between two (or three?) suppliers, to avoid single source problems. (If your management insists on one source, at least have a backup qualified.)

- Avoid frequent switching of supply back and forth between suppliers.

- Keep looking for better sources.

- Stop buying from a supplier who doesn't do a good job. The supplier may be the largest in the world, but not serve you well.

- Tap supplier technological innovation first.

- Select and evaluate suppliers and *motivate* them to supply.

- Consider and foster use of offshore sourcing when economic to do so.

- Promote standardization and simplification of components and products.

Long-term commitments should help. But, beware. Unless there is an ongoing rapport and performance measurement, these "commitments" often vanish when a shortage time occurs.

Future strategic importance of purchasing and supply management should increase as future events unfold with the managers of external supply seen as key elements of the business strategies.

To review too many specific strategies or tactics in this chapter would destroy this book's continuity. There's much more to strategies and tactics that follows. Many strategies will present themselves to the reader as we review the components of good buying; for example, as detailed in the chapters about quality or negotiations.

5

Buying From the Right Supplier

The ability to select reliable suppliers is a mark of successful purchasing. To paraphrase an old saying, "Tell me who your suppliers are, and I'll tell you what kind of a purchasing department you have." It's not always easy, however, to identify good suppliers. There is no substitute for an objective means of supplier appraisal.

What should buyers look for in a "world class" supplier? The term has come to mean those suppliers who can deliver their goods anywhere globally at competitive cost in all marketing arenas. Some other considerations affecting source decisions are the stage of economic development of the supplier, the buyer's expectations, and preferences for geographical location. Bulky items can be costly to transport long distances.

Source Selection and Development

Sourcing breaks down into two categories: source selection and source development. Source selection can be day-to-day buying for items now available on the marketplace, or looking for lower cost suppliers.

Source selection to get the "right" supplier runs the gamut from liking a salesman and believing you have a good supplier (the halo effect) to the formalized and technical evaluation reserved for high tech or military procurement. Neither extreme suits most companies. The three steps of source selection are: search, screen, and select.

Anyone can call a supplier and say, "Hey Joe, what's it cost for 100 mops?" That's why everyone figures they can buy—It's easy! But evaluation of suppliers is relevant *before* the buyer buys! Anybody can start a business relationship and find out it doesn't work. The trick is to do it in advance, long before any requisition hits the buyer's desk.

From our initial search, buyers have identified several potential suppliers to screen to find the final source. After doing the homework, the selection process is completed with the negotiation, agreement, and issuing of the purchase order.

Request for Quotation (RFQ)

A good approach when no established market prices are published is to decide whom to invite to quote. Much wasted time is avoided by picking the most logical sources for inquiry, and this brings into play the experience of the buyer. Most companies use a simple request for a quote (RFQ). This is not to be confused with a request for bid (RFB) that is for special projects, and which will be reviewed in a subsequent chapter.

Buyers prepare their RFQ form, which typically includes date, control number, name of company and buyer, description of goods wanted, quantity sought, any special patterns or dies requirements, any tooling now available by the buying company, delivery destination, special handling and shipment, packaging, delivery date for goods, and finally a deadline to receive a reply. Buyers may want to include additional special requests, such as:

- How long price holds firm
- Request for supplier's blueprints or other documents
- Request for alternate proposals
- Any special materials or supplies to be used
- Any special tests or quality standards

The buyer lists potential order quantities, and asks for price breaks and discounts. By indicating a willingness to consider substitute items, the seller is encouraged to make creative suggestions. Ideas to save money might include grouping of items into blanket orders, packaging, or design changes. But, the buyer must take the initiative to search the market, and not wait for a sales pitch.

International purchases require special attention. Unlike a domestic inquiry, additional details need to be given. ASME or UL codes have to be spelled out, along with any special tests to which parts will be subjected. The buyer may have to provide the codes themselves as the international supplier may not be be familiar with them. Local suppliers know these things from experience, but foreign suppliers may be groping in the dark, hesitant to admit it, since they want to please.

Comparing current quotes with past prices paid and to other competitors' pricing is a fundamental technique of buying value. An example of statistical comparison of prices would be for a commodity such as foundry castings. A chart is prepared showing all suppliers under consideration, price quoted by each, shipping costs, pattern charges, tool cost, and any other factors. If all suppliers quoted to identical requirements, the decision is simple. But usually, there are brands, quality, pricing, and so on. So, judgment is needed, and clarifies alternatives in deciding the supplier to select.

s might cause a buyer to discard a low quote and select a higher lternative? One survey stated: quality 84%, delivery 84%, service 38%, past experience 32%, reputation 12%, facilities 11%, technical ability 11%, financial responsibility 8%, failure to meet specs 6%, and to keep multiple source of supply 3%. (Surprisingly none suggested errors.)

Buyer's Checklist for Selecting New Suppliers

Before deciding on the "right" supplier, consider the specific supplier concerns below. This checklist gives buyers some ideas to build upon. This same list can also be used for supplier evaluation that is reviewed in a later section.

A. *Reliability*
    1. Is the supplier reputable, with a proven track record?
    2. Have the supplier's ability and integrity been proved by past performance?
    3. Is the supplier giving me savings along with product improvements?
    4. What is the quality of the supplier's management team?
    5. What is the supplier's position in the industry? Is it a product leader?
    6. What is the supplier's previous delivery history with the company?

B. *Financial and cost factors*
    1. What is the *total cost* of using the supplier's product?
    2. How is the product priced, and how stable is it?
    3. What is the total cost of using the product, including transportation?
    4. What is the supplier's financial position and credit rating stability?
    5. Does pricing meet company targets?
    6. What will be the inventory costs if the supplier's product is not readily available?
    7. Is the supplier willing to negotiate?
    8. What, if any, cash discounts are offered?

C. *Technical capabilities*
    1. Will the supplier provide application engineering or design assistance?
    2. Will the supplier provide analytical engineering that will help improve the efficiency of my basic processes?
    3. Can the supplier handle special needs and designs?

4. Does the supplier contribute to general advancement through basic research?

5. Does the supplier have special technical capability? What has been accomplished recently?

6. What are the operating technology characteristics, such as manufacturing capacity, component design, and techniques used?

D. *Delivery and availability*

1. Will the supplier ensure on-time delivery?

2. Are stocks available locally? On short notices?

3. Does the supplier offer a broad line of commodities?

4. Is the supplier's location an advantage to me?

5. Does the supplier plan shipments to minimize my inventory?

6. Can the supplier be depended upon to provide a steady flow of products or materials?

E. *Buying convenience*

1. Does the supplier offer a full line of related products?

2. Does the supplier package their product conveniently for my use?

3. Does the supplier have a local sales contact?

4. Are they qualified to help me? Can I call upon specialists for my difficult problems?

5. Will the supplier help me cut acquisition costs such as qualifying visits, telephone calls, lab tests, incoming inspections, spoilage and waste, rejects, and complaints?

6. Will the supplier promptly respond in answering queries?

F. *Quality factors*

1. Quality—does it meet the specification? Will it do so consistently?

2. What is the performance and life expectancy?

3. What quality sampling plans are used?

4. What overall quality control system is in place?

G. *Sales assistance*

1. Does the supplier help develop mutual markets? Will they recommend our products?

2. Will the appearance of supplier's product enhance the value of my own product?

3. Will my queries receive personal attention of supplier representatives?

H. *After-sale service*

1. Does the supplier have a service shop organization available when and where I may need it?
2. Is emergency service available?
3. Will renewal parts be available when I need them?
4. Does the supplier provide training and education aids in the use of the product or services provided?

I. *Service factors*

1. Will supplier provide timely information on progress of purchase orders?
2. What is the supplier's labor relations record? What is their a history of strikes?
3. What is the supplier's attitude toward our buying organization?
4. What are the warranties and claims policies?
5. Will the supplier promptly handle rejected materials and credits?
6. Will the supplier comply with *my* procedures?

Teamwork and Cooperation

PMs are unanimous in agreeing that teamwork and cooperation are essential to achieving effective source selection. What are some on-the-job activities buyers actually undertake to keep their companies competitive? A survey[1] indicated how buyers rated importance of several activities, with the percent reporting for each item as follows:

• Bringing suppliers in for candid discussion of needs	93%
• Reducing the number of suppliers	88%
• Train suppliers in just-in-time (JIT) deliveries	85%
• Solicit suppliers' value analysis help	85%
• Source overseas more extensively	85%
• Encourage suppliers to use quality control techniques	80%
• Cut back on sole-sources	38%

There may appear to be a contradiction in the above where some are reducing the number of suppliers, while others are cutting back on sole-sources. But this is not the case, for in the past many buyers gave all suppliers who visited the chance to compete. So, companies find they have too many sources for certain buys. More of a problem are sole-source situations, for experienced buyers know that lack of competition costs them leverage in lowering prices.

---

[1]Excerpts from a *Purchasing Magazine* 1985 survey pertaining to sourcing issues.

Qualification of New Suppliers

Qualification of suppliers is based on a satisfactory assessment of selected criteria that are essentially identical to those quality considerations used when selecting new sources or evaluating current ones.

Before making a major buy, it makes sense to "qualify" any new supplier. When placing a trial order, it's wise to do a source located inspection before the first major shipment. Meeting with quality control and other people who do the job helps gain confidence in their integrity and get their commitment to quality. Take a good look at the supplier's process, and examine their production methods and equipment. It pays to periodically visit and review events with key suppliers.

A strategy to develop needed new sources may evolve simply because they don't exist. Then investment in and subsidizing the cost of development and testing may be sensible. Getting closer to a supplier's product development is a key activity for the purchasing engineering function. Selection of source, along with negotiating the price, are purchasing's greatest challenges!

Using Multiple Sources of Supply

How do we *spot check* prices? Do we strive to have *at least two suppliers* of any item? The implication of these questions is that the purchasing manager should consider setting a policy about using multiple sources of supply, as a precedent to deciding from whom to buy.

Why have more than one source? If you split the business, how do you determine who gets what? Should you use two sources if one is more expensive? Are you expecting a supplier to burn down or be in a flood? Whether to use single or multiple sources is a controversial subject. Some buyers argue that multiple sources reduce risk while increasing costs. Without question, some American companies today are using fewer sources based on the philosophy of a monogamous marriage consistent with partnership principles.

A major impetus to single source thrust has been quality legend W. Edwards Deming. One of Deming's 14 points about quality is to have a single supplier. He proclaimed you're lucky if you get one company who can make what you want. While honoring his contribution to quality, Mr. Deming was probably not an expert on the economic marketplace. A glimpse of his idea of a contract comes from an acquaintance who personally dealt with him. A spokesperson told how Deming refused to visit with General Motors until they agreed in advance to keep him on the job for a long time based on the probably correct assertion that the "transformation" would require a long-term commitment. The spokesperson mentioned that Deming didn't know what the PO read, but quoted him as saying, "I will bill you from time to time based on my belief of your commitment to my principles."[2]

---

[2]"W. Edwards Deming: The Prophet of Quality," 1994 Wootton Productions' TV program.

Others have agreed with Deming's position on single sourcing, and some American automakers who sole-sourced some items say the practice cuts down on component dimensional variability. They claim to be able to work more closely in meeting design and quality requirements if using fewer suppliers. They also claim it's easier to insist on a process for failure analysis when the supplier has total responsibility.

Today, believing the Japanese have only one source, some buyers jump on the bandwagon of the sole-source philosophy. But the truth is, the Japanese almost always have back-up suppliers. After 4 years of single sourcing with Inland Steel, Honda of America added both Armco and Bethlehem Steel as suppliers. As Honda's VP for Corporate Planning explained, "These new sources give us greater flexibility to meet our increased production and expanding operations."[3]

What are some practical arguments for a single source of supply? It's easier to use a single source, and many times that is a must. Other reasons are:

- It's easier to work out delivery schedules as may be needed for just-in-time (JIT) delivery requirements.

- Sometimes no one else is able or willing to supply.

- Concentrating purchases with one good supplier provides advantages of "economy of scale."

- Special die tools, molds, or setup charges are often too expensive to duplicate.

- Requirements may not be large enough to warrant the added expense of testing and inventorying with another supplier.

- Suppliers who know they are solely responsible may be more inclined to meet your needs.

Yet, when only one source is used, competition is eliminated beyond that which may have existed at the initial point of partner selection. A major deterrent to using maximum economic leverage is when the marketplace is a sole source, or buyers *have not qualified* a second source.

And, experience teaches that it is competition that keeps a supplier's performance top notch. Also, the possibility of a fire, strike, or a new product introduction by another supplier are still factors to consider. For buyers to use leverage, there must be acceptable supply options.

Single sourcing puts 100% burden on the supplier partner, and in practice, once fully understood, the supplying partner will step up to the challenge of true partnership. Some other quality experts might point out that if a backup source is available, each source will feel relief of responsibility.

---

[3]*Purchasing Magazine,* April 10, 1986, p. 28B7.

A distinction can be made between sole versus single source. Sole source is said to mean there is no one else qualified or available. Single source means the buyer chooses to use only one of several available sources. So, a sole source may be beyond the ability of the buyer to change without a sound source development process.

Not all buyers have embraced the single source philosophy. Most experienced buyers prefer a backup. Typical reactions from buyers have been, "What if my supplier goes on strike, or burns down, or gets flooded out?" Those are good questions. Whether to have a backup source or use a single source depends largely on whether there is time to recover from delays or problems. Buying for a high-volume assembly line favors an alternative. If buying for resale, or the buyer can wait for new shipments, perhaps a single source is enough. You will need to decide, and formalize your decision in the form of a policy statement based on your specific situational needs.

Arguments for multiple (does not imply many!) suppliers are:

- Competitive supply provides leverage to ensure performance at reasonable price levels.

- Reliability for assurance of supply may be increased.

- Buyers have greater flexibility should a supplier's quality slip or they fail to maintain delivery schedules.

- Keeping multiple sources allows the buyer to become knowledgeable about competitive technical innovations. Unless the item is basic, how do buyers know which supplier will come up with technological innovation? This is relevant when buying sophisticated electronics and tight tolerance mechanical items. Locked into a supplier who does not innovate could put your company at a great disadvantage.

Clearly a factor in determining a company's sourcing strategy is the degree of trust in a source, and the quality of the relationship with the supplier. If a buyer wants to use a single source, but still have backups, here's one way of achieving both objectives: Divide the business, say castings among two foundries. Give each supplier half the total volume, *but* all of the volume of each pattern. This gives maximum item volume production to each supplier. Have an understanding that capacity will be made available on other sizes each does not currently supply, in case of an act of God or dire problems.

Provide some stability to the supplier's production runs. Removing a pattern from a foundry for some time often loses the expertise to make that casting. Much skill and know-how comes from uninterrupted production. Change suppliers carefully.

A stated policy to use only one source removes much economic leverage. The goal should not be to eliminate suppliers (unless there are too many); rather, it should be to obtain good pricing control for the quality of materials needed.

Certain higher risk environments not only justify but also support a multiple sourcing strategy. Each commodity or item should be judged on its own.

Prime Sources of Supplier Information

The buyer can find new sources for items that may be available primarily from (1) catalogues, (2) sales contacts, (3) other buyers, (4) trade journals, (5) trade directories, sometimes (6) advertisements or timely literature—and recently—the Internet.

Sources of information available to the buyer are:

1. *Thomas' Register of American Manufacturers* by Thomas Publishing Co., 461 Eight Avenue, NY, NY 10001. Issued each year, this has long been the most comprehensive set of volumes available. It cross-references leading manufacturers, offices, and personnel, and the type of commodities manufactured.

2. *Regional Industrial Buying Guide.* As an example, consult the Upstate New York Regional Guide issued by Thomas Regional Directory Co. Inc., 5 Penn Plaza, NY, NY 10117.

3. *Sweet's Catalogs.* This comprises several complete sets of catalogs, published annually. Contact Sweet's, F. W. Dodge Division of McGraw-Hill, Inc., 330 W. 42nd St., NY, NY 10036.

4. *MacRae's Blue Book,* which indexes addresses, trade names, and advertisers.

5. *Canadian Trade Index,* which is of particular use to buyers dealing with Canada. This is a database of more than 13,000 manufacturers, their products, trade marks, and brands. The cost is approximately $112.00 from Canadian Trade Index, One Yonge St., Suite 1400, Toronto, Ontario M5E 1J9, Canada (416) 353-7261.

6. *International Yellow Pages,* sorted by country, city, and product. An 800 number found in the local phone directory can get Yellow Pages and White Pages from anywhere around the world. An example is the *Italian Yellow Pages for the U.S.* directory that is issued annually in English, and free upon request from AT&T, 412 Mt. Kemble Ave., Morristown, NJ 07960-1995.

7. *1997 U.S. Custom House Guide,* by North American Publishing Company, 401 N. Broad Street, Philadelphia, PA 19108-9988. The cost is approximately $300. (Contains Harmonized code, customs regulations, port cargo-handling capabilities, and other data.)

8. *Sourcing Guide for Importers,* which is a "how-to" guide available free upon request, from UNZ & Co., P.O. Box 308, Jersey City, NJ 07303.

9. *Visual Search Microfilm File,* which includes a retrieval system scanna-
   ble by viewers; by VSMF, 800 Acoma St., Denver, CO 80204. A
   library of 16-mm microfilms contains over 100,000 pages of supplier
   product data.

10. Search the Internet! Magellan McKinley's Internet Directory lists over
    1.5 million sites, and this number is growing rapidly! Use web ad-
    dresses, such as Dun & Bradstreets' [http//www.dbisna.com]. This is
    but one of dozens available.

NAPM's *Purchasing Today* (formerly *NAPM Insights*) includes its Economic
Survey and commodity reports on various markets such as aluminum, foods, and
paper. These are short overviews provided by experts within its Commodity
Survey groups. Also listed are items in short supply, and those that are up or
down in price. Another feature is a regional business survey report that breaks
down the economy around key U.S. cities.

Sales contacts are another excellent source of information and provide much
of the information needed to keep buyers posted on new items, features, and so
on. Buyers have to be mindful of time constraints and not bog down into idle,
wasted conversation. In other words, they should be choosy about whom to see
and how much time to spend with such representatives.

Buyers from other companies are good sources of information on capable
sources. For the global buyer, the following sources of information are also
available:

1. Chamber of Commerce of the U.S., U.S. Customs Service, 1301 Constitution Ave. N.W., Washington, D.C. 20229. (202) 566-8195.

2. Dun and Bradstreet, 99 Church St., NY, NY 10007. (212) 349-3300.
   D&B offers free information on economic trends. [http://www.dbis-
   na.com]

3. International Chamber of Commerce, U.S. Council, 1212 Avenue of
   the Americas, NY, NY 10026. (212) 354-4480.

4. Superintendent of Documents, U.S. Government Printing Office, Washington, D.C. 20402. (202) 512-1800. [http://www.access.gpo.gov]

5. U.S. Superintendent of Commerce, Industry and Trade Administration,
   Bureau of East West Trade, Washington, D.C. 20230. (202) 377-5500.

6. U.S. Department of Commerce, Maritime Administration, Office of
   Public Affairs, Room 3895 Washington, D.C. 20230. (202) 377-2746.

7. U.S. Department of Commerce, National Technical Information Service,
   5285 Port Royal Road, Springfield, VA 22161.

8. U.S. Office of Small Business, Washington, D.C. 20523. (202) 235-
   9155.

9. Office of International Trade, 1441 L Street, N.W., Washington, D.C. 20416. (202) 653-6543.

A wide variety of timely supply literature is also available in professional journals and magazines. Examples include: *Purchasing Magazine, Electronics Purchasing,* and *NAPM's International Journal of Purchasing and Materials Management.* Furthermore, much current data with respect to employment statistics and wage trends can be obtained from *The Wall Street Journal, USA Today, Business Week, Forbes Magazine, Dun's Review, Newsweek, Time, The Journal of Commerce* (issued daily, with a biweekly International edition), and your local newspaper. For those with a global outlook, check out the short sourcing reviews extracted from Brigham Young University's "Culturegrams." Several other sources—especially international banks—provide detailed economic reviews of all nations.

Supplier's Financial Stability

Let's suppose that a favorable price for a vital component is quoted by a supplier not known to the buyer. However, extensive tooling must be funded before production begins. If delivery problems should arise later on, shipment of the end item to the customer will be delayed; as a result, promotion and marketing of the using company's product are delayed and customers who have placed orders are dissatisfied.

To prevent all this, a visit is often made to the new supplying company. Quality and engineering personnel may concur in judging the company a good source, but it is still the purchasing managers' job to ensure that the supplier can perform as promised. And, until satisfied with the company's financial stability as well as its technical ability, the purchasing manager or buyers cannot be confident that the source will be reliable.

Unfortunately, the amount of financial information available becomes less as the need for it becomes greater. Consider that data from Standard & Poors, Dun & Bradstreet, and from stockholder reports are available for large, strong companies, but often little is available about the smaller firm—where the need to be cautious may be greatest! This is a concern, as about 90% of all U.S. corporations have assets less than $1 million, according to the Department of Commerce. Yet these smaller companies are often excellent sources of supply, usually being highly flexible and eager to help make items that larger corporations may have no interest in.

If a potential supplier refuses to provide a financial statement, that does not necessarily mean there is a situation being hidden from the purchasing manager. However, it would be questionable buying practice to place $1 million worth of business with a company having a sales volume of $50,000, or with one that doesn't give assurances of its stability. A shaky supplier faced with business failure may have to increase its prices sharply or allow lower quality by using cheap substitutes; the only other alternative may be to close shop. The supplier's financial problem may make the owner desperate to accept an order even at too low a price, hoping to fulfill it—only to find the company in deeper trouble leading to inevitable collapse. Hence, the PM must be alert to the financial stability of his or her suppliers.

Credit Rating Reports

Many small companies, especially when privately held, do not issue financial statements. In such cases, a Dun & Bradstreet ("D&B") credit report can help by advising:

- General information on the supplier's facilities. If the report is clearly unfavorable, this can save the time and expense of a personal visit.
- The company's credit rating.
- Description of the company's major products. If the company is already making something similar to what you propose to buy, it's less likely that you will have quality or delivery problems.
- Data on financial strength and profitability. A company with a healthy profit in a competitive industry is generally an efficient one. Conversely, the company with a record of losses is to be suspect for future business transactions.

Credit executives, too, can help the PM just as he or she helps the sales manager—and in many of the same ways. They can:

1. Analyze any suspect current supplier in relation to size and management progress.
2. Classify suppliers according to their volume of sales, reputation, dependability, and performance.
3. Help handle the problem supplier who, for one reason or other, must remain on the active list.
4. Analyze any suspect current supplier in relation to size and help buyers assist limited suppliers who are worth doing business with, but who have special internal financial problems.
5. Give objective operational information that the PM can use to better understand the supplier's facilities and performance capabilities.
6. Reduce supplier turnover and help eliminate unsatisfactory one-shot purchases.
7. Advise on new prospective global sources' trade practices and offshore reputation from banking connections.

It should be recognized that D&B ratings often report data given them by the supplier itself. Similarly, vital information can be withheld; and, while the practice is not, fortunately, too common, information may be falsified. The PM should recognize the potential weakness that either situation implies. If a D&B report is suspect, the PM can ask the supplier for bank references, or for the sources of money supplied to them, and follow their advice. Also, customer references can be of value in analyzing a supplier's condition.

Usually, published data are based on a period of one year, either a fiscal year or the normal calendar year. It is usually enough to make only a simple analysis of the material as described below, but in questionable cases the PM should call on the financial department for its expert opinion.

Let's look at a typical financial statement to determine what it tells us. On the left side of the balance sheet, Table 5-1 shows the assets column, listing all

Table 5-1   A. Balance sheet—December 31, 19— (simplified and hypothetical)

Assets		Liabilities	
Cash	$ 2,000,000	Accounts payable	$ 1,800,000
Government bonds	4,000,000	Accrued taxes	1,700,000
Accounts receivable	1,675,000	Total current liabilities	3,500,000
Inventories	4,500,000	Long-term liabilities	5,300,000
Total current assets	$12,175,000	*Total liabilities*	$ 8,800,000
Property, plant and	$ 6,500,000	Net worth	
equipment (net)		Preferred stock	$ 1,000,000
Goodwill and patents	1	Common stock	2,575,000
		Retained earnings	6,300,001
Total assets	$18,675,001	*Total liabilities plus networth*	*$18,675,001*

B. Profit & loss (or income) statement

Net sales		$13,000,000	%
Less			
Cost of goods sold:			
Material	6,450,000		(49.6)
Direct labor	1,400,000		(10.7)
Plant overhead	650,000		(5.0)
Selling and administrative expense	1,200,000		
Depreciation	1,700,000	11,400,000	
Operating profit		$ 1,600,000	
Other income (dividends and interest)		275,000	
Total income		$ 1,875,000	
Less interest on bonds		290,000	
Profit before Federal taxes		$ 1,585,000	
Less income taxes		824,000	
Net profit (or income)		$ 761,000	(5.85)

goods, owned property, and any expected receipts. On the right-hand side are the liabilities—those debts that are owed, some payable soon (current liabilities) and others over the longer term (such as bonds to be redeemed). Net worth includes stockholders' equity which is the money put in by the owners of the business, as well as the earned surplus retained by the business to permit growth. The total assets must equal (or balance) total liabilities and net worth.

By reviewing the balance sheets for several years, significant changes can be detected. For example, new loans may have been necessary, or old loans may have been paid off. Inventories may have been increased to take care of increased sales, or reduced to show better performance.

The profit and loss (income) statement shown in this same table depicts the financial position of a company for a particular date. It shows the receipts from selling goods and from other income, such as interest on bank deposits or stocks and bonds. This statement matches these incoming funds against the costs of goods and other expenses in operating the company for one year; the net profit, after tax, is what is left for the year. Of course, it is also possible to show a net loss, which would be a prime concern to any buyer.

Ratios as Guides

Ratios that show the relationships of various financial data help provide a clearer picture of a company's financial position. Some of the ratios used in determining a supplier's financial strength are:

- *Working capital ratio*: Current assets divided by current liabilities. Indicating the amount invested in current assets compared with the amount of current liabilities at a particular time, this is a general measure of a company's liquidity.
- *Acid test ratio*: Cash and receivables divided by current liabilities. Comparing the amount of cash and receivables with the total current liabilities, this measure is more exacting than the current ratio in determining the firm's ability to meet its obligations.
- *Return on investment ratio*: Net profit before taxes divided by fixed debt and equity, this measures the return on capital investment to produce profits.
- *Profit ratio*: Net income after taxes divided by net annual sales, this shows the rate of earnings, after taxes, on net sales. Low profit may worry stockholders; what is more important to the buyer is the regularity with which a company has made a profit—evidence that it can stay in business.
- *Inventory turnover*: Cost of goods sold divided by average inventory. Showing the number of times a company turns over, or receives and sells, its average inventory.

- *Net worth to total debt ratio*: Comparing the capital invested by owners with the capital obtained by borrowing, such as at year end. When this ratio is less than one, it shows that the equity of the owner is less than that of the creditors. As this puts a strain on management, unexpected loss of sales volume, rapid cost increases, or catastrophe may force the company to take undue risks to maintain operations.

Applying some of these ratios can provide some interesting information. How can the PM tell if the implications are positive or negative? Let's apply some of the above ratios to a hypothetical company, Amanda Kay Products (AKP), whose P&L statement and balance sheet were already shown in Table 5-1.

As previously stated, the supplier's strength can be judged by a study of its balance sheet, together with its profit and loss statement. In this case, the working capital ratio—which shows what ability the company has to meet its obligations and still provide for future growth—is 3.48, which compares favorably with D&B's median of 2.76. (See Dun and Bradstreet's "14 Important Ratios in 72 Lines of Business.") If it was less than one, the assets of the company would not be enough to cover the current liabilities. An old rule of thumb says that minimum safety requires current assets to be at least twice the amount of current liabilities.

The acid test ratio for AKP, cash and receivables divided by current liabilities, shows a ratio of 1.05. This means the company has the financial strength to meet all obligations presently due. The profit ratio is 761,000/13,000,000 = 5.85%, which is quite healthy when compared to 3.64 for others in its field.

Inventory turnover is 8,500,000/4,500,000 = approximately 1.9, which raises a question about the company's inventory position. The size of the inventory appears unusual when we compare the other favorable ratios—but perhaps there is good reason for high inventory this year. Remember, inventory turnover will depend on the type of business and time of the year for cyclical businesses. Large inventories are dangerous because price drops can cause losses; they may indicate a high percentage of finished goods that can't be sold. Other ratios should also be checked; a trend of several years is more significant than a single year's report, since strikes or such other one time problems as fire, flood, or debt repayment can make the one year misleading.

Changes from one year to another show whether management is being made to "look good" for a short period of time. A company can show a profit yet be borrowing money, deferring payment of bills, or postponing purchases of needed equipment; or it may show a small loss in order to clear out a high-interest debt or provide improvements designed to place the company in a better long-range competitive position. Because of the complexities involved in interpreting financial data, it would be wise, when in doubt, to check with your financial officer to ensure accurate conclusions are reached!

Search for Low-Cost Suppliers

Because of the high impact of material costs, the purchasing function has pushed aggressively to attain "world-wide cost leadership." A strategic emphasis has been to maintain market share, and this has resulted in an increased emphasis on purchasing as part of an integrated global corporation's strategic management.

Purchasing managers and buyers have to use their knowledge of the "ins and outs" of sourcing, both domestic and offshore. Manufacturing, cost of product, and quality have become focal points of corporate strategy. Those companies that can deliver a product anywhere at the lowest possible cost will survive and grow—while others will fall by the side.

Let's look at our U.S. labor cost versus that of other competitors as shown in Table 5-2. As indicated in this table, Japan's wages were in eighth place in 1989, and 89% of the U.S. production worker's wages. By 1994, their wages of $21.42/hour were up to No. 3 worldwide and 125% of U.S. workers.

Recent U.S. gains have been at a lesser rate. The almost 10% yearly wage gains in the early 1980s have dropped to about 4% currently. Average hourly pay in manufacturing rose to $17.10 in 1994, which remains in fifth place worldwide. NAFTA partner Canada at $16.58/hour has dropped to eighth place—a dramatic improvement that should boost their exports. Note the advantage of Mexico—now allied within NAFTA—with labor rates far lower than the others listed!

This relative lowering of American labor cost is not solely the result of smaller

Table 5-2   Hourly compensation costs in various nations

Manufacturing Production Workers						
	1989			1994		
	$/Hour	Percent	Rank	$/Hour	Percent	Rank
United States	14.31	100%	5	17.10	100%	5
Canada	14.71	103	4	15.68	92	8
Mexico	1.72	10	13	2.61	15	10
Japan	12.68	89	8	21.42	125	3
Germany	21.00	146	1	27.31	160	1
United Kingdom	10.48	73	9	13.62	80	9
France	12.75	89	7	17.04	100	6
Italy	13.20	92	6	16.16	95	7
Sweden	17.48	122	3	18.81	110	4
Switzerland	18.12	127	2	24.83	145	2
China				0.37	2	12?
Russia				0.60 *	4	11

Source: Copyright DRI/McGraw-Hill. Reprinted with permission.

*Wall Street Journal August 5, 1996, p. A15.

U.S. wage increases. Where a foreign currency such as the German mark has risen, labor costs in that country rise versus American. Translation of foreign currency into dollars for comparison to U.S. wages causes much of the change.

Computing Total Landed Cost of Acquisition

A key criterion to consider in making any source selection relates to total landed cost of acquisition. Following is an example that demonstrates the importance of considering *total* costs: An engine crankcase is furnished by two suppliers who have comparable prices. However, Supplier B has experienced a higher rejection rate and as such appears inferior to A on the company's quality report. It might cost an extra $5 each to cover inspection. However, on the production line, A's crankcases require sorting, and extra machine time to overcome machining difficulties because of "hard spots." So, when total cost of quality is included, supplier B's casting may be $30 more economical than A's.

Lifecycle costs should be considered as another factor in total landed cost. If model A wears out at an average in 5 years, and another model B lasts 15, in the course of the lifetime of model B, three Model A's will be needed. So over that span of time, A's lifecycle cost will be three times that of B.

The professional buyer knows price alone is not all that must be analyzed, based in part on the above example. Here is another example that indicates total landed cost for a foreign purchase of a single power generator:

Generator price	$5,000.00
5% Buying commission	250.00
Insurance	98.00
Freight forwarder/broker	125.00
International freight	1,880.00
Domestic freight	540.00
Invoice total	$7,893.00
Plus Customs duty	150.00
Total landed cost	$8,043.00
Versus net item price	$5,000.00
Extra charges	$3,043.00

In this example, the "extra" cost equals 38% of total!

As an aid to consider total landed cost, the following checklist may be helpful to the buyer in identifying, analyzing, and quantifying total landed cost. Although this example assumes an offshore buy, many of the items will also be relevant to a domestic purchase as well:

- Price in U.S. dollars
- Export packing, marking, and container costs

- Commissions to Customs broker/freight forwarder
- Fees for consultants or inspectors
- Terms of payment costs and finance charges
- Letter of Credit fee
- Translation costs
- Exchange rate differentials
- Insurance premium
- Customs or other documentation charges
- Import duties
- Transportation costs
- Taxes imposed, state sales, foreign VAT
- Extra inventory itself, plus inventory carrying costs if, for example, the foreign purchase requires a larger company stock than for domestic supply
- Extra manpower needed to buy overseas based on greater documentation; time considerations
- Increased costs of overseas business travel, international postage, telex, FAX, and telephone rates
- Miscellaneous and hidden costs: obsolescence, deterioration and spoilage, losses to damage and theft, and longer delivery time frames

U.S. companies keep buying offshore to good advantage. However, the pendulum of costs has shifted. Any decision to source overseas should be made based on the best ultimate value. In many cases the "extra" cost can range from 25% to 40% of the quoted price. Based on the significant list of possible cost drivers indicated above, it should be clear that price should be judged in perspective to the *total landed costs* incurred.

Postselection Supplier Evaluation

How do buyers manage their supply sources? Assume a company has sales of $1.00, and purchases of $.53, thereby indicating a productive value-added of $.47. In such a case, if a company doesn't manage its suppliers, it is managing only about half of the cost of products sold. Many purchasing managers believe the buyer *needs to manage his or her sources* of supply.

Throughout the performance period, buyers must tell suppliers what is expected. How high is high? A buyer can manage suppliers by using available options, such as:

- Increasing or decreasing volume bought
- Getting local stocking of items, for faster shipments and lower inventory
- Using competition to get the best package price, lead-time, and quality
- Giving incentives for better supplier performance
- Dropping a supplier for poor service
- Taking legal action—as a last resort, hopefully (rather drastic)
- Making factual presentations—quality performance data, delivery, and rejection rates as actually recorded

The term "managing suppliers" may bother some buyers. Defining managing as "the art of making things go right" is the proper attitude. With good job performance, the following desirable results are signs of effective supplier management:

- Low rejection rates—at receipt and forward through the life of the end item delivered
- Reasonable prices paid
- Good supplier relations
- Reputation of "Firm but fair!"
- The ultimate test—high customer satisfaction level

Some people reject the idea of tracking of supplier post-award performance on the grounds that the only list they'll keep is one for suppliers they're going to eliminate, believing it's the suppliers job to perform. But underlying this conviction is often the concern that an elaborate system is needed, which is not usually the case. There is value in knowing a supplier's performance throughout the performance period.

If buyers are to award business based on performance there has to be some standard of judgment. We are interested in a moderate, reasonable way to identify those suppliers that perform both well and poorly. How we use the system is key. The focus is not on punishment, initially, but on communication to improve performance for the benefit of both parties.

Let's take the case of a supplier who has performed poorly, yet makes a commitment to get back on track. Surely, there is nothing more discouraging for them upon inquiry to be told, "We *still* think you're doing poorly." Conversely, nothing is more gratifying than to have the buyer formally acknowledge a positive turnaround. The emphasis, then, is a positive one which can bring about improvement. Good suppliers can be superior ones. However, the buyer has to *know* how they're doing to help them to achieve superior results.

Upon being surveyed,[4] the following list was compiled from those who used

---

[4]Seminars at the World Trade Institute, New York, Chicago, and Los Angeles, 1987–1993.

a supplier rating system. Purchasing managers rated in priority, on a scale of 1 to 10, the importance they attached to various aspects of supplier performance:

1. Quality of product   9.7
2. Competitive prices   9.4
3. Delivery dependability   9.0
4. Services given: 8.0
   technical services, etc.
5. Total cost reduction help   7.7
6. New product ideas and R&D help   6.2

Some of the information analyzed by companies, but not used in their supplier measurements, were:

- Financial strength   5.2
- Geographical location   4.3
- Reputation   4.2
- Other factors   2.0

A Sample Rating Exercise

One supplier measurement system that persists is the purchase performance index. This index attempts to reduce all basic factors into one numerical percentage, or "Ideal Index." A typical rating is composed of the traditional supplier performance areas of quality (assigned 40 points), price (35), and service (25). The percentages will vary according to the importance given each area in relation to the whole. Any such rating is composed of both subjective and objective factors. Figure 5-1 shows an example of an "Ideal Index" for supplier ratings, combining numerical ratings in the lower right hand box.

Let's actually rate a company. The Amanda Kay Products Co. (AKP) supplies $35 controls for air conditioners. If all their shipments were acceptable over a period of time, a value of 40 points (maximum) would be assigned to quality, which indicates optimum performance. If some lots were not acceptable, the 40 points would be reduced proportionately. During one quarter, AKP supplied 2000 acceptable valves out of 2500 shipped. The quality rating would be 2000 divided by 2500 times 40, which is 32 points.

The price rating is based on a maximum of 35 points. A list is compiled of all unit prices from each major supplier of *similar* interchangeable controls. To the list, transportation cost and the cost of nonrecoverable defective purchased material is added. While AKP will replace the 500 rejected controls, they usually will not make up the loss (assume $500) that resulted from removing defective controls from units that had been assembled before the defect showed up. The

QUALITY RATING

KIND & CLASS-IRON-CL2 PERIOD REPORTED 1st QUARTER

VENDORS	3	16	21	27	35			
FACTORS	X	X	X	X	X	X	X	X
RECEIVED	126	243	132	98	57			
REC. INSP. REJ.	10	28	31	36	2			
LINE REJ.	5	12	3	4	1			
TOTAL REJ.	15	40	34	40	3			
% ACCEPT	88.1	83.5	74.2	59.2	94.7			
RATING (% ACC. x 40)	35.2	33.4	29.7	23.7	37.9			

COST RATING

KIND & CLASS-IRON CL2 PERIOD REPORTED 1st QUARTER

VENDORS	3	16	21	27	35	
FACTORS	X	X	X	X	X	X
PRICE 1 LB.	.19	.18	.16	.16	.20	
+DISCOUNT (10%)	.019	.018	.016	.016	.020	
+TRANS.	.171	.162	.144	.144	.180	
+VARIANCE CHGS.	.021	.046	.051	.039	.032	
	.033	.056	.123	.142	.011	
NET	.235	.264	.318	.325	.223	
RATING	33.2	29.6	24.5	24.0	35.0	

SERVICE RATING

KIND & CLASS-IRON CL2 PERIOD REPORTED 1st QUARTER

VENDORS	3	16	21	27	35	
FACTORS	X	X	X	X	X	X
PROMISES KEPT	97	93	89	86	100.0	
RATING	24.3	23.3	22.3	21.5	25	

VENDOR RATINGS (CONSOLIDATED)

KIND & CLASS-IRON CL2 PERIOD RATED 1st QUARTED

VENDORS	3	16	21	27	35	
FACTORS	X	X	X	X	X	X
QUALITY	35.2	33.4	29.7	23.7	37.9	
COST	33.2	29.6	24.5	24.0	35.0	
SERVICE	24.3	23.3	22.3	21.5	25.0	
CONSOLIDATED RATING	92.7	86.3	75.5	69.2	97.9	

Figure 5-1 An "Ideal Index" for supplier ratings.

new unit cost for each supplier is then determined. The lowest ultimate cost always will be given the full 35 point value. The price factor for AKP is 35. To proportion a competitor supplier's rating, the lowest cost is divided in turn by each of the other higher costs. The resultant ratio times the full 35 is the rating for each of the other suppliers.

The final rating is for service that is usually a percentage of delivery promises met. The *delivery promise date* from the supplier is the standard for measurement, and not the requested delivery date. If a supplier never missed a delivery, the full 25 points are awarded. This rating may be adjusted based on such factors as outstanding sales help or expert engineering advice. As an example, the buyer supplies this subjective factor to adjust the 25 points. AKP has delivered all lots on time, but has failed to take prompt corrective action on a leaky washer. So, 22 points are awarded by the buyer's judgment.

The composite rating, 100 points for perfection, is the total for the three measured areas. AKP scores 89, made up of quality 32, price 35, and service 22 points. A rating of 90 to 100 is excellent, 80 to 89 is good, 70 to 79 is fair, and below 70 is not acceptable. So, AKP is considered to have a rating of "Good."

As previously noted, variations on the areas and points awarded can suit the specific company and its situation. For example, for some companies a designation of 50 might be more appropriate for quality, while the delivery weight a 20, cost competitiveness a 20, and service and reliability a 10.

How Valid Are These Ratings?

On the plus side of the ledger, ratings are useful in assisting suppliers to maintain required quality levels. Discussing ratings with a supplier will make them aware that their performance is watched. Again, communication has its mutual rewards! In most cases, and this is key—they will try to conform more closely to require- ments if the ratings are *valid*. Moreover, reviewing the findings at the supplier's plant is one good way to know that company's management. Further, why not ask the supplier what they think of you as a customer? This often leads to some honest talk about problems that may have been causing needless friction!

A high rating to the superior supplier becomes a source of pride, while a lower rating can motivate the supplier to meet or better the competition to avoid a failure that could cost business. It is important to point out specific areas where suppliers are not up to standard; how can there be expected improvement without knowing the shortcomings? Unexplained ratings will seldom result in correc- tive action.

Price is probably the most difficult attribute to quantify. Some advocates of the system suggest awarding all points to the low-price supplier and none to the others. There is serious question about the wisdom of including data on price, although some do just that and believe it works for them.

Service is usually promoted by salespeople, but it is difficult to assign a relative value, with the possible exception being broken shipping promises. Many intangibles exist in this area, such as the type of supplier help given, research and development facilities made available for tests, and the like. At best, service is subject—at least partially—to personal buyer judgment.

Trouble often occurs when trying to consolidate the individual ratings into a composite Ideal Index. In doing so, both subjective opinions and objective facts are combined. Who has the authority to say that quality is worth 40, 45, or 50 points? Is it worth anything to buy a worthless item at a low price? What happens if a buyer gets an excellent item at a good price, but receives it too late to meet the customer's need?

One suggestion would be to rate only statistically measurable factors. However, what about other factors such as assurance of supply? Also, a delivery in time to avoid a cost penalty might increase the value of the service factor versus quality or price.

Building Rapport

This chapter has focused on the process of selecting the right supplier for the job, followed by in-process evaluation of performance. But truly world-class performance cannot be achieved without building a world-class relationship with your suppliers—and this implies a long-term commitment.

6

Develop a Global Vision!

The American short-term goal of profitability encourages the option of either buying offshore or producing there to take advantage of lower labor costs. Some domestic companies have found themselves unable to compete in world markets. Companies have been caught in the squeeze of trying to stay competitive while satisfying customers who are themselves striving to meet the flood of foreign competition. The movement to buy product from lower cost international sources has upset some of the older supply channels. Global buying is perhaps the single most important development in purchasing today that helps keep the company competitively in operation.

Throughout this book purchasing is portrayed from a global outlook, but that does not imply that buyers should set their strategies or goals to *buy* offshore. Rather, the buying process is broadened and improved by a global buying perspective. Even if a buyer never buys, or has the chance to buy offshore, having a global outlook will give him or her greater insights to better handle domestic buying. Buyers don't know they've got the best buy unless they are looking at their offshore options.

Competitive advantage exists when a company makes products efficiently, and they buy what others can make more economically. It's not enough to make goods in the native country alone. If these products are sold elsewhere, they must be globally competitive.

By definition, world trade is, "To buy and sell worldwide." If a company sells worldwide, can it buy solely from domestic sources? Not likely. We need to be mindful that the political reality of foreign trade is important as sovereign countries promote policies to protect their economic growth, increase employment, and maintain price stability. The following summarizes[1] some developments affecting trade:

---

[1]Victor H. Pooler, *Global Purchasing: Reaching for the World,* Chapman & Hall, New York, 1992, p. 9.

- World markets are more complex, but provide new market opportunities
- Increased worldwide competition is a reality
- Bilateral trade agreements have emerged that aim to improve world supply by dropping trade barriers
- Countertrade in purchasing has become a necessity in many markets
- There is ongoing redeployment of capital and human resources on a global scale
- Today, we are seeing continuous company reorganization with fewer people and a new flexibility

There are advantages and disadvantages in worldwide buying and selling that need to be both understood and adapted into an integrated worldwide purchasing and supply management strategy. International competition can be healthy! Be aware of what's going on out there. The challenge is to put your buying leverage on the global bargaining table.

Gross Domestic Product

Let's begin with a look at some economic data pertaining to the United States and its trading partners. Table 6-1 shows the United States has the world's largest national economy. With a gross domestic product (GDP) at $7.42 trillion, the U.S. ranks 1st, and its foreign trade alone ranks as the world's fifth largest economy. Japan and Germany rank second and third, respectively. The GDP indicates the annualized growth rate, adjusted for seasonal change and inflation. In February, 1996 the first quarter GDP was +2.8%, and includes many things such as value of new homes built, capital investments, and consumer buys such as cars and food. However, stocks and bonds, welfare spending, social security

Table 6-1   GDP and export trade of major nations

(In $U.S. billions)	GDP 1995	Nominal exports	Percent world trade
USA	7,418	804	13.07
Canada	566	212	3.44
Mexico	250	63	1.02
NAFTA total	8,234	1,079	17.54
Japan	5,129	484	7.86
Germany	2,417	556	9.04
France	1,539	361	5.87
Italy	1,088	272	4.42
United Kingdom	1,104	309	5.02
Russia	2,000 (est.)	52 (Value understated by barter)	
Total all international exports $6,153 billion			

Data source: Copyright DRI/McGraw-Hill. Reprinted with permission payments, and Medicare are not included. Work done at home as well as underground economic activities are not measurable in dollars so are not included.

In terms of the current world trade between all nations, all international exports totaled $6.156 trillion in 1995. Europe, the United States, and Japan make up almost 70% of the free world's gross national product.

As the economic leader of the free world, Americans champion "free trade." An analysis of the U.S. international merchandise trade deficit shows ebbs and tides. From a high of $167.1 billion in 1986, the deficit was reduced to about $100 billion in 1991, and as of 1995 was back running at an annual rate of $162 billion. The Congressional Budget Office states that the budget deficit will be lower in 1996 for the fourth consecutive year. However, unless spending can be cut, the respite will soon be over. The deficit was 5% of the GDP in 1992, and projected at 2% in 1996, but rising to about 3.5% by 2006.[2]

So, there we have the scope. A nation in decline is not one that is the envy of the entire world! The U.S. destiny is global, with its sphere of influence greatest under the North American Free Trade Agreement (NAFTA) begun in 1993.

North American Free Trade Agreement

NAFTA puts under one grouping the GDP of Canada, Mexico, and the U.S. Think of it—360 million people with a productive output of more than $8 trillion. The president's enterprise for the Americas initiative seeks to expand the NAFTA type agreement throughout North, Central, and perhaps South America.

Just what does NAFTA cover? Key provisions call for:

- Tariffs on farm produce are eliminated over 15 years.
- After 8 years at least 62.5% of autos must be produced in North America to remain duty-free.
- Limits on bank ownership will be out by the year 2000.
- Environment, health, and safety laws cannot be overruled.
- Professionals and executives can operate freely, but limits to Mexican emigration will remain.
- "Rule of origin" requires that all garments are made from yarn or fabric made in North America.
- Free access of trucks to cross borders will be in place by 1999.

Although much has been written recently regarding our trade partners south of the border, Americans often underestimate the extent of our trade with our northern partner in Canada, which accounts for approximately $200 billion of trade between our countries. The U.S.-Canada trade partnership has prospered,

---

[2]*Syracuse Herald Journal,* May 12, 1996.

with the two countries making up the largest single trading partnership in the world. Japan is the United States' second largest partner and closing rapidly.

Total Canadian nominal exports of goods and services for 1995 were $212 billion. Exports to the United States make up about 75% of all Canada's exports, and the cross-border movement of goods continues to grow.

Mexico is a distant third among America's trading partners with $35 billion. Mexican reforms make their economy attractive for trade and investment, although recent financial problems have been troubling to some would-be investors. Seventy percent of Mexican trade is with the U.S. Mexico can be an attractive alternative to the Pacific Rim because of low labor rates, relatively minor bureaucratic regulation, and gradual reduction of corporate taxes to 35%. Also, customs duties have been substantially reduced or eliminated.

What Can Purchasing Do?

Believing that buying overseas is too complicated, some buyers hesitate to try it. After all, many buyers are inclined to buy in town, in state, or in the U.S. rather than internationally. Others mistakenly conclude that global buying is little different from buying locally, and that procedures for doing business abroad are much the same as doing business in town. Look at it this way: If a buyer lives in New York, buying from Los Angeles isn't quite as easy as buying locally. When buying offshore, the sourcing issues can become greatly magnified.

The task of developing global supply alternatives is a part of the procurement planning process. The best suggestion is to talk with other buyers who now buy internationally. Go to a seminar on this subject, and attend any meetings sponsored by purchasing groups. Buying Guides for most major foreign trading countries are available.

There are advantages and disadvantages in worldwide buying and selling. What's wrong with local buying? Nothing, provided good value results, but, as noted previously, the buyer won't know this without also testing global markets.

The Expanded Role into Global Purchasing

When buying offshore, the objectives of purchasing are the same! But, the scope of the job expands greatly. Today's buyers must conscientiously seek to expand their outlook toward global buying. When a child picks up a lump of coal he sees a rock to throw. In the same lump of coal the engineer sees a source of heat energy, the BTUs to cook a meal. The nuclear scientist sees enough pent-up power, if released by nuclear fission, to propel a ship across the Atlantic.

Likewise, the buying job may look the same to some, but global purchasing is an expansion of an already complex job. There are few limits to the variety and type of global buying arrangements that buyers can carry out. It's a matter of outlook. What do you *see* when you think of global purchasing?

The purchasing manager's and the buyer's vision can no longer stop at our national borders. Purchasing should be viewed within its global environment. Table 6-2 breaks down many of the major changes affecting global companies.

Emergence of the Global Corporation

Joint ventures and the quest for world trade growth have led to the emergence of the "global corporation." A *joint venture* is a co-production effort to manufacture in a host country that might supply land, raw materials, brick and mortar, and labor. The U.S. partner often provides technology, some production machinery, and perhaps financing. Output is shared by the partners.

Other countries, particularly developing countries, want part of the trading action. Trade has now increased from state-controlled economies. American buyers often must deal with governments in these managed economies.

Far Eastern countries seek access to America's technology, but they often lack dollars to purchase it outright. So, in effect they said, "We'll buy from you, but you should buy from us. Of course, you (the buyer) must pay us in dollars." To make sales, the seller must go by their rules because they've built it into their contracts! This is known as countertrade and it is found in perhaps as much as 20% of today's world trade.

What Is Countertrade?

Countertrade can be defined as, "Any transaction involving exchange of goods or services for something of equal value." Sometimes cash is used to pay for any value differences. There are a variety of types of countertrade including barter, counterpurchase/buyback, and offset.

Barter is a direct swap of materials or goods without funds. An example would be an exchange of Russian oil for American wheat.

"Counterpurchase," or "buy-back," is when the seller agrees to buy partial value of an initial sale from the buyer. Twenty-six percent are this type arrangement in which the sale of a company's product is tied into a separate agreement. The seller agrees to buy, from the country to which the sale was made, part or full value of the sale.

"Offset" is the most common form of countertrade, making up about 43% of countertrade volume. The term comes from the activity in which a seller is obliged to "offset" the sales value, usually by purchasing a set percentage of goods, materials, or services produced in the buyer's country. For example, to make a sale of military planes, the seller may agree to buy the tail wings, or some other subsystem, from the buying partner. Alternatively, indirect offset may take place which entails a transaction not directly linked to the sale. This can become truly creative! Examples of actual offset purchases have included panty hose, vacation excursions, and wine!

Table 6-2 The environment/culture: "What's going on around us"

Culture	Four major "revolutions" in business*			
	Technological revolution	Materials/purchasing revolution	Quality/productivity revolution	Work force/mgt. revolution
United States	First to lead internet	Supply mgt. with emergence of *Purchasing*, difficult to structure in company	Surpass Japanese Re-emphasized quality productivity	Individualism Theory X & Y Downsizing "Lean and Mean"
	Electronic data processing E-mail	Material Requirement Planning (MRP) Manufacturing Resource Planning (MRP II) JIT Delivery Approach	Computerization SPC Zero-defects philosophy	Reengineering
Japanese	Copied United States and improved	Kanban—"Just in time" Improve quality & speed-up deliveries	No. 1 objective in life Attention to details Quality circles	Theory Z *Consensus* Worker involvement-groups

*Revolutions defined by Dr. Vitali, Univ. of Milan, Italy.

Note: Purchasing managers and buyers must work within framework of a global concept that brings all the above into play.

It is clear why countertrade activities impact the purchasing function. U.S. companies embrace countertrade to help ensure future sales of their products overseas. They can meet foreigners' demands that sales be matched by purchases from them in some way. And, sometimes this is the only way to make sales to poorer countries, who essentially use countertrade to finance their major foreign procurements.

These newer trade tactics affect the buying job in a significant way. Over half of those responding to a survey[3] said their company made such deals in the past year. Another survey showed that 83% of buyer respondents are partners in countertrade activities. In 34% of the responses, the purchasing function is responsible for finding internal uses for countertrade goods. Fifty percent reported they can use 100% of accepted goods within their firms. The other half had to search for distribution channels for disposal of goods and services acquired through countertrade.

Offshore sourcing often yields 15% to 25% lower prices than solely buying domestically. As a general rule, material cost savings of less than 15% may not offset the added nonmaterial related costs to buy internationally. As always, purchasing's aim should be to buy the right quality at the lowest total cost. As we begin to consider constructing a global program, the buyer should review the following foreign sourcing issues:

1. Incentives to consider foreign sources

2. How to start buying offshore

3. The foreign purchase contract and documents used

4. Customs regulations

5. Cultural and business differences

What incentives exist to checkout offshore sourcing in worldwide markets? When surveyed about reasons for offshore buys, managers reported as follows:[4] Price (74%) was the major reason for going offshore with price advantages of 20% to 30%, and in a few cases approaching 40%. Quality (46%) came in second, and uniqueness (41%) was third. Fourth was increased number of suppliers (35%) where there was inadequate domestic supply (better deliveries), fifth was increased exposure (23%) to worldwide technology, sixth was the need to become globally competitive (21%), and seventh was the need to meet supplier's "offset" requirements (5%).

Other reasons for overseas sourcing are that it provides a wider choice of suppliers, and provides exposure to worldwide technology. *Foreign sourcing*

---

[3]Victor H. Pooler, *Global Purchasing: Reaching for the World,* Chapman & Hall, New York, 1992, Ch. 1.

[4]Global Purchasing Seminars. World Trade Institute, 1987–1993.

keeps domestic sources competitive! Often, the mere threat of buying internationally brings price reductions and service improvements from domestic sources.

How to Start a Global Program

Let's assume you're just starting to source overseas. The following steps provide a useful checklist:

1. Sell yourself on the concept by testing the marketplace.

2. Decide what you want to buy. Start with simple, noncritical items, as early efforts need to be successful.

3. Gather all internal information–specifications, drawings, and samples.

4. Determine need—quantity and timing. Unlike a domestic supplier who can ship within a few weeks lead-time, a foreign supplier usually works with a much longer lead-time. Decide what proportion of annual usage to source abroad. Have a domestic backup source allowing for occasional shipping problems.

5. Define quality requirements, including packaging. Don't underestimate the importance of knowing exactly what's needed. Packaging that is satisfactory for a domestic truck shipment won't necessarily hold up on a freighter in rough seas.

6. Communicate with others involved. Don't go it alone. With international buys, others also have increased difficulties. They must overcome new barriers to communication. Contacts abroad need to be developed carefully. And, it takes time!

7. Set a target price. To be advantageous, price should be 15% to 20% under current cost, including freight. Some companies won't source overseas unless there is at least a 20% improvement, while others will settle for 10%. A total dollar volume target is also needed.

8. Decide how you will buy:

    a. Direct from the foreign company

    b. Through local representatives

    c. Through trading companies

    d. Through specialized independent agents or brokers

    e. Through affiliate companies or another in-house division with contacts or experience in various international markets.

9. Prepare yourself for discussions and negotiations as a team. Allow adequate time to explore fully all details. Experienced overseas buyers tell of how many a deal was botched because someone assumed something would be done that wasn't.

10. Visit suppliers only when your volume warrants and you have firm leads or quotes and are ready to buy. Supplier visits may not be needed, but if they are, be well prepared.

Study literature, foreign business methods, and culture. Do your homework. Experience has shown some disincentives or roadblocks to successful offshore sourcing are:

- Language barriers
- Nationalism—that is, local source preference
- Lack of knowledge of the foreign supplier's culture
- Customs regulations and duties
- Currency exchange rate confusion
- Lack of proper planning and buying strategies

When buying globally, it is important to consider the differences that affect buying offshore. Routing of shipments through foreign countries and clearing through Customs and paying the proper duty are examples of procedures not required for purely domestic buying. International purchasing is more complex because of transportation distance, language, terminology, relative value of the dollar, customs duties, methods of payments, and practices. Also, legalities differ between the two contracting parties operating across national boundaries. The following compares the major purchasing issues and activities between offshore and domestic suppliers.[5]

Purchasing activity or issue	Domestic	International
Political/government	Seldom involved	Often more vital
Business environment	Stable rules	Multiple environments, diverse and changing
Sourcing	Homogeneous market	Fragmented markets, much more complex
Legalities	U.S. Law, UCC	GATT, and treaties
Scope of buying job	Broad	Far more expansive
Supplier relationships	Important	More demanding, time consuming
Countertrade	Illegal	Part of marketing strategy
Determine need	Sales, manufacturing	Longer forecast

[5]V. H. Pooler, *Global Purchasing: Reaching for the World,* Chapman & Hall, New York, 1991, p. 12.

- Inventory impact   Asset dollars   Usually larger; longer supply lines
- Specifications   Quality impact   More specific
- Information sources   Accurate data   Data not always available
- Communications problems   One language   Translation
- Dispute settlement   Negotiations   Potential arbitration
- Negotiation   Key activity   Many cultural customs to complicate process
- Placing the PO   Routine   Added clauses
- Documentation   Routine   New forms to execute
- Payment   Open account   Credits, letter, and documentary drafts
- Exchange restrictions   Single currency   Currency risks, varied value and stability
- Tariffs   None   Customs regulations
- Distribution   Air, rail, truck   Same, plus ocean transport
- Insurance   Blanket   Marine

In addition to the added complexities, there are many hidden costs in foreign sourcing. Ordering and administrative costs are higher than for domestic purchases. More purchase documentation and extra paperwork are used. Increased costs result from overseas business travel, international postage, telex, FAX, and telephone rates.

As can be seen from the foregoing, the cost and complexity differences between domestic and international sourcing would appear to be significant and daunting! But there are also rewards if the buyer is willing to invest the time to master the challenges of global buying.

Within their own companies, buyers are exposed to every other department to some degree. They work with different people with varying temperaments both within and outside of their companies. But who has the need for a broader outlook more than global buyers who deal with other cultures and business practices? They encounter greater technology, varied products, and ways to conduct business, as well as the complexity of global transportation and the legalities of international business.

In the ideal example of global buying, a company that has divisions in 15 countries seeks to get maximum value. In selecting sources, buyers don't solely use other divisions' volumes to enhance their own division's purchases. Truly global buyers use competitive advantage to see that the minimum total landed cost results for all buying operations, worldwide, which in turn affects the cost of products purchased.

Using the global marketplace, the buyer gains leverage to keep domestic suppliers' prices competitive. Exports provide capital and jobs for the local economy, while imports provide capital and jobs for offshore suppliers. Buying goods abroad at a lower price and better quality increases U.S. consumers' collective buying power. As a result, real income rises, giving a higher standard of living.

Entry Steps to Clear Customs

One of the complexities in global buying not encountered in the domestic case is the Customs clearance process. This section identifies the steps and specifics involved. There are five customs clearance steps: (1) entry, (2) valuation, (3) examination, (4) appraisement, and (5) liquidation. Entry can be made through almost 300 ports of entry into the U.S. Imported goods are not legally entered until the entry process is completed. Entry for consumption consists of filing documents to determine whether merchandise may be released from Customs custody, and to allow duty assessment and the gathering of government statistics.

Delivery of the merchandise has to be authorized and estimated duties paid. Within 5 days after the cargo has become available, an entry permit, Customs Form CF 7501 obtained from the U.S. Government Printing office or commercial printers, must be filed with the inspector at the incoming pier or airline terminal, along with the estimated duty payment. A commercial invoice is also needed to compute the amount of duty owed. Goods may be entered by the owner, buyer, or licensed customhouse broker.

A bill of lading, airway bill, or carrier's certificate stating the consignee gives evidence of shipment and the right of the consignee to make entry. Usually a shipment is consigned to a specific company, individual, or "To Order" (to the bank or to shipper). It depends on the method of payment. If consigned "To Order," the bill of lading properly endorsed shows the right to make entry. An original bill of lading is needed for the Steamship Company Release.

Details on the invoice are prepared according to Section 141.86 of Customs Regulations, and commercial practice. Customs wants the Harmonized code number shown on the left-hand side of the invoice, close to the item's name. Any discounts, rebates, commissions, and royalties must be shown on the invoice. While the invoice may state quantities in weights and measures used in the United States, the Customs entry must state quantity in metrics.

Immediate Delivery (I.D.) Entry

An article for urgent display at a trade show, or perhaps delicate equipment susceptible to damage, can be immediately released by using special permit Entry/Immediate Delivery Customs CF 3461. I.D. Entry certifies that a bond is current, and requirements for entry have been met. Upon approval, the buyer is free to take over the shipment, but within 10 days of arrival you must still file an Entry Summary CF 7501.

"Demurrage" is the payment for holding of goods beyond the allowed time. Goods not cleared within the prescribed period are considered unclaimed. Customs sends unclaimed merchandise "into General Order," that is the storage warehouse. The cost to reclaim merchandise can be quite high. If not claimed within one year, goods may be sold by auction.

Mail Entry is used for parcels valued under $1,250. The Post Office delivers to the consignee, collects the duty at that time, and makes the entry. The packages must have a customs declaration attached, and this form is available at post offices worldwide. The package must contain a statement of value and be marked, "Invoice enclosed."

Types of Transportation Entries

Customs routinely advises carriers that goods are subject to inspection by "Transportation Entry and Manifest of Goods Subject to Customs Inspection and Permit" CF 7512. A short serial numbered card, Transportation Entry and Manifest of Goods CF 7512-C, is checked to show the type of entries listed below:

- Immediate Transportation Entry
- Transportation and Exportation
- Warehouse Withdrawal for Transportation
- Immediate Exportation

This same form is also a permit to move goods to a duty-free zone. To clear Customs at a different port than arrival, the merchandise may be transferred "in bond" to that other Customs area. An example would be unloading goods in the Port of New York, and delivering part of the shipment by bonded carrier to Canada.

A Customs bond is a signed contract that ensures performance imposed by law. The bond may be in negotiable or non-negotiable form. There are usually three parties to a Customs bond: (1) the principal (your company), (2) surety, and (3) the beneficiary (the U.S. Customs Service). Surety is a third party who agrees to pay if the conditions of bond are not met, meaning the principal can't or won't pay.

An Immediate Exportation or I. E. Entry is prepared when merchandise is exported immediately from the same port of entry. These special type entries are indicative of the arrangements that can be worked out.

Customs Duty Valuation

A tariff is a "list of duties," a schedule or system of fees. Duties are determined by Customs, usually at an "ad valorem" (according to value) rate, and are a percentage of the dutiable transaction value. Transaction value is defined as "the price the buyer actually pays the seller," which includes packaging costs and the value of any "Assists" that are not included in the price itself.

"Assists" includes any materials or items that are part of the finished imported item, as well as any supplied tools, equipment, dies, or molds that were used in production.

Examination

Before the goods are released, the Customs district or port director may choose to examine the merchandise. Examination may be made on the docks for bulk shipments, at container stations, cargo terminal, or your premises. Examination is to determine:

- The value of the goods and their dutiable status
- Whether goods are those that are invoiced
- Whether the goods were marked with the country of origin or require special marking or labeling and if done properly
- If any articles are prohibited
- Whether the goods are properly invoiced or are more or less than ordered

Perhaps 5% of goods are physically inspected.

Country of Origin Marking

Section 304 of the Tariff Act states that each imported article is to be marked in "a conspicuous place as legibly, indelibly, and permanently as the nature of the article permits, with the English name of the country of origin, to indicate to the ultimate consumer in the United States the country in which the article was manufactured or produced." This marking must be permanent, and it must be large and legible enough to "be read easily by a person of normal vision." The supplier must use the words, "Made in . . ." or "Product of . . .". Adhesive labels aren't recommended, but are acceptable if approved.

Exempted from individual marking of country of origin are articles that: (1) can't be marked, (2) would be damaged, (3) would be excessively expensive to mark, or (4) entered into warehouse for immediate export.

Certificate of Origin

An UNCTAD Certificate of Origin Form A is often needed for goods more than $1,000 in value. A certificate permits buyers to gain duty-free or reduced rate under the GSP provision or other trade arrangement. To secure reduced tariffs, a minimum of 35% of local content is usually required. When required, it is proof of the origin of any materials and labor used to produce the goods. It also helps deter the seller from subcontracting or farming out work without the buyer's knowledge.

The Exporter's Certificate Of Origin, Customs Form 353 used by Americans and a similar bilingual form for Canadians is important. While it does not have to be used for entry, it must be produced upon Customs request. One of the Rules of Origin requires that 50% of the value of the goods must be either U.S., Canadian, or Mexican origin to be duty-free or get special duty under this agreement. These are elaborate rules detailing phased tariff reductions of specific items. The buyer will want to get a copy of this agreement published by Customs.

Usually, the Certificate of Origin is issued or approved by the Chamber of Commerce from the shipping country. They are sometimes signed by consulates and trade associations officials.

Appraisement

After entry is made, but before liquidation, the Customs Service finalizes its appraisal decision. To compute value of shipment for Customs declaration purposes, any foreign currency denoted must be converted to a U.S. dollar amount by using Customs conversion rates. Conversion is per provision 31 U.S.C. 5151. The *date of exportation* is used to certify a rate regardless of time of payment for the goods themselves. These rates are set by Customs and must be used. For estimation purposes, they are close to the published exchange rates in the *New York Times,* etc.

Liquidation

Duties are not official until "liquidated" (completed) after several weeks or months. Customs has one year from date of entry to liquidate, or tell the importer that the entry is to remain open. Any under or overpayment is rectified.

Methods of Payment

The "open account" method of payment, normally used in U.S. domestic trade, means the goods are sold on credit. (Buyers pay after they receive the goods.) Payment is made without any documents other than an invoice. Delays in processing payments across borders tie up suppliers' capital, so open account usually isn't allowed by most offshore sources, and is prohibited by law in many countries.

Most European and some South American suppliers don't wait for buyers to pay by invoice. Rather they present a draft to a bank that triggers payment against the buyer's funds. A draft is simply a check-like form drawn on a bank. This is called "payment by collection," a method that is less expensive than a formal Letter of Credit.

Although the offshore supplier typically prefers payment before shipping (preferably cash), most buyers prefer to pay after they use or sell the goods (consignment). Credit worthiness becomes a dominant issue in offshore buys. Several credit payment methods built on the concept of "constructive delivery" are used to break any standoff between buyer and seller. Banks give their assurance of payment provided the supplier presents certain documents as stipulated in the buyer's conditions.

Documentary Credits and Letters of Credit, often termed simply "Credits," means any arrangement by which the payment stalemate is broken. Banks in more than 160 countries subscribe to agreed rules for documentary credit banking procedures, as last amended in 1983. The International Chamber of Commerce spells out the details in its UCP 400, or "The Uniform Customs and Practices for Documentary Credits."

All credits must clearly state whether they are available by sight payment, by deferred payment, by acceptance, or by negotiation. For most offshore buys, we can place payment methods into three major groups used by businessmen for international trade: (1) Collections, (2) Letters of Credit, and (3) Banker's Acceptances.

Collection consists of payment upon tendering to banks of the proper documents associated with a purchase. The financial document is the sight or time draft. This collection method is easier than the formal Letter of Credit procedure and costs less.

The draft method is either:

1. A clean collection (meaning no other documents are required beyond the draft)

2. Part of the documentary collection explained above, consisting of the financial document, plus specified commercial documents such as a bill of lading, invoices, and certificates of origin. Sometimes other certificates such as inspection and insurance are needed.

The draft cannot be canceled without agreement between the parties. It resembles a bank check, and two types are used. The first is called *Documents Against Payment* (D/P), where the documents are released to the buyer upon payment of the draft. The other is called *Documents Against Acceptance* (D/A), where payment is made when the goods are accepted by the buyer.

The draft will be either a (1) sight draft, or (2) a time draft. A sight draft is commonly used. It means payment will be made upon presenting, or on "sight" of the draft. A "time draft" is a payment to be made within a stipulated time after being presented. *Tenor* is a term applying to the time delay in payment, normally 30 or 60 days. An "arrival draft" is a special type of sight draft that is payable only after goods arrive at a named port.

About 35% of all world trade use some form of Documentary Draft Collection as the means of payment when there is a trusting relationship. The Letter of Credit is more binding and preferred by some suppliers.

Letter of Credit

Many offshore suppliers want an alternative payment method called "Letter of Credit" (L/C). The L/C is primarily for the protection of suppliers. Sometimes buyers can negotiate to have the supplier waive the credit. However, certain governments require a L/C by law, and the parties have no choice but to comply. Buyers should know how to make the L/C work for them.

At the request of the applicant, the buyer's issuing bank arranges to make payment to a third party beneficiary. The supplier's "advising bank" actually makes the payment to them after receipt of the funds from the buyers' "issuing bank."

The supplier will be paid if contract conditions are met. It protects the supplier as the bank assumes the obligation to pay against presentation of required documents. There are many variations of such credit arrangements that are separate transactions from the sale of goods.

Credits may be either (1) revocable or (2) irrevocable, but most credits are issued as an "Irrevocable L/C," which means they cannot be canceled without consent of the supplier.

Letters of Credit must be arranged by the importing buyer, and executed by the "issuing bank" that guarantees payment. This bank commitment is usually required by many foreign suppliers before they will make or ship. This protects their payment risk and transfers it to the bank. About one third of offshore payments use this method.

The buyer fills in data on the bank's application form and forwards it to the bank for execution. Figure 6-1 shows the Letter or Credit sequence of events required as explained below:

- Supplier and buyer agree on the purchase.
- Buyer applies to his "issuing bank" for a L/C.
- Issuing bank prepares the letter and forwards it to supplier through supplier's foreign "advising bank."
- The advising bank forwards the letter to the supplier.
- Supplier prepares shipment and presents goods to carrier.
- Supplier then sends the draft for payment to their advising bank.
- Supplier forwards document copies to buyer or buyer's broker to clear customs in advance.
- Advising bank forwards draft and documents to issuing bank.
- Issuing bank reviews documents and honors supplier's draft by making payment.
- Issuing bank gives shipping document packet to the buyer, who is free to take goods (if not already cleared).

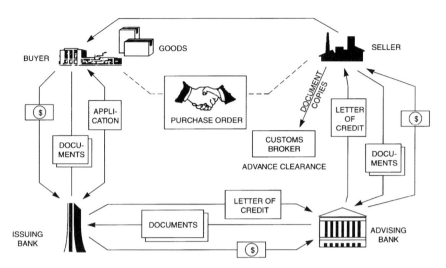

Figure 6-1 The Letter of Credit process.

The cost to the buyer is about one-tenth of 1% of the invoice price, with a $65 minimum charge.

A Standby Letter of Credit, with its deferred payment credit, is, from a banker's point of view, an unsecured loan. When used, it is accepted by the issuing bank. Standbys differ in that neither party expects to draw against the credit. They expect the account party will honor its payment.

The Standby L/C means the bank will pay, but will take title until the merchandise is paid for. An actual example will serve to illustrate the point. A U.S. firm needed a major purchase from Japan to be shipped to its Brazilian plant. However, the Japanese refused to accept a Brazilian purchase order, mindful of a then-poor credit rating for Brazil, where the government dictated a delay of payments. The solution was the Standby L/C. If for any reason, the Brazilian division did not make a payment on time per its contract, the U.S. parent guaranteed payment within 24 hours by wire to the Bank of Tokyo. This broke the impasse and allowed the buy to proceed.

Another alternate is a "revolving L/C" that permits flexibility for payment of any shipment up to a certain value, say, $5,000. As payment is made, the amount of credit returns to the original amount.

Banker's Acceptance

Bankers acceptance provides financing by the bank's promise to pay the face amount of the draft to any holder who presents it at maturity. Acceptance is created from either a L/C or time draft drawn independently. Acceptance shows a willingness to pay a time draft or bill of exchange. The bank has the importer/buyer simply write the word "accepted" on the time draft or bill and sign it.

Generalized System of Preferences

The generalized system of preferences (GSP) is a program for free rates of duties for merchandise from beneficiary developing independent countries to help their economic growth. The United Nations Conference on Trade and Development (UNCTAD) formally approved GSP in 1968. Startup required a waiver in 1971 of Most Favored Nation clause of GATT that forbade discriminatory international trade. Today, 27 countries grant GSP benefits to help developing nations improve their economic status through more exports.

Under the Generalized System of Preferences, duty-free entry is allowed for more than 3800 tariff schedule subheadings, from over 130 "Beneficiary Developing Countries" (BDCs). Industrialized countries are encouraged to import from the emerging nations by benefiting from their duty-free treatment.

Bilateral and Multilateral Trade Agreements

The most famous of the multinational treaties is the Geneva Accord on Trade and Tariff (GATT), which extended the same customs and tariff treatment given to the most favored nations (MFN). When buying from a country with MFN status, a favorably low duty, usually less than 4%, is levied.

Often subject to political changes, MFN tilts buying decisions away from nations without that status by having duties levied of 25% to 45%. MFN status for a given country changes with the times. As an example, Congress often debates taking MFN away from China, unless they change their human rights position. Now, Russia has MFN status since they espouse a more open market approach.

Other examples of multinational treaties are the free trade associations that foster unrestricted trade among its members. Among well known associations are those countries in the Pacific Rim that formed the Association of South East Asian Nations (ASEAN). Members include Indonesia, Malaysia, the Philippines, Thailand, and Singapore, all countries that are also listed as beneficiaries under GSP.

The European Free Trade Association (EFTA) includes Austria, Denmark, Norway, Sweden, Portugal, Switzerland, and the United Kingdom. The Latin American Free Trade Association (LAFTA) includes Argentina, Bolivia, Brazil, Chile, Columbia, Ecuador, Mexico, Paraguay, Peru, Uruguay, and Venezuela. The Caribbean Free Trade Association (CARIFTA) members are the United Kingdom's Cook Islands and includes Guyana, South America.

The Caribbean Basin Economic Recovery Act, known as Caribbean Basin Initiative Act, CBI, was designed to help 22 smaller nations by eliminating duties on U.S. buys. Most products from the area are eligible, but must meet a 35% of appraised value requirement. The Israel agreement is a bilateral agreement of importance to buyers and importers signed in 1985 that calls for duty-free or a reduced rate of duty for imports from Israel, and elimination of most tariffs.

These agreements are intended to strengthen and benefit the U.S. and our friendly neighbors to promote productivity, full employment, and friendship. Further, they are expected to contribute to expansion of world trade.

Quotas and trade agreements try to balance trade, though they're not doing the job very well because conflicting national interests are at work. Foreign trade, viewed as an engine of growth, is often subjected to much political influence. All governments, including that of the U.S., try to provide favorable conditions to win jobs and greater exports.

Harmonized Tariff Schedule of the U.S.

Buyers should learn if their commodities can be brought into the U.S. duty-free or with special lower tariffs. Buying from a country with "Most Favored Nation" (MFN) status, as defined by the Trade Act of 1974, means that U.S. buyers may be relieved from paying most, if not all tariffs. Buyers can determine the benefits specific to their situation based on a review of the HTSUS.

Table 6-3 shows an example of the information provided in the HTSUSA that spells out differing duties for various classes of goods from various countries. U.S. Customs Schedule A determines and identifies those countries and items getting favorable duty rates. For example, under the "Rates of Duty" column are sublistings 1 and 2. Column 1 divides into "General" and "Special." The General column shows the percentage duty as used for countries with MFN status. The Special column is used for countries with special agreements. In this column, A denotes duty-free entry under GSP (General System of Preferences) for developing nations. E is Caribbean initiative, CA is Canada, and IL is Israel. So a chest freezer imported from the United Kingdom would take a 2.9% MFN duty rate, while the same item from Israel is free. But from Bulgaria (column 2), a 35% duty is charged! Buyers are influenced by the political realities to buy from those countries friendly to the United States.

U.S. Programs Benefiting the Importing Buyer

Trade policies affect rates of duty charged. Penalties imposed on exporting nations take the form of higher duties that hurt the buyer. In similar fashion, benefits may be given to other nations that give buyers reduced costs. The result is that buying decisions enforce the intended aim to encourage or discourage imports. Let's focus on U.S. Programs benefiting the importing buyer. Buyers should ask themselves if they are aware of these benefits, and are they taking advantage of them?

Customs regulations that benefit buyers include Bonded Warehouse Entry, Duty-free Reentry Of Goods Sent For Repairs Or Replacement, and Partial Duty Exemption Section 807 of the HTSUS. In addition, the United States has created

Table 6-3 *Harmonized Tariff Schedule of the United States (annotated for statistical reporting purposes)*

Heading/ subheading	Stat. Suf. & cd	Article description	Units of quantity	Rates of duty 1 General	Rates of duty 1 Special	Rates of duty 2
8418		Refrigerators, freezers and other refrigerating or freezing equipment, electric or other; heat pumps, other than the air conditioning machines of heading 8415; parts thereof (con.):				
8418.30.00	00	3	Freezers of the chest type, ...	No.	2.9%	Free (A, C, E, IL) 2% (CA)	35%
8418.40.00	00	1	Freezers of the upright type, ...	No.	2.9%	Free (A, C, E, IL) 2% (CA)	35%
8418.61.00		Other refrigerating or freezing equipment; heat pumps: Compression type units whose condensers are heat exchangers	....	2.9%	Free (A, B, C, E, IL) 2% (CA)	35%
8419		Machinery, plant or laboratory equipment, whether or not electrically heated, for the treatment of materials by a process involving a change of temperature such as heating, cooking, roasting, distilling, etc.				
8419.11.00	00	5	Instantaneous gas water heaters	No.	4%	Free (A, E, IL) 3.6% (CA)	45%
8419.50.00	00	6	Heat exchange units		4.2%	Free (A, C, E, IL) 3.3% (CA)	35%

a number of incentives to encourage companies, both foreign and local, to manufacture in the U.S. Unfortunately, sometimes it is a foreign competitor that has learned best how to work the system of incentives. As an example, consider the case of the Japanese, from whom we should learn: (1) Japanese management and labor are not openly confrontational, and (2) they take advantage of tax breaks, use of duty-free zones, and other concessions designed to encourage development of business within the U.S. The case of typewriter manufacturer Smith Corona shows the strange twists of global competition. Smith Corona (SC) got relief in 1974 when it charged rival Japanese manufacturers with dumping typewriters in the U.S. market. Since moving manufacturing to Singapore, SC changed from the U.S.'s largest typewriter manufacturer to its largest importer. Meanwhile, the Japanese assembled typewriters in Tennessee.

In 1991, Japan's Brother Industries filed charges under U.S. law alleging Smith Corona dumps its Asian-made products in America. Claiming prices were cut below costs, the Japanese said, "While we've been investing in the United States and creating jobs, they've been migrating to Singapore, taking jobs with them."[6]

Benefits from Foreign Governments

Benefits provided to offshore suppliers by their native governments to encourage exports often result in benefits to American buyers in reduced costs. Ask if your supplier has access to subsidies or reduced taxes. Or, does the supplier's country offer insurance covering exchange rate risks? Another example: Mexico's "maquiladora," foreign-owned plants. Mexican workers now earn just about $2.60/hr. The Mexican "maquiladora" approach fits into the supply system of many American companies. Components and subassemblies that are made in the U.S. by sophisticated technology can be shipped into Mexico duty-free for final assembly. Upon completion, the products are returned to the U.S. for sale. Any duty charged will apply only to the "value added" labor.

Foreign "Free Trade" Zones and Subzones

Buyers can use trade zones to improve their company's cash flow and reduce costs too. Technically, a FTZ or foreign trade zone is a secured site legally considered outside a nation's customs territory. Goods can be brought into the zone without duty. Goods within a U.S. FTZ, for business purposes, remain within the International Zone of Commerce. There is no time limit with respect to the time you may keep goods in a zone. The *prime aim is to create American jobs.*

There are about 185 FTZs now in use within the U.S., with still more applications being processed. In these trade zones, goods may be stored, exhibited, assembled, processed, sorted, manufactured, repaired or altered, and repackaged,

[6]"Typewriter Firm Tastes Its Medicine," *Syracuse Herald Journal,* April 19, 1994, p. 86.

all without paying duties or taxes, until the goods are moved into a country's Customs territory. Any duty then due is assessed only on the import value.

Every port of entry may have a zone within which any state and local inventory taxes are waived. Typical is Onondaga County's zone, in the vicinity of Syracuse, New York. The Greater Syracuse Foreign Trade Zone, Ltd. is a 64,000 square foot zone segregated in an independent warehouse. Subzones are smaller locations that may be owned by a city or a specific company. In this case, 172 subzones exist.

Duty Drawback Savings

A benefit that results only *after duty has been previously paid* is termed Drawback. Drawback is an old concept going back to the U.S. Tariff Act of 1789 that was enacted by the First Congress. Its purpose has always been to encourage American commerce or manufacturing. Drawback helps a manufacturer to compete in foreign markets without having duty as part of product costs.

Drawback is covered under Section 1313, Title 19, HTSUS Code. Drawback is a refund of U.S. Customs duties paid upon importing materials or goods that are sold abroad at a later date. Ninety-nine percent of the amount of duty paid can be recovered under drawback. The one percent is retained by Customs to defray their costs. Interestingly, government statistics show that drawback rebates are often about 10% of what U.S. companies could claim. How much profit is your company giving up?

Well into the future there will be further evolution of the buyer dealing in global markets with economic acumen. So, we need a global outlook since the marketplace, customers, and competition are global.

This book is a companion to *Global Purchasing: Reaching for the World* in this publisher's Materials Management series. It should be clear from the foregoing information that the amount of detailed information on the subject is truly extensive and can only be summarized in a single chapter. Should you begin offshore buying, you will want to refer to that work for the detailed discussions inclusive of sample forms and full importing procedures.

Chapter 7 will look in detail at how we can evolve the supplier relationship to top level status. We will explore the natural frictions that exist in the buyer/seller interface, and further explore ways to smooth those frictions for mutual benefit.

7

Building Rapport with Suppliers—Transition from Supplier to Business Partner

Relationships with key supplier personnel deserve special consideration. It is tempting to play "hard ball" with a supplier, especially one who wants to maintain business. The experienced buyer learns that every so often, a special favor or extra help is needed in the long-range interest of both parties. So, being unreasonable or discourteous often hurts the buyer in the long run.

The increasing use of partnerships and alliances requires a strategic purchasing orientation. Increasing complexity in doing the materials job will require buyers to become ever more knowledgeable about their source's supply capacity. A challenge is to keep competitive leverage while maximizing mutual goals.

As *Purchasing Magazine* Publisher Jack Connor has said,

> "The growing complexity of buy-sell relationships demands ever more intensive partnering, both internal and external. Here's what's happening: Smart buyers are transforming buyer/seller dealings into multi-level, multi-disciplined relationships. They're opening the proverbial and much-maligned 'backdoor', the side doors, the front door, and any other passageway they can find to facilitate the flow of ideas and information between buyer and seller company."[1]

Consider what suppliers want and expect from buyers. Buyers have both a need and the right to get cooperation, but to get it *they have to offer something in return*. Goodwill has long been recognized as a business asset, and tact is a necessity! Openness and friendliness cost little, and will pay off in maintaining a sound relationship. As one experienced purchasing manager said, "The supplier only offers deals to those they like!"

One of the potential problems of partnering is that in multiple locations, a supplier may provide good service to one and poor service to another. By routinely funneling all business to the preferred supplier, complacency can set in.

---

[1]"Purchasing Outlook," *Purchasing*, Feb. 12, 1987, p. 43

This is an era of extreme cost competition with relatively low inflation. Buyers have long-range concern about the availability of materials. Partnerships have been formed for long-term survival. There can be no question that a strong joint effort to meet customers' requirements is worth the effort. American companies have forged new business partnerships and formed joint ventures and other international arrangements to share the costs and growth opportunities. Making it possible are rapid communication, computerized information, and better transportation along with international business acumen.

A purchasing engineer may request much presale technical services and engineering samples. A supplier might have to spend significant time and effort working out specification details. Perhaps making early samples requires some investment in tooling or even dies. Of course, suppliers hope to recover such costs from future business, but perhaps after receiving samples, the buying company fails to test or doesn't give them a fair trial. Is there any obligation to the seller? Would you consider this to be a "sharp practice"?

Supplier Partnering Relationships

There are certain areas of the purchasing function that should be given special attention—those friction areas where no hard-and-fast rules can be applied. Tact and goodwill often are the only tools available to management in its constant efforts to promote cordial and effective supplier and trade relationships, especially in cases where public criticism and controversy hit hard at purchasing policies.

Good supplier relationships are of paramount importance to every purchasing manager. Those companies who serve PMs are also potential buyers of their company's products, so it makes good common sense to keep relationships with any supplier as cordial as possible even if the company has never made any purchase whatsoever. People who are friendly toward a buyer will often go to bat for her, perhaps by taking steps to help meet a tough but necessary delivery date or locating a source for hard-to-get material. As a contact point and showcase for a company, purchasing definitely affects the corporate image insofar as those salespeople who visit with the buyers are concerned; that corporate image will depend on the image created by the buyers, and no amount of public relations will overcome any bad impression they may make.

There is a natural friction and stress in the buyer/seller relationship based on the inherent nature of the acquisition process. Practical experience and response from buyers at various seminars shows the following negative aspects sometimes experienced by buyers in dealing with salespeople:

- Sales reps who don't have product knowledge
- Sales engineers who design the product for our engineering

- Salespeople who lay "guilt trips" on buyers ("You don't want to save $10,000?!")
- Salespeople who are too "foxy" for engineers during negotiations

Achieving good relationships isn't simply a matter of avoiding conflicts. While it is mandatory that buyers follow the law, we cannot dictate the world's moral or ethical posture. (We can, however, set a good example.) The idea is to use the inherent power in the buying job tactfully and ethically.

Some lost sales may be traced to something that happened to upset the buyer/seller relationship. Some salesmen claim they are shut out of a certain company because the buyer is a friend of a competitor. A friendly, intelligent salesman is of great value to any company, but a buyer can ill afford to buy on friendship alone. Buyers must receive for their company products or service values equal to the money spent. Both parties must profit.

Often, discussion between buyer and seller is not as open as it should be. Consider the true example of two distributors in New York State—one who got 99% of the business from an industrial customer. They were equal in size. The sales vice president, after not receiving significant business over nearly 15 years, finally got the courage to discuss a run-in a former salesman had with a buyer 15 years ago. The story made no sense whatsoever to the PM; in fact the buyer didn't even know the salesman who supposedly was visiting weekly! For 15 years this distributor accepted a salesperson's excuse about why their competitor got ½ million dollars more per year than they did.

Behavioral scientists have shown that strength and weakness are mirror images. As such, the qualities that make buyers valuable in some situations are often their worst faults. A buyer doggedly persists in a cost reduction, and may be successful, but if not, may stubbornly persist and antagonize valuable suppliers. Another senior buyer's quiet confidence in troubled times make him the choice to run the department. Then he turns out a poor manager because of failure to communicate.

Salespeople should be given a chance to tell their story, thereby keeping competition alive and fair. To them, their products are the most important in the world—don't belittle them even if they are inferior to others. Constructive criticism is something else—if it will help that supplier to improve his position as a future supplier. It's natural for a salesperson to be disappointed at not getting an order, but courtesy and friendly tact may pay off in the long run for all concerned.

Many buyers allow salespeople to call repeatedly without the slightest possibility that they will be interested in their products based on the company's needs. It is only fair to advise the salesperson at the earliest moment. Honesty pays off in the long run! Give the reasons why, rather than let them believe that they can one day be of service.

An opportunity to explain your company's problems, product requirements, and specific applications arises when a new salesperson visits. This will open a door through purchasing, and the salesperson will soon sense what channels of communication are likely to be most profitable. This is the time to advise what is expected and how the company buys. It is also an excellent occasion to begin cultivating good supplier relationships.

"Backdoor" Selling (How to Handle Difficult Salespeople)

Buyers can have about as much authority as others will allow. When he or she has little authority, the buyer's results can be poor, and when he or she has enough, the results can be gratifying. Top management support of the purchasing function encourages others within the company to cooperate. Without that cooperation, it can be difficult if not impossible to operate efficiently. "Backdoor selling" raises such an emotional conflict because it tends to destroy the buyer's communication channels necessary to effectively control expenditures.

Purchasing people have long complained about backdoor sellers—the salesperson who sells to others outside purchasing without maintaining contact with the buyer. While it does exist, it is questionable whether this complaint is justifiable in many cases.

Why are there so many complaints about this issue? The authors have frequently discussed with salespeople their complaints about buyers to better understand the persistent use of backdoor buying. Here is an example of a specific complaint: A circuit breaker is obsolete and superseded by another, but the buyer doesn't know what that means technically, and the sales engineer doesn't know whom to talk to. The buyer takes information over the phone, but the problem is to translate the technical information so the buyer will be able to communicate with engineering. Sometimes, "It's like talking to a brick wall."

Typical complaints mentioned by sales engineers concerning buyers have been: (1) disorganization, (2) intimidation, and (3) inability (or unwillingness?) to act. Perhaps the most common complaint is, "They don't really know *what* they're buying." So, the sales response is to bypass such buyers.

Here are some specific true-life examples of complaints from the selling side of the desk.

- A sales engineer, now part owner, selling for an electronic supply distributorship, comments, "When a buyer is highhanded, I can't trust her." He believes the buyer is getting his price and giving it to others who gain an unfair advantage. This SE believes 70% of buyers give "unfair advantage" or "the last look" in auctions. Interestingly, he likes those who do it to him because he sells in a "cat and dog" market, with a product readily available from several stocking distributors!

- Another pet peeve is the government buyer who wants a common screw obtainable at any hardware store, but they can't deviate.

- Another sales engineer stated that some buyers "don't know anything" and won't let him talk to engineering. After several attempts, the SE says he'll wait enough time so the buyer forgets him, and then will call on the engineer directly. He recounts a case where he broke into a new account while a buyer changed jobs, before a new one was selected. After telling the engineer he had no one to talk to, the sympathetic engineer tested samples that were approved. The new buyer priced them and awarded him the account.

- Still another SE advises that when he backdoor sells, 9 of 10 buyers go along with it, because it didn't put them out. He contends that "many are lazy."

An unmistakable trend is that the buyer, under pressure to combat the ever present profit squeeze, and with top management support, is making more final decisions about what is bought than ever before. The key to a given company's purchasing power is held by the buyer who knows what his or her company needs, and what it takes to sell it. If the job is handled competently, buyers are the ones who control, or at minimum approve, what the company buys. The buyer should be in sales' corner if they have something to offer that will do a given job better or more economically.

There can be strong temptations for the buyer to backdoor buy just as for the salesman to backdoor sell. Both exist because to some extent the acknowledged proper channels are not producing results. Many buyers "backdoor buy" continuously, because of the complexities and speed with which information must be secured and passed on; that is, the buyer is often forced to go around the salesperson to get information from suppliers. Usually, the salespeople could care less since they get credit for the sales gain anyway.

We need to do a better job at the vital buyer/seller interchange. Consider that both the buyer and seller have much to lose if the salesperson is not able to sell through proper buying channels! This is a shared responsibility to ensure those channels are properly accessible for the benefit of both parties.

Failure to see salespeople promptly, although not unethical, is cause for irritation. As a guide, nobody should be kept waiting more than 30 minutes. Not that they can expect to see anyone immediately coming in off the street. But, if buyers are tied up, visitors should be so advised by the receptionist; if they do wait, it will be their choice. Visiting hours can also present a problem. Some companies insist that sales people call between limited hours. However, because this makes things especially difficult for those sales people traveling some distance, thought should be given to the effect of such a limitation on others. In large cities, the supplier who is restricted by one company's visiting hours can always find another buyer willing to see him. Elsewhere, establishing arbitrary visiting hours may cause hidden resentment and give the impression that the company's buyers consider themselves excessively important.

Dealing with salespeople is a part of life for buyers. Though usually proficient and a valued member of the partnership, not all sales representatives are perfect. On the "lighter side," let's look at some facetious categories compiled[2] on types of salespeople. We've added ways to handle some of them:

1. The *wind-bag*. This is the back-slapper, joke-teller, or the time-waster. Drops in as he "just happened to be in the neighborhood."

   a. Simply stand up, shake hands, and while talking, walk him out the door.

   b. Some have their secretary say, "They're waiting for you in the meeting, Ms. Jones." (The authors don't condone this practice).

2. The *technocrat*. Thinks of himself or herself as a "marketing engineer." Uses lots of "engineering-ese" to impress you with knowledge. If he doesn't have a simple answer ready, ask him to put it in writing and send it in.

3. The *name dropper*. Just talked to your Mr. Jones (your president). "He and I are planning some fishing this summer, you know."

4. The *silent type*. Just sits there and waits for your lead. Lay your problems on him.

5. The *"newsboy."* Typically arrives with attaché case loaded with brochures, catalogues, and bulletins. Ninety percent of what he offers you is of no interest.

6. The *"know-nothing"*. Arrives totally unprepared. This often happens with newer salespeople. Suggest they visit only with specific items to present.

7. The *"order taker."* Unlike the know-nothing, is familiar with what you need and simply wants to write up the order. He's often good at this, but can't answer status of any orders received last week, or month, and is not interested in any follow through.

8. Ms. or Mr. *"Peepers."* Learned to read upside down at an early age. One solution is to have a large blueprint handy to quickly cover your entire desk before she or he is admitted. Of course, you'll not leave any written prices exposed.

Again, the majority of salespeople are proficient, but recognizing the poor ones and turning them around does companies a favor!

Conflict Resolution: Working with Others

The Boy Scout rule is that the campgrounds are always left in the same or better condition than they are found. This is a positive example to follow! Likewise,

---

[2]Somerby Dowst, *Basics for Buyers,* Professional Procurement Co., Mohegan Lake, NY 10547, 1987, p. 139.

generations of Maine woodsmen, upon arriving at a shelter station, chop wood as fuel for heating for the next arrival. As applied to our profession, when a manager vacates his role in purchasing, will the profession have been somewhat enriched by his or her contribution?

Some department's functions cause more natural friction than others. The production process itself, plus many unexpected events, can cause trouble between purchasing and manufacturing. That's because these functions may be measured by conflicting yardsticks. Purchasing is typically out to get the lowest possible materials costs, often in direct conflict with production control's efforts to hold down inventory by stocking smaller quantities. Add to this the character of a good production control person who generally is a driver; otherwise they would not be successful. In any case, the two functions can collide with buyers who are inclined to more diplomatic relationships with others. Again, the answer lies in service. The higher goals of purchasing can be achieved only when production requirements are met. Purchasing is ultimately responsible for *all* functions and activities regardless if another function is delegated to expedite or monitor quality. Ultimately, the blame for poor supplier selection and performance will fall on purchasing, which must face up to this responsibility.

As purchasing is a conflict-producing job, there is a need for statesmanship—both with supplier's representatives and fellow employees. Take the example of a salesperson who has worked hard to get his products specified by an engineer. Sooner or later, most PMs one day will get a phone call along the lines of, "I just asked your buyer about the status of the expected go ahead, and he told me he gave the order to my competitor who quoted a lower price. I've put a lot of time and effort and cost into this job. Your company owes me. You've treated us poorly. You've got to make good on this." Does this salesman have a legitimate beef? What is your best course of action, if any?

One of the secrets of dealing with difficult people is to be able to keep your emotions under control. Dealing with issues and not personalities is sound advice, and it helps to recognize the basic style of those with whom we work. Understanding the type of personality can help buyers and managers to make some assumptions that are likely to be correct when you don't know the individual you're dealing with well.

Always go to visit the highly dominant person. Confront him or her directly. It is sound advice not to attack a person's basic values, but to follow this advice you first need to understand what those values are. Conflict management varies with different types of people some of whom we might characterize as follows:

- *Passive*: They may offer a weak handshake, dead-pan face, and blank stare. They avoid any controversy and never let you know where you stand.

- *Dictatorial*: They are bullies who intimidate and are blunt, constantly demanding their way. They can be brutally frank and critical.

- *Yes-people*: These are the opposite of the bully. They agree with any proposition or commitment, but rarely perform. Always sorry for this, and pleasant, but you can't always rely on them.

- *No-People*: They take an opposite position as a reflex action. Inflexible, resistant to change, they're quick to prove why something can't possibly work.

- *Complainers*: Negative and nit-picking, they turn others off. They almost never do anything about things they love to complain about.

- *Know-it-alls*: They come to a seminar and know far more than the instructor. They let everyone know during the meeting, and especially the breaks, how little the instructor knows! Arrogant, this type has a ready opinion on any subject. Yet, when wrong they blame others or are defensive.

You may recognize some, if not all of the above characteristics in the people you work with, live with, or buy from!

A Time to Do Nothing!

A Rube Goldberg is the term for doing something with extreme complexity what could and should be done simply. It is often as important in our business world to know what *not* to do as it is to know what to do. Sometimes there is a time to tell what needs to be done, a time to seek advice on what should be done, and a time to solve the problem in a cooperative manner.

Recall trying to open a stuck window? Instead of forcing the window to open, it makes better sense to bang the window shut. Greater force is easier to apply to break the bond. Then, the window opens freely. So too, often in the buying situation, continued forceful thrust only produces friction.

President Eisenhower told how Churchill notified him of the intent to be with the first troops setting foot in Normandy in the invasion of Europe during World War II. Ike tried to persuade him this was out of the question, as he was too valuable to the cause.[3] Churchill felt it was his prerogative, and he asked Ike if he had complete authority over the entire invasion. When told that was true, Churchill stated that since the British Navy was a part, he had a right to be on a ship as a member of the crew.

Rather than confront the situation directly, word was sent to King George, who promptly sent a note to Churchill. Churchill wasn't ordered not to go, but the king wrote, "Splendid idea Winnie. I intend to be at your side when we step together on the soil of France." Churchill saw at once the danger to a lost king,

---

[3]Several versions exist, but this is how Eisenhower himself described it in a TV interview January 26, 1967 with Alistair Cooke.

and said not another word to Ike about crossing with the troops. This is a good example of handling a conflict without directly challenging the person causing it.

When someone is upset, let them know you are too, but don't feed into that pattern. Stay calm! You have to disagree sometime. Doing so does not require that you prove the other party is wrong. Direct the discussion toward why you need to accomplish your goal.

The challenge is to learn to deal with difficult people. How to handle complaints and anger might be found from these steps to diffuse:

- Disagree without arguing.
- Use questions to diffuse anger from disagreement.
- Buy time to allow emotionalism to calm down.

Scenario: Buyer Dealing with Boring/Lost in Space Salesperson

Let's consider a humorous case that should provoke some thought on dealing with and improving relationships with sales people.

Your assistant reminds you that Mr. Sharpsell is waiting to see you. A feeling of futility passes over you as you think of Sharpsell, who is a sales representative for Christianson Manufacturing. They are one of only two suppliers who make a precision switch component for you. He visits about every other month, as your company does substantial business with Christianson in spite of the representative.

Each of Sharpsell's visits has been unpleasant to you. He is overbearing, sloppy, and long winded. You invariably become bored and frustrated as he routinely regales you with stories on his hobbies in which you have no interest.

You're in your office awaiting his arrival, and have hardly begun to think of what excuse you will use to avoid another long, grueling session, when Sharpsell walks in with a big smile on his face, saying . . .

> "Hi pal! Boy, what a weekend. We took in the best-of-breed dog show Sunday. . . Our little Midge came in 2nd. She should have gotten the blue ribbon, but one of the judges favored this widow's terrier. Some say he's on friendly terms with her, if you get what I mean. Say, did you hear the one about . . ."

What would you say and do with Sharpsell? Some suggestions might be:

- Cut off the front legs of the visitor's chair?
- Move to get up while walking him to the door?
- See him only in the lobby?
- Have Sharpsell phone from the lobby?
- Ask him to limit visits to every other month?
- Receive visitors based on dollars spent with them?

No doubt some of these ideas, though in some cases offered tongue in cheek, provide some creative solutions. And though there may be many other creative alternatives, the underlying challenge is to minimize areas of friction.

In addition to the above areas of friction relating to personality, areas of friction between buyer and seller include the following: specifications and tolerances that are too close, specifications changed without warning, late payments, cash discounts taken but not earned, unreasonable delivery demands, and excessive "bureaucracy." Also burdensome are lack of technical knowledge on the part of purchasing personnel, an absence of loyalty to the supplier, ignorance of small supplier problems, frequent changes in personnel, and attempts by buyers to get free technical and engineering services as well as ideas from suppliers while intending to buy elsewhere.

The small supplier, in short, cannot work effectively with the large company buyer unless that buyer is able to represent his company fully and properly. The lenient or easy-going buyer may leave dealings with others in the company to the salesperson who may have neither the time nor the ability to get a decision from them.

Conversely, there are some buyers who go overboard on what they term "good relations," often finding themselves more interested in protecting the suppliers' interest than their own company's. This type of individual may be constantly battling the production and engineering departments, urging them to accept what the supplier furnishes even if it isn't quite what they want. In situations where there is a discrepancy in goods furnished, and where considerable unraveling is needed to determine what corrective measures are necessary and who will pay the costs of faulty supplier performance or poor engineering specifications, the buyer sometimes appears to his company colleagues to be in the supplier's corner. This is proper when the buyer is aware of facts that support that position and is acting in good faith to settle a dispute through negotiation—but he or she had better be able to explain his or her reasoning.

Buyers frequently must defend the supplier against unwarranted criticism and rejection of materials, since the buyer is often the only one in a position to have heard both the company's and the supplier's interpretations. In any such situation "firm but fair" should be the guide.

Surveys indicate that suppliers are more important today than just a decade ago. In a recent survey, 90% of purchasing managers agree, 70% of design engineers also agree, and 60% of engineers view purchasing's role on their design team as more important. In times of extreme cost competitiveness, there may be a temptation for some buyers to force suppliers into unreasonable concessions. But genuine long-range concern about materials availability should balance any such tendency. Improvement is needed, not simply in good supplier relationships, but the broader "supplier partnering" concept—a shared responsibility to meet the buying and selling companies' needs.

"Supplier partnering" is the term being used today to indicate closer cooperation between buying and selling companies to achieve joint benefits. In this context, the suppliers are viewed as an integral part of the manufacturing process. Partnering is not just meeting a buyer's stated immediate requirement. It is also providing new products, methods, and materials to improve quality and keep costs low. The competent buyer will use the suppliers' product development and research to improve supplier productivity. One way is to invite key suppliers to a series of meetings where competitive parts or items are scrutinized, wherein the aim will be to mutually identify cost reductions or quality improvements.

A type of partnering agreement used primarily for MRO items is the systems contract explained in Chapter 15. It is an agreement to supply all of a family of goods, at a level of price. The goal is to save purchasing time and paperwork, reduce inventory, improve flow of goods, and still achieve best pricing.

The advantages of partnering have been asserted by many in the field. One analysis indicated the following benefits from partnering[4]:

1. Inventory reduction
2. Reduced paperwork
3. Reduced acquisition costs
4. Typically standardized prices for longer term decisions
5. Improved quality

Advantages to the seller were indicated to be:

1. Increased business
2. Increased efficiencies within the seller with higher sales
3. Better inventory turns with better planning
4. More stable customer relationships that are renewed and reinforced

Interestingly, the advantages to the seller often translate to buyer advantages, which supports the wisdom of the practice. Another survey[5] of partners reported that their reasons for partnering were as follows:

1. Reduced inventory   (76%)
2. Cost control   (75%)
3. Dependable supply levels   (70%)
4. Reduced lead-times   (67%)
5. Reduced paper processing (46%)
6. Improved quality control   (43%)
7. Technical support   (23%)

[4]"Partners for Profit," *Purchasing,* April 28, 1988, p. 63

[5]*Purchasing Magazine,* July 28, 1988, p. 23

Strategic supplier partnering provides a competitive edge to improve not simply supplier relationships, but also the broader shared responsibility to meet your company's needs. As expected, there are some problem areas that both partners report. One is failure to treat partnering type agreements any different from other deals. Another is failure to study the needs of the other party, and how each will change to help the partner.

As previously stated, partnering is not just meeting a buyer's requirements; it is providing new products, methods, and materials to improve quality, while keeping costs low for the buying company. There should be more joint design efforts between the engineers of both buyer and seller, looking for cost reduction or quality improvements. What's in it for suppliers? Benefits sought by suppliers are maximum buy levels, longer term contracts, and access to future production plans.

About half those who practice partnering bring suppliers into their product planning process early on. This practice is consistent with concurrent engineering emphases, and often focuses on projects aimed at value analysis (VA) improvements.

A "certified supplier" is a supplier—generally defined as "world class"—that meets or exceeds your company's accreditation standards. This may be based on the company's rating system defined earlier. Reward outstanding performance with certified supplier status along with increased business volume if suppliers continue to perform well! Certified suppliers should feel confident to invest to keep up with the "state-of-the-art" as they have assurance they have a partnership that will not lead to being dropped without good grounds.

These services could be provided as rewards by the buying company to its suppliers who achieve certified status:

- Long-term contracts
- Manufacturing engineering service support
- Quality control assistance
- Productivity gains in support of other sales
- Human resources planning
- Investment in facilities and equipment
- Tie-in on purchases from raw material suppliers

By working with suppliers to correct deficiencies all the way back to their operation and production processes, the buyer can assist in improving production yield. In turn, this should provide cost savings to the buyer.

Ethical Issues in Buying

Ethical issues continually affect buyer/supplier relationships. Buyers are custodians of their company's reputation, and need to resist any impropriety. The buyer must distinguish between what is considered acceptable and what is not.

Is any other position so suspect? Yet fewer lapses of honesty probably occur in purchasing than in other positions. But the buying function is always under close scrutiny primarily because of the flow of the company funds through a PM's department. Buyers spend others' money to buy products, materials, and services they don't usually use themselves. So, is it any wonder the buyer is under scrutiny of the boss, subordinates, suppliers, and those who seek to supply, as well as the consumer of what they buy?

High personal integrity and strong moral convictions are, on the whole, typical, but not all people in purchasing, unfortunately, live up to the professional norms. This can cause them unforeseen trouble, and further erode confidence in the profession for the rest of us.

Ethical questions center around distinguishing between legitimate sales promotion and inducements meant to influence buying decisions. Like it or not, this is a potential problem area for anyone engaged in the buying profession. Ideally, decisions should be made on price, value, and service considerations, with freedom from outside influences.

In sports, if you don't play by the rules, you're penalized. In football, if you clip you're assessed 15 yards; if you strike a low blow in boxing it may cost you the round; so too, in business the rules of the game must be adhered to. In the supply game the rules are not always clearly defined or well known. And the courtesies of the road are sometimes a matter of opinion.

Where to Draw the Line

Ethics, simply put, is a standard of how you will act in certain circumstances—"basic principles of right action!" One's actions in dealing with others create an impression, whether accurate or not. Obviously, a person is going to be judged on the ethical standards of the person doing the judging, and what appears proper for one person may be quite offensive to another. This is why gray areas exist.

An auditor, asked for an opinion of purchasing, once said, "You have to find out who's getting the graft." When questioned, he admitted that he didn't quite mean this—at least there was nothing specific in mind. The answer is typical of the emotional response when some business people think of purchasing. A former salesman, after becoming a top manager, may recall "wining and dining" the buyers he used to deal with. So, if there is any area where the "Simon Pure" should prevail, it is purchasing. There might be less of a double standard in business ethics if everyone remembered that they must answer for their behavior not only to the company but to themselves.

In creating a positive atmosphere conducive to a successful supplier partnership, here are a few questions that the PM should consider. Does this department subscribe to and display the "Principles and Standards of Purchasing Practice" (Domestic and International) as adopted by the NAPM? (see Table 7-1). Is the ethical policy of the company given in writing? Do the buyers and purchasing people feel free to discuss ethical conduct among themselves and with those with whom they come in contact? Does the department notify suppliers, in writing, of its policy on acceptance of gifts?

Probably the most important factors that determine ethical practices within a company are the traditions of the industry, one's personal convictions and values, the behavior of the individual's superiors, and the behavior of one's equals.

Table 7-1   Principles and standards of puchasing practice:
Loyalty to your organization
Justice to those with whom you deal
Faith in your profession

From these principles are derived the NAPM standards of purchasing practice. (domestic and international)

1. Avoid the intent and appearance of unethical or compromising practice in relationships, actions, and communications.

2. Demonstrate loyalty to the employer by diligently following the lawful instructions of the employer, using reasonable care and only authority granted.

3. Refrain from any private business or professional activity that would create a conflict between personal interests and the interests of the employer.

4. Refrain from soliciting or accepting money, loans, credits, or prejudicial discounts, and the acceptance of gifts, entertainment, favors, or services from present or potential suppliers that might influence, or appear to influence, purchasing decisions.

5. Handle confidential or proprietary information belonging to employers or suppliers with due care and proper consideration of ethical and legal ramifications and governmental regulations.

6. Promote positive supplier relationships through courtesy and impartiality in all phases of the purchasing cycle.

7. Refrain from reciprocal agreements that restrain competition.

8. Know and obey the letter and spirit of laws governing the purchasing function and remain alert to the legal ramifications of purchasing decisions.

9. Encourage all segments of society to participate by demonstrating support for small, disadvantaged, and minority-owned businesses.

10. Discourage purchasing's involvement in employer-sponsored programs of personal purchases that are not business related.

11. Enhance the proficiency and stature of the purchasing profession by acquiring and maintaining current technical knowledge and the highest standards of ethical behavior.

12. Conduct international purchasing in accordance with the laws, customs, and practices of foreign countries, consistent with United States laws, your organization policies, and these Ethical Standards and Guidelines.

Everyone leans on the boss to some extent in finding out what is expected in this regard. Unless the top people show a good example, how can others be expected to do so? Buyers are prone to pick up the group's ethics; if most buyers do not accept gifts, newcomers are likely to follow the lead.

A newspaper editor wrote that much can be said in favor of politicians publicly announcing any favors or gifts. Then there is a minimum of gossip, a minimum of suspicion. "Having a complete fill-in, we ask no questions. The fellows who get into trouble are those who try to sneak out of town on a yachting trip and conceal the source of their vicuna coats and Oriental rugs." Perhaps a good guide is for the PM to act as if everything he or she does will be reported in the local newspaper!

Purchasing managers and buyers alike must beware of extremes in ethical behavior. What of the buyer who smokes but won't accept a cigarette offered by a salesman? He is going to extremes when he places a supplier's representative in the embarrassing position of looking as though he were offering a bribe. Most salesmen are naturally friendly and outgoing; and, while few buyers with good business sense will accept excessive gifts and lavish entertainment, fewer still will object to small tokens.

Certainly, accepting money is bribery and unlawful, such as when a sales person arranges for a special "kickback" to the buyer in consideration for business received. That's an open and shut case. But distinguishing between the gratuity and a bribe is sometimes difficult. One PM jokingly puts it in this way: "If you can't use it, it's a bribe!" But this is no joking matter; bribery is punishable under law. It would be naive to state, however, that it doesn't exist. The problem must be faced, and it is the PM's duty to be constantly aware of any situation where trouble might occur.

Deciding what is a legitimate expenditure for trade promotion, sales, and advertising as compared to gratuities isn't always simple. A salesperson's rightful purpose in contacting a buyer is to influence his or her choice on the basis of the superior features of product, price, or service. To do this, he or she will employ advertising, catalogues—and persuasion—all of which are necessary. On the other hand, gratuities in the form of gifts, entertainment, and so on, apart from quality, price, or other considerations, are sometimes used to influence the buyer. The intent is to sway the buyer's judgment so that the results are favorable to the seller.

A conflict of interest is not always easy to define, but the following are possible conflicts:

- Investing personal money in a supplier's business
- Borrowing or lending money to a supplier
- Accepting excessive gifts and entertainment
- Misuse of privileged information

- Having outside work that affects effort provided your employer
- Playing the commodities market for materials you buy
- Divulging company proprietary pricing or other data in a group setting where non-company personnel are present (as at an industry association meeting)

Whatever the form, attempted supplier influence on employees is as difficult to eliminate as it is to locate. Purchasing people are by no means the only recipients of such attention; superintendents, foremen, engineers, management, inspectors, and rank-and-file manufacturing employees who are in a position to influence sources of supply may also become involved. Where lack of control enables the minority of unscrupulous suppliers to approach factory employees directly, they may, through small inducements such as an occasional fifth of whisky, persuade employees, who might not realize it, to find fault with competitors' products so that a particular one will be favored. For example, a large foundry had to discharge a foreman because even nominal gifts, such as cigars and pencils, influenced his judgment. The seller was asked not to call again.

Buying Practices

Failure to give unsuccessful bidders an honest reason why they have not been awarded a purchase order is one factor contributing to an unethical purchasing image. There can be no excuse for not supplying such information, except in the most unusual of circumstances. It may be in the interest of the PM's company to withhold certain facts; however, the PM never should willfully mislead a supplier in cases where business has been placed elsewhere.

Knowledgeable purchasing people know that giving competitive prices to suppliers is a breach of business etiquette. It may be advisable to advise that the price was "5% too high," so that they have an indication of where they stand; then the pencil can be sharpened the next time they have a chance to bid (Although some PMs will disagree, saying this is unethical—going beyond the limits of proper discourse.)

Regardless of the ethical implication, buyers interested only in securing better prices may also find it to be common sense not to give out prices paid. As an example, if a potential powder metal supplier is told that a casting is bought for $5.40, they are in an enviable position with respect to their competitors. Knowing that the buyer wants the powdered metal, and is interested in savings, upon receiving their product cost and pricing data, the supplier may choose to submit a price of $5.20. The supplier's cost could allow a price as low as $4.00 but, sure of this market, they set the price just low enough as an incentive for the buyer to award the order.

From the PM's standpoint, putting specific price information in the hands of the supplier is poor buying, even if no ethical consideration is involved. There may be special instances where setting "ballpark" prices may be acceptable practice, especially when a fair amount of investigation and development is necessary before quoting. If it makes sense to use a second source of supply, certain facts may have to be provided to induce a new potential supplier to put real effort into their quotation. Practically speaking, however, only in an exceptional few cases should ballpark prices be given, and in no case should the actual prices paid be divulged to a competitor. This may run contrary to some peoples' concept of partnership.

As noted earlier, requesting price quotations from suppliers with whom there is no serious intention to place an order is another questionable practice. Such requests for price imply that if quality and price are acceptable, an order will be forthcoming. Failure to adhere to this expectation often invites suspicion; salespeople want to know why they lost out. They may blame bad ethics—and they could be right. Remember, for every satisfied supplier in a three-bid situation, there are two who may find cause to complain.

The habit of supplying misleading information with inquiries also should be avoided. Falsifying the volume of business that may be forthcoming simply to get a lower price is one example, as is giving misleading information regarding the ultimate end use of a product. For instance, a buyer, faced with the problem of a rubber product that has been causing him trouble for some time, goes to a new supplier. But the supplier isn't told about previous rejections blamed on the partner's design. First the supplier quotes a price, and then is hit with the magnitude of the problem during the production process.

A troublesome conflict arises when a supplier works on a new product design with engineering, only to find that the buyer has placed the order with a competitor. Company policy should ensure against such occurrences. Some companies make it a policy to explain to the supplier that their product will be used until the investment is recouped. After that time, others will be allowed to bid in free competition.

Any supplier about to be dropped from active source supply deserves adequate notice, as they will have manpower and tooling to adjust, and a need to reschedule. The smaller the supplier and the larger the purchases, the more reason for such adequate notice. Depending on the circumstances, the buyer may be morally responsible for working out a reasonable cut-off date, even if no legal obligation exists. Be wary of a short-term profit at the expense of the long run. Shifting purchases from a faithful supplier to an untried one should occur only after reflecting that the new supplier may be quoting an unreasonably low price just to see what happens.

Receipt of Gifts from Suppliers

A buyer can't meet or visit foreigners without being given an occasional small gift. It is difficult to refuse, and often would be an affront to the supplier based on local custom. Make sure it's of minimal value, and reciprocate. Unlike Americans, many cultures around the world like to give and get small token gifts. They're not bribes! An occasional token gift can enhance the business relationship.

Lack of knowledge of the foreign supplier's culture has long been a weakness of American buyers. Too often we are seen as too direct and impersonal and in a hurry to conclude an agreement—which often offends the sensitivities of foreign business people. That result is clearly unintentional.

In the U.S. and Britain, there is the "old boy network," while in India, the interactions usually follow along lines of the caste system. Individuals in developing nations usually classify others as "ins" or "outs." In China, members of a particular dialect group are "ins," while those outside the circle are the "outs." In some societies there is an obligation to repay a favor, and obligations remain until repaid. If someone has given a favor such as a contract, the next favor must come from the receiver. This process—though somewhat different from our own—is one basis for conducting business on a personal level. Some foreign businesspeople explain that such practices sweeten their enjoyment of doing business. Gift giving in non-Western cultures has developed into a modern business tool intended to create obligation as well as genuine affection.

Many CPOs seek to discharge obligations, but some suppliers enjoy creating them. Many suppliers say that gift giving intends to create both short-term pleasure and long-term bonds of friendship and loyalty. Gifts trigger future favors and have long-range implications for the friendship.

Christmas gift giving, once common domestically, is down considerably in the United States. Not only have tough economic times tended to make people cut down on these type expenditures, but the National Association of Purchasing Managers' campaign against this practice has also gotten results. Often, management will exhibit a double standard—offering gifts to their own customers, while looking with a questioning eye at anything received by their buyers. This is not unusual, management needs to ask itself how it can rightly reconcile these otherwise inconsistent behaviors!

People who have no gift problem are the only ones who find the solution easy. That is why a college professor could tell an advanced purchasing class there was no room for compromise. Later he said, "By the end of the session I could see some dents in my armor of moral righteousness. The ethical problems involved in buying and selling are complex and difficult to solve."

It is debatable whether business gifts are illegal or unethical. If gifts can be tax-deductible (as they are), they're legal. Presumably they influence or affect new business—and, if this is so, it should be unethical to give and accept them. Some feel the practice should be made both illegal and non-tax-deductible, believing that this would eliminate the gift problem. Yet people who give Christmas gifts have every right to spend their money as they see fit. Most claim their purpose is to show goodwill and appreciation for business received. From the purchasing manager's viewpoint, the chief harm they do in making their gifts is to create suspicion (and jealousy)—to the detriment to the buyer's company. Suspicion, then, is really the heart of the problem, and, if the PM's ethical image is to be improved, suspicion should be eliminated.

The PM and buyer find themselves inheriting a custom that has existed for years. It is difficult to know where to draw the line without offending others. Legally, any payment, gift, favor, or gratuity received by the agent, without the knowledge and consent of the principal, belongs to the principal. This is the rule under the general law of agency.

Christmas gift surveys show that about half of all companies have a policy on receiving and giving gifts; one third of these companies require the return of any gift unless it takes the form of an advertisement. (One buyer reported a supplier who got around this restriction by sending a bushel of apples wrapped in individual papers, with the company name imprinted on each.) Somewhat less than a third acknowledge the gift, but ask that the practice be discontinued in the future, while the balance take no action and accept the gift. Purchasing people should ask themselves whether the acceptance of a simple gift merely increases respect and admiration for the donor, or whether it makes it a bit more difficult to be truly objective when making buying decisions.

Professional buyers have long tried to eliminate gifts. After all, the buyer should be above suspicion, both in the eyes of your suppliers and your management. And sellers who lose the order often tend to be suspicious of the buyer's decisions, especially when they don't agree. People judge on their prejudices. When someone is in a decision making job, such as buying, appearances may be far more important than reality—in fact, *perceptions are reality*!

Lucky is the buyer whose management states an outright policy against giving and receiving gifts, for it's no longer an issue. If this is not the case, the buyer's best interest is to adopt this as policy, regardless. However, as previously noted, the buyer will find there will be international practices that run contrary to domestic ethical norms—and these differences need to be acknowledged and accommodated.

Lunches and Entertainment

There is nothing inherently wrong with a business lunch and occasional modest entertainment when a buyer visits a supplier. Sometimes a business lunch can be most productive as a way to smooth relationships and get better acquainted. Only the abuse of such courtesies should be questioned. Excesses, such as time away from work, and a too cozy relationship with favored suppliers are obviously objectionable.

What may appear to be a casual business lunch or cocktail may be viewed with suspicion by those looking from the "outside in"; management may think its purchasing officials are too lax. Moreover, to a third party—perhaps another supplier or potential supplier—the relationship may not appear to be so ethical.

For example, the buyer may be having dinner with a supplier as part of a business meeting. The situation is perfectly legitimate and ethical; however, to the third party who happens to see them together the other supplier may seem to have an "in" with the buyer; the third party may feel that it's not getting any business due to this apparent cozy relationship.

Some companies avoid such incidents by having rules against lunches at suppliers' expense and substituting invitations to dine with the buyer in the company plant; when an outside lunch is necessary, the check is picked up by the buyer. In fact, one of the surest ways to help the buyer keep his position with suppliers is to allow an expense allowance. This allows the buyer to reciprocate where luncheons and the like are deemed appropriate.

Double Standard of Ethics

A Mother Superior tells the story of a little boy crying, "Fresh Maine lobsters! Get your fresh lobsters!" Thinking the nuns would enjoy a special treat, she stopped to make a purchase. The boy came over and whispered, "Sister, don't buy 'em—they ain't no good." Then he resumed his cry, "Fresh lobsters! Get your fresh lobsters!" Some business people are like that boy; they have a double set of ethical standards.

A meat-packing company sent out a friendly letter to its supplier list, asking for cooperation with its no-gift policy. Two weeks later, a sales letter was sent to the same list of suppliers to advertise its products as suitable gifts to give customers.

Another company's lunch policy was made to look ridiculous when the buyers heard that a supplier's president annually took their own chief executive on a boat trip to Florida. Can the president of a company, its vice president, or its top purchasing officer be entertained freely when the buyer is reprimanded or fired for accepting the same courtesies?

It is difficult for any PM to convince buyers that they should accept no luncheons or gifts when their own sales department makes a regular practice of handing out gifts and has an authorized budget to cover the expense of the program. Here is an indication that the company does not want those who spend its money to be approachable but, at the same time, considers it good business to foster its own relationships with its customers' buying people. There is something hypocritical about this common way of thinking, which is explained by some as "business logic."

But what distinction is there? Where are the guidelines about what is acceptable and what is not? From several polls asking purchasing people whether they accept entertainment, 60% reported that they accept lunches from suppliers, 25% dinner or theater invitations, 10% ball games, and 15% golf. (The total is more than 100%, because some respondents checked more than one answer.) Seventy-five percent stated that business is transacted during such off-business contacts. About

10% regularly entertain the supplier at the buying company's expense; 65% do so occasionally; and 30% never pick up the tab.

As to what effect such contacts have on business negotiations, 37% claimed to be uninfluenced, while 58% reported the benefit of getting to know their suppliers better, and 20% felt they were being placed under an obligation. When asked if they felt the practice should be eliminated, 35% said yes and 65% said no.

It has been said that you can't make a rule that will cover every situation; it takes careful weighing of specifics and circumstances. Issuance of a company policy against gratuities and gifts is like writing the rule, "Thou shalt not sin." This rule is unenforceable, yet it exists to set a necessary example.

Do's and Don'ts of Dealing with Suppliers

In this chapter we have attempted to provide real-life examples to support recommended action. Perhaps we can summarize this section with a list that will provoke further thought in our quest to improve this vital relationship between supplier and buyer.

There are any number of actions that can be taken to improve the relationship between buyer and salesperson, and that are consistent with concepts of common courtesy. On the other hand, there are actions and behaviors that should be avoided. The following is a list of practical "Do's" and "Don'ts" that have proven worthwhile. They should assist the buyer in his or her dealings with supplier sales representatives:

DO

1. See salespeople promptly.
2. Advise unsuccessful bidders why they lost the business.
3. Respect any confidential data given to you.
4. Introduce salespeople to anyone in your company who may help.
5. Suggest other companies in your vicinity that might be able to use their product.
6. Keep salespeople apprised on your assessment of how well you believe they're performing for you.
7. Explain your policies, procedures, and buying methods.
8. Take the salesperson on tour of your plant or inventory facilities. They will be pleased to see where their products fit into yours.
9. Explain your quality and inspection methods.
10. Share expenses—reciprocate in picking up the check in the case of business luncheons.
11. Let salespeople use you as reference if you appreciate their services.

DON'T

1. Don't let phone calls or visitors interrupt your meetings.
2. Don't be overzealous of your buying prerogatives. As appropriate, allow the salesperson to meet with your technical people or others who can assist.
3. Don't play favorites based on personality issues.
4. Don't readily go over the local salesman's head. Keep the salesman posted on developments relevant to his company's performance.
5. Don't threaten a company with punitive action unless you absolutely intend to take it.
6. Don't keep salespeople in the dark on new products you need.
7. Don't expect or induce entertainment or gifts of any kind.
8. Don't let any salesperson be so successful that his or her company becomes too dependent on you for most of their business.

Personal visits to key suppliers are frequently mentioned in surveys as actions well worth the investment in time and money. There is no substitute for first-hand knowledge of the supplier's capabilities. Consider an on-site evaluation both prior to making the award and perhaps again, midstream in the manufacturing performance period. A visit is a wonderful way to strengthen the bonds of partnership!

Timing the visit is important, so plan it carefully. The supplier should know the reason for interest, and why they should be interested in seeing you. Meetings should include different levels of the supplier's management, so they can all share an understanding of the relationship.

It's timely that we now take a fresh look at the issue of quality versus price in the next chapter.

8

Buying the Right Quality

Purchased materials, components, and assemblies directly affect the quality of a company's end-product sold to its customers. To achieve acceptable quality, a program of continual quality improvements is needed. This requires close working relationships and communications that benefit both the supplier and the buyer.

Everyone is for quality, but how would most of us define it? Survey responses given by many top practitioners in purchasing, purchasing engineering, and sales engineers included:[1] reliability, function, customer needs, consistency, meeting engineering specs, changing engineering specs, process control, transferable variability, cost savings, and cost control. This highlights that quality has to be defined specifically in terms of each item bought.

Perhaps no person has had more influence on current quality management thinking than the late W. Edwards Deming, whom the Japanese memorialized with their prestigious Deming Award. Deming said in essence that the key is to "think differently and break our patterns of thinking. . .making what the customer wants. Each gets more for less. . .the heart of the Deming philosophy." He went on to conclude that:

> "people must visualize and understand why they're doing something. They should ask themselves, 'What are we doing, and why are we doing it?' "[2]

Quality Defined

Let's review and summarize what we've learned about the elusive nature of "quality." People have tried to explain for many years, and some have tried to reduce it to a formula, such as:

---

[1]Pooler & Associates's Seminars 1985–1993, World Trade Institute.

[2]"W. Edwards Deming: The Prophet of Quality," 1994 Wootton Productions.

$$\text{Value} = \frac{\text{Function}}{\text{Cost}}$$

While the above calculation cannot be proved mathematically, it's intuitively obvious that value can be increased by improving function or decreasing cost.

Another authority on quality, J. M. Juran, has given 13 meanings for quality. The importance of knowing exactly what's needed can't be underestimated, and we have to define quality requirements in terms meaningful to us. Quality today has come to mean, "compliance to requirements." Suppliers have an obligation to meet the standards, and the buyer has the obligation to see that they do!

"Quality Circles" became popular as American firms studied Japanese quality successes. Small groups or "circles" with various functions as members, not unlike Value Analysis teams, work on problem areas to find solutions. Circles are effective at tackling problems between two or more functions that require a constructive cooperative solution. Circles are usually formed to solve a specific problem and then are dissolved.

Let's compare the Japanese versus American approach to quality, as analyzed over the past decade:

Japan	*U.S.*
• Supplier selection:	
Co-destiny approach	Adversarial
Excel at relationships	Price is major selection criterion
• Management philosophy:	
Communicate to workers	Little worker communication
Lots of training	Minimum training
• Product development:	
Up-front design reviews	Minimum design reviews
Frequent prototype trials	Minimum prototype trials
• Long-term quality commitment:	
Commitment to quality	Changing to commitment
Quality comes first, production second	Production first, quality second
Top quality measurements	Failures too often ignored
Process capability	Improving
Root cause corrections	"Patch" corrections
Commitment to technology	Strong
• Price and delivery	
Lesser importance	Major factor

The above differences in Japanese and American management practices paint a striking contrast: however, Americans have adapted some of the best of the practices of Japan over the past few years. Today the differences between the two countries have been significantly narrowed. More particularly, current thought as it relates specifically to quality can be summarized as follows:

Traditional thinking	Newer thinking
Within specification	Uniformity around target
Inspect, sort, and rework	Quality built into design
Zero defects	Use as philosophy to reduce defects
Go/no-go tolerance	Reduced process variability around nominal dimension
Just-in-case	Just-in-time
Status quo	Constant improvement

"Suitability for a purpose" is a good description for economic quality. "Suitability" means that quality alone cannot be isolated. Contrary to espousals of "quality at all costs," quality cannot be divorced from the intended *end-use* and *cost*! Consider the example of a beautiful gold tie clip versus a paper clip. They both will do the intended job of holding a tie in place, but one is much more attractive yet far more expensive than the other. Although in this case some peple might opt for the gold clasp for "prestige" purposes, the professional buyer will not be swayed by excessive quality beyond the actual need. The lesson is clear: excess quality is undesirable if costs go up.

Higher than projected material costs may be caused by unneeded quality requirements, such as a high gloss surface finish that cannot be obtained economically, or tight specifications that are not commercially available. Buyers may find it difficult to control the cost of defective materials or back charges, which if not collectible from the supplier are losses to their company.

Deciding What to Buy

Before a decision about buying the right quality can be made, several questions should be answered about what to buy. Is the item regularly made to some standard or specification? Can the product be found in suppliers' standard catalogues? Is the item a critical repair part for equipment, such as a pressure relief valve, or an item used by itself, such as pliers? Some items demand high quality, while others can be replaced easily if they fail.

Price is what you pay, while quality is what you receive. In fact, often the brand with the highest price tag is the lowest in quality. This is especially true for such maintenance type items as soap, toilet articles, and foods. Suntan lotions, frozen pizzas, and children's clothing show the highest negative correlation between price and quality. While these illustrations relate to consumer goods, experienced buyers have learned the same lesson when buying contractor type items. It is more difficult to get the facts from manufacturers who sell parts through wholesale outlets.

Specifications

Buyers must have some standard, or specification to buy. Lacking this specification the buyer will find it difficult to shop for comparable quality from alternate suppliers. Ideally, the "spec" will allow more than one supplier to furnish.

A specification is simply a description of the item wanted. The spec can be a written description, detailed drawing, or picture of what is wanted. Quality can be described in a number of ways in the purchase order, such as by: (1) brand, (2) grade, (3) sample, (4) physical and chemical constituents, (5) method of manufacture or production, (6) materials used, and (7) performance.

Buying by brand name places all the trust in the supplier. Some brand products are widely advertised and have a wide market appeal, and product quality acceptance is already present. In-house sales and management have much influence on these considerations. A buyer needs guidance as to what is desired.

Some companies buy by sample. Their spec reads, "as per engineering approved sample." But this often creates a problem. When problems arise, the question is "what is the approved sample," and "where is it"?

Difficulties can arise from taking too many samples from suppliers. Who pays for the sample? If free, is it without obligation or does it obligate the buyer to a response as to the sample's acceptability? Is the sample given for a specific test period? Whether free or paid for up-front, who pays for running the tests? Though there is nothing wrong with accepting legitimate samples, choose them well to save headaches for all concerned by accepting items only when there is a legitimate interest. If buyers pay for samples, they won't request any unless they really want them!

A contrasting approach to customer-defined detailed specifications is "specification by performance" that holds the supplier responsible for the purchased item functioning correctly. This type of specification probably should be used more often, but sometimes it can be difficult to enforce.

While there is a need for a complete and accurate spec, it can be overdone. The military is not alone in providing often embarrassing examples of excessive wording. Consider an actual situation where a conscientious engineer was supervising the move of his testing equipment from an old to a newer nearby plant. While driving to work, this engineer noticed his equipment on a parked truck with the driver inside a coffeehouse. The next day a new spec was received by the buyer amending instructions to include the clause, "All moves are to be continuous, i.e., drivers are not to take coffee breaks while transporting equipment between plants." This was excessive—a phone call would have sufficed to solve this problem! The spec should be simple, while describing the quality as precisely as possible.

Most importantly, the specification should allow the receiving department to check that what was received was precisely of the quality intended. Companies should avoid using "as is" approvals repeatedly for off-spec goods that have been rejected. Ideally, buyers should educate engineering and quality personnel to review the spec and correct it consistent with the concurrent engineering concept. Otherwise, the same problem will repeat itself, and by often deviating we teach suppliers that our commitment to quality is weak, and inferior items are acceptable.

The goal is to maintain *adequate* standards of quality. Contrary to current thinking by some, there is a cost associated with quality. Advertisements have long told us that when it comes to the real world, the more expensive a product, the better the quality must be. You get what you pay for! Right? Wrong! Many studies confirm what many consumers have long suspected, that high price and high quality don't necessarily go hand in hand.

Efforts to Ensure Quality Through International Standards (ISO 9000 Series)

Buyers' use of quality standards gives confidence that recognized quality procedures and standards are being met. The American National Standards Institute, Inc. (ANSI) issues standards that are based on a "consensus of those substantially concerned with its scope and provisions." The standard is a guide to help manufacturers, consumers, and the general public achieve quality assurance. Cooperating with this effort, the American Society for Quality Control (ASQC) set their quality assurance standards ANSI/ASQC Q90-94 series *Guidelines for Selection and Use*. In the interest of harmonizing global standards, they've achieved "technical equivalence" with Europe's ISO 9000-9004 series. This has been adopted within the U.S. as the ANSI/ASQC Q90-94 series which uses English language terms and denotes the practices used. A cross-reference points out where differences may exist.

Buyers now will contend with the ISO codes, so they should become familiar with them. Standards are governed by the International Organization for Standardization (ISO), Geneva, Switzerland. Forty-two nations are on the committee that defines minimum requirements for a quality system.

The ISO issued its ISO 9000 series to define minimum requirements for a quality management and assurance system. Though not as well known domestically, about 10,000 companies from about 30 nations have been registered by ISO. Since the standards have been adopted within the U.S. as the ANSI/ASQC Q90 series, the number of U.S, companies that hold ISO 9001 registration, the highest rating, has increased rapidly. (Even UPS' Air Letter envelope states "ISO 9001 Quality registered".)

Following are the five international ISO 9000 standards for quality management and assurance:

1. ISO 9000 Guidelines for selection and use of quality management and quality assurance standards
2. ISO9001 Model for quality assurance systems in design/development, production, installation, and service
3. ISO9002 Model for quality assurance systems in production and installation
4. ISO9003 Model for quality assurance in final inspection and test
5. ISO9004 Guidelines for quality management and quality system elements.

ISO9004 supports other registrations. Interestingly, this includes sections on selection of qualified suppliers, provisions for settlement of quality disputes, and other verification methods for quality with suppliers.

The choice of 1 through 3 above depends on your business. For example, if a product is designed, produced, sold, and serviced by your company, only ISO9001 can be used.

A company meeting the ISO 9000 quality standard is better positioned to sell to European firms that recognize the requirements. In the Greek language, ISO means "equal." Presumably, meeting this standard means the quality system equals that which is desired.

Once registered, a company must pass periodic inspections that are determined by the third party agency selected. The four steps to begin are:

1. Set policy with a management commitment.
2. Develop a work manual—how to do the job.
3. Develop Standard Operating Procedures, by departments—how they are to do things.
4. Develop individual work instructions—details on doing the job.

It is best to discuss a preassessment of your operation with an ISO registrar. The fee is $15,000/year. It is hoped this third party accreditation will increase offshore sales, as Europeans have used this standard for some time and are familiar with it.

For those with access to the Internet, further information can be received at the following site: [http://www.iso.ch]. This site contains detailed information on ISO 9000 and related publications.

Total Quality Management

Total Quality Management (TQM) is a concept developed in the 1980s as the United States became enlightened to the need for improved quality as a competitive initiative. Total Quality starts with management commitment to formal goal setting, quality system analysis, and a measurement system. Specific quality strategies used by professional purchasing departments are:

- Implement Statistical Process Control (SPC).
- Establish supplier quality programs—consider zero defects philosophy.
- Know your company's cost of quality.
- Raise quality levels of products.
- Increase automation and reduce variability.

Aspects that are tracked by some companies to measure suppliers' quality performance have been reported by survey[3] and include:

- Rejects   86%
- Production stoppages due to poor quality   56%
- Rework in dollars or hours   54%
- Scrap generated in use of the material   49%
- Customer complaints   47%
- Material acceptable without deviation   42%
- Warranty costs resulting from failures   36%

Cooperation with the Quality Function Pays Off

Sometimes, purchasing managers think of the quality assurance (or control) function as interfering or impinging on their authority in dealing with suppliers. However, a progressive purchasing manager recognizes the important role of the quality control people and cooperates fully with them. They can be one of the best allies in the business world.

Purchasing and quality control working together can improve acquisition by concentrating on (1) design, (2) manufacture, and (3) purchase. Control of the "cost of ownership" begins in the design phase by choosing suppliers who can meet the required quality levels. Quality improvements often reduce scrap and rework and will ultimately lower the customer's costs.

Quality can't be inspected into any product, but must be inherent in the design, and care used when it was crafted. Let us recall the four basic responsibilities usually assigned to quality control: (1) to assist engineering in establishing quality standards; (2) to measure how well these standards are met; (3) to see that corrective action is taken when necessary; and (4) to plan improvements in quality when substandard quality is evident.

---

[3]*Purchasing Magazine,* Jan. 29, 1987, p. 29.

Let's look at each of these areas in some detail:

1. *Assist engineering in establishing quality standards.* Quality standards in the form of blueprints and other specification media are set by the engineering department. However, some factors—such as cleanliness, parallelism, perpendicularity, and the like—may not be clearly specified. A certain amount of confusion is inevitable, since every small detail is not readily recognizable at the time of the original design, and the quality people are in a position to help clarify these confusing points. If there is no quality group, then purchasing itself must assume this responsibility by taking matters up directly with engineering. But, the job can be made easier by recognizing the contribution of the quality function and literally putting it to work.

The Quality function generally has the responsibility of specifying sampling plans and indicating the degree of protection against failures these plans will provide. By deciding a day's production is a batch, finding defects by sampling would cause rejection of the entire lot. This makes it tough on suppliers who perform poorly; but, at the same time, it points out exactly where improvements must be made. Finally, Quality advises the inspection people how to inspect. By detailing all critical, major, and minor characteristics, inspectors can spend their time most profitably.

2. *Measure how well standards are met.* In measuring how well supplier standards have been met, Quality uses tools of the statistical trade, such as control charts, the standard deviation, and the audit inspection. They may use a reliability test laboratory to check both purchased and manufactured components for longevity, or possibility of failure. They may random sample for overall control of quality. In the course of their work they often uncover supplier problems. So, Quality asks suppliers for corrective action. If too many individuals are speaking to the supplier, confusion can result. Here the buyer's coordination role comes into play.

From time to time, quality people may be off base or otherwise mistaken in their evaluation of a supplier's product. In this case, the buyer must take the opposite side to protect the buying company's policy of firmness and fairness to the supplier. Communication is, as always, essential to gain an understanding of the buyer's problem. Buyers should explain their reasoning and position to the quality people and any others involved. In this manner, buyers will retain the respect, support, and cooperation they must have.

3. *See that corrective action is taken as necessary.* Corrective action is required of both the using and the producing companies if problems are not to recur. Here, again, Quality can be a good partner in straightening out the "kinks" that are an inevitable part of all operations.

4. *Plan improvements in quality.* Whereas corrective action is a matter of "putting out fires," the planning of improvements is more analogous to "fire prevention." This function is probably quality control's ultimate goal; certainly it is much more productive and interesting than continual "fire fighting," although

sometimes the results are difficult to assess or measure. Examples include process capability studies, variance analyses, quality reports, and statistics of all kinds.

Poor supplier quality has many repercussions. It disrupts the production schedule and ties up floor space while units are awaiting the repair or replacement of defective parts or materials. Often, too, the cost of such repair or replacement is not completely recoverable from the suppliers. Purchasing is primarily responsible for keeping losses in this area to a minimum.

Cost of Quality

To some, the definition of quality means "conformance to requirements," or "meeting the specification." The system is "prevention," the performance standard is "Do it right the first time." The measurement is Cost of Quality (COQ).

Costs associated with quality are traditionally buried in various departments' budgets. Assembling these data allows managing the variables through a multi-functional team approach. COQ becomes a tool used to improve quality of both products and services provided to customers.

Cost of quality identifies the cost of "preventing": errors and mistakes and failures, both within the company and when product is in use with customers. The various costs of quality can be broken down into appraisal, prevention, external, and internal failures costs. Further, they can be broken into those quality costs picked up by accounting systems and those costs not normally picked up.

Accounting systems pick up: warranty, scrap/repair, and inspection or testing. Those costs not normally picked up include: Lost sales, switching customers, retrofit field trips, settlement expense, improper applications, time in transport, higher inventory, obsolete materials, and expediting costs, as well as excess labor costs due to clerical errors, employee absenteeism and high turnover, poor quality information and processing, poor management decisions, errant strategies, and so on.

Lengthy design cycle time, engineering redesigns, down time, high setup time, queue time, and poor supplier plant layouts all contribute to higher costs of quality.

The COQ draws attention to the need to reduce costs. With this knowledge, a measuring stick can be established to set goals and chart progress. The COQ report is normally under the guidance of finance. The report should be compiled using costs from:

1. *Prevention costs*: Expense of running a system to ensure that products conform to the customers' requirements, including: specifications, procedures to hold dimensional tolerances, training costs for quality purposes.

2. *Appraisal costs*: Cost of testing, sampling, and audits to detect errors, including staff related to quality improvements, measurements and control.

3. *Internal failures*: Cost connected with a rejected or failed product, including extra inventory carrying costs, labor, materials, scrap, and wastes.

4. *External failures*: Warranty claims costs, transportation and handling of returned products. Costs of rework or "doing it over a second time." Costs of engineers' trips to customers to solve problems.

There are also other costs, but the above covers the majority of them.

Working with Suppliers to Manage Quality

When sourcing for components to be used in products that are to be sold in the U.S. and Canada, such components must conform to the proper codes. Canadian marketed products must meet the Canadian Standards Association (CSA). Other worldwide markets sometimes require local code approvals, such as for example the German TUV code.

Example of specialized U.S. technical codes are electrical Underwriters Laboratories (UL) and ETL Testing Laboratories codes. These codes are designed to protect consumers, and should be in the specification or the buyer's purchase order. ETL testing laboratories will recognize UL approval, but UL will not recognize ETL approval.

There are other specialized technical codes that are commonly required in the U.S. such as: ASHRE (American Society of Heating and Refrigeration Engineers), ASME (American Society of Mechanical Engineers), SAE (Society of Automotive Engineers), API (American Petroleum Institute), and ASTM (American Society of Testing and Materials). These need to be understood so they will be used only when applicable, avoiding unnecessary cost. Approval of these agencies takes place in advance, and usually requires a stringent test procedure.

Certification Clause

A buyer must assure his or her source's products and components meet code criteria. Therefore a clause such as the following should be stated in the purchase order:

> "Purchaser will submit their products to obtain UL, ETL, (or other agency) approval. Seller must submit proper certificate that its products comply with these (or DOE, FTC, OSHA, DOE, FTC, AHAM, SAE, ASHRAE, ASME, etc.) requirements and achieve published rated capacity and efficiency per Seller's submitted specifications."

Sometimes customers impose quality standards or procedures that force purchasing to take special steps with suppliers. For example, the buyers' company may have to keep records tracking quality from its sources. For military projects, this is essential. The original manufacturer is required to be able to trace quality through the manufacturing process.

All suppliers should be urged to maintain a first class quality management program. The use of statistical methods of documenting quality should be requested when appropriate.

Quality and Reliability Clause

Use a Quality and Reliability clause in the purchase order. These key clauses should be considered specifically for major technical or foreign buys. Those that follow are representative examples only and suggested as a training aid. The buying company is responsible for its own proper wording, based on negotiations with the supplier and the specifics of the goods bought. Sample wording might be something like the following:

> "Seller shall use effective quality and reliability control techniques in monitoring their processes and products. Seller shall provide and maintain a quality control system that will, as a minimum:
>
> - List all critical and major characteristics
>
> - Specify details for quality audits, including characteristics to be inspected. Follow with agreed representative sample of all lots and frequency of inspection
>
> - Tender only supplies that have been inspected in accord with the quality control system and found to conform with the requirements of this agreement
>
> - Provide for qualification of new and revised products, and re-qualification in case of major product deficiencies
>
> - Provide for disposition of rejected samples."

State the option:

> "Surveillance may be by appointed representatives of Purchaser at Seller's plant. Buyer may choose to inspect products by Purchaser or its representative at any reasonable time during business hours. (Each company will specify details consistent with their purchases here.) Purchaser has the right either to reject or to require correction of non-conforming products. The purchaser shall accept or reject products as promptly as practical after delivery."

> "Seller's compliance with this paragraph shall in no way relieve it of its responsibility and obligations otherwise assumed under the terms and conditions of this agreement."

Among items that may be checked for quality are the processes being used, the techniques and controls on the finished product, plus test methods and test data that support the product ratings. Any allowances for deviations or substitutions should be clarified. Any penalties for failure to meet quality standards should be spelled out.

Early Supplier Involvement

About 70% of production savings occur from improvement in design. Begin by using some of these steps:

1. Coordinate engineering/purchasing/supplier meetings.
2. Analyze product development projects and time to go into production.
3. Study test procedures to analyze supplier failures that can be reduced to allow elimination of incoming inspection.

Below are some quality tactics that can be tracked:

Tactics	*Results tracked*
• Parts per million (ppm) approach	• Changed quality reports
• Train people	• Quality and SPC awareness
• Improve quality Purchased Fabricated	• Cost of Quality reduced
• Quality circles	• Number of circles operating
• Buyer/supplier programs	• Programs ongoing
• Certify suppliers for results	• Number of suppliers certified
• Use of personal computers	• Failure analysis
• Quality task force teams	• Teams report action for correction

Qualification and Prequalification

Qualification of components or materials for both existing and new products is the direct responsibility of design engineering. The economic and supply considerations should be introduced by purchasing before the final source selection. And this information should be early in the source selection process.

Source qualification can range from a simple to quite complex system for hi-tech state-of-the-art hardware. When placing a trial order, it is wise to perform an inspection at the supplier's facility before the first major shipment. Meeting with a supplier's quality department and others who do the job helps gain confidence in their integrity and a commitment to quality.

Buyers must represent supplier input, such as pricing, availability, and so on. Buyers search out globally and screen new potential world-class suppliers. The mission is to have available such information in advance, so it can be quickly fed to engineering as needed. Purchasing should provide a window as to new components and materials suppliers. Buyers must work themselves upstream in the decision making process.

It makes sense to qualify any new supplier before anything is bought. Buyers can spearhead a "prequalification" effort to identify new sources, and also new processes or methods of production. A plan for Source Qualification of components is often established by large manufacturing companies.

Multiple source prequalification of important suppliers provides an escape valve to reduce risk, so changes can be made without a drastic effect on quality. The buyer who has prequalified suppliers doesn't wait for emergencies or troubles to develop.

Zero Defects Program

A Zero Defects Program seems unattainable in the real world. However, it is an effective means to prod lax suppliers by motivating them to strive for perfection. Zero defects as a goal forces a change in attitude to recognize that things must be done right the first time; operations must be made error proof, and it is necessary that capable process be maintained in a state of control. This goal requires rigorous buyer communication with suppliers.

The subject of zero defects is not to be confused with common incoming inspection sampling plans that require zero defects in the sample inspected. The late W. Edwards Deming, in one of his books, goes through a rigorous mathematical proof that shows there are only two optimum cost sampling plans: (1) 100% inspection or (2) zero inspection. The result of this analysis is the obvious conclusion that suppliers must attain a low enough defect rate that costs of defects in production, assembly, and field failures is less than the cost of inspecting quality into the product. Certified, conforming material from the suppliers is the optimum situation.

The history of zero defect sampling plans starts with the use of MIL-STD-105D sampling procedures. 105D plans each carry a prescribed acceptable quality level, or AQL. If a supplier is delivering product at or near the stated AQL, then there is only about a 5% chance that the 105D plans will reject the lot. This is called the "producer's risk." What many in industry often fail to recognize in these plans is that there can be a rather large probability for the customer accepting defect rates much greater than the stated AQL. This is the "consumer's risk."

Consider the following example. Suppose you had a large container of marbles. Most are white, which will represent good product. Evenly mixed, and representing 10% of the total, are green marbles which represent defective material. If say 20 marbles at a time are sampled, over and over, you would sometimes find no green, sometimes one green, sometimes two green, and so on. The laws of probability govern the result.

Drawing from the various plans in 105D, for a 1% AQL, we find a plan that calls for a random sample of 80 pieces with a reject number of 3. That is, if we find zero, one, or two defectives, we accept the lot. Three or more defectives cause the lot to be rejected. Figure 8-1 shows the operating characteristic curve (OC curve) for two plans. The horizontal axis is a scale of actual (but unknown to the consumer) defect rates. The vertical axis is the probability of accepting (finding fewer than three defectives) for each of the actual defect rates. Note that if the defect rate is equal to the 1% AQL, there is a probability of 0.95 that we will find fewer than three defects and hence accept the lot. What is frequently not given proper attention is that this plan provides a probability of 0.10 (10% of the time) for accepting defect rates of about 6.5%! That is, there is a 10% chance that we will find fewer than three defects in our random sample even when the actual defect rate is near 6.5%

To improve our odds as the consumer, plans have been developed that will accept the lot only if zero defectives are found in the sample. Typically, these plans have an OC curve that passes through the same consumer's risk point for a 0.10 probability of acceptance, but offers better protection for the consumer for all defect rates to the left of this point. This plan is shown along with the previous 80 sample 105D plan as shown below. With this 34 sample size there is only slightly better than a 71% chance of accepting a product with a defect rate equal to the AQL.

For the above reason, when a defective is found in a zero defects plan, inspectors do not reject the lot, but rather they *withhold acceptance*. The lot is now given further investigation by others to determine the appropriate action. Note that the equivalent "accept on zero defects" plan requires a much smaller sample size, in this case 34 versus 80 in the 105D plan.

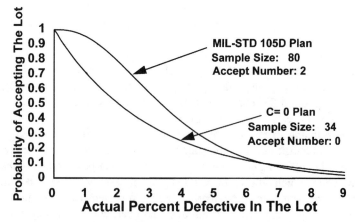

Figure 8-1 Operating characteristic curve for MIL-STD-105D and C = 0 (zero defects) plans.

The advantages of a zero defects sampling plan are:

• More pressure on the supplier to do it right the first time.

• Significantly less inspection than that required by 105D as the required sampling sizes are far less.

• Improved protection for the buying consumer from high defect rates higher than the AQL value.

Many commercial companies set an AQL that the buyer will accept in the future. If recent results are, say, an AQL of 3%, a defects target might accept 1% or less.

An AQL is often set around 1 or 2%. Currently, working to Mil-Q-9858A the AQL concept is not accepted. Many hi-tech commercial companies also consider this AQL unacceptable today in light of Japanese standards of "parts per million".

Statistical Process Control

Statistical Process Control (SPC) is the application of statistical methods of charting key dimensional tolerance measurements to determine the process capability and condition of the process at any time relative to its inherent variability and mean performance. Use of SPC by a supplier is indicative of potential for world class performance.

• *Statistical* is the science of drawing inferences and making decisions from variable data.

• *Process* is any combination of machines, tools, methods, materials, and people used to get the qualities desired for products or services.

• *Control* is a managerial process of setting and meeting standards.

SPC might be likened to the game of chess. The rules are simple, but the strategy for developing a control for a given process can be quite complex. If buyers are not familiar with the fundamentals of SPC, a supplier can easily present great looking control charts that have little real meaning.

Figure 8-2 shows the X-bar portion of a mean and range chart. Averages from small samples of consecutive units of production are plotted on the chart. As long as these means fall between the statistically derived control limits and do not exhibit significant trends, it can be assumed that the process average has not changed. Control limits are not specification limits. Control limits are a function of the process capability, not the specification. A point that falls beyond the control limit does not necessarily mean that defective product has been produced. A properly designed control chart for a capable process allows the operator to take action when an out of control point occurs but before the specification is

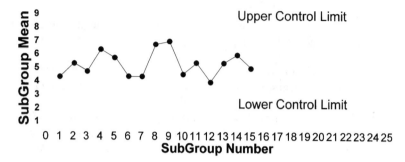

Figure 8-2 X-bar control chart.

violated. If you never get an out of control point, maybe you don't need the control chart!

The distribution of individual measurements produced by an in-control process frequently takes on the shape of the classic normal distribution or bell curve. See Figure 8-3. Two numbers or parameters describe the shape of the distribution. The mean (or average) is the midpoint or center of gravity on the horizontal axis. The other parameter is the standard deviation. As the standard deviation increases, the normal curve gets wider, indicating more variation in the measurements relative to the mean value. The height of the curve at any point on the horizontal axis is a function of how often specific dimensions are expected to occur. Most observations in the normal distribution fall fairly close to the mean.

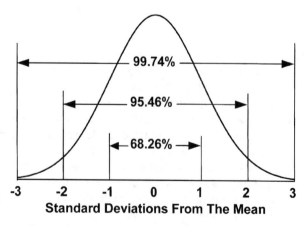

Figure 8-3 Normal curve with standard deviations.

Note in the previous figure that more than two-thirds of all dimensions in a normal distributed process fall within plus or minus one standard deviation from the mean. More than 95% will fall within plus or minus two standard deviations, and essentially all (99.74%) are contained within plus or minus three standard deviations.

The use of statistical analysis and the normal distribution allows buyers to make a factual assessment of a supplier's capability and performance. Figure 8-4 shows three different normal distributions and how they relate to a dimensional specification. The curve titled "Desired Process" shows the process is perfectly centered. The mean is coincident with the midpoint of the specification. The range of dimensions within plus and minus three standard deviations of the mean are using up only about 70% of the available tolerance. (In SPC jargon, this is a process with a 70% Capability Ratio, or a Cpk of 1.43.) Should the process begin to drift in one direction or another, a properly designed control chart will alert the operator to make an adjustment before the specification is violated.

Supplier A's process is properly centered, but by having a larger standard deviation, this supplier is using up all of the tolerance. This kind of supplier should make buyers nervous for any change in mean performance will yield defective material.

Supplier B, on the other hand, has very little process variation. The entire six standard deviation spread uses up only about half of the total tolerance allowed. However, the mean value for their process is well above the midpoint of the specification, so poor targeting is evident. All of their product meets the specifica-

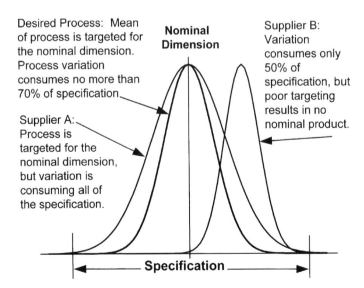

Figure 8-4   Typical SPC bell curve charting of key dimensional tolerances.

tion, but almost none of the dimensions are near the optimum midpoint of the specification. Left as it is, buyers should again be nervous about this process. Having the supplier B retarget the process average to the midpoint of the specification will put this supplier in an enviable position relative to the other two curves. B has the potential of being the superior source as they have shown an ability to closely control production tolerances.

The senior author, responsible for large quantities of motors, recalls how his company cooperated with several American motor companies to check the relative merits of Japanese motors. The bell curves for American shaft diameters were within tolerance similar to supplier A's. The bell curves for the Japanese suppliers were consistently narrow, similar to that shown for supplier B. This was the only detectable difference between Japanese and American electric motors at that time when they first began to compete.

State-of-the-art quality producers use standard deviations from the ideal as reviewed earlier. Individual machining centers maintain online charts that track and record results as parts are produced. Using SPC allows suppliers to monitor and control measurable characteristics. Prompt detection, improvement, or degradation allows knowledge about quality. The results of using SPC (as shown in the steps identified in Table 8-1) are increased conformance to requirements and decreased costs of getting them.

Table 8-1   Steps in Using SPC

Activities	Methods
1. Define problem and set priorities.	1. Charts and graphs 2. Pareto analysis
2. Understand process.	1. Histograms 2. Run charts 3. Diagnostic use of control charts
3. Determine causes of process behavior.	1. Cause-and-effect diagrams 2. Scatter diagrams 3. Regression analysis 4. Analysis of variance 5. Design of experiments
4. Identify alternate solutions.	1. Brainstorming 2. Teamwork
5. Implement solution.	1. Who, what, and when 2. Measure results
6. Test solution.	1. Data collection 2. Before and after comparison 3. Statistical methods
7. Defect prevention.	1. Process control charts 2. Permanent solutions 3. Help people do it right

A Case Study on Quality

Let's conclude our overview of significant quality issues with a thought-provoking case study:

Amanda Kay Products (AKP), an electronic distributor, buys components such as switching relays to extremely close tolerances for a computer assembling company. Because of the tightness of the specs, buyer Bryce Bradley narrowed down the number of relay suppliers he could depend on to three companies. These shared equally in AKP's requirements.

To get this business, AKP was able to offer customers "just-in-time" or JIT service. The relays could be delivered within 24 hours, so the customer had virtually no inventory. But, zero-defects quality standards must not suffer. While considered unusual for a distributor, both AKP and their suppliers were required by their largest customer to conduct 100% inspection. However, as sales for circuits increased, buyer Bryce felt inspection of each piece at both the manufacturer's and his receiving location became increasingly expensive and cumbersome.

Statistical inspection was considered but was abandoned for reliability reasons as AKP management had agreed on surveillance inspection at their warehouse. This inspection wasn't to be 100% but rather a continuous spot check of all the processes in making the relays.

What was the plan? Bryce and the management felt a shift to source inspection would do the following:

1. Eliminate a special inspector at AKP's receiving inspection. With training, regular receiving people would cover. This would provide a substantial savings of manpower and costs.

2. Reject defective relays at source, to reduce the material now being returned after in-house inspection.

3. Eliminate several sets of duplicate testing equipment, since only a minimum would now be needed for spot checking.

The plan is to be put into operation, and discussed with each of the three suppliers. Two gave wholehearted approval, and a schedule was agreed upon for starting source inspection. However, the third major source refused. Magnatron Manufacturing was the leader in its field, and set the standard of quality others had to match. The Magnatron brand name was often cited when AKP salespeople pushed their product with their customers.

This refusal threw a monkey wrench into the new inspection scheme. Buyer Bryce wanted the advantages to be gained by source inspection, but was afraid for the success of the program when his largest and most important supplier declined to cooperate. He wanted to keep Magnatron, but his management wondered how suppliers could be compared as to quality or price performance when inspection was being performed by different ground rules. Bryce faced a quality dilemma. Before considering your advice to Bryce first consider the following questions:

1. What are the advantages and disadvantages, as you see them, of AKP's source inspection plan? Would you use this plan or maintain the original inspection procedures?

2. Should Bryce go ahead and buy despite Magnatron's refusal? If so, on what basis should AKP accept or reject relays from the suppliers?

3. As a general approach, do you believe buyers should concern themselves with the matter of providing "checks" on supplier quality control?

There is no perfect answer to this case, nor your on-the-job quality decisions. We need to tailor quality requirements to your needs.

The introduction of probability theory to quality control and random sampling techniques has mushroomed with computer applications. Now complex algorithms can be routinely used where previously judgment (guessing?) made the decision about when and how much to order, and that is the subject of the chapter that follows.

9

Purchasing's Strategic Approach to Inventory Management

The purchasing department's task, as already defined, is to procure all the goods and services required by the organization. Generally, the purchase of items falls into three major categories: (1) capital equipment and services, (2) maintenance, repair, and operating supplies, and (3) materials and components used to produce a final product. Current thinking emphasizes pull systems, minimum lot sizes, and shorter lead-times as *essential to better inventory management*!

In manufacturing environments, the bulk of purchasing's expenditures is for materials, components, and supplies that become part of a final product. As planning and control systems drive requisitions for purchased items, purchasing's role is to communicate this information to suppliers in a timely manner, and verify that the suppliers have the capacity to supply as scheduled.

Management of these supply items directly affects the goals of the organization concerning production efficiency, inventory costs, quality, cash flow, and return on investment. So, the relationship of purchasing and operations planning is key in supporting and achieving these goals. This chapter will focus on providing a conceptual understanding of planning and control activities and inventory management strategies to address the question of *when*, and *how much* to buy.

Types of Inventory

There are four basic divisions of inventory used throughout the production process:

1. *Raw materials.* Any material or part required from outside the company for use in the manufacturing process. Economics of purchase generally dictate a sufficient acquisition of material that will last over some period of time.

2. *Work-in-process.* WIP consists of raw materials that are being worked on, or in various stages of completion in the factory. Levels of WIP

will vary greatly from company to company depending on their planning system, and the cycle times of their manufacturing processes.

3. *Finished goods.* Products and goods that are completed and ready for delivery to distribution centers or directly to customers.

4. *Maintenance, repair, and operating supplies.*

Managing the inventory levels of these four inventory groups is vital. In most manufacturing organizations purchased inventory represents 30% to 60% of the cost of goods sold; the percentage is even greater in retail businesses. The planning and control of purchasing is as important as the planning and control of internal production activities.

Who controls inventory? Control in larger companies is usually with Production Planning and Control, or Materials Management. In many companies, the purchasing department is responsible for inventories; regardless, purchasing will exert a certain amount of influence on many inventory decisions.

Depending on the type of business, and whether most inventory is in-process goods or finished products, whichever is the most important may determine who controls overall inventory. When inventory control is a purchasing function, it usually doesn't cover the finished product. Perhaps the marketing department will be responsible for finished goods inventory.

Management of distribution inventories is handled separately. Decisions regarding levels and number of distribution centers have to be settled with marketing. Distribution Resource Planning (DRP) seeks to locate facilities closest to customers to be serviced. Should distribution centers be company owned, private or public warehouses? Considerations include alternate modes of transport, and so on. DRP develops a schedule that provides future product requirements back to manufacturing.

Whether the PM controls inventory or not, at a minimum, PMs had best understand some of the existing concepts (all of which are not theory, but in practical use by some companies). And, if they do not have direct control, they had better not be the roadblock who will have to be removed to make way for someone who will do something about this continuing management problem of adequate inventory control. Whether inventory controls are placed within purchasing or controlled elsewhere depends on organization policy and structure of the company served. There is no escaping the inventory challenge. Once materials are bought they have to be stored somewhere before being shipped.

Inventory Objectives

Most companies have a keen interest in the creation of inventory, but management is generally dissatisfied with its control. Whether inventory is an asset used to achieve the objectives of an organization, or viewed as a liability, depends on how it is managed. The primary objective of inventory is to decouple[1] customer demands and production capacity. It is safe to conclude that there is a large gap between sophisticated inventory control concepts and actual practices. Few managers are satisfied about the present state of inventory results being achieved.

The objectives of creating and controlling inventory are generally in conflict, but must be resolved through negotiation, based on management decisions regarding inventory as a whole. Two major company objectives that underlie the need for inventory are (1) customer service and (2) product and procurement efficiency.

The need to provide quick delivery of goods and the ability to ship as promised are fundamental service objectives of all companies. To remain competitive, inventory is often held to buffer against market uncertainty. Inventories allow delivery even if demand exceeds what was forecast. Uncertainty regarding supply and how fast goods can be replenished also contributes to uncertainty for which inventory can compensate.

From the production point of view, most factory managers are measured by the amount of products they produce. If equipment is not running or being setup, it is considered nonproduction. It is believed that long production runs are more efficient than short runs. So, the creation of inventory, which may be held for a longer time, is needed to improve factory performance. From a purchasing standpoint, buyers often buy in larger quantities than immediately needed to minimize transportation costs, and realize savings through quantity discounts. Such buyer attempts to save money result in increasing inventory. So, we see the objectives regarding inventory are often in conflict.

Conflicting Pressures on Inventory

Let's take a look at some of the conflicting pressures that underlie the need for inventory and the countering pressures to eliminate it. Among the forces that tend to push inventory up are:

- Customer service goals—trying to deliver on time, guarding against market uncertainty, and providing a variety of products to many customers
- Inability to accurately forecast requirements
- Taking advantage of lower prices for larger quantities
- Longer production runs to reduce manufacturing cost
- Building inventory in anticipation of seasonal demands or possible contract problems with labor
- Safety or buffer stock to hide factory inefficiencies or absorb variations

---

[1]This term is used to denote work-in-process inventory that acts as buffers between operations in a factory.

in workcenter queues due to the mix of parts or products being worked on. Also, to meet continuous production with a minimum of stock-outs and work stoppages

- A lack of knowledge or use of planning, control, and measurement techniques to control inventory
- Older "push" systems where items are manufactured or purchased as required by a schedule in anticipation of future sales

Some of the factors and efforts that will tend to push down or reduce inventories are:

- Desire to improve return-on-investment
- Need to reduce investment or release capital
- Realizing that inventory carrying charges cause heavy dollar penalties
- Anxiety over obsolescence, spoilage, and deterioration
- Space limitations and higher taxes
- Contemporary management programs such as JIT to reduce lead-times and achieve high-velocity manufacturing
- Implementing demand "pull" systems that trigger material movement to a workcenter only when that workcenter is ready to work on it
- "Kaisen" initiatives—the Japanese term for continuing improvement, involving everyone from managers to workers to eliminate waste in machining, labor, and manufacturing processes

To keep these conflicting pressures in balance and to control inventory effectively, the following questions may be considered:

- How many of the items will be required on the basis of sales forecasts or production schedules?
- What is the item's lead-time, including time to process internal paperwork?
- How many of the item will be used during the lead-time?
- How many are on hand now?
- How many are on open purchase order?
- What is the inventory policy?

The simple truth is that inventory is expensive to hold. Company funds are tied up that could be more profitably used elsewhere. Today, most high-level managers strive to have none, but that's seldom possible. However, the benefits of a properly managed inventory far outweigh the cost of maintaining it. From an idealized control of inventory, a company would get material from a single source, located in town, who delivers exactly as requested. The supplier is totally dedicated to the buyer's wants. But, the real world calls for achieving lowest total costs, being globally competitive with high-quality products, available quickly to meet customer's demands.

Asset Management (Cost and Control of Inventory)

Management attention has shifted from traditional "P&L" management to "balance sheet" or asset management because many companies cannot generate sufficient return on invested capital to survive. A judgment is that about 25% is required, based on replacement costs. Inventory is reflected on a company's balance sheet as an asset, and is usually the largest single entry, so management attention naturally focuses on it.

Because inventory ties up capital, has to be stored, needs to be handled, can spoil or become obsolescent, is taxed, and sometimes lost, it can be considered a huge liability. Furthermore, inventory often compensates for poor forecasting, poor supplier delivery performance, and poor ordering practices. If the wrong items are in inventory, the situation is magnified.

Raw materials, WIP, and finished goods inventory are considered short-term assets as they are expected to be consumed or sold in a short period of time. MRO supplies are generally written off against income as an expense and are not expected to be used in the production of a finished product.

Capital equipments are considered long-term assets and must be depreciated according to IRS rules, so they too are not considered as part of inventory. The average U.S. company has about 30% of the firm's working capital tied up in inventory, which represents a large portion of the total costs of goods sold. The same percentage holds true for most distributorships' inventories.

Inventory has a multiple effect on company results since it is a factor in both the investment turnover and the profit margin. Since ROI is obtained by multiplying investment turnover times the profit margin, its importance is clearly seen, as *it has a double-barreled effect on company performance.*

Record Keeping Systems

Successful inventory management requires administrative, physical, and financial controls. These controls are achieved through record-keeping systems, inventory valuation methods, and warehouse practices.

- Periodic inventory systems are used by many manufacturers that review at regular time intervals, perhaps weekly, monthly, quarterly, or annually. This system is used for MRO supply items, or "C" category inexpensive production components.

- Perpetual inventory systems keep records current, and are used by retail stores, wholesale distributors, and some manufacturing companies.

- Four-wall inventory systems are used by manufacturers where storage time may be short or nonexistent. Items are recorded as received, and not subtracted from inventory until they leave in finished goods.

- Visual inventory systems may be informal, and require users to reorder as needed. Visual systems are used to manage office supplies, and other inexpensive MRO supplies.

Methods of Inventory Valuation

The costs of inventory items must be valued for financial reporting and various control functions such as ABC analysis. The most common methods for determining the cost of inventory are:

- *First in, first out (FIFO).* This method assumes that the oldest items in the inventory will be used first. Using FIFO methods in periods of changing costs would tend to keep the inventory costs on the balance sheet closer to current market value, but the cost of goods sold would be at the lowest recent cost.

- *Last in, first out (LIFO).* This method assumes that the last items received in inventory will be consumed first. Value is based on the most recent quantity put into inventory. Using LIFO in periods of rising material prices tends to understate the inventory value on the balance sheet. However, the cost of goods sold is closer to current market values. Cost of goods sold is at lower cost than their replacement cost.

- *Average cost system.* This method seeks to average between the balance sheet and the P & L income statement.

- *Standard cost system.* This method assigns a single value for an item throughout the year. Inventory assets and cost of goods sold are reported in consistent terms. In periods of rapid price increases (28% in 1982) failure to foresee increased costs of goods created highly inaccurate P&L statements. In concept, standard costs seek to equal the actual costs at time of usage.

- *Replacement cost system.* This method assigns inventory cost based on the next receival. This is important if items stay in storage for long periods of time as a company's prices might not cover the current cost of the items sold.

- *Actual cost system.* This is most desirable, but seldom used. Large projects or government procurement may require it, but it's difficult to achieve actual costs when many items are flowing through a high-volume manufacturing operation.

The time value of inventory costs needs attention because a dollar received today is more valuable than a promise to receive a dollar a year from today. Inflation erodes buying power. Time-value charts[2] have been published for quick computation should they be needed.

Once an accounting decision has been set to cost inventory, the IRS does not allow shifting back and forth to take advantage of current economic conditions.

Physical Controls of Inventory

There are a number of issues related to the physical control of inventory. They are dependent on accurate inventory records, and their maintenance. Accuracy involves item identification, physical storage and location of materials, storeroom management, and physical inventory counting practices. The consequences of poor inventory records include unplanned shortages, surpluses, productivity loses, high inventory levels, excessive expediting, and most importantly, lost sales and missed customer promises.

Finance normally will require an annual physical inventory review, but the preferred method of control is daily cycle counting. Planning and replenishment systems rely on accurate record data, so it is critical that on-hand balances are verified as often as possible. The goal of any counting system is 100% accuracy, but more importantly it is to detect discrepancies between record data and what is physically available.

Cycle counting uses full-time specialist(s) and allows detection and correction of causes for error resulting in better records. The most common criterion for triggering a cycle count is the ABC classification reviewed later. High-value A items are counted more often than lower value B and C items. World-class companies strive for 99.8% of A items, 99% for B, and 95% for C items.

To accelerate the updating of inventory records, the trend is toward automated systems to display database information in real time. Barcoding, magnetic stripes, optical reading devices, and automatic counting devices are some of the tools currently being explored and used by many organizations.

Goals of Inventory Control

The basic goals of inventory control are measured in terms of customer service and inventory investment. The task is to produce the greatest possible return on investment *while meeting customer needs*. The primary function of inventory management is to have items available, to maintain the flow of goods through

---

[2]NAPM's *Purchasing Handbook,* 2nd ed., pp. 29–42,

the production process to the customer, while minimizing the costs to achieve this service.

One of the most successful distributors, Hughes Supply of Orlando, Florida, uses their founder's statement, "You can't do business out of an empty wagon." That says it all! There must be enough materials or goods to sell. The challenge is not to have too much. There has to be a balance, some rules for keeping enough, but not too much. Inventory flexibility is greatest when the inventory is in raw materials and the least when in finished goods.

In addition to maximizing the return on investment objective, other goals to be considered are:

- To achieve an acceptable inventory dollar investment, based on annual sales or planning forecasts
- To meet delivery schedules, satisfying sales goals
- To minimize production delays because of stock-outs, to keep production lines operative, and to maintain employment stability
- To achieve adequate control through simple management reports that allow proactive, not reactive, action, rather than use meat-ax approaches if inventories get out of hand

Financial Analysis of Inventory

The size of a company's inventory depends not only on sales volume but also on the type of business and the time of year. If a car dealer has a large stock at the height of the buying season, he is said to be in a strong inventory position. Yet, the same inventory during August places the dealership in a vulnerable position, because the new year's models will come out in late September. A large inventory can be vulnerable to losses due to sharp price drops. In short, correct inventory size depends on many factors. Without a measure of inventory investment, companies are operating in the dark. For this reason, turnover rates, or "turns," is widely used to measure inventory investment relative to the cost of goods sold.

The sales to inventory in dollars denotes sales generated by a unit of inventory. The effect of inventory turnover on inventory investment can be made simple. Using this method, if $1 of sales is divided by $1 of inventory this is a turnover of 1. If that turnover is increased to 2 turns, the inventory investment is decreased to $.50 or by one-half; 5 turns reduces inventory to $.20; 10 turns to $.10. The higher the inventory turnover, obviously the less inventory. At up to 8 to 10 turns the effect is pronounced, but further increased turnover has a less dramatic effect as the reduction in inventory is a diminishing percentage.

Inventories are one of the principal barometers for the economist and management to use in determining the health of the company and the economy. As an economic upturn lengthens, the sales curve falls off or may actually drop, while the inventory accumulation cannot yet be cut off. Watching the ratio of sales to inventories provides a signal for action to prevent excessive inventory from causing financial damage to the company.

Demand should be anticipated as best as possible. Seasonal factors affect construction sites that in turn bring heavier than normal requirements. While the goal is to have just sufficient inventory to meet demand, it's impossible to be always that precise. Inventory policy decisions must be made on how much stock to carry. One way to set the lot size is determined by EOQ.

An inventory budget may be prepared for a plant or for various work centers. Typically, the budget will display allowable dollars that can be held in inventory based on production output. A monthly inventory budget value may be determined by the formula:

$$\text{Inventory \$} = \frac{\text{Monthly Production (\$)} \times 12}{\text{Desired Inventory Turnover}}$$

The desired turns for each work center can be determined by past performance or set jointly by management and those directly held accountable for inventories.

Let's assume a model situation where a company has sales of $12 million per year ($1 million per month), and a net profit of $600,000 (a 5% profit margin). Total assets are $6 million of which 30% or $2 million is in inventory.

$$\text{Investment Turnover} = \frac{\text{Sales}}{\text{Total Assets}} = \frac{\$12,000,000}{\$6,000,000} = 2$$

Historically, the model company's inventory turnover is 6 turns. Applying the formula will provide a dollar level of inventory against which to measure actual results.

$$\text{Inventory \$} = \frac{\$1,000,000 \text{ (Monthly Production)} \times 12}{6 \text{ (Desired Inventory Turnover)}} = \$2,000,000$$

If management believes the turns should be increased to a target 6.5, this would lower the new target inventory to about $1,850,000. In this way, any desired change in turns can quickly be converted to the amount of budget dollars management approves for inventory purposes.

Basic to good control is knowledge of future requirements, not merely information about past sales. Often the data available and used are past performance figures that may not allow for future expansion or contraction of sales volume. Some other financial inventory ratios used, are:

- *Profit to inventory* is a measure of return on inventory investment.
- *Committed (against sales orders) inventory* to total inventory is a measure of how much inventory is stocked for customers.

- *$ Inventory to $ monthly shipments* (or production) defines available-for-sale inventory to outstanding orders.
- *$ Inventory to net working capital ratio*, if too large indicates that difficulty may be experienced in meeting current financial obligations.
- *Current debt to inventory* is an indication of how much the business relies on funds from disposal of unsold inventories to meet debts.
- *Available inventory to inventory* predicted by the models as a standard.

In some cases, other standards might be more suitable. By themselves these ratios are not always meaningful. However, comparison over time, or against standards, is essential for complete understanding. A word of caution! Trying to check the turnover for a hardware store using data from a chemical company or a machinery manufacturer may prove nothing. Ratios are meaningful only if similar companies are compared.

Inventory Turnover

High inventory turnover is desirable but at some point low inventories will cause increased production problems and costs that, in turn, will reduce profit and return on investment. There is an optimum dollar turnover for existing sales, and it isn't always the maximum turnover. Herein lies a conflict, for if management is measuring inventory performance arbitrarily, by either dollar value or turnover, the results may not produce the best return on investment. A turnover of four "turns" means that goods are bought and sold on an average of four times per year. That doesn't tell whether the inventory mix is correct. Some items could be out of stock, while others are in excess.

Comparison of one company's turns to another is meaningful only if they are in similar businesses. Inventory turnover ratios vary from industry grouping to individual company within the groups. As a generality, a turnover of 4 is on the low side, while 15 would be quite high, and a good average might be about 8 to 10. As examples of specific industries: auto parts 5.3 turns, chemicals 6.6, drugs 4.9, electrical components 4.8, foundries 10.5, machinery assemblers 5 to 15, metal stampings 6.5, paper 7.3, and petroleum 9 turns.

Dun and Bradstreet, Inc. has for many years issued important ratios for more than 70 lines of businesses that are compared over a 5-year period. Charts are of some use in detecting trends or in checking month-to-month or year-to-year performance. They do not so much control inventory as they raise questions about why the inventory may be rising at this time when in other years it has held steady, and the like. Action then may be taken as required.

How Can Inventory Be Controlled?

Inventory control may be considered on two levels, the dollar level and the unit level. Financial officers are primarily interested in the dollar level, because money tied up in inventory is not available for other uses that may be more fruitful or more urgently needed. Naturally, they want as low a dollar value of inventory as possible. Because manufacturing requires specific quantities of items to meet production schedules, the PM, interested in dollar value, is a party to making these units available. The immediate goals are to maintain sufficient stock to keep manufacturing supplied, to keep stock-outs to a minimum, to prevent losses because of obsolescence and spoilage, and to hold down costs of owning inventory.

Specialized areas controlled by purchasing and supply management are closely linked to inventory planning. When the company has the same people making the purchasing and inventory decisions, it's easier to approach the concept of supply management. This allows the trade-offs between balancing the cost to procure and cost to inventory, while considering the end customers' service needs.

Usually a small number of inventoried items account for the largest portion of total inventory value. This fact has led to the use of the ABC system, whereby inventory is classified into groups of high value (A items), medium value (B items), and low value (C items).

ABC Inventory System

Items can be divided into "ABC" categories as seen in Figure 9-1. Different authorities use different percentages. It's the concept that matters, and company's percentages vary. What control should the company get through using the ABC system?

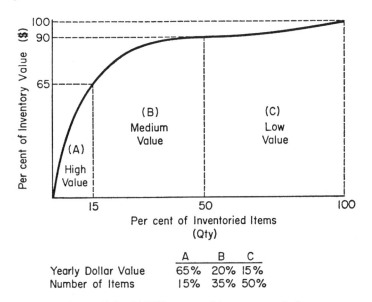

	A	B	C
Yearly Dollar Value	65%	20%	15%
Number of Items	15%	35%	50%

Figure 9-1 "ABC" system of inventory analysis.

1. Close control for high-value A items (buy minimum quantity, or only order as customers request), which are about 10% to 20% of items but 65% to 80% of the cost.

2. Buy economic purchase quantity for medium value B items, which are about 20% to 35% of the items and 20% to 30% of the cost.

3. Buy larger economic quantities of low value C items, which are 50% to 70% of the items, but only 10% to 15% of the cost.

Inventory carrying costs will be about 25% of an item's value, but this can vary greatly from one company to another. For the ABC analysis, some companies use a Days of Supply measurement rather than simply a certain quantity.

Deciding When and How Much to Buy

When you come right down to it, there are just two basic decisions in inventory control that must be made: (1) when to buy and (2) how much to buy.

Planning and control systems provide the requirements based on forecasts or production schedules. Many different replenishment systems are available and combinations are appropriate under different conditions. There are three basic methods of deciding when to buy:

1. Statistical reorder point (ROP)
2. Time-phased order point (TPOP), and
3. Material requirements planning (MRP).

The method a company will adopt depends on the demand characteristics of their products. Independent demand (finished goods or distribution inventory) is usually planned and controlled with conventional methods such as ROP and TPOP, whereas inventories subject to dependent demand (raw materials and components) are usually planned and controlled through MRP.

Statistical Reorder Point

The statistical reorder point (ROP) system is one of the oldest methods known for determining when to replenish or buy. The purchase quantity is usually a fixed order quantity or lot size based on past usage, to meet production demands. The ROP method requires the use of perpetual inventory data displaying current on hand balances and quantities already on order. A sawtoothed graph is a classic model of inventory behavior when usage is relatively constant. Figure 9-2 shows a sawtooth diagram of inventory levels with continuous receivals and usages. This is helpful in determining when to order to ensure the arrival of a new shipment before the minimum stock level is reached.

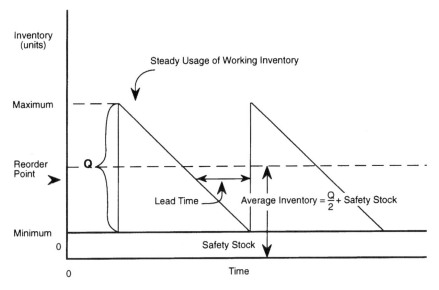

Figure 9-2   Sawtooth diagram of inventory receival and usages.

Determining the reorder point is what triggers the requisition of a replenishment order. The ROP can be described as the sum of the demand through the lead-time. For items with fluctuating demands that exceed the lead-time resulting in a stock-out, or lost sales, some safety stock is usually added to the equation. The final ROP formula becomes demand through the lead-time, plus safety stock, and is expressed as: ROP = DLT + SS.

If an item is ordered once per year, one can envision a sawtooth chart as a single tooth with high inventory costs. Ordering each working day would produce about 250 teeth. Cost to procure and ship would skyrocket, but the inventory would be low.

This reorder point method makes some general assumptions about demands placed on inventory: that the demand is fairly constant and predictable, and independent from the demand of other items. ROP is not adequate for managing dependent demands for raw materials, components, and subassemblies. Materials requirements planning (MRP) techniques were developed to handle these items.

The ROP requires a mechanism to alert buyers when the order point has been reached, and it's time to reorder. Two mechanisms commonly used are perpetual inventory records and visual review systems such as a simple "min/max," or bin card systems. The two-bin system is the most common visual review method. How does it work? When the first bin empties, it triggers a new order for more. It is generally used for the management of low-value items with short lead-times, such as office supplies or hardware. A major advantage is elimination of paperwork, although storage space used is larger. This method is still widely in use, but many companies now use time-phased order point rules when determining when to buy.

Time-Phased Order Point

Time-phased order point (TPOP) is a method for determining inventory replenishment action based on the time-phased grid used in MRP. The purchase quantity is usually a fixed lotsize, but TPOP does allow for buying discretely, meaning only what the exact demand is.

The data that drives this type system includes a forecast of requirements, the lead-time of the item, and the order quantity. How does TPOP work? Forecasted demands, scheduled receipts, and available on-hand quantities are projected by week or periods over the planning horizon (usually 3 to 6 months). In each period the quantity available, plus the scheduled receipts, minus the forecast for the period equals the projected quantity available.

When the projected available inventory becomes negative, the need for a replenishment order is triggered. There are a number of advantages in the use of TPOP. It enables the use of predictable future requirements, rather than historical data for order actions. It provides future visibility of when purchasing or production orders need to be issued. Forecasts can be adjusted for seasonality, trends, or discontinuous demand.

Materials Requirement Planning

The Master Production Schedule (MPS) drives materials requirement planning (MRP). It specifies the products the organization anticipates manufacturing or buying each period. So, the MPS is the plan for producing the supply to meet the customer demands. Production Control and Inventory Planning use the Bill of Material (BOM) in conjunction with the MPS to explode demands and identify requisitions and production orders that must be released.

MRP uses many of the techniques of inventory management already reviewed with ROP inventory control using the ABC system. Companies that have large in-process inventories use MRP that was designed for computer application in its infancy. MRP was a time-phased effective technique to determine the timing of demand to produce a schedule of planned order releases to cover expected shortages in both in-house manufacture and external purchased components.

A flaw in early MRP was the inability to consider the capacity needs of manufacturing. That gap was filled with the creation of capacity requirement planning, known as CRP. The capacity for work centers is derived from the number of machines or workers, and the planned working hours per week.

CRP uses routing and lead-time data to develop work center profiles to aid in identifying bottlenecks and underload. By smoothing out the workload across work centers and over time, bottlenecks along with lead-times can be better controlled. The feedback from CRP closed the loop between the forecasted plan and the actual production and supplier performance. This helped determine if corrective action was required, and what action was most appropriate. A more sophisticated MRP was born that was called manufacturing resource planning, or MRP II.

MRP II is a formal manufacturing information system that links Marketing, Finance, Operations, and Purchasing. It converts resource demands, such as equipment, manpower, and material into financial requirements and converts product output into monetary terms. The major benefit of MRP II is that it can evaluate an organization's ability to execute the plan financially, and evaluate the merits of the plan in terms of return on investment (ROI), and profit.

Manufacturing Resource Planning

Manufacturing resource planning (MRP II) ties in with capacity requirement planning (CRP). CRP compares the timing when the units are required on the production floor; considers machine hours, rate, and labor hours by work centers; and facilities usage for shop-floor control. Through corrective action, workers can be shifted to different jobs as production within a company changes to meet customer demands. There should be a balance between the capacity of the plant to produce and the materials needed to operate. Various reports are generated to track these functions. Though a most important production function, the details are usually of little concern to purchasing people.

In summary, an order can be initiated in several ways: an item reaching its order point, the arrival of a planned order release date through a time-phased MRP system, or a Kanban trigger in a JIT environment. A computerized system may generate a requisition on the planned order release date or when the inventory reaches its order point. The timing of a req requires that all aspects of lead-time be considered. The planner's time, the buyer's time, the supplier's time to process and ship the order, receipt of the product, and the move time to stores or to the required workcenter all must be factored in. Additional time may be needed if the item has never been purchased before as quotations and negotiations are needed.

The conventional approach of when to buy has historically centered around demand-push systems such as ROP and TPOP, and MRP as described above. These methods tend to load machines to maximum efficiencies and output, resulting in excess WIP inventory and waste. The shift of emphasis in industry today is on demand-pull manufacturing that responds to customers' needs, which can be highly variable. Material movement to a workcenter or the authorization to procure goods is triggered only when they are required for use.

Implementation of the just-in-time philosophy emphasizing total quality, employee empowerment, reduced setup time and costs, flexible resources, and more frequent deliveries from suppliers has led to demand-pull concepts such as Kanbans to trigger the need for a purchased item.

The Japanese "Kanban," or card system, has been widely studied, and some U.S. companies have adopted it. Kanban was pioneered by a Toyota Motor Co's VP who visited American supermarkets to study how they replenished their shelf stock. As the shelves emptied, the VP noted it "signalled" employees to bring out more stock. The Kanban means a card that triggers, or signals, the need for replenishment as a *pull* system since the customer's demand causes the need.

How Much to Buy

The question of how much to order has been the most thoroughly researched subject in the literature of planning and inventory control for many years. Still there are different options that can be applied to this important issue. A company may purchase an item for different reasons—in response to receiving a req for an item (make to order) or in anticipation of customer orders (make to stock). In a make-to-order environment the buyer usually purchases only the quantity needed by the customer. For make-to-stock, the rules governing order quantity are primarily a function of the item's demand characteristics. A fixed order quantity, usually the ROP discussed earlier, is appropriate for managing independent demand (finished company products).

Dependent demand items (raw materials and parts) are usually managed best by an MRP system. Often, the right quantity is a hybrid of ROP systems and MRP management systems.

Money tied up in other than bare essential inventory should be justified just as fully as any new investment. General considerations about buying the "right" quantity are as follows, in random order:

- Knowledge of customer requirements
- Company policy on inventory
- Knowledge of market conditions
- Supplier's economical manufacturing quantity
- Economical shipping quantity
- Standard purchasing unit (barrel, pail, carton, etc.)
- Manufacturing lead-time
- Transit time
- Cost of issuing orders
- Quantity price differentials
- Storage facilities available
- Cost of handling inventory
- Interest cost on investment
- Insurance premiums to protect the inventory

- Depreciation and obsolescence
- Turnover target, and balance of product mix

Buying the right amount usually is a compromise of many of the above considerations. But, every quantity decision is based on the comparison of two different costs; the cost to carry the inventory versus the cost to place and acquire the order. The cost to place orders with suppliers is inverse to the cost to carry inventory.

Applying the Economic Order Quantity

The most widely used method to determine order quantity is the economic order quantity (EOQ), which is used for items with level and continuous demand. When forecasted demands are "lumpy" or discontinuous, the EOQ formula doesn't provide the best estimate of the quantity to buy. Several methods have evolved over the last few years to determine the best order cycles and quantities under these conditions. Some of these methods are lot-for-lot, periods of supply, period order quantity (POQ), least unit cost (LUC), and least total cost (LTC). Our focus will center around EOQ.

The original formula for EOQ was introduced in 1915, and altered to its present form in 1922. Despite the mathematical formula, EOQ is not difficult to grasp, and is simple to apply once basic principles are understood. Use of the technique is facilitated by using a high-speed computer that can perform the calculations in split seconds, as well as simple charts that can be easily read by clerical people.

EOQ can be applied to all inventory items, and is ideal for service type buying and MRO items. In manufacturing, however, it is usually applied first to the medium value B items that have much leverage. How much of an item should be purchased at one time can be answered by balancing (1) the cost of carrying the inventory and (2) the cost of completing a purchase. When these two factors are equated properly, the result is the lowest total cost to the company. A buyer knows that if she buys less of an item, there is a decrease in inventory carrying charges but an increase in the cost to procure; conversely, if she buys larger quantities, there is an increase in inventory carrying charges but a reduction in the cost to procure. There is a "right" economic ordering quantity (EOQ), expressed mathematically, that will produce the minimum cost.

PMs may not use the EOQ technique more frequently because it hasn't been mathematically proved to their satisfaction. Also, the square root computation causes doubt. The economic order quantity, or EOQ, occurs when the total cost is at a minimum as shown in Figure 9-3. The mathematics to derive the formula is relatively straight-forward, and is shown in Table 9-1.

Buyers rightly should ask "Does it work?" At a college workshop, 35 experienced business people pitted their skill and judgment in inventory control against one professor in a game of simulation. Penalties for stock-outs (items not available

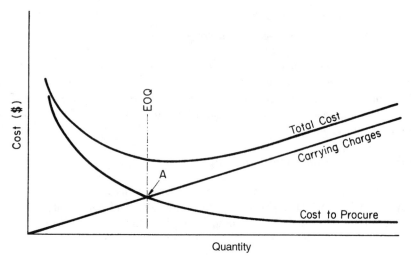

Figure 9-3 When EOQ occurs.

when required for production) were incurred and, as each period of usage rolled by, total costs were accumulated. The usage figures were provided by spinning a wheel of chance, certainly as erratic a method as any production schedule could offer. At the end of a simulated year, the total cost of procuring and carrying inventory was computed. The professor had beaten all his competitors, using tools of mathematical probability about the chances of stock-out, and the economic ordering quantity (EOQ) formula. EOQ worked in this game of simulation just as it is working in many companies today. However, the difficulties of getting

Table 9-1 *Derivation of the EOQ Formula*

Where EQQ = economic ordering quantity in units;

  A = usage per year

  S = cost in dollars to procure each order or release;

  I = annual cost of carrying inventory expressed in decimals (%); and

  C = unit price of item in dollars.

(1) Cost to procure inventory = inventory carrying charges. (This is when EOQ occurs.)

(2) $\dfrac{AS}{EOQ} = \dfrac{\dfrac{ACI}{2^*}}{\dfrac{A}{EOQ}} = \dfrac{ACI\,(EOQ)}{2A}$

(3) Simplifying algebraically $(EOQ)^2 = \dfrac{2A^2S}{AIC} = \dfrac{2AS}{IC}$

(4) $\therefore$ EOQ $= \sqrt{\dfrac{2AS}{IC}}$

  The total carrying charges are computed on average inventory, since the average amount of inventory is half * of the total from one shipment to the next.

actual cost and other data make it more complicated in real life than it seems in the classroom.

EOQ is affected by such actions as a boost in the discount rate, causing higher borrowing costs. As seen in the formula, as carrying costs go up, the EOQ will be reduced, signaling the need to lower the inventories, and to order somewhat less.

Order size changes inversely with the interest rate. Tighter money policies would allow the dollar level of inventory to remain the same, but the quantity (units) level would have to be decreased to keep the total value the same. This is the basis for the belief by some economists that inventory fluctuations can be influenced sharply through credit control.

Purchasing managers not familiar with the principles of EOQ will want to find out about adaptations to mathematical formulas that companies have developed. For example, using a purchase order cost of $10, and an inventory carry charge of 25%, let us follow the example in Table 9-2.

A, or annual usage, is the expected quantity of the item that will be required; it is taken from the production schedule. *I,* or carrying charges, may be secured from the controller. Should data on carrying charges not be readily available, these can be closely approximated by addition of the individual percentages as shown in Table 9-3.

The blanket ordering system, using a yearly PO and releasing quantities as required, creates no problem. Cost to procure (*S*) is based on the individual lot shipment received, and not on each order placed. The reason: EOQ seeks to balance the procuring costs as a whole in relation to the cost of carrying inventory. Some companies use a set S value for each of their high-value items, and an average *S* value for medium- to low-value items.

Among the functions to figure cost to procure (*S*): preparation of purchase requisitions, source selection, routing selection, method of shipment, order preparation and placing, expediting, receiving, inspection and similar reports, in-plant movement, stores, inventory records, invoice payment, freight rate check and payment, and application of accounting charges to proper accounts. Included in these functions are such items as buyers' salaries and clerical wages, use of computers, office supplies, telephone, FAX, postage, and travel expense.

Table 9-2   Practice example for EOQ

Given the following data, what is the economic order quantity?

Cost to procure per order (*S*)	$10
Usage per year (*A*)	120
Price per piece (*C*)	$ 1
Carrying charges (*I*)	.24

$$EOQ = \sqrt{\frac{2AS}{IC}} = \sqrt{\frac{2(120)(10)}{.24\ (1)}} = \sqrt{10,000} = 100 \text{ pieces}$$

The quantity to order is 100 pieces, which is 10 months' supply or a value of $100.

Table 9-3   Carrying charges (Composite of estimates made by a number of experts to show (1) factors involved in carrying charges and (2) their possible magnitude

Cost of Component	Range in Per Cent per Year
1. Interest of investment	5 to 6
2. Space charge	¼
3. Handling charges	1 to 3
4. Supplies	¼
5. Insurance	¼
6. Taxes	¼ to ½
7. Obsolescence	5 to 10
8. Depreciation	5
9. Deterioration	3
10. Use of money elsewhere	4½ to 8
Total in Pct. per year	12 to 24½*

*The lower percentage generally would apply to metalworking or manufacturing industries; the higher, to higher-profit, fast-moving industries such as electronics, chemicals, or services.

For a given operation, the value of S and I may be constant. In that case there are only two variables, A and C, that change with each item considered. The formula can be simplified by determining the constant (K) that equals the square root of $2S/I$. Then the formula becomes EOQ = $K \times$ square root of A/C.

Many managers ignore the EOQ believing it has to be computed for each item or buy. Not so. It's irrelevant what is bought! After finding the K value, charts can be prepared that eliminate even simple arithmetic. The economic quantities can be put into chart form for easy reference on-the-job as shown in Table 9-4. This table is based on a $K = 10$. For another case where the K factor might be

Table 9-4   EOQ chart used for any purchase

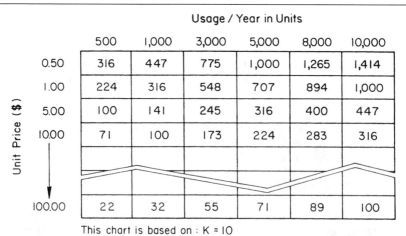

	Usage / Year in Units					
	500	1,000	3,000	5,000	8,000	10,000
0.50	316	447	775	1,000	1,265	1,414
1.00	224	316	548	707	894	1,000
5.00	100	141	245	316	400	447
10.00	71	100	173	224	283	316
100.00	22	32	55	71	89	100

Unit Price ($)

This chart is based on : K = 10

7, the chart can be converted by dividing each quantity by 10 and multiplying by 7 (or multiplying by .7).

The buyer simply takes the price for any item, and based on the annual quantity used, comes up with the amount of that item to buy. Keep in mind that the chart is tailored to a particular operation, and can't be universally applied.

How to Gauge Price Breaks

An alert buyer will try to take advantage of volume discounts to get lower prices; but does this produce a better buy? EOQ can provide an answer, but the formula must be worked one step further when price breaks exist. Of several methods that have been tried, the most exact is to compute total variable cost (TVC) for each quantity where a price break occurs. The result is as many EOQs as there are price breaks, but only one of them will produce the lowest total cost. This multiple-equation solution can be combined into a single formula, but this procedure usually is attempted only by those companies with sophisticated data processing capability.

We will stick to solving the EOQ formula for each price break. Total variable cost (TVC) is the total ordering cost for the period, plus the total cost of carrying inventory. When we reduce this to a formula, using the same symbols for factors already included in the EOQ formula:

$$TVC = AS/EOQ + EOQ/2 \times C \times I$$

where

$$A = \text{annual usage;}$$
$$S = \text{cost to procure;}$$
$$C = \text{price per piece; and}$$
$$I = \text{carrying charges.}$$

Applying the formula to an example, we find TVC for each price break. For example, 75 valves cost $5 each, but 100 valves cost $3 each. A is 500; S is $10; C is $5 and $3; I is .24. EOQ for the $5 price = 91; and EOQ for the $3 is 118. First, compute TVC for the price of $5.

$$TVC = AS/EOQ + EOQ/2 \times C \times I = (500 \times 10)/91 + 91/2 \times 5 \times .24 = \$109.60.$$

Since the TVC for the price of $3 = $84.44, and is less than that for the $5 price, the quantity to buy is the EOQ for the $3 price, or 118 valves. For each additional price break, TVC is computed in the same way.

Pitfalls in Application

Some companies using EOQ have in fact found themselves carrying higher inventories than management thought practical. To counteract this objection several adjustments have been used. One way is to reduce all quantities in figuring EOQ by an arbitrary percentage. As an example, if the inventories are about 5% too high, reduce all quantities by automatically introducing this into the formula. Some companies that did this felt the results made the formula more acceptable to them. This solution might be compared to the use of a safety factor by the engineer (though it also could be interpreted as ignorance of a better solution).

The economical order quantity cannot be dismissed by those interested in sound inventory control, nor should it be plunged into blindly. Experiment first! To start, the basic formulas should be applied where there is enough money to make it worth the effort.

By proper timing in placing the purchase order, buyers can decrease the need of higher inventory and safety stocks. Lead-times will influence timing of placing of orders as well as stock-on-hand, to last until the next shipment is received. Maintaining and updating a supplier's lead-time listing is a necessity. Deterioration, shelf life, size and weight, and the like are all considerations.

Economic Purchase Quantity

There is a possible conflict between the most economical order quantity and the supplier's most economical manufacturing quantity. Few companies buy to a set economic order quantity formula. They are guided by factors such as the suppliers lead-time, production schedule, in-transit time, and so on.

Another fact of life is that severe pressure to reduce inventories causes many production managers to refuse purchasing requests to increase quantities to lower costs. Their prevailing philosophy is that if a supplier can give a lower price for higher quantities, the buyer should get the lower price anyway. The idea is the supplier must find a way to lower its cost and so price, or risk losing the business to another supplier who will do so.

So, while there should be chances for buyers to adjust the desired quantity, to allow for quantity price breaks, minimum buys, combining items in shipment, and the like, they may have to struggle for that privilege. Of course if top management dictates a policy of always buying a minimum, that has to be respected. Yet, judgment should be used to modify the quantity to an "economic purchase quantity," or EPQ.

The Just-in-Time (JIT) Approach

In the 1980s, many American managers found themselves losing ground in the manufacturing "race" with the Japanese. They believed a primary reason for Japan's success was a concept termed "just-in-time" (JIT). Early on, a common misconception held by many managers was that JIT, in a narrow sense, was another planning tool that simply required all the supplies to ship components exactly as needed and on time. The result was many early failures until the realization that JIT is a broad-based philosophy of management, which embraces the president of the company on down through manufacturing to the workers on the shop floor. The process ranges from supplier to customer in a never ending journey toward the elimination of waste, defined as any part of process cost that does not add value to the product. Examples include excess inventory, unneeded quality inspection, excess material handling, and so on.

Reports have been glowing about the success of JIT, such as: inventory levels have been reduced by X percent, throughput times have been shortened, work-in-process (WIP) is reduced substantially, downtime reduced, increased use of labor and equipment, and flexibility in scheduling and productivity improved. Who can quarrel with such results?

JIT is a combination of philosophy and process that takes years to implement. No two JIT implementations are ever the same. While it is primarily equipment manufacturers who are pursuing JIT, there are lessons that can be used in MRO contract buying.

A successful JIT program involves total quality surveillance, JIT manufacturing techniques, and an involvement of people. JIT is a philosophy that crusades for total elimination of waste through the cooperative effort of everyone in the company. As a result of continual searching out inadequacies of the inventory system used, changes are made in work order, according to lead-times, and the like.

JIT goals are consistent with normal inventory control goals, but represent a tightening up philosophy. Distilled to its essence, JIT programs attempt to tighten the record keeping, and to carry minimal stocks by receiving frequent shipments. Receival is planned as close as possible to need, with 100% reliability.

All phases of manufacturing from design to delivery are fair game for improvement. Statistical process control (SPC), line stopping devices, visual checks, and ways to correct one's own errors are part of the strategy to ensure that no defective products are produced. Perhaps perfection may not be attainable, but its pursuit is urged by striving to eliminate waste.

JIT calls for empowering employees and using their experience and knowledge to achieve quality at the source. Treating employees with respect, keeping them informed, and responding to their ideas for improvement are essential ingredients. Cooperation is absolutely essential for success, so managers should create an environment conducive to problem-solving by providing the training, education, and support to develop their employees' potential.

JIT is hailed as creation of a flexible environment that keeps things simple (KISS—keep it simple, stupid!) As expected, advocates have reached out to encompass already proven techniques and programs that work well. JIT does not replace MRP, EOQ, etc.; rather, it emphasizes execution of them.

JIT wisely calls for: a team approach. Others *must* get on the bandwagon. JIT engineering, JIT purchasing, JIT management all are needed to get on the team. On the shop floor, execution strives for the continuous flow of materials all the way from the suppliers to the customers who are the market demand. This can be achieved through developing strong relationships with suppliers to reduce their own setups, shorter lead-times, and lower inventories.

Buying for Just-in-Time Delivery Requirements

The ability of nearly all manufacturing organizations to produce quality products is limited by the timing and quality of incoming materials and components. So, JIT requires that buyers pay close attention to their supplier base. As any company's internal processes are brought under control, buyers need to extend and sell the JIT philosophy back to their sources. Suppliers are viewed as an extension of the company's own operation. Any failure to perform affects the entire system. So, long-term relationships are based on gaining mutual trust and becoming partners to serve the company's goals. Here are some suggested ways buyers can assist using JIT.

- Involve suppliers up front with the design of new products to take advantage of suppliers' capabilities.

- Buyers are seen as coaches to help suppliers to realize improvements and lower costs.

- See that any of your company's technical support and know-how is available to the suppliers.

- Be aware that nearby suppliers reduce lead-time and delivery time, allowing receiving in frequent smaller quantities.

- When there is assurance of supplier quality programs, the need for incoming inspection is reduced.

- Use of standard shipping containers for incoming parts eliminates counting.

While there are many strengths, we should be aware of potential weaknesses. Many contemporary articles raise questions about JIT that should be addressed. "Someone who feels that perfection must always be attained has created stress before the job begins."[3] Stress can result from lowered buffer stock. When problems are solved, the inventory is reduced again to isolate more problems. As the inventory is lowered, defects from components becomes more onerous, and can no longer be tolerated. "Kaizen," or constant improvement *must* follow. That is said to keep people from being complacent. It's also a way to ensure stronger unionization.

JIT calls for employees making the decisions. Line-stopping strategy is used

---

[3]A. F. Scott, J. H. Macomber, and L. A. Ettkin, "JIT & Job Satisfaction: Some Empirical Results." *Production and Inventory Management Journal,* 1992, p. 56.

to ensure "quality at the source," and less rework needed. The line is to be stopped to fix problems just as the Japanese do. Stopping devices are included in the plants such as whistles and bells, "poka-yoke" (failsafe), and on-call buttons. "Andon" is a term for visual shop floor lighting that like other signaling devices is designed to alert others to help fix the problems. But, as some anxious employees report, "God help me if I pull the plug."

On the down side, a philosophy that seeks perfection as a never-ending quest is bound to cause high employee job stress. This is ironic as a stated JIT goal is to improve employee morale and well-being. Proponents have grafted a Japanese cultural approach to American values. The Japanese group orientation and dedication is not inherent in American culture. When American workers' take-charge styles enforce JIT, it can easily come across as, "You will be happy." "You will reduce inventory," and so on.

The following are some other comments that were noted: "Buyers with fewer suppliers have more free time to work in "value-adding activities," such as progressive delivery innovations." There is a need to "eliminate artificial economies of scale." Managers are cautioned not to hinder JIT with "contradictory performance measures." Negotiations should "include penalty clauses for compliance failure." Also, traditional accounting systems *must* be changed. Performance measures based on standard costing are said to promote waste. And finally, "World class JIT performance is achievable only with a successful total business approach."

The JIT philosophy applied wisely with employee participation is a valid and proven success. JIT is a way to compete with anyone worldwide, and with reasonably low inventory!

Purchasing's Role in Supporting Inventory Objectives

PMs have to be aware at all times of their company's inventory problem and to contribute to its control. For purchasing can't escape accountability for manufacturing inventory results even when not solely responsible for it. PMs and buyers should be sensitive that the American Production and Inventory Control Society (APICS) has embraced the JIT approach. Controlling inventory requires, no *demands*, purchasing cooperation!

At the same time, PMs and buyers must maintain their focus also on other important company goals that they alone can fulfill. There is need to balance lower inventory against the higher cost of acquisition, effect on material purchase price, and transportation costs. Then the buyer can evaluate total delivered costs. Here are some factors to which purchasing relates:

- Markets and pricing situations cause changes in timing of placing purchase orders and adjusting quantities.

- Quantity buys—carload, truckload, barrels, all affect inventory volume.
- Supplier lead-times will alter safety stocks carried.
- Economic supply conditions, for example, a pending steel strike, or industry shortage will also have an effect.

Buyers often suggest changes in requisition quantities to take advantage of volume discounts. Knowledge of market conditions and pricing structures allows the buyer to adjust the quantity of an item to be purchased, for example, to beat a foreseen price rise, or to wait for an imminent price decrease. At the suggestion of purchasing, inventories can be increased by buying carload lots instead of truck lots, by the tank car instead of in barrels.

Only the buyer can supply the following information. The first three items are *always* needed:

- Lead-times
- Standard packaging quantities
- Volume discounts and price-breaks
- Odd-lot or broken-package surcharges
- Combination-orders possibilities
- Pricing updates
- Special tooling or set-up charges (Set-up time does not contribute to value-added activities.)

Since the above factors change from time to time, a way to advise Inventory Control is needed. Limits of liability should be clearly defined, to shorten the lead-time and reduce the inventory carried.

Use of Local Stocking Arrangements

Inventories can be reduced drastically when the buyer can get the supplier to carry the inventory, referred to as "pushback" of inventory—from the buyer to the supplier. A warehouse normally provides this service; but increasingly, in times of excess capacity and severe competition with just-in-time demands, many suppliers of special items do so. It ensures them of future business and is a big plus from the buyer's viewpoint. The practice can produce highly satisfactory results. The supplier can make items as their workload permits, ensuring immediate deliveries and a continuous supply to the buyer.

As a result, many suppliers have been encouraged to build warehouses near buyers consuming locations. So, inventory costs are shifted to the suppliers. Would we expect to see this cost reflected in the prices buyers must pay to single sources?

"Stockless purchasing" is similar to systems contracting, and is used when suppliers carry in-stock sufficient quantities of items so that the buyer may operate its production processes without considerable inventory of its own. These stocking programs are usually negotiated to save by reducing the physical space needed for, and dollar value of, the inventory needed to operate.

Shortsighted Inventory Minicase

This minicase is about a myopic JIT and single source supply policy, and brings out some practical issues. Danny Mack Supply Co.'s management pushed just-in-time deliveries from suppliers. They learned how other supply houses are talking about single sources, low inventories, and stressing "supplier partnering." These other distributors said they do this and save money. Management asked, "Why can't our buyers do the same?"

Buyer Michael David finds that the price for bond paper is 30% lower from an off-shore Norwegian papermill than from his previous paper distributor located nearby. Michael sets up a program to split a carload shipment with another local customer. He gets a good price savings and is commended by his management.

After the first year of the new 3-year paper contract, Michael is advised of possible mill labor trouble in June. The mill suggests their customers plan a stocking program, saying they almost always have a walk-out every fifth year when the union contract expires.

Michael takes in extra inventory. The strike does occur and isn't quickly settled. Outside buys are needed to keep stock available. After 60 days the papermill resumed production, but Michael's inventory is still too low. Michael tries to negotiate for increased mill deliveries, but the mill is reluctant, citing their "capacity problems."

Then a worldwide paper shortage develops. Michael is having difficulty in getting his supply. The Norwegian mill orderbook is backlogged, and Michael's company is put on allocation. The mill assures him that he'll get what is promised, but Michael doesn't feel confident at all he'll get what he needs.

You be the buyer. It's a tough time to find *any* new source, much less a reliable one. Seldom can inventory be judged solely by itself, as is seen by answering the following questions:

Q1. Should buyer Michael have had a stronger contract?

Q2. Should Michael have single sourced offshore for paper, or for any major supply item? (Remember, his management urged it.)

Q3. Certainly this mill has helped reduce the inventory (in fact it's too low), but how about assurance of supply?

Q4. How could this situation have been avoided?

Q5. What do you do now?

This simple case brings up several conflicting and confusing issues. Isn't that the case on the job? Does DMS's failure to handle the situation reflect on their lack of inventory know-how? Did their management show little interest? Isn't it true that the failure was one of *execution?*

Usually a buffer inventory or backup source is required when offshore sources are pursued. Inventories are reportedly higher, to allow 4 weeks in-transit time from Europe and 5 to 6 from the Far East. Bulkier materials come by ship. More expensive, smaller items travel by air.

Domestic suppliers can ship within, say, the 13 week lead-time built into many MRP systems. Offshore suppliers usually work with a year's forecast that's not easily obtained. Decide the percentage of annual usage to source abroad. A company cannot afford to shut down its production lines, or run out of what it sells. Consider a domestic backup source allowing for occasional shipping problems, and to ensure competition.

Even good goals and programs can go astray. As we reflect on it, there are no single or simple answers to questions about inventory. There are, however, many proven techniques to use. The importance of inventory impact on every company's return on investment makes these issues a challenge for alert purchasing managers and their buyers. Certainly, "ROI" is the *king* of inventory management.

10

Buying at the "Right" Price

Some prices are rigidly set and no amount of skill or negotiation will change them. Fortunately, many items are competitive or can be negotiated, leaving the buyer to find the "right price" from the "right supplier."

The seller is usually under pressure to ask for a higher price; recall he or she tries to eliminate the competition. It's smart to first settle on the desired quality and then get the item at a fair price rather than think of, "How much will this quality cost?" A higher price will *not always* bring better quality.

It is not solely an issue of pricing versus quality. In a competitive world, quality is frequently independent of costs. Price may rise but total costs may be lower. Price is not the only criterion in reaching proper purchasing decisions.

Price schedules normally reflect better economics to the seller, allowing him or her to sell at a lower price to get a higher volume from the buyer. Schedules will vary with the quantity bought, size of your shipment, containers used, channels of distribution, and special discounts. Trade discounts are given for different customers in the distribution network. So, eliminating the "middle man" can sometimes bring better prices, a 5% discount for example.

Existence of price schedules for standard items doesn't prevent negotiations for discounts or better deals. Obviously there are those times when the buyer has insufficient volume to change existing price levels. Price breaks allow you to choose between buying larger quantities, thereby getting lower prices, or lower quantities at correspondingly higher prices. This can be tricky. Elaborate formulas have been developed to produce the "economic order quantity" to buy. Common sense is used to keep within the inventory rules established and a good price.

How Prices Are Set

A firm price should normally be sought. Escalation of prices or "price at time of shipment" as well as "cost-plus" deals should normally be refused except for unusual purchases. An exception would be if cost is "managed" by customer and supplier together, as it may yield true savings for both parties on a cost-plus basis. However, the agreement *must* include the terms of how cost improvement will be accomplished and tracked.

When studying prices, consider the question, "What is a price and what is its purpose?" Price is the monetary value at which ownership of an item is exchanged. The following approaches to price, while offered with tongue in cheek, give an insight into true pricing methods.[1]

- "Tag-along" studies all competitors' price sheets and matches them exactly.

- "Ratio specialist" believes established percentage profits are valid, so everything has to get the same profit multiplier.

- "The mathematician" creates charts and trend lines, weights, averages, and standard deviations. Prices are precisely where the lines intersect.

- "Psychologist" figures, "If I do this, this will happen, then the probability is this will result. So, I'll start by asking for this price."

- "Quick change artist" reacts to all competition and suggestions without much forethought. If a better price exists across town, then prices shift to meet the moment.

- "Novelist" doesn't believe in worrying about price structure. He or she quickly comes out with any "safe" price, but expects to haggle over discounts, just enough to get the sale.

As with most humor, there is more than a shred of truth in the above. If you still believe prices are based on costs, ask yourself the following:

- When traveling in the same aircraft, why are there 10 or more different fares paid by the people on board?

- Why is electricity distributed to different customers at different rates— by volume, but also by classification, whether factory, municipality, or home?

- Why are transportation rates different for various commodities, while costs to haul may be the same?

- Why are identical products priced differently for different customers?

Buyers should ask themselves why profit margins for products within a company vary so much. How costs are set can vary widely. Early stage costs are typically high and gradually decline as competitors enter the market. Experienced

---

[1] Adapted from Victor H. Pooler, *Purchasing Man and His Job.* American Management Association, New York, 1964.

buyers know well about price flexibility. Also, they've learned that suppliers don't always know their costs—at least accurately.

These points should give us reason to doubt that prices are cast in concrete. One of the first things to understand is, "Most prices are flexible and can be changed!" Effective buyers have learned that it depends on how many people want the item! Knowing what potential buyers think it's worth is a major factor.

The price is never low enough to suit some buyers. That's not always bad, but has made some suppliers believe that all most buyers want is the lowest price. They might contend that "It's gotten so we can't afford any service on what we sell." However, mostly that's an inaccurate contention, as no business would exist long without quality and service, which are of utmost importance.

The senior author recalls a college roommate who has one of the largest car agencies in Maine. I visited him one day and was told he was out back doing service work in the garage. Bill has 28 men in his two locations (since expanded to six) and more than six well-dressed salespeople out front, but he still sells more cars out in the back garage than all of them together. When I found him, Bill explained, "You can really sell 'em when you service 'em. I know when they need a new car before they do. Further, when a guy's car is in trouble he wants advice and he's listening." The same applies to the industrial buyer— when in need of service, he or she will buy from the source that provides help. Many major buying decisions often are swayed by stories of past service.

Some suppliers' prices will be "what the market will bear." It's difficult to know whether a price is "right" and fair, allowing a profit to the supplier yet ensuring the price gives a value to the buyer. People who actually produce an item usually have little concept of what costs are incurred. Many prices are set with extremely arbitrary allocation of costs, particularly with respect to overhead. Buyers should challenge suppliers' allocation of costs, and should strive to learn how to judge what allocations are reasonable.

Purchases for the government may require a supplier's purchasing system to include price and cost analysis. The Federal Acquisition Regulations (FAR) contain data on price analysis techniques such as (a) comparison of price quotations; (b) comparison of prior quotations for the same or similar items; (c) use of such yardsticks as dollars per pound or per horsepower; and (d) comparison of proposed prices with estimates of cost prepared by purchasing personnel together with engineering and manufacturing.

The government has an interesting position on pricing. If prices are:

- Too high—suspect monopoly and the Sherman Antitrust applies.

- Same as others—suspect price collusion which reduces competition so the Clayton Act applies.

- Much lower–suspect undercutting of rivals, thereby forcing them out of business (dumping), so Robinson-Patman will prevent.

In reality, excess or advantage of any kind usually is a violation of the law.

Put a Price Adjustment clause in your purchase order. A buyer may have to call for periodic review of prices on long-term contracts. If a blanket order price is subject to change, fix a ceiling to the amount of escalation by using the following pricing adjustment clause stating to the effect:

> "Purchaser has the right to approve all price increases in advance. Any price increase is limited to:
>
> - A (named) maximum percentage
> - Shipments after (a set date)
> - A (percentage) of the U.S. Producer Price Index for (site the specific items to be adjusted)
> - A (maximum amount) increase allowable"

When you discuss the above escalation, also negotiate a discount for higher volume, and spell out those terms here.

Here are other suggestions about pricing clauses:

1. *Most Favored Pricing clause*: "If Supplier gives any buyer a lower price for like or similar item(s) prior to completion of this purchase order, Supplier will promptly extend to Buyer the lower price, providing granting of such lower price is not in violation of any law."
2. *Pre-price increase notification clause*: "In the event of price escalation, Supplier must notify Buyer 30 days in advance and review with Buyer reasons for changes with intention to negotiate."

Although these clauses are intended to keep downward pressure on future price increases, no knowledgeable buyer would *always* buy at the lowest price. Often a truly low price could be a warning something is wrong. Some prices are pinned to cost of ingredients, so in such a case the buyer must keep abreast of market trends. A buyer of copper tubing must know the daily price of copper, a baker the price of wheat, and so on.

Meeting Target Costs for New Designs

Factors that contribute to total product price are cost of the materials or components. Materials and components can be studied during design development to establish a target cost that acts as a benchmark to evaluate original and future price quotations. Target costs are useful in negotiations stating expectations about the range of prices needed to meet the design objectives.

Setting a target price strikes a bogey for you to measure performance. A good rule of thumb in setting a target price is that an offshore price should be 10% to 20% under current cost, including freight. That's roughly the point where offshore buying becomes advantageous. Also set a total dollar volume target. Reducing a price, say 80% and saving $100 total, makes no sense if the purchase administration costs increased an extra $200.

An example of "sharp practice" is where a buyer gets supplier A to go below supplier B's price. Then the buyer asks B to do better. This auction keeps up for some time. As one salesperson said, "I don't mind auctions, just so long as I get the last chance to bid!" Any salesperson who asks for a last look, or buyer who gives it, should be shown the door!

In the above auction situation, or when there is reason to feel the prices are out of line, a good tactic is to *give all suppliers the same opportunity* to price again. Buyers should always try to get a supplier's lowest price the first time; otherwise, they may be wasting time and money. Contrast this with a situation where seller A's price is $100,000, and seller B's is $80,000. Buyers should reserve the right to negotiate with seller A, who may have features that are desirable, to see if they can't be purchased at nearer seller B's price. Buyers would be failing their responsibility if they did not do this. In this case, let's assume seller A drops to $75,000, it would be unethical to go back to B and try to better the price again. Of course, the issue is whether both should have the same opportunity.

Price Inflation: The Key to Price Forecasting

Marketplace uncertainty demands competence. You must solve material supply problems, economically—which leads us to suggest considering purchasing's responsibility for economic supply assurance through improved forecasting.

Forecasting can be informal. The chosen method may be judgmental or intuitive and may be based upon opinions and knowledge of a few key buyers. These can be fairly accurate short-term if these people know their markets, and use available data.

When asked how he felt about the future, the economist replied, "Optimistic." When asked, "But, why are you so gloomy?" he replied, "Because I'm not so sure my optimism is justified." That makes a point. Forecasting is not an exact undertaking and is still partly an art. Yet, if forecasts are to help companies, they must be soundly based. Beware that forecasts can show trends, but *rarely can they accurately predict a turning point.*

Many times in meetings, management ultimately turns to finance for answers. It's easy for them to look back, but it's another matter when it comes to looking ahead. The buyer is responsible to answer management's concern about future materials, supplies, and cost relationships.

Significant inflation can be defined as a rapid rise in prices over a short time. The result is a sharp erosion in buying power of the currency used to buy. Economists distinguish between two types of inflation:

1. "Demand-pull," when more people want what you want.
2. "Cost-push," when rising costs incurred are reflected in the prices charged.

An aerial navigator learns that if you watch your compass heading and know the wind direction and velocity, you will always know where you are. You can compute where you are relative to the ground. Inflation is like economic wind-age—if buyers know, or can project the inflation for their commodities, they can forecast prices somewhat accurately. However, as one economist said, "Forecasting is difficult, especially when it's in the future."

Why worry about inflation? History teaches us the disastrous results of runaway inflation. When inflation has gotten out of hand, governments often try to freeze prices by fiat. But this has never worked, as prices finally break out and go through the roof, until they readjust. In July, 1923, 3.5% of the tradespeople in Germany were unemployed. By September the number jumped to 9.9% and by December, over 28%. Eventually, it cost millions of marks to mail a letter, and subsequently, Hitler became an acceptable leader.

Inflation has been around for a long time. A chart has been drawn that shows 700 years of world inflation. While inflation is well under control today in the U.S., currently about 3%, it hasn't eased worldwide, and has intensified in some regions of the world. From a global perspective, it's estimated that the world's prices are increasing at about 15%/year. But much worse are those of some developing nations, at about 50%.

Buyers are not helpless to fight inflation. Set a competitive environment to prevent unreasonable price increases. Here's a tactical checklist for managing price increases:

- Refuse to pay increased prices! Just don't accept increases without some discussion and justification. Stand up and be counted if you believe the prices are not justified.

- Be responsive to supplier pricing actions. If they lower prices, favor them. If they raise prices, react!

- Expecting an increase? Don't wait! Ask suppliers for reductions before they can ask for increases.

- Consider giving the business to someone else, but only after warning— and discussion.

- If every fact is not known, make some assumptions and give it a go. Suppliers give a second thought to increasing in the face of strong objections.

- If a supplier gives you a good deal, don't brag to others about it.

- Be sure to advise marketing and finance of price changes to be sure they can cover them in your company's pricing to ensure profitability.

- Ask for a cost breakdown to let you assess the need for increases.

- Compare the amount of increase with the Producer Price Indexes available.

- Follow magazine publishing cost indices and percent price changes, or make your own calculations and track them.
- Monitor industry pricing announcement patterns to identify the suppliers most likely to lead an increase.
- Use the "pricing formula" to be sure the increase is tied to reasonable overhead and profit.
- If an increase is inevitable, ask the supplier for alternatives or cost savings ideas.
- Don't give a supplier who leads in initiating an industry increase a chance to meet a lower price granted by a competitor, as this goes counter to competitiveness.

Perhaps you can think of other ideas. Although some of the above would appear to fly in the face of a supportive partnership, buyers must nevertheless always remember that there has to be economic parity and fairness. Buyers are responsible for their companies' costs! Remember: the buyer's job would be unnecessary if every supplier could be counted on to sell at fair prices.

Price, Cost, and Value Relationships

The price to be paid to accomplish the task has to be weighed against the time to finish. Time can be compressed and shortened with higher expenditure of resources; conversely, time can be stretched by the setting of the priorities. An excellent example was the $24 billion to reach the moon within Kennedy's prescribed 1970 deadline. Perhaps it could have been done at half the cost if Americans would have waited until 1980, but that was not acceptable after the early Russian space success was achieved.

To play an important role in cost reductions, start by considering the relationship of price, cost, and value, and remember that value often has little relationship to cost. As an example, a one cent and a 50 cent postage stamp cost the same to make, yet one's value is 50 times the other's. Another simple illustration is a common ball point pen. Ask most people what its value is, and they'll ask, "What did it cost?" Assume $1. Now take out the spring, pull it to twice its length, then break the filler by bending sharply. You've now added labor. The cost has gone up, but what about the value? As a writing instrument, the pen may be worthless.

So value depends on the usefulness, and on factors other than cost! Buyers should think in terms of constantly changing values, where there is no such thing as a firm price. Price is seldom constant, often depending on how many people want an item! The psychology of what people think it's worth is a major factor, as value can depend on:

- Desirability (psychological, aesthetic, artistic, pleasing, prestige, esteem, and uniqueness)
- Location
- Time
- Use—collector, or for utility (Note that price escalates sharply when a desire to own exists!)

An example of prestige value can be illustrated in the 1996 Sotheby's auction of Jackie Kennedy Onassis' memorabilia which was advertised as "a piece of Camelot." Ordinary items went for what many would believe are astronomical prices. Examples included $48,875 for a tape measure, and $18,000 for a salt and pepper shaker. A lighter expected to fetch $3,000, instead brought $48,500.

President John F. Kennedy's rocking chair was expected to bring $3,000 to $5,000, and was instead sold for $453,500, while a cigar humidor went for $574,000 to a collector. Perhaps most remarkable were Jackie's fake pearls shown in a picture while she was holding her son, John. A comparable three-strand necklace sells for about $65 at Macy's, but the Franklin Mint paid $211,500 to display them in their Philadelphia museum. Now they're selling replicas at a reasonable price to all.

In the real world or in industry, it is a popular belief that the more expensive a product, the better the quality must be. Whoever said, "You get what you pay for" is guilty of utter nonsense! The buyer of the 1990s knows the truth—Costs do not determine prices, rather *prices determine the amount of costs that can be incurred* by the manufacturer or distributor and still stay in business! Price is what you pay for *value*, which is what you receive!

Cost and Price Analysis

Price analysis is the bottom line judgment of which of several sellers' prices is the most reasonable and acceptable. It involves comparing (1) bids, (2) past prices, and (3) prices for similar products.

Experienced buyers know that it's not sufficient to simply consider the price of what is bought. Each challenge of a price naturally will lead to a study of costs. A new product may command large premiums as a reward for supplier ingenuity until a competitor catches up.

The ultimate goal of cost analysis should be to engineer out unnecessary features through an understanding of component costs. A change in any of the three factors of design, materials, and methods can produce savings. Cost and price analyses are ways to get at the facets of cost making up a price so that the price can be better negotiated.

An Exercise to Compute Price of Paint

Let's consider an exercise where price analysis will be used. You are new to buying paint. Having received a requisition for 100 gallons of paint, you've gotten three quotes. The lowest price is from supplier A, but you know industrial paints are thinned based on the application when applied. This is similar to buying concentrated orange juice and not paying to ship the water. Industrial paints are specially formulated and have varying viscosities, and dilution with paint thinner is needed based on spray equipment used and drying time. The maker of brand A suggests a thinning ratio of 3 parts paint to 1 part thinner and his product is priced at $9.00/Gal. Brand B's ratio is 4 to 3 and his product is priced at $14.00/Gal; while brand C's ratio is 3 to 2 and his product priced at $10.00/Gal.

Make the following computations:

Brand	$ Price	Mix Ratio	Price Thinner	As used Actual price
A	9.00	3:1	$2	(Fill in prices)
B	14.00	4:3	2	
C	10.00	3:2	2	

Assume thinner costs $2.00/Gal and coverage of all brands after thinning is identical. Which is the best buy—brand A, B, or C? Please work the computation before reading the footnote answer![2] Is the lowest price the best buy?

Analysis forms the basis from which the buyer can question and probe. Getting as many specifics as possible will assist you in making a case for lowest ultimate cost. Information disclosed for cost analysis can be used only in a completely "above the table" approach to maintain good buyer and seller relationships; that is to say, suppliers who give up information that is used to muscle them later soon learn to withhold data! Buyers have to creatively search out the available tools to apply on the job.

To conduct a cost analysis obviously implies the availability of such data, but what if you can't get detailed costs? Not every supplier will readily provide data on his production costs, and, in many cases, it simply will not be available. In such cases, similar machines and equipment can be analyzed on a "cost/horse-power" basis. A scattergram of known prices allows a trend line that permits estimates of a variety of sizes. Compare new proposed prices versus estimates of your cost targets.

The old formula of "price per pound" comparison for engines, compressors, and the like still has some merit. This relatively simple method of price comparison is certainly not as accurate or acceptable as a specific breakdown analysis, yet when nothing else is available, it can be helpful. In the absence of better data, use it regardless of the product being analyzed. For example, knowing that a jet aircraft in the 1970s cost around $21.27/lb provides some background to estimate a current model's cost. An index can be used to update that price. In this manner,

---

[2] Brand A's application cost is $7.25, B's $8.85, and C's $6.80 makes for the best buy.

any previous price may be updated. A specific application of indices will be shown later in this chapter.

A buyer's own plant can often estimate likely production costs of a supplier so the buyer can show the supplier where he is out of line. The supplier may then reduce his own costs, perhaps by changing methods of processing. A typical example of open cost analysis resulted from advising a manufacturer his price was too high. By mutually reviewing the costs, the two determined that some "fringe quality" the engineers desired could be given up without lessening the functional quality of the end-product. This is not a rare case. An engineer may ask for a plus or minus .0005 inch tolerance in the specification, but upon learning about the cost disadvantage, may loosen the specification where the attribute is not critical.

Cost Analysis Tips for Buyers

Here are the general steps to take along with some hints to consider when performing a cost analysis:

- Review the specification with Engineering and Quality.
- Visit the supplier's plant to learn how the item is processed or assembled.
- Search out your company technical specialists and use their expertise.
- Get information from the supplier of either raw materials or components used in the manufacturing process.
- Break out the components of costs as best you can.
- Together with your team, make estimates where data are lacking.
- Compare the current prices requested by the supplier with your best estimate of what prices should be.
- Negotiate if you have grounds to raise questions.

Every price should not be suspected as padded or watered. It would be short-sighted to challenge all prices and tabbed a price haggler. Sellers often catch on to this, and build a pad into the initial quote—so in fact this can be a self-fulfilling prophecy! There should be a basis to believe the price is high. Profit is essential to the seller for the relationship to endure, but go for the "fat!"

The challenge is to determine whether a price is *fair*. These techniques of analysis can be used. To get as much information as possible from the supplier, use the simple pricing formula:

$$\text{[Manufacturing costs]}$$
$$\text{Price} = \text{material} + \text{labor} + \text{labor burden} + \text{SG\&A} + \text{transportation} + \text{profit markup}$$

In the above formula, selling general administrative costs (overhead costs) include general offices; executive salaries; office rental; and most non-manufacturing costs such as selling, and advertising. Should you be paying advertising costs for other standard products? These are the sorts of questions to pose to the supplier.

Profit is considered a "cost" of doing business. It's the reward for taking the risks and producing something of value. It is a return to those investing in the effort, and it is an element of cost that must be built into pricing or the business may fail.

Material cost includes that which goes directly into the product. Because it is often a large part of purchase price, the buyer should delve into what material will be used, as well as at what prices and in what quantities. It's important to know whether a material burden is used. In an actual dispute a buyer agreed the supplier would invoice "at their cost," which would include labor and burden, but no profit. Both parties felt it a fair settlement until 2 weeks later when an invoice called out "costs" as including a 50% material burden. In the eyes of the buyer, material burdens were unheard of, whereas the seller claimed since they had little labor, a large burden on material was always used. Be careful of all facts early in the negotiation game.

Direct labor cost is that needed to directly fabricate, assemble, and finish the product. This includes not just the wage rate, but also cost of fringes, benefits, and direct supervision. So, a wage earner at $10 per hour might have effective wages of $13.50 per hour.

This simple formula has reduced many a price for knowledgeable buyers who use it. At the very least, such analysis forms the grist around which the buyer can question and probe. Getting as much data as possible assists in making the buyer's case for lowest ultimate costs.

While some costs are usually classified as "fixed" and others as "variable," many accountants apply them as "direct costs" and "overhead costs." To accurately analyze a supplier' costs, buyers must distinguish between these type costs. Direct costs (fixed) include material and direct labor, and they are those accounted specifically to each unit produced.

Overhead cost (indirect and variable) includes material handlers, depreciation, repairs, and the factory costs—taxes, insurance, management salaries, and all else.

When monitoring price increases, it can be seen that a 5% increase in labor costs cannot justify a 5% increase in product price when material costs are holding steady. In a relevant example, upon being questioned about a company's announced increase, a supplier's president became flustered, and responded, "It's too much trouble; keep the price as it is." Another got so confused about his costs in a negotiation that he said they'd stay with present prices until they could study their cost completely. A year later the price remained unchanged.

If a supplier is charging research and development expenses to your job, but he is making the design your company has developed, get those costs out! Why should you pay for part of the supplier's development for other items?

Suppose the buyer has furnished certain components for assembly by a supplier. Should such a supplier be allowed burden on this material you've bought? Not unless he's expended time and effort and has the risks for spoilage, or other justifiable rationale.

Scrap and spoilage is another area for potential abuse when claiming high production costs. This means the price may be inflated, and is a difficult area to negotiate. Make sure the value of high-cost material scrap is deducted from product cost. Data in the *American Metal Market, Wall Street Journal,* and *New York Times* are close enough on base materials to allow judgment. Failure to eliminate excess scrap means you're paying inflated prices!

Among elements of costs are:

- Design engineering of product and manufacturing engineering of process

- Special tools, dies, and fixtures needed to make the product

- Facilities and equipment not used in other manufacturing

- Plant layout changes needed to produce

- Training of employees to meet new tasks and processes

Some definitions that buyers may confront, are:

- Economic costs refer to future cost of doing something relative to an alternative. If it cost $100 to build a machine 2 years ago, which has a further life expectancy of 3 more years, then an accountant would say its value is currently $60. But if the machine isn't needed, a salvage sale might bring $100. That amount is the economic cost.

- "Opportunity cost" is another term used to describe possible future economic benefits. It is a measure of the alternative earnings potential of funds that are tied up in doing a project instead of being invested elsewhere.

- Depreciation is the write-off of costs of an investment, or startup, that has been capitalized. This cost doesn't necessarily reflect actual cost outlays in any period.

Startup costs are charged to a specific production run, but are unaffected by volume produced. These costs can be added to direct costs, or treated as overhead. In either case, *failure to get these costs out of repeat business* easily disguises prices that are too high. Tooling and engineering costs are often separately stated within manufacturing costs, if they are a large part of expenditure. In such a circumstance, it may pay to buy special tooling outright, to remove it as an element of cost that won't be in future prices.

Fixed and Variable Costs

Using standard accounting procedures, the accountant groups overhead into fixed versus variable, and direct versus indirect cost elements. Some useful financial terms used in accounting are shown below.

Fixed costs are those the supplier incurs even if he didn't get your order, such as depreciation of the building, machinery, rent, etc. Even if nothing is produced, he still must pay such costs. *Period costs* are costs incurred that are spread over a certain time interval. Interest cost is an example.

Variable costs may be incurred specifically because the supplier fulfills your order. This may include materials consumed when processing, such as machining coolant, and abrasive disks. As with fixed costs, variable costs can be expressed in terms of a "per unit" or "total" basis.

Some costs are combinations of fixed and variable, such as:

- Margin costs (also called incremental costs) are extra costs resulting from making an extra unit of quantity. They include direct variable costs and any fixed costs if there is a new step level of costs.

- Full costs (total fixed and variable on a per unit basis) are established by adding the two unit costs together or dividing the total fixed and variable cost by the number of output units.

- Step costs vary with volume, but are fixed for short segments of volume spans.

- Semivariable are those partly variable, and partly fixed, such as heat, light and power, postage, and repair of equipment. Most accountants would include them in the variable category.

The challenge for the buyer is "How does a supplier allocate the above types of overhead costs?" If a supplier devotes a specific plant solely to the buyer's production, allocating the burdens can be straightforward. But usually other products are in process, so the supplier uses a percent allotment. The buyer must be sure he or she is not charged too high a percentage of these costs, which can be difficult to detect given that overhead rate estimates are often much less accurate than estimates for direct labor and materials.

Statistical and Graphic Analysis

Some buyers use statistics like a vagrant uses a lamppost—more to lean on than for illumination. There is some truth in this humorous simile. However, when properly applied, statistical analysis can provide valuable tools to the buyer when forecasting. Sometimes it's useful to know the average price, weight, or size of items bought. The average temperature in New York might be stated in degrees, but it doesn't tell you much about the highs and lows. The median is found by arranging items in order of magnitude and taking the magnitude of the midpoint of the total number.

Graphs are often overlooked as simple devices to study basic pricing structures. Figure 10-1 is an example of a statistical price comparison chart. It depicts two valve suppliers' prices along with proposed price increases.

Heuristic algorithms are a technical method for the application of numerical evaluations on heretofore subjective items. These algorithms use probabilities of risk. For an application example, if costs of copper increases processing costs of spiral fin tube, how will sales be affected? Most answers given on the job would be, "about the same" or "about a 10% increase." An algorithm would apply numerical probability evaluations in answering such a question; for example, an 80% probability that a 10% increase in price of tubing would cause a 5% loss of sales.

The NAPM PMI report is a good example of a *subjective assessment approach* to measure the manufacturing economy's changes. It is a compilation of selected specialists' opinions taken from various key industry purchasing chiefs. Surveys and decision trees are other examples of subjective approaches.

The *Delphi Forecast* is an intuitive method for collection of predictive statements circulated to experts, followed by successive rounds refining the opinions. The approach uses collective wisdom with anonymity, feedback of reasoning, and statistical control (to give the degree of confidence and unanimity). It's a means of projecting the earliest date something is likely to occur, as well as the average date and finally the latest estimated date. An example might be the answer to the question about when the computer would allow elimination of all

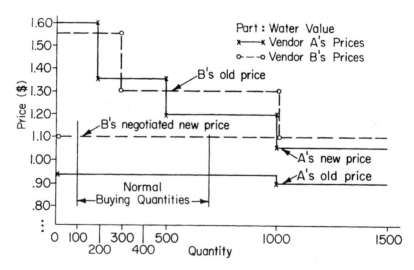

Figure 10-1 Price comparison of two suppliers' price breaks.

buying paperwork. In this remote example, the earliest might be the year 2000 and the utmost 2100! However, some believe it can be sooner.

The idea is to get estimates from a group of experts, none of whom are identified. By feeding back the results of the survey, letting them digest it, the experts resubmit their opinions. Some say this feedback should be repeated *ideally* three times. But, after two rounds, further refinement is usually seen as wasted effort—consistent with the concept of diminishing returns. Experience indicates that as experts learn the reasons for the others' opinions they modify theirs; and, as a group prediction accuracy is improved. It has been shown that three people's judgments are generally superior to one, so stimulation of ideas will produce more ideas.

While this method is useful, it is not necessarily reliable. There are objections to statistical treatment of nonquantifiable predictions such as "never." But Delphi, followed by face-to-face discussions, is said to almost always improve accuracy.

Other Mathematical Techniques

Technological forecasting is the process of using logical, reproducible methods to predict in quantifiable terms, the direction, characteristic rate, implications, and impacts of technological advance. An important part of measurements and statistical data is not the mere collection and graphic display of such, but the judgment and perspective so essential to interpret what is shown.

Technical forecasting can be broken down into: (1) expert opinion, (2) trend extrapolation (we touched on this earlier with the discussion of time series data and methods of predicting future prices), (3) systems analysis, (4) mathematical models, and (5) supplementary methods.

Other techniques of possible use are: (1) queuing, (2) gaming, (3) systems simulation, and (4) statistical decision theory. These are reviewed briefly below.

1. *Queuing.* Queuing develops waiting-in-line relationships, etc. Operations research finds the cost of the wait and compares it with the cost of doing something else to avoid the wait. An example would be determination of the preferred economic choice between increasing the number of service facilities or improving the handling speed of existing ones.

2. *Gaming.* Gaming features teams and score keeping. This can be a good training tool, though it's usually difficult to get realistic environments at the speed with which a game needs to be run. Games omit the pressures of performance, as "real life," rumors, personalities, relationships, and company policies are not usually brought into play.

3. *Systems simulation.* Systems simulation is the duplication of data by high-speed computer of the business or some aspect of it—such as its distribution pattern. Historical relationships are used to decide what will

happen if changes take place. Simulation differs from gaming in that in gaming, the buyers make the decisions, whereas in system simulation, buyers set the decision rules, and the computer sifts the data to provide the decision. The costs, revenues, profits, and other data affected by supply and purchasing actions are studied. A merit of simulation is that it is performed fast, so many different situations can be tried quickly.

4. *Statistical decision theory.* This is a means to determine if buyers have enough information to reach a decision, and the risk they take. It can help in evaluating whether a decision should be reached now, or deferred, and what would the costs be to wait?

Linear Programming

Linear programming is an operations research technique that is used to find how to make the best use of limited resources such as materials and labor. One use in purchasing is to determine how much material should be bought from several possible supply sources, when none of them can supply it all. Prices may vary from various suppliers and the technique will help supply the one answer that results in ultimate lowest cost, showing what quantities should be bought from each supplier.

Linear programming has proved useful in evaluating proposals for setting up distribution, or warehouses in different locations. Taken into consideration are transportation costs, flexibility for future growth, and the like, to gain efficiency, reduce costs, and improve customer satisfaction.

Break-even Analysis

Break-even analysis is a useful tool to the supplier when trying to determine when a production run turns a profit. The break-even point is defined as the point on the chart where total revenue equals total costs. Any volume below the break-even point loses money, while those volumes above it will make money. The buyer, armed with this information, can use these data in determining buy quantities and in negotiations of pricing. With respect to the latter area, the implication is that the supplier well within the high-profit area can afford to reduce his price.

Figure 10-2 diagrams how break-even is computed for an example of solving for X the exact quantity to achieve break-even. It may be computed as follows.

Given: (1) Break-even occurs where total costs = total revenue

          (2) Total costs = fixed costs + variable cost × no. of units

          (3) Total revenue = no. of units × unit price

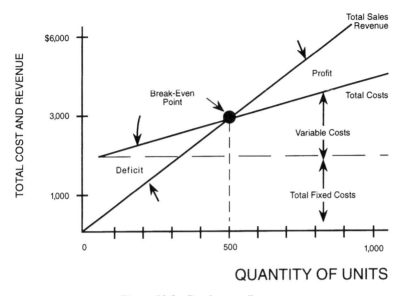

Figure 10-2   Break-even diagram.

Assumed facts: cost of item = $4.00, fixed costs = $1,000, and selling price = $6.

Total costs = $1,000 + $4.00 × X
Total revenue = $6.00X

So, 1,000 + 4.00 X = 6.00X

2 X = 1,000
 X = 500 units

In this example, the supplier's break-even is at 500 units. By changing the quantity we buy, we can see the result on the supplier's profit. If prices were raised to $7.00, the new break-even would occur at 333 units. But if labor costs (variable costs) rose, it might increase cost/unit to $4.50, so the break-even point would increase to 400 units.

Break-even is a tool to check sensitivity of prices and costs. Should prices be raised, what is the effect on other factors?

Producer Price and Consumer Price Indexes

The government provides useful tools known as the Producer Price Index (PPI) and Consumer Price Index (CPI). As an analogy, consider the homemaker's typical shopping basket for which prices of the same items are noted each month and a composite index is created of how food prices change. The government does exactly the same thing with industrial commodities, the result being a producer and a consumer price index issued by the U.S. Department of Labor, Bureau of Labor Statistics. These indices are useful tools to show price trends, and to update a previous price to a current target. Should a supplier quote a higher price than the target, the PPI gives a benchmark for negotiations of price. The PPI is arranged by stage of processing and by commodity, so as to be relevant to specific commodities.

The PPI is the composite price level for industrial and contractor goods. How is it created? Why should we care? Because this knowledge will be used to create our own company's market basket index (CMB), which will be useful as a buying performance measurement tool. Monthly price surveys are taken by the Bureau of Labor Statistics as of "the Tuesday of the week containing the 13th day of the month," which consists of about 1,250 individual commodity indices. Each number, 02 to 1599, is weighted for its impact on the overall price level. The PPI is our only realistic measure of industrial pricing levels on a national scale.

A current PPI of 1.279 for June 1996, which when compared to the reference date, 1985,[3] when the index was set at 100, tells us that what cost $1 in 1985 now costs $1.28. That's a 28% price rise. The PPI rise since January 1, 1996 was only 1.3% for the 6-month period.

Buyers can compute price inflation for any specific period of time by taking the difference between the numbers and dividing by the oldest number, which is then multiplied by 100 to give the change in percentage.

The CPI is a standard measure of the price level of retail goods and services. Computed similarly to the PPI, it includes consumer items such as insurance, housing, and food, to tell us the "price of living." The CPI index was 146.0 on June 1996. Since the base year of 1982 was equal to 100, that means that for every dollar it cost to live in 1982, it now costs $1.46, or 46% more than in the base year.

The CPI Detailed Report is issued monthly at $7.50 per copy, or $24 annually, from the U.S. Government Printing Office. For those buyers with contracts containing price adjustment clauses based on these indices, they can be read on the Internet at a subscription price. The site location is [http://stats.bls.gov]

Your Company Marketbasket Index

A company can create an index of its own purchases. It is computed by first determining the percentage of each major commodity purchased, as compared to total purchase volume. Then that resulting ratio is multiplied by the appropriate individual commodity government index within the PPI. The sum of the major commodities (about 15 or so for most companies will suffice) will give a single

---

[3] The official base years are the average of 1984 to 1986.

index number, which is the company composite index. Plotting this index monthly will provide a trend of the marketplace in which your buys are made.

This index can be used in highly inflationary times to determine appropriate price escalation. Also, it can be used in determining performance measurement based on difficulty of buying in the marketplace. However, it cannot be used as a true measure of purchasing performance since certain market price changes and product design changes in general are considered beyond the control of the individual buyer.

Some companies apply the above analysis to the overall materials budget. They have called this result the purchasing power index. This index relates price changes to the purchasing budget by reviewing relative buying power of dollars today compared to a past date. For example, for a CMB with a current index of 118, use this formula to determine the company's relative buying power:

$$\text{PPI} = \frac{100}{\text{Current index of item}} \times 100$$

This shows the company's buying power is about 85% of that in the base year. This type of information is useful for price negotiations as an aid to judge whether it's a buyer's or a seller's market. Without an understanding of the difficulty of buying, how can a management determine its cost savings or price reductions are valid and at levels that they should be?

Use of Standard Cost

Standard costs come into play in two ways. One is in price forecasting and the other is as a measurement in purchasing performance which is reviewed in Chapter 18.

A standard cost is the most commonly available method that companies use to monitor their costs. Anyone who had managed during the late 1970s and 1980s, when inflation was rampant, knows how management depends on accurate future cost projections. An inflation factor must be anticipated, or the company profit objective will be unattainable.

Under the standard cost method, prior to a new fiscal year the purchasing department uses its judgment (similarly to the Delphi forecast) to arrive at the percentage changes expected in the prices of all major categories of purchased goods during the 12 months when the standard cost will be in effect. One method is to rely on the buyers' judgment to evaluate expected percent changes of price of major purchases for the coming year. These figures can be reviewed with finance or management, who may concur or make alternative recommendations, usually on the basis of historical data or other meaningful criteria.

A monthly Purchase Variance (PV) report is prepared by finance, showing whether the department paid more or less than expected for any given item. If the expenditures follow the "standard," then purchases are "on target." A "favorable variance" at the end of the year may indicate good buying (or poor forecasting?). In any event, these data are useful for sales to adjust their product pricing in anticipation of rising costs. Table 10-1 shows a standard cost systems PV chart broken down by major categories, such as steel, copper, and motors. Note that $229,800 less than standard was paid for electrical items, for a 2.6% favorable variance. Overall, variance for all purchases indicates 1.7% of expected purchase cost was not paid out.

PV provides buyers a check to see how items were bought compared to the standard. This provides good question-raisers. If a plastic fan's price advanced

Table 10-1   Purchase variance from standard costs

	Standard cost performance			
	Purchases at standard cost	Purchases at actual prices paid	(Favorable) variance	%
Class 1: Steel				
Plate	$ 294,470	$ 264,785	$ (29,685)	(10.5)
Sheet	1,826,575	1,749,570	(77,005)	(4.2)
Bars	82,720	78,970	(3,750)	(4.6)
Total steel	2,203,765	2,073,325	(110,440)	(5.0)
Class 2: Nonferrous				
Copper	5,406,505	5,380,435	(26,070)	(0.5)
Aluminum	1,766,205	1,731,375	(34,830)	(2.0)
Total nonferrous	7,172,710	7,111,810	(60,900)	(0.9)
Class 3: Casting and Forgings				
Ferrous	2,697,005	2,618,175	(15,830)	(0.6)
Nonferrous	772,670	774,370	1,700	0.2
Total castings, etc.	3,469,675	3,455,545	(14,130)	(0.4)
Class 4: Electrical				
Motors	7,708,720	7,483,840	(224,880)	(2.9)
Starters, controls	994,210	989,290	(4,920)	(0.5)
Total electrical	8,702,930	8,473,130	(229,800)	(2.6)
Class 5: Fabricated products				
Fasteners	647,710	619,615	(28,095)	(4.3)
Stampings	1,048,350	1,042,765	(5,585)	(0.5)
Machined parts	377,645	376,045	(1,600)	(0.4)
Compressors	1,424,905	1,430,935	6,030	0.4
Total fab. prod.	3,498,610	3,469,360	(29,250)	(0.8)
Class 6: Miscellaneous				
Rubber and plastic	627,410	633,565	6,155	1.0
Miscellaneous	1,319,000	1,297,000	(21,495)	(1.6)
Total misc.	1,946,410	1,930,565	(15,340)	(0.8)
Total commodities	26,994,345	26,534,485	(459,860)	(1.7) Favorable actual $ less than standard

15%, a good question is "why?" Answering will tell something about the price change, problem with the fan, or possible error in the report.

PV is falling from favor in many companies as a means of measuring buyer performance, because it is so difficult to separate forecasting ability from the subsequent management of cost as the mechanism that produced the favorable variance. Tracking of variance is of value, and seeking the reason for high variances, however, remains valid.

PV provides management with a means to forecast profitability, and whether the company is able to meet cost estimations. The report is usually monthly, computerized, and broken into individual items for study. A 3-year PV trend chart provides continuity. A pitfall is to extend these data too far into the future, which leads to misleading information.

Certainly by now we can agree that prices are highly flexible and subject to continual change. By choosing from a wide range of purchase analysis techniques, buyers can rightfully claim to be the watchdog, or the keeper, of prices.

Strategy of Hedging Versus Forward Buy

Offshore buying confronts buyers even when they know the exact price to pay. For once the price is set, how can we make sure that price ends up as the amount we will pay when foreign currencies are involved? That becomes a critical issue when buying offshore. When a buy is in another currency, the possibility of translation losses affecting profitability becomes a significant management concern. The buyer will need to decide whether to buy in U.S. dollars or in the foreign currency *before* placing the order.

Before getting into the details of the hedging versus forward buy strategies, let's consider some basic definitions. "Currency" is the medium of exchange, such as coins, money, and bank notes. Hard currency is expected to rise versus the U. S. dollar, while soft currency is expected to drop versus the U.S. dollar. To decide in which currency to buy, buyers should study the exchange rate. That's the price at which one currency is bought (exchanged) for another. Factors that influence the rate are:

- Inflationary or deflationary trends of the two currencies.
- Relative value of the U.S. dollar to other currencies (current exchange rates).

If an increase is inevitable, getting advance warning allows the buyer to stock up at the old price.

Currency value has both a *level* and a *volatility* factor to be considered. Level is the number of pounds or marks required to buy one dollar, while volatility measures the rapidity of those currency fluctuations or level changes.

"Foreign exchange" is conversion of funds of one country into usable funds from another. The rate at which the exchange takes place varies frequently. Daily rates are published in most major newspapers for the prior day's trades on the International Monetary Market (IMM) of the Chicago Mercantile Exchange.

A "bid" is the price at which a price maker is willing to purchase a foreign currency. An "offer" is the price at which a price maker is willing to sell a foreign currency. The "dealing date" is the date that the deal was made. The "value date" is the day the deal is to be settled by either delivery or receipt of funds.

When an exchange takes place with other currencies, the issue of relative value occurs. As an example, a purchase order is issued in January with price in U.S. dollars. By the time shipment is made from Japan, let's say that the value of the yen has dropped 20% versus the dollar. From the Japanese perspective, they will receive 20% less value if dollars must be converted to yen. By the way, this is one reason the Japanese were buying American real estate rather than take translation losses as the yen lost so much value versus the dollar a few years ago.

The buyer has to determine in which currency to buy. When asking for quotes, it is a good idea to get the prices in both U.S. and foreign currency. Then, the buyer should consult with finance before making major buys, after becoming knowledgeable and up-to-date on currency fluctuations.

Ways to Minimize Risk

When buying in the foreign currency, buyers can try to negotiate a 50/50 currency fluctuation in their contract to help maintain balanced long-term relationships. Such risk sharing is used by about half of the buyers surveyed recently. Currency adjustments might be negotiated in advance and inserted as a clause in the purchase order. Such a clause might cover any of the following provisions:

- Equal sharing of gains or losses resulting from exchange rate changes
- A band or window set for currency adjustment: "If the exchange translation value varies + or − 5% from the price as of the date of this PO, an offsetting adjustment of that percentage will be made."
- An adjustment to be made at the time of delivery
- Adjustments for blanket orders to be made each month, quarter (or as otherwise determined appropriate)
- Use a forward buy, or
- Hedge through the use of futures or options

Using a "Forward Buy" Contract

The sooner buyers freeze the value at the time of payment, the better. By using the tactic of making a "forward buy" contract, buyers can protect their foreign currency exposure by buying or selling currency for future delivery. Buys can be made for delivery in 30, 60, 90, or 180 days. Special quotes for longer times can be obtained from the banker.

A forward buy contract eliminates the risk of exchange rates moving unfavorably to the buyer between the time the deal is made and the actual delivery date when funds are needed to make the purchase. For instance, if buyers know they must pay Italian lira in 90 days, they can make the deal today and be assured exactly what their costs will be. There is no separate fee charged as the bank's profit is in the price charged. This locks in the exact product costs and so the company's profit is secure.

How a Futures Hedge Works

Another buyer tactic is the "futures hedge." A financial futures contract is a buyer commitment to buy or sell a set amount of that currency at a future time. Futures contracts are commitments to buy ("long") or sell ("short") at a time in the future. Though exchange rates are not too predictable in the short range, they tend to move in cycles. The price is free to change with the market until the settlement date on the futures exchange.

A critical issue is when the contract is canceled by selling it. Although about 1% of contracts expire with the buyer taking possession of the currency, most will cancel by selling. There is a small commission fee paid and margin to be deposited when a futures contract is created. A gain or loss results from this financial transaction that will almost exactly cancel the corresponding opposite gain or loss from any exchange rate change in our purchase order transaction. Figure 10-3 depicts how the futures action cancels the price change.

In effect, the original profit expected based on the cost of products purchased was ensured. The fluctuation of currency was eliminated, or hedged, as the buyer froze the price level at close to the quoted price. The small fee paid is the insurance cost of eliminating risk. Note: some may hedge only half the total buy value, and accept the risk on the other half.

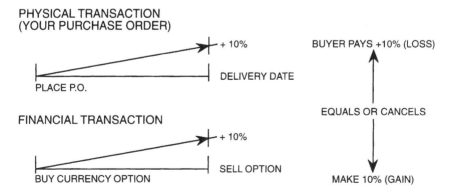

Figure 10-3 How the hedge action cancels out price changes.

Of course, if buyers take no action, and the dollar strengthens, they will come out with an extra gain. That's considered a speculation by many financial types, as we must remember that the *object is to be certain of costs—that is, to minimize fluctuation risk.* Companies are divided about the degree of risk to allow. These hedging activities are sophisticated tactics. Because high volumes of money can be made or lost in this manner, people doing the buying must not take the risk alone—they must have financial and management concurrence.

11

Negotiations—Keystone of Effective Buying

If we had to agree on only one key personal trait a professional buyer must possess, it would be the ability to negotiate. Most of us tend to underestimate our power to influence others.

Buyers need to negotiate proactively, taking the initiative. Simply sending out inquiries to potential suppliers asking, "What price would you charge us?" is not doing the job. This is only the first step. When all the quotations are in, it's up to the buyers to tell the suppliers what price they will pay. Once the prices are in, negotiations may begin. At this point, the difference in margins often spells success or failure. Some buyers are timid about price negotiations, thinking such discussions degrade themselves or their company. Others fear being labeled "price buyers." If the buyer is not getting better prices than anyone else could, then the buyer is not doing the job with optimal effectiveness.

Buyers in U.S. companies are often dealing with foreign governments who must approve and shape the deal. Negotiating with governments is more complicated than simpler negotiations with individual companies.

Offshore suppliers expect to do what we call "haggling" or "horse trading." Many offshore suppliers love to negotiate, seeing it as an act of "friendship and honesty." Americans call it an "auction" when a buyer gets supplier A to go below supplier B's price, then asks B to do better—this keeps up for some time. Buyers should always get a supplier's lowest price the first time, or else they may be wasting lots of time.

A negotiation is communication between the parties. Though not an exact science, techniques have been found that are of use to experienced negotiators. Webster defines "negotiate" in three ways:

- "To discuss a matter with a view to coming to terms about it"

- "To procure or arrange for by means of a discussion of terms"

- "Negotiation" is "a parley or conference regarding terms."

A powerful leverage effect is available to keep suppliers competitive when the buyer uses the marketplace. Negotiations in buying change depending on their intended purpose. These could include:

- Set a specific contract price.
- Revise existing prices either upward or downward.
- Change prices to meet adverse costs or operating changes.
- Get agreement in advance on terms and conditions.
- Settle various unforeseen commercial problems.

While most buying negotiations involve prices, many things other than *price* are negotiable; for instance, terms and conditions of the PO, changes in packaging, reduction of overhead rates, settlements of disputes and damaged goods, and so forth.

In face-to-face meetings, psychologists tell us that if you have a choice, take a chair where there is no barrier such as a desk between you and the other party. The removal of barriers serves to relax the participants.

The Negotiation Environment

Does a time constraint exist? If you must buy, and do it quickly, you are at a distinct disadvantage. We have to be prepared for negotiations to take longer. If it takes one hour, day, or week, to negotiate with Americans, it may take two times that with Europeans, and about six times that with the Japanese. It is possible to conclude a contract in 3 days, but only if most of the details are settled well in advance. Major agreements may take four, five, or more rounds of thorough discussion.

Be sensitive and tolerant to the time needed to reach consensus decisions— especially when dealing in the international environment. The American may perceive vacillation while, in reality, consensus is being reached.

Location of the meeting and channels of communication are important. It is not always desirable to negotiate in your host's office. Set the meeting to begin at a time that will allow for a relaxing lunch at a proper time. People are always more agreeable (though sometimes drowsy) after eating.

Personal characteristics give us clues to the tendency to take risks, or play it safe. Is there a tolerance for ambiguity or not? How interested is the seller in making a deal? Sometimes a negotiation is fruitless, especially when one side isn't interested in settling or agreeing. Both sides must want an agreement to succeed.

Do your homework thoroughly! There is no substitute for advanced planning leading to a sound negotiation strategy. Some advance thought should be given to such questions as: What information is to be given? Have goals and priorities been set? What are your target prices? Are there concessions you'll make?

A tremendous negotiation lever is available to keep domestic suppliers competitive when the buyer uses the global marketplace. Don't overlook it. Basics of negotiation don't change because the buyer is negotiating internationally. Yet, there are differences to explore in an expansion of procedures.

Negotiation Strategy

Negotiation strategies can be broken down into these six key activities:

- Prepare for negotiations—database/forecast.
- Define objectives—your position limits.
- Organize your team.
- Develop a strategic plan.
- Control the climate or behavior.
- Seek alternative solutions to achieve "win–win" results.

Many buyers think that for them to win the negotiation, the other party must lose. Not so! In fact, most successful negotiations are "win–win." The buyer gets a measure of what he or she wants and so does the seller, though perhaps neither achieved everything they'd wanted. Recall a negotiation is a mutual bargaining discussion, to arrive at terms that are *agreeable to both parties*.

What are your expectations? Who has the authority to make final decisions? Be aware of restrictions on the seller's authority. Can he sign or negotiate agreements without approval? Ask him! Sense the relative power of the parties—who is the boss? But more important, *who makes the pricing decision?*

Most of us don't plan for negotiations as well as we should. Plan the agenda ahead to your advantage. Brief team members beforehand so none of them tips your hand, or gives up a point before you do. Make sure your negotiation team agrees on the overall strategy. More specifically, ask yourself:

- Have goals and priorities been set?
- What are your target prices?
- What is the location of the meeting and channels of communications?
- Who will do the talking?
- Who will keep minutes for distribution, etc.?
- How will you handle disagreement among your team members?
- Who has the authority to make final decisions?

Does trust exist in the business relationship? Ask yourself if you believe there is a basis for negotiation. Does the supplier have something to give? If there's no room for give and take, the negotiation may be a waste of time, as both sides must want an agreement. It pays to work for a trusting and open relationship. You must meet the right people. If people don't know you, it doesn't matter what the proposal or price is. So, buyers must first establish good relationships based on trust.

Let's now apply some limited cultural issues to our negotiations. Most effective negotiators focus on what they *need to have*—not stated *wants*. For example, if someone says, "I want an apple"—his or her stated position may be that he or she *wants* an apple—but actually, the need is based on *hunger*. Your bargaining chips are that you have a sandwich and banana. Offering either will fulfill his or her underlying need to overcome being hungry.

Another example: two chefs both want an orange, but you have only one. Based on their *wants* you can't win, but upon exploring their *needs* you find one needs an orange for juice while the other needs grated rind for pie flavoring. Applying that to the job—a salesperson tells you, "I *want* a higher price, but in reality the need is greater profit! Offering greater volume or lower manufacturing costs may satisfy that need.

As previously noted, while negotiation techniques may be used worldwide, the major challenge is to *apply them with an understanding of the cultural and business practices* of the other party. Cultural variations are not right or wrong—simply variations that must be recognized.

Professional purchasing managers usually leave lawyers out of actual negotiation meetings. So, consult them and follow their advice, but consider leaving them at home when negotiating a domestic as well as an overseas purchase. Having a lawyer present may be seen as a threat to sue and as a lack of confidence in the negotiation outcome.

Define your position limits by setting targets and goals as a team. Commitments must not be given before the resolution of major negotiation goals are met. Have reasonable goals and expectations—usually a minimum and maximum position.

Remember that personal values of the negotiator are non-negotiable. Successful negotiations are the result of dedicated effort to improve by following proven techniques.

Implementing Tactics and Negotiation Checklist

Tactics of buying change depending on whether it's a buying or selling market. One commodity may be easy to get, while another is in scarce supply. In the latter case, buyers must often "sell" to get the goods instead of someone else. This is where partnerships can help!

In a seller's market, the skilled buyer/negotiator with better interpersonal skills—with the ability to set up trusting relationships—will shine, as he or she is politically adept at getting along well. In this market, a tough purchasing manager may be seen as out of touch by his management, so to be truly effective, buyers should adapt their style to suit the situation at hand.

Negotiation Checklist ("Do's and Don'ts")

This time-tested tactics checklist[1] provides ideas for conducting a win–win negotiation strategy:

Do

- Find out if the seller is interested in making a deal. There is a time when negotiation is fruitless, especially when one side isn't interested in settling or agreeing.
- Negotiate with those who can make concessions. Often a seller has a range of prices to submit. They may be able to drop prices, say 5%, without prior management approval.
- Negotiate at home when possible—and be seated somewhat together. (Don't be trapped into swiveling your head as at a tennis match!)
- Be patient! Patience is one of the most important attributes of the negotiator. Few successful negotiators plunge in and try to wrap everything up too quickly.
- Enlist the aid of team specialists in manufacturing, finance, and engineering to help evaluate tooling and other special costs. Purchasing research will help supply basic data necessary for negotiating in depth.
- Expect to get some concessions. Be confident of facts presented. Divert attention if the negotiation hits your weak points. Shift to minor points that you may choose to concede later.
- Use techniques such as cost and value analysis that provide grist for discussion on how to reduce prices.
- Negotiate for the long pull—not the short-sighted advantage that may backfire at the first turn of economic conditions.
- Remain silent at times! Often greater concessions result from a seller's fear of losing business. Suppliers may talk themselves into a better settlement than the buyer expected.
- Know what you can expect to gain by negotiating. Keep that target in mind. Be reasonable about what the supplier can give.

---

[1] First published in the late 1960s when the senior author wrote the American Management Association's Bulletin #50, "Developing the Negotiating Skills of the Buyer." This updated version is timely today.

- Plan ahead! Prepare the agenda to your advantage. Brief team members beforehand so none of them tips your hand, or gives up a point before you do.
- Set the meeting to begin at a time that will allow for a coffee break or perhaps a relaxing lunch. Call a recess if talks hit a snag!
- Confirm the agreement in writing, and *always be fair!*

Don't

- Tip your hand too easily!
- Accept the first thing or idea tossed out. When acknowledging the other side's point of view, the buyer doesn't have to agree with it.
- Get so bogged down in details that the overall objectives are lost. Many a session occurs where agreement was there, only to have someone keep negotiating and lose it.
- Use information you know is wrong or weak that strains your credibility as you are forced to acknowledge the facts.
- Try to prove the supplier is wrong! You may succeed in embarrassing them and winning your point, but you've damaged your relationship.

Negotiation Fundamentals from a Global Perspective

Even if we conduct most of our business domestically, a global perspective can help us to better understand the subtle cultural differences between the parties of a business transaction. As an example, consider that business is conducted at a different pace in New York City than in the rural South. Moreover, distance between the parties increases the chance of misunderstandings. But unlike the obvious cultural differences we recognize when working internationally, sometimes we experience such differences even in the domestic arena. Our global awareness, then, can help us to become more sensitive to those differences, even when they are more subtle in nature, as in the case of the New Yorker doing business with the individual from Louisiana. The point is that even local negotiations require a sensitivity to your business partner's cultural differences to be effective. However, because cultural differences are magnified when dealing overseas, we will focus primarily on these international differences as they provide stark examples of the point made.

Lack of knowledge of the foreign supplier's culture has long been a weakness of American negotiators. Too often, our American buyer is seen as too direct and impersonal. In a hurry to conclude an agreement, his or her impersonal approach often offends the sensitivities of foreign sellers. That result is clearly unintentional. Better understanding of others' culture and practices through study, travel, and experience all help overcome this roadblock.

Cultural similarities and differences have been documented and studied. Though we have such a diversity of ethnic cultures that borrows from all races and nations, business culture in the United States is unique. For example, we do business first, then build a relationship. Business people in virtually every other culture in the world *build relationships* before doing business.

Americans often inadvertently make blunders. When you meet someone do you touch his shoulder or grab his arms? People from many cultures (notably those in Europe and the Far East) feel ill at ease when touched—other than when shaking hands. Do you pass food with your left hand? That's highly offensive in some countries, where the left hand is used for bodily functions, leaving solely the right for eating.

We have to be slow to criticize and not offend or insult any visitor or host. "Loss of face" is not just an issue relevant to the Far East. Many American buyers believe in fairness and "playing by the rules," though sometimes we exhibit a tendency for "one-upmanship." We have "win/lose" value systems— if he wins, then I must lose. Competition is revered in America! Competitive skills are honed not only in our sports, but also in our businesses. Children naturally "keep score." "Who has the most marbles?" Who's the strongest? It's natural in our culture, but the knowledgeable buyer must recognize this is not the case worldwide.

It was no fluke that Americans got to the moon first. We pride ourselves on being No. 1. We're idealists and romanticists. We believe in the American dream—anyone can come here and make it if they persevere. Some American buyers are described as having a macho "I'm in charge" style, and are often referred to as "John Wayne" negotiators—"take it or leave it!"

We can't hope to know all cultures, and can't include them here. In this section, we will focus on the Canadian, Mexican, and American cultures, as the North American Free Trade Agreement (NAFTA) frames our collective destinies to work together.

Canadian Culture

Most Americans don't consider Canadians foreigners, so they may believe there are no cultural differences. Americans have to be mindful that Canadians can be sensitive about French and English relationships. Canadian culture is entwined with American because of geographical closeness and strong trading relationships. Coupled with the close contacts, the background of many Americans parallels the Canadian experiences. The same European powers played an important role in shaping the U.S. as well.

"Canada" is an old Iroquois Indian name meaning "group of huts." Early French settlers founded "New France." The French/Canadians had to escape the

222 / Purchasing and Supply Management: Creating the Vision!

fierce Iroquois Indians to the South. Canada's early settlers battled along with the British and French who were both vying for new territory. New France was heavily populated and settled by soldiers, and even the civilians bore arms. This fit into their culture of a militarist type government. In fact the governor's chief duty was to fight the Indians.

"New France" in the St. Lawrence valley and "New England" each encouraged settlement to maintain their claims. Though caught up in England's and France's wars, since the War of 1812, the U.S. and Canada have maintained what is regarded as the longest open and friendliest border in the world.

Following American independence in 1776, many Americans loyal to the Crown moved into Canada. Some Canadians of French heritage moved into the U.S. but most remained where they were, with divided loyalties. Canada has two basic cultural heritages. About half of all Canadians are of British descent, while one-third are descendants of earlier French immigrants. French Canadians have kept their language and customs.

Two-thirds of Canadians live in the St. Lawrence and lower Great Lakes lowland regions. The French-speaking Quebecois have in the past threatened to establish a separate nation. The Separatist movement is active and always present in eastern Canada. Accommodations have been made to keep the country unified, but it remains a struggle.

So, there are cultural differences that over the years have tended to meld into what some might call a North American culture. Some Canadians say they have picked up some of the best traits in their heritage from contacts with the British, French, and Americans. They mention leaving behind some of the negative aspects of these three societies.

Canadians like a polite and perhaps slower pace in getting into business details. They use first names, but wait a bit with new acquaintances. They will invite you too, when they detect you're being polite and friendly. Be wary of coming on as being too overpowering in your relationships.

Canadians sometimes express a dislike of being talked down to by some Americans. Americans are perceived as being somewhat arrogant, often lacking knowledge and appreciation of Canadian culture. In business, more appreciation by Americans about the importance of the strong relationship of trade with Canada would be welcomed!

Canada's government is committed to free-trade principles. NAFTA will gradually eliminate all restrictions between these two great trading partners. While benefiting both nations, some Canadians express worry that being "too cozy" could result in gradual loss of their cultural identity. The American buyer should be sensitive to this concern.

Certainly negotiations would not be unlike in the United States, but in dealing with a French-speaking company, an interpreter might be helpful. And although lack of easy conversation will make for more formality, most all companies have bilingual employees to ease communication difficulties. This is particularly the case outside of French-speaking Quebec.

Mexican Culture

Like Canada, Mexico is a valued, though smaller, partner under the NAFTA umbrella. Spanish influence affects its cultural norms. However, unlike other Latins who say they are descendants of the Spanish, Mexicans say, ". . . when we were *conquered* by the Spanish." Many Mexicans consider themselves as having an Aztec heritage.

Protocol and social competence are admired. Shake hands upon meeting business people, but wait to see if women offer theirs. A slight bow may suffice for some.

Direct contact within Mexico is preferred and much business will be done through acquaintances in place of official channels. Friendliness and courtesy together with sensitivity to Mexican culture and independence will help to smooth relations.

Mexico's official language is Spanish and the predominant religion is Roman Catholic. Mexicans have strong feelings about their neighbors to the north sometimes bordering on paranoia. As one explained, "When we look at a map we always see the big U.S. sitting on our shoulders." Unless there have been previous contacts, there can be a suspicion about Americans motives. As is said, "We sleep with one eye open." As with most cultures, Mexicans can be sensitive to comparisons and condescension. They most certainly don't like to be reminded of the U.S. border invasion by a small subset of their countrymen. Proud of their independence, they sometimes understandably complain when the word "America" is applied exclusively to U.S. citizens.

Decisions are highly centralized. Managers decide without much consultation with lower levels. Prices can swing considerably. So negotiate them down! The Mexican negotiator may be selected by his social standing and not his technical talent. It may be more important that he have the proper family ties and political influence.

Because trust and compatibility are important in Mexican negotiations, center heavily on personal aspects. Deliberations are usually cautious and a better deal will often be forthcoming. Although on occasion Mexicans may appear to be overly dramatic and emotional to Americans, they see themselves as more reserved than brasher Americans. They prefer behind-the-scenes bargaining, and may see little value in direct negotiation exchanges.

Mexicans expect you to socialize with them before dealing. And business schedules should not preclude involvement with their family or friends. In formal meetings, informational charts, samples, and models are of help and appreciated. Some Americans report that after verbal arrangements are concluded, they are rescinded later, so as elsewhere, there is no substitute for a formally documented agreement. Some Americans feel Mexicans are too relaxed in their scheduling of appointments. You must allow for more time to conclude arrangements and be patient.

Most businessmen take no siesta, but use the 2 hour time for lunch and socializing. Between 2 and 5 p.m. is the time for the main meal. Dinner is around 8:30, and it's not courteous to arrive early. The spouse is often invited. If you go to the home, flowers for the hostess are always welcomed. A thank you and a phone call afterwards are common courtesies.

Certainly the above are sketchy ideas on complex cultural issues for the major cultures American buyers most likely will engage. They serve to point out cross-cultural frictions Americans tend to overlook. Hopefully the next time you deal with our trading partner suppliers, recalling some of these cultural issues will help you be a more sophisticated global negotiator. And, being more sensitive to American culture will help us on our home ground.

Americans want people to get to the point; after all, a favored expression begins with "the bottom line is". We are in a greater hurry. Foreigners are repeatedly told to plunge right into the subject. Conversely, the advice to Americans is to "count to ten" when waiting for replies to questions. In fact, the single most important piece of advice in dealing with foreigners is *"Be patient!"*

Communication is almost always the greatest problem for most negotiators worldwide. Shockingly, many Americans upon travel abroad find that despite much progress in recent years, many foreign people still speak foreign languages! Seriously though, for most negotiators worldwide the primary impediment to getting a good deal is lack of communication.

Address Alternative Solutions to Gain Concessions

When making a concession, don't give it too quickly or easily! Moreover, "Quid pro quo"— *ask* for something in return. And when conceding, do so graciously without haggling. Remember, when it's all done, *both parties should be reasonably satisfied about the deal.*

If the negotiator asks no questions or doesn't know what's going on, then he or she is not performing the job effectively. Ask lots of questions! Questions are far superior to statements that may offend. They allow a touchy point to be put on the table in an inoffensive manner. And, they help when probing for information.

"Why?" and "Why not?" can be effective questions, as well as "What do you want?" Another approach is to make a statement that implies a question. Here are other simple questions to use—What if we:

- Give you a 1- or 5-year contract?
- Drop your warranty?
- Allow you to manufacture during off-season?

- Supply you with technological help?
- Change your contract to a long-term blanket order?
- Make progress payments?
- Change our specs to what you'd prefer to make?
- Provide certain materials and components?
- Buy a higher quality?
- Double our order?
- Buy all your output?

Perhaps you can think of many others! All these questions give the supplier alternatives that make it easier to perform. Most importantly, they provide the buyer with issues to discuss. Asking questions is a sound technique toward finding solutions of mutual satisfaction.

Despite the best of planning and intentions, a negotiation may reach an impasse. Sometimes buyers have to learn not to plunge ahead without slowing down. You might liken it to driving a motor boat through seaweed. Gradually the motor propeller fouls and turns ever slower as the boat slows to a crawl. You can't get out of the weeds by racing full speed ahead. By reversing the propeller the debris is cast off. Then you can resume full speed. In business, sometimes the negotiator makes no progress heading straight at the problem. Turn around, go into reverse until the hazard clears. Then go ahead once again toward your target. In this light, an impasse may be acceptable—and even planned—as part of the negotiation strategy!

Avoiding the Pitfalls—How Not *to Blow It!*

We can learn from negative negotiation actions. Save some bargaining chips to use to get rid of a stumbling block, especially if parties begin to change previously agreed positions or issues.

Members of a team can provide unknowing obstacles to successful negotiations. The following is a list of stumbling blocks guaranteed to blow any negotiation:

- Letting the supplier know there is no other source available. (Of course, this is somewhat at odds with supplier partnering, if single sourcing is practiced)
- Boasting how much money you will make on your deal. The supplier will feel he has a good share of that coming to him, so it's better to stress how competitive your marketplace is, and your concern that the supplier must help you meet that market.
- Divulging authority limitations. Making a statement such as, "I've got to clear it with the boss" weakens your negotiation power. Moreover,

it may cause the seller to visit the boss! (However, divulging authority limitations may be acceptable in limited cases where the buyer is being pushed into an untenable position that requires a temporary escape!)

- Not knowing what you want. Letting the supplier do the selecting can be acceptable in some instances. However, it usually allows the seller to get the best deal regardless of your true needs. As in a store, you won't often get the best buy unless you know exactly what you want and go after it.

- Waiting until the last minute to spring a major issue. Better to outline it early—otherwise, the late admission may submarine the entire negotiation!

- Giving up information on the seller's competition. Casual statements over lunch, such as "They can't furnish the plastic models we want," or "They quoted us $10 each" ensures you'll get prices just a small amount lower. Moreover, if you'll talk about the seller's competition in the seller's presence, he will always wonder what you are telling the competitor about his company!

When an agreement is reached, always reduce the discussions to writing. Your record keeper should be accurate. Simple language should be used with short sentences for clarity. Joint memoranda of understanding prepared while negotiating can be signed by both parties. By jointly agreeing to the final wording, this becomes part of the negotiation process as loose ends are tied together.

Sales are made in part with emotions, and not solely logic. Emotions can be studied by body language. Some experts claim that 90% of communicating is by other than word meanings. Someone may say something that he does not mean, but his mannerisms will give him away. Body language is an overlooked part of communications, which can be broken down into various categories: facial expressions, eye contact, posture, movement, speech, tone of voice, and attitude. We can learn from these nonauditory cues:

- *Facial expression.* We tend to like someone with a ready smile.

- *Eye contact.* We rely on our perceptions of others. Many of us believe that someone is more honest if he maintains eye contact. Didn't your mother ask you to "Look me in the eye and tell me you didn't eat those cookies?"

- *Posture.* Someone who leans forward is seen as interested, when compared to someone laid back and relaxed with legs crossed. Crossed folded arms sometimes tell us a person is unfriendly or closed to change or suggestion.

- *Movement.* Drumming your fingers, fiddling with rings, or tapping your foot are all distractions that give others a feeling of impatience, or little interest in their ideas.

- *Speech pattern.* Rate, volume, and clarity of speech affects how your message is received. Advance preparation allows you to speak comfortably. People can listen at 400 words per minute, yet we speak at about 200. Listeners have "free time" to notice many little distractions while speakers think about what to say next.

- *Tone of voice.* What you say is often lost in how you said it! Tone of voice conveys more meaning than words. Nervous people raise their voice, so if so inclined, you need to be confident to convey a positive upbeat tone.

- *Attitude.* Attitude is important! You will need to be a good communicator, patient, even tempered, and not easily frustrated. A sense of humor may help. To achieve a successful negotiation one must use persuasion and arguments, both emotional and logical.

Buyers need to watch out for symbols and gestures that may not be what we think! The "V" for victory is usually recognized, but many other symbols aren't. Be wary of using hand signals as they may not convey the message intended! Tapping the side of the head in some parts of Europe implies "something is crazy here," while a similar gesture in the Netherlands conveys the message, "How clever, or smart."

In ancient Rome, the thumbs down symbol said it all! Hitchhiking with a fist and the thumb is an obscene gesture in Australia. The thumbs-up symbol, given with a quick clockwise jerk of the right hand, is a Brazilian's way of showing approval. But to an Iranian, it is the filthy sign.

The hand symbol of 0 with three fingers means "OK" in the U.S., "zero" in France, and "money" in Japan, while in Germany and Brazil its meaning is an obscene reference. Consider this true story about the dedication of an American company's new Brazilian operation. The government officials were present along with local plant officials and their wives and families. Public relations, wanting to be dramatic, decided to have their top executive whisked away in a helicopter from the assembled crowd after the dedication ceremonies.

The helicopter hovered above as the excited crowd below watched with impressed interest. The American executive leaned toward the window and with a big grin, gave the Brazilians the infamous hand symbol. Imagine the repercussions!

A Negotiation Settlement

A true-life negotiation settlement may help bring together some of the issues just reviewed. A large metal fabricator was unable to keep up with the volume of self-made parts for a new product. The company turned to a smaller nearby company to help. Needing the work, the smaller company struck a friendly agreement to begin at once.

An engineer was placed at the disposal of the subcontractor to clarify details about the special nature of the work required. Because of urgency, a verbal approval to begin work was given. A purchase order followed shortly, approving an hourly rate, plus the cost of various materials to be itemized.

Several weeks passed with no parts being approved as acceptable to the large company's quality people. After joint efforts to solve the problems, exasperation began to set in. The subcontracting supplier felt his reputation was at stake, and resented being pushed by the larger neighboring plant. Soon, it became evident that the standards of the buying plant were not being met, so by mutual consent the contract was canceled, since only one acceptable unit was produced out of 30 started.

An invoice was submitted to the buyer amounting to $12,000 based on work performed. Twenty-nine units were scrapped, so the one acceptable unit cost $12,000 instead of an in-house cost of $400. The smaller company felt they had tried to help to the best of their ability, and did not believe they should lose money on this venture. They said their interpretation was that the buyer had simply purchased their labor to do the job; further, because the buying company had its engineer located at their production facility, and because this engineer dictated the methods of operation, the subcontractor was not responsible for output and performance. They went on to add that if they could have used their own judgment and methods, the quality would have been satisfactory. They contended that they could have produced to the required standards had they been in charge.

How would you view the basic issues of this case? How would you go about negotiating a fair settlement? Consider these questions before reading the actual settlement, which follows.

A settlement was reached that provided that the subcontractor be reimbursed for the materials and labor expended. The buyer believed the supplier had acted in "good faith" in trying to "help out" in an emergency, so should not suffer a loss. He negotiated an allowable profit that was a third of that expected. All unused materials were promptly returned. Both parties agreed not to blame the other, or hinder a possible future relationship. Obviously, poor preliminary work in spelling out the agreement caused a good deal of the trouble in this case. The moral is that even in emergencies, it's always best to anticipate possible problems and cover contingencies in the purchase order.

Negotiations remain the heart of the purchasing job. It is a never ending task. How well it is done determines to a large extent the difference between a paper-placing function and a profit-oriented arm of management.

Regardless of outcome, even if a disappointment, remember to part on friendly terms (unless using disappointment is a specific short-term tactic to achieve a long-term result). It pays to work for a long-term and open relationship, as there will always be another day and another buy.

12

Global Supply Demands Technical Buying Cooperation

The new global buying game is technologically oriented! Using the greater *worldwide technology* exposure helps a company to become globally competitive. The technical buyer and purchasing engineer jobs become more vital as the supply base problems become more technical. For "partnerships" between suppliers and buyers to flourish where companies work together instead of as adversaries, managements expect increased technical expertise from their buyers.

On the lighter side, this would appear to be a difficult task given the difficulties of interaction between the players, as indicated in the "old chestnut":

> "An engineer is said to be a person who knows a great deal about very little, and who goes along knowing more and more about less and less until finally he or she knows practically everything about nothing, whereas:

> "A salesperson on the other hand, is a person who knows a very little about a great deal and keeps knowing less and less about more and more, until he or she knows practically nothing about everything;

> "A buyer starts out knowing practically everything about everything, but ends up knowing nothing about anything due to association with engineers and salespersons."

On a more serious note, purchasing managers (PMs) must ensure that their department is provided with the technical know-how to work successfully with operating departments, or that buyers can do the job themselves. Purchasing must be proactive, taking the initiative, or it will be relegated to accepting the role of a clerical "confirmor" of what others decide to do.

Purchasing research is the systematic study and analysis of any purchased item or procedure. The goal is to either improve the purchase or reduce costs. About one-third of U.S. companies have used a small research staff of one or two people, while about two-thirds report they have no staff research personnel but depend on the buyers to handle their own commodities. The larger a department the more likely it is to employ researchers. One survey reported an average of about seven staff personnel in a large company, though the function has been hit by recent downsizing initiatives in American industry. If advantages of research are not to be lost, each buyer has to become more technically knowledgeable.

Analysts may participate with the buyer during negotiations to provide data backup. If a supplier submits a low-ball price, research delves into the situation with manufacturing and engineering to make sure the supplier is not trying to buy in on the business only to increase prices in the near future. Analysts are particularly helpful in make-versus-buy analyses. An analyst can uncover the facts that help buyers negotiate with suppliers.

Through analysis, purchasing has been able to procure materials at lower cost and acquired better control of long-range buying. Further, newer materials can be placed in engineering hands more quickly, and be in the company's products at an early stage in their development.

The Reengineering Process

"Reengineering" was defined in Chapter 2. What better place to use it than when giving thought to purchasing and engineering's joint role? Unlike other business functions that *must* work together, engineering can exist quite well within its own confines. If a cooperative effort is to exist, usually it will be purchasing that has to initiate the contact. And, it is purchasing that must create the vision!

This chapter delves into the serious relationship between the purchasing and engineering disciplines. With both working with the supplier's salespeople, a triangular relationship is formed.

When reengineering, it helps to review proven existing programs and techniques to adapt to today's demanding challenges. Some say, "Do whatever adds value and/or eliminates waste. In short, keep things 'clean and mean' ". That's a philosophy that has led to outsourcing, downsizing, and reengineering.

Although many artists and scientists and other individuals are quite prolific until very late in life, tests indicate that creativity generally drops 90% between ages 5 and 7, and by age 40 an individual is only about 2% as creative as when at age 5.[1] Psychologists believe that the filtering process is so strong in most people that they tend to block out new and creative thinking because of inhibitions or fear of ridicule. The thought is that if the filtering process could be detached from the creative generation of ideas, creativity would be enhanced—a contention that has led to the concept of "brainstorming"—allowing someone to express whatever comes to mind without fear of ridicule or of being analyzed.

When someone comes up with what later proves to be a great idea, the thought almost always is expressed as an analogy with another situation known to the

[1]"Business Probes—the Creative Spark," Niles Howard. *Dun's Review,* January 1980.

group—that is, it is an adaptation of another concept. For example, the idea of packing seeds in a dissolvable tape to be planted in the ground is said to have resulted from association of a machine-gun belt!

Creative responses do not always come from the engineer's logical 1, 2, 3 approach, but rather from the releasing of repressed ideas from free association where ideas may fly off in every direction. Every music pattern consists of no more than 12 notes, yet look at what Chopin and Beethoven have written with them! The pianist picks up sheet music 100 years old and the melody is played exactly as it was composed. The notes, or "symbols," unlock the door!

Our language is put together with only 26 letters. Paintings use only three primary colors. All mathematical equations have but 10 Arabic symbols, and computers differentiate simply between 0 and 1. All sculptural and mechanical inventions are confined to just three spatial dimensions; so when we look at something as "new," or creative, we are only looking at different shapes, forms, and patterns that have already existed before in some basic form.

We need more symbols in the business world, more pictures or images, more recognition of roles to play, to better understand and coordinate business conditions. And business people often find that difficult! Like something a child makes with building blocks, all progress is pyramidal.

The development of the personal computer is a classic study of assembling building blocks. IBM first made its neglected small PC models by simply assembling existing components. Then Steve Jobs adapted the "friendly" visual image projection developed by Xerox's Palo Alto Labs. IBM enlisted Bill Gates to let them use Microsoft's DOS operating system, then developed their own OS/2. Microsoft subsequently developed the popular Windows® platform which remains the industry standard today. And the beat goes on . . .

Creative management begins with a commitment, involvement, and motivation. With our minds on innovative thoughts, we're now ready to grapple with the practicality of the job situation. The basic techniques of purchasing change little over time. However, our vision changes. Critical success factors for technical buying or purchasing engineering are listed below:

- Awareness of the global environment
- Knowledge of your products and processes
- Knowledge of suppliers' capabilities
- Education or experience (engineering background desirable) to comprehend the technology
- Experience in interpreting drawings and specifications
- Ability to perform make-versus-buy analysis
- Ability to perform cost/price and value engineering analyses
- Ability to access information through your company—engineering, manufacturing, quality, etc.

Engineering is one of the true cornerstones of a company's success; without good engineers the company will be mediocre at best. And engineering must be supported in its search for new products and ideas, as it must approve changes that result in improved products or cost savings. For its part, engineering must translate research ideas into marketable products, a process that requires the balancing of many factors to achieve reliable commercial design.

The Design Engineering Process

New designs are continually conceived. Testing and evaluations need to be reviewed with suppliers, and adjustments made when: (1) customers demand changes after a design is in production, (2) a manufacturer provides a replacement for obsolete parts, or (3) a supplier stops making certain components.

Supplier technology should be used, not avoided! Innovative materials, components, and products should be explored during development and design change times. The degree of complexity often determines the extent of interchange. Design review teams, with qualified suppliers participating, are often needed for military or technical products. This should preferably be done before the design is finalized.

Design integration and cooperation between the specifying and supplying organizations is needed to achieve a balance between the product's quality, cost, and value for the end-use customer. Per a sales engineer, "If someone says they have a problem—and they're cooperative, I'll give an extra pound of effort." She maintains she'll stay in the office until late in the evening to help out the cooperative customer. You build "credits and debits" with the customer.

Need for Follow-up of Design Engineers

If new product design target costs were not achievable on early production models, cost reductions can still be achieved. Changes must be made with purchasing knowledge so a supplier's price increase can be minimized. If a certain change makes the product easier to make, perhaps a price reduction is in order. But buyers can't expect the supplier to speak up—so the engineer must consult the buyer, who can make the price adjustment.

Purchasing often represents the supplier input, such as pricing, availability, etc. Purchasing should take the lead to search out and screen world-class suppliers. Its mission is to make available such information in advance, so it can be quickly fed to engineering as appropriate. Engineering and purchasing together must see that information is fed into the process of designing and developing new products.

Table 12-1 shows who will handle the purchasing/engineering interface based on the objective being addressed. The priorities given to various joint objectives by a purchasing and engineering team change, depending on whether the design is in existence or is new.

Table 12-1   Purchasing/engineering technical interface matrix

	Purchasing best performed:		Priority	
Objective	Plant	Headquarters	New product	Existing
Source selection	Best done where design engineer works		#1	#5
Make-versus-buy decision	x		2	3
Maximum purchasing power		x	3	1
Promote standardization	x		4	4
Initiate cost reduction	x	x	5	2
Support global procurement		x	6	6

About 70% of production savings occur from improvement in design. Begin by taking these steps:

1. Review suppliers' performance in giving technical support to solve problems.
2. Evaluate their capabilities to give technical leadership.
3. Coordinate engineering/purchasing/supplier meetings.
4. Analyze product development projects and time to go into production.
5. Set up future production delivery schedules for planning.

State-of-the-art technology designs increase the cost and potential for quality problems. Such risks, however, should be minimized if the suppliers are recognized and rewarded for valuable contributions to the buying company. If two competing suppliers both contributed, both should get an equal opportunity for future work.

Earlier supplier involvement is a fact.[2] Suppliers are becoming involved earlier in the design cycle. Why? To capitalize on suppliers' expertise, on the latest technology, and because the design cycle is getting shorter. What are the biggest benefits of early involvement?

1. Better quality results
2. Better manufacturability
3. Lower costs
4. Latest technologies available

Prequalifying suppliers is one way to get earlier involvement. A stated objective is the qualification of components for both existing and new products. Although this may be the direct responsibility of the design engineering organization, there

---

[2]"Design '88: Teaming Up," *Purchasing Magazine,* March 10, 1988.

are economic and supply considerations that must be introduced by purchasing. This must occur early in the process—prior to source selection.

Strategic Technical Support Activities

Before reviewing ways to improve relationships between design engineers and buyers we should give thought to what has been learned about natural frictions that exist. Based on experience and investigation with others, we found the following underlying root causes for roadblocks to cooperation by some design engineers:

- A feeling that the proposal of a new method or material represents criticism of decisions engineers have made in the past.
- A fear that adoption of the proposal will downgrade the quality of the product (or component, material, or system) for which they're responsible.
- Many engineers have made changes that backfired on them, to their embarrassment.

What have some buyers complained about when dealing with design engineers?

- Some designers will specify parts, materials, and processes that are familiar to them. They may not want to risk an unproven alternative.
- Designers have a lower interest in economic factors than buyers.
- Design engineers sometimes specify just one supplier for a given requirement.
- Some engineers are reluctant to accept buyers' suggested supplier recommendations.
- Their design process is complicated and some engineers resent any suggestions that may lengthen development time.
- They often put new design objectives above product redesign goals, believing that it could be too costly to redesign simply to save material; they prefer to work changes in when they design a new model.
- Sometimes engineers fail to supply full and complete specifications, or specify tolerances that are too tight.
- There is a lack of respect for the time required by purchasing to do the buying job. The same design engineer who took 3 months to design something will expect the buyer to buy it tomorrow.
- There are too many engineering changes in design as the project continues—often with conflicting or incorrect specifications.
- It is sometimes difficult to get information from engineers.

- Engineering sometimes damages negotiation opportunities for purchasing, by letting suppliers know, "We like you, and will specify your product."

- Contacts with suppliers are not documented fully.

- Engineering is too strict in its definition of quality requirements. Engineers often "gold plate," which runs counter to cost containment.

The above comments are the expressed reactions of buyers in attendance at seminars conducted by the authors. Certainly there is some venting in the above listing, yet buyers can expect some of the above forms of defensiveness from some design engineers. Buyers should work to encourage the engineers to take some reasonable degree of risk, but remember, the *design engineer is always responsible for the integrity of the design!* Don't underestimate that responsibility.

Here's a short scenario illustrating an interaction with salespeople and engineering. Let's assume you are a technical buyer, and have found two new possible sources for cooling fans. Though the sources are confident they can make the motor at the price quoted, they're not sure of the exact electrical characteristics required to match your application. Savings of $50,000/year are possible, but costly tests will be needed unless torque curves are made available from the prime source.

You now have two new possible suppliers eagerly awaiting the curves to match the motor correctly. Together with your design engineer, you're anxious to resolve this quality design issue, so you've insisted that the current supplier give you the data. Their salesperson said at that time, "I'll do my best to bring them on my next visit."

Aware the motor is now single sourced, the domestic manufacturer is reluctant to give up technical information, afraid they will have competition. If they don't provide the data, they figure the design can't be competed against. The salesman arrives on the agreed date to bring the curves, saying, "Sorry, but the lab is tied up and I can't get them yet. But, I've brought you some new price lists not too much higher than they've been. We need to talk about tying down just how many cooling fans you'll want this coming year. We're pretty busy now."

What is your response? What do you do—hold him to the commitment? Give this some thought before proceeding. Perhaps a more important issue confronting this buyer is the relationship with the design engineer.

Some Complaints by Design Engineers

This is a two-way street. What do engineers say bothers them about purchasing?[3] In order of most frequently mentioned, complaints are:

---

[3]Compiled by authors during many seminars.

- Lack of product knowledge
- Price buying
- Poor follow-up and feedback
- "Going by the book"—inflexibility
- Unwillingness to try new suppliers
- Conflicting documents between what is on the specification and on the agreement to buy
- Procurement degraded to "paper pushers"
- Some buyers have an "attitude problem"
- There's a lack of performance in meeting our needs

So, there has been some dissatisfaction on both sides of the issue! Good relationships between purchasing and engineering are vital. Despite all the above complaints, many buyers, purchasing engineers, and design engineers do get along well because of enlightened managers of these operations. As an example, a vice president of engineering who was aware of frictions issued guidelines in cooperation with the director of purchasing. Although aimed primarily at the engineering staff, these guidelines also provide purchasing managers with some insights that may be helpful. Below are the written instructions prepared by this chief engineer for his department:

- The purchasing department should be informed of correspondence with suppliers. This means that copies of any such correspondence should go to purchasing. And when correspondence is received from suppliers, either the original or a copy should be given to purchasing.
- The engineer should call in a purchasing representative whenever an important discussion is to be held with a supplier, even though it relates to some future design.
- It is essential that no engineer advise any supplier directly relative to changes of prices or specifications on current production models. Any negotiations with or advice to suppliers on products must be handled by the purchasing department.
- No engineer should take it upon himself to change any existing purchase order either by verbal or written instructions to a supplier. Correspondence concerning any existing purchase orders must be handled by purchasing. Any necessary technical transmissions should be done only with the agreement of purchasing, with copies to the appropriate buyers.
- Any discussions that lead to prices being mentioned should have written confirmation (a copy of which should go to purchasing), or a record of the conversation should be made by the engineer and furnished to purchasing.

- It is necessary that the engineer talk tentative price and cost in conversations with suppliers in connection with new products and in the process of selecting and qualifying components or parts. If the engineer is to be cost conscious, this is definitely part of the job.

- Confidential information or quotations provided by one supplier should not be passed along to another and the confidential disclosure of new developments on the part of the supplier should be respected.

- It is essential in conversations with suppliers that the engineers make it perfectly clear that they do not make the decision to buy and that the purchasing department is completely responsible for such a decision.

Engineering usually requires more services from buyers than from other departments. The capabilities of engineering and purchasing should be combined. Here is how some buyers build rapport with design engineers:

- Supplier catalogues are made readily accessible to engineering.
- Buyers invite engineers to visit supplier plants with them.
- Purchasing will act quickly to place and attain delivery for developmental buys.
- A special buyer or purchasing engineer provides interdepartmental liaison (larger organizations only).
- Purchasing's supplier evaluation system stresses design suggestions.
- Keep routine contact between buyers and key engineering sections.
- Maintain dialogue with suppliers' engineers.
- Achieve design integration by being part of the design team process.
- Attend key engineering design meetings.
- Spearhead standardization efforts with engineering.
- Jointly search for less costly substitutes of equal or better value.
- Analyze product development projects and timing to go into production.
- Arrange test procedures to analyze supplier failures that can be reduced and might allow elimination of any incoming inspection.
- Participate in joint plant source selection boards for major source selection.

So there is plenty of room for improvement ideas to rid the company of such frictions. It is clear that the activities of design engineers can materially impact the buyer's sourcing options. So, if the buyer can help the engineers with several constructive alternatives—early in the design process—the payoff comes in lowered material costs. How can buyers and purchasing engineers ensure cooperation with engineering? They should look for ways to satisfy: (1) reliability, (2) technical capabilities, (3) service availability, and (4) supply availability. Design engineers indicate the aspects of supplier performance that are most important to them include technical assistance, fast delivery of test items, a consistency between samples provided and production lots, good after-sale service, and ability to maintain competitive pricing.

There are two extremes in purchasing's relationships with engineering, neither of which is optimal. One is the situation where the purchasing department insists that it must make all supplier contacts, handle all correspondence, and decide whether or not a supplier may see an engineer; in the other the engineer is a free agent who on his or her own introduces changes in contracts, makes commitments to suppliers, and approves costly changes without proper authorization from purchasing. Under this latter scenario, some engineers fail to realize when they are within purchasing's domain and ignore the effect of their actions on the company.

The optimum situation allows the engineer sufficient access to supplier "know how" and advice without eliminating the buyer from the process. An engineer may be "just looking," but before he is through he may have set a price and made firm commitments, "forgetting" to key the buyer in. This must be fought if for no other reason than to avoid the resultant higher cost in materials expenditures. To illustrate: A production manager phoned a PM and complained loudly that delivery of promised widgets was late. As a consequence, the line had to be shut down and several hundred people were sent home. Confused, the widget buyer called the supplier and was told an engineer had given orders not to produce the widgets until it could be decided whether to add a corner molding for appearance. When contacted, the engineer advised he had no idea his call to the supplier would cause such a problem and was unaware of the delivery requirement.

The normal inclination is to give the engineer who exceeds his authority a verbal lacing, but it is far better to preserve good relationships and explain why he should not contact a supplier without advising the buyer. Again, the key is tact—you may need this same engineer's help tomorrow!

Review of the Technical Buyer and Purchasing Engineer Jobs

The purchasing engineer's task is to assist the buyer in making a good buying decision, using his technical knowledge and skills. To do this well, purchasing engineers should try to see the buyer's point of view. What sort of things should progressive buyers and purchasing engineers seek to do?

- Purchasing engineers and buyers must know the seller, but in addition, must understand modern purchasing strategies and tactics, so as to be part of the purchasing team.
- At the same time hi-tech buyers and purchasing engineers must be aware of the plans and programs of importance to the design or manufacturing engineers.

Questionnaire for Purchasing Engineers[4]

The following questions were designed to draw out discussions about issues that affect purchasing engineers, analysts, and buyers, and focus on their responsibilities. Reviewing this list raises appropriate issues:

1. What is your company ratio of purchase engineers to buyers?
2. Do your suppliers submit cost breakdowns when requested?
3. When do you begin price/cost analysis, upstream or after drawings are issued and "firm"?
4. Do you find it more rewarding to go downstream? Experiences?
5. How do you determine burden rates for suppliers?
6. Can you target price if your specifications and sample units are not defined reasonably?
7. How long will you track a key component for which a target price was set?
8. How do buyers get new prices to the engineers? By phone, electronic media, or written forms?
9. How do you measure performance versus target price for key items?
10. Do you measure versus target only, or versus base quote and a target?
11. Do analysts participate in make-versus-buy decisions?
12. Can analysts contact suppliers directly for cost data, etc.?
13. Do purchasing engineers assist buyers in source selection? Do process engineers get into the act?

These questions, when addressed by purchasing engineers, force a confrontation with the various aspects of the job, including some of the frustrations. Responses from seminars revealed the following summary of such frustrations as expressed by buyers and purchasing engineers in attendance:

*   Difficulty bringing in qualified suppliers versus local sources
*   Difficulty recruiting buyers' support for their ideas
*   Coordinating activities within a decentralized organization
*   Finding measurements to prove why new purchasing ideas are important

It's said that much of the information purchasing gets on new products comes directly from salespeople. But some salespeople will tell you buyers often don't

---

[4]Prepared by John Burlew for Pooler & Associates seminars, "The Job of the Purchasing Engineer: Working with Design Engineers, Buyers and Suppliers," and "The Technical Buyer and P.E.," presented at the World Trade Institute, 1988–1990, New York and Los Angeles.

understand the technical aspects of their offerings. The purchasing engineer job came about from the realization that otherwise effective buyers may find it difficult to communicate in a technologically complex situation without an engineering background. The sales counterpart is the sales engineer.

The above questions were used in an actual setting of purchasing practitioners. Following study of the questions posed above, the group drew up their strategies and tactics. Actions to be taken by the purchasing engineer or progressive technical buyer are suggested below:

- Determine cost targets.
- Perform cost/price analysis.
- Work with Quality and Reliability functions.
- Attend key engineering design meetings.
- Search for less costly substitutes.
- Assist purchasing to conduct "pooled buying" studies.
- Follow up with engineers for specification approval.
- Work closely with electronic design engineers.
- Visit supplier sources, as appropriate.

The senior author got into purchasing because the chief engineer thought nobody in the purchasing department knew what the engineers were talking about. Some engineers no doubt still find that's the case. The purchasing engineer operates within the purchasing sphere, but has key interfaces with design engineers as well.

A job description for the purchasing engineer is in the Appendix. Study of the specific listed duties will clarify the role.

Make-Versus-Buy Studies

All businesses may be thought of as a store. The choice is to get products from within ("make") or from outside ("buy"). Balancing the pros and cons allows an objective decision.

Make-versus-buy can be a complex analytical tool. But it is simple in concept, answering the question, "Should our company make this item, or buy it?" Competitive advantage exists when you make products efficiently, and you buy what others can make more economically. As such, wise make-versus-buy decisions are vital to the success of any manufacturing company.

There are many factors to address to make a good make-versus-buy decision. Following are some of the conditions that are generally supportive of a "make" decision:

- Your product has valuable in-house technology, particularly proprietary processes.
- Your product is unusual or complex, and direct supervision is needed to ensure direct control over quality.
- Assurance of adequate supply is critical so as to preclude outside buy.
- Absorption of fixed capital investment is of such critical importance as to preclude outside buy.
- A "make" decision will allow for preservation of the employment base.
- In-house manufacturing is determined to be a lower cost alternative to purchasing.
- A "make" designation is supported by your company "know how," your equipment, and experience, and is consistent with company growth goals.
- Control of design parts changes, inventories, and deliveries are of critical importance so as to preclude outside buy.
- The design or its processing is confidential, and considered key to the company's future competitiveness.
- Idle capacity is available to use to absorb overhead.
- The part is delicate and/or hard to transport.
- Your company does not wish to depend on an outside source of supply—regardless of the reason.

To the contrary, many items are best purchased outside the company. Conditions supportive of such a decision include the following:

- Cost studies show lower costs to buy than to make in-house.
- Space, equipment, time, and/or skill are not readily available to develop the production operations.
- Supplier(s) provide unique process or design technology.
- Supplier(s) have unique patents.
- Supplier's product reflects value improvements fostered by the competitive supply marketplace.
- Capital is not currently available.
- The customer has expressed a brand preference.
- A "buy" decision puts the buyer into play in the market, thereby providing knowledge of changing market prices and conditions.
- Because of small volume or other capital priorities, investment in a "make" is not attractive.
- The company wishes to avoid direct exposure to seasonal, cyclical, or risky market situations.

- There is a need for special techniques and/or equipment, thereby making "buy" the more attractive alternative.

Capability to manufacture specific in-house (make) products will be inherent in the company business strategy. Some manufacturing people think buyers want to "buy" everything, and buyers sometimes think manufacturing wants to "make" everything. Paradoxically, there is much more to buy when a company manufactures than if it buys the component. Consider that when a company buys a compressor, this is a single item to purchase. Making the compressor may require thousands of purchases of the subassemblies, components, and materials, such as castings, connecting rods, piston rings, and lubricating oil.

Purchasing should have a systematic way to reach these make-versus-buy decisions. It's important to have a written format to ensure that all proper factors are considered efficiently, and that all critical considerations are analyzed. In addition to pure cost factors, nonfinancial factors need also be considered, which ultimately may override cost in reaching a final make-versus-buy decision.

Many companies have constructed forms similar to the one below which focuses the buyer on the data relevant to a sound make-versus-buy decision:

Make Versus Buy Analysis

I. Cost to make (per piece)

    a. Direct material (incl. freight, handling, and scrap) _____

    b. Direct labor at projected actual rate _____

    c. Indirect or variable burden (incl. engr. and mfg.) _____

    d. Depreciation (if new capital or tooling needed) _____

    e. Total variable cost to make (a + b + c + d) _____

    f. Fixed burden on estimated plant loading of ____% _____

    g. Profit desired (30% of e above) _____

    h. Total cost to make (e + f + g) _____

II. Cost to buy (per piece)

    a. Purchase price _____

    b. Freight/handling & purchase order costs _____

    c. Supplier tooling/engineering _____

    d. Other (specify) _____

    e. Total cost to buy (a + b + c + d) _____

III. Other non-cost considerations with implications and conclusions:

_____

_____

_____

_____

IV. Annualized savings: Make $_____ versus Buy $_____

V. Final decision is to: Make _____, or Buy _____

Decision review date: _____

In conducting make-versus-buy analyses, quality and cost are, of course, prime considerations. Other major factors are service and security of supply. These are some of the situations that trigger the need to conduct make-versus-buy evaluations:

- Technology change to certain hardware or processes
- New source availability change—quantity, quality, location, or price
- Company goals for vertical integration (own our core business)
- Review of strategic manufacturing strategies
    1. Plant facilities. Do we have idle space?
    2. Idle funds?
    3. Employee relationships
    4. Legal conflicts? Patents?
    5. Supplier relationships

Cost to buy, made up of the price of the item, transportation, cost of handling, and storage should be weighed against cost to manufacture, made up of the out-of-pocket costs of material, direct labor, and direct burden (supplies, indirect labor, perishable tools), which vary with the product in question. For make-or-buy decisions whose dollar value is relatively small and that do not greatly affect plant capacity, this comparison may be sufficient. But when we are considering a bigger decision where plant capacity may be idled or new facilities may have to be built, then to the cost of manufacturing must be added period (or fixed) costs, which do not fluctuate with the volume of products produced but are part of the cost of being in business. Some such periodic expenses are the salaries of additional supervisors, capital expenditures for machinery and buildings, depreciation of equipment, taxes, and insurance.

Elimination of sales expense and the supplier's profit should favor making an item if it can be done as economically as the supplier would do it. However, with increases in company specialization it becomes more difficult for the using firm to be as efficient as the specialist in say, metal stampings and castings.

Sometimes the decision may be to both make and buy. To illustrate: Special

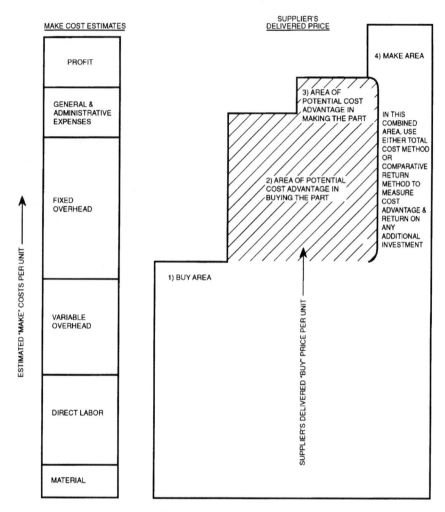

Figure 12-1 Chart of "make" costs with supplier "buy" prices.

fittings are converted from standard ones by drilling oil grooves and openings; so a more favorable overall lower cost results than if they had been either purchased as a finished product or manufactured completely by the user. Another alternative may be to make a portion of an item while buying the remainder.

Figure 12-1 diagrams a comparison of "make" costs with supplier "buy" prices. Its framework has settled many on-the-job situations.

Purchasing's Role in Make-or-Buy

Who makes the decision to make or buy depends to a large degree on the dollars involved. One person might make the decision, but most often it is made by several individuals or groups. This is especially true when plant additions or capital expenditures are at stake; then top management makes the final decision. With less extensive expenditures, purchasing or engineering and manufacturing officials may settle the question individually or jointly. Sometimes a committee makes or reviews important decisions. Such a committee may be headed by the manager of the project and often consists of representatives of major company functions. Purchasing must take part, and cooperate with manufacturing engineering, estimating, design engineers, finance, and others to review major projects. Here is a checklist showing who will most appropriately be tasked to perform the data collection.

Issue	Responsibility
A. Proprietary items	Engineering
B. Term of investment	
Production life	Engineering/marketing
Payback required	Finance
Cost advantage life	Manufacturing
C. Quantities required per year	Production control
D. "Make" costs	
Material	Purchasing
Direct labor content	Manufacturing
Variable overhead	Finance
Expense tooling	Manufacturing
Fixed overhead	Finance
Sales, general and admin.	Finance
E. "Buy" costs	
Purchase price including freight, etc.	Purchasing
F. Cost to qualify component	Engineering
G. Any inventory obsolescence	Production control
H. Make investment	
Inventory	Production control
Capital/tooling/equipment	Manufacturing
I. Alternative use of existing equipment, or scrap value?	Manufacturing

Although important make-or-buy decisions might be decided by top management, purchasing managers do have a team role here. At a minimum, they collect the cost data for these decisions; and, when a member of top management, they may actually be the coordinating officer and spearhead the decision themselves. Many items that are studied stem from buyers' suggestions for cost savings.

Purchasing will advise on cost comparisons; manufacturing will specify needs and capacities; finance will tabulate manufacturing cost data; engineering will check technical specifications, quality, and suitability; and marketing may advise on trends and the likelihood that sales volume will be affected by the decision.

It should be recognized that cost accounting generalities may not be able to address all the issues relevant to a comprehensive make-versus-buy analysis. Labor relationships can be affected. In some instances, when it is known that a part is to be removed from manufacturing and bought outside, jobs are affected. There has yet to be devised a simple, infallible formula to guide any company. Moreover, conditions are always changing. Suppliers' prices vary according to their need for volume and with other economic factors; so, a make-or-buy decision made one year may be invalid the next. Obviously, a company cannot change back and forth repeatedly, which emphasizes the need for a systematic approach in decision making.

A study shows that a lower price for one alternate make-or-buy decision produces a 100% return on investment, while alternate B will produce 80%. This makes alternate A appear as the logical choice, until further study shows that the life of product A is projected as just one year, as it's expected to become obsolete, whereas the 80% return should exist for at least 5 years. In this case, the duration of the return is a factor. In summary, if it makes more sense to buy, buy it; or, if it is more economical to manufacture, make it. But don't make a change unless your study decisively favors the alternative, for hidden costs may eat up expected economies.

And conditions do change. In the 1930s the ice man had a secure business as people needed ice to stop food spoilage. The iceman collected ice in winter, stored it, and then in the heat of summer he drove around looking for an "ICE" sign in the window. Stopping, he'd chip off the 50 cent size, leave it, collect, and move on. He was secure—then somebody invented the refrigerator.

Like the iceman, our buyer might find himself obsolete if he only can pick ice or process requisitions. It becomes increasingly evident that the routine of buying must be done with minimal effort, and the computer does help. The buying role is emerging as a managerial coordinator of materials and planning. And, that coordination must include engineering for by far the greatest cost reductions come from the original design, or a value engineering approach to existing products. Managements want alert, aggressive, and intelligent purchasing personnel who practice modern techniques of buying as team players.

13

Using Cost Reduction Techniques

Because the quality and suitability for a specific purpose can be based on technical considerations, the buyer must work closely with the design engineer. And consider the effect of resulting cost reductions on both costs of products and inventory. For example, a reduction in price of any commodity decreases inventory, thereby increasing capital turnover. At the same time, the same "better buy" reduces operating costs, increasing the profit generated by each sales dollar. The combination of an increased turnover of capital—as shown on the balance sheet—with an increased profit percentage (as indicated on the P&L statement), causes resulting ROIC to be doubly enhanced. This phenomenon can be seen schematically in Figure 13-1.[1]

The need to search out ways to control and cut expense is a given. Perhaps the term Economic Value Added (EVA) is a more appropriate term. Value can be enhanced in different ways. The following are some traditional tactics used by professional buyers to increase profits:

- Stockless purchasing

- Blanket order (annual volume contracts)

- Systems contracts

- Trade discounts

- Rebate programs

- Freight cost reductions

---

[1]Victor H. Pooler and David J. Pooler, "Purchasing's Elusive Conceptual Home," *Journal of Purchasing and Materials Management,* Summer 1981, p. 17.

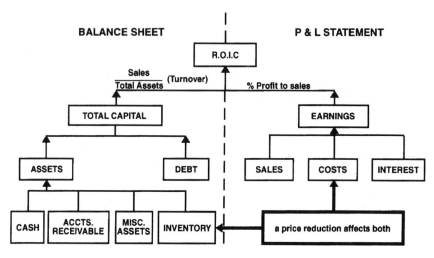

Figure 13-1   Effect of cost savings on profitability.

Purchasing must be an important contributor to profit and growth through active cost reduction efforts. Buyers can strive to achieve strategic global competitiveness for their company by using some analytical techniques and tools on-the-job, such as:

- Strong long-range source development
- Team buying: local, national, and global
- Cost and price analysis
- Statistical and graphic analysis
- Make-or-buy analysis
- Standardization and simplification
- Value and cost analysis
- Lease-versus-buy
- Learning curve
- Forward buying versus hedging

It's known that only a small amount of activity produces most of the results. A few salespeople produce most sales, a few engineers most of the good designs. Likewise, a few buyers produce most of the savings in purchasing. Productivity is a matter of effectiveness on-the-job, not just how hard one works.

The more difficult programs require a more technical approach. What are the advantages and disadvantages of each? How can the manager recognize the need and problem areas in this area of cost reduction?

Should top management fail to set broad strategic cost reduction goals, then the purchasing manager or buyer should set his own high standards of performance and do his best to achieve them. A few suggested strategic goals might be the following:

1. Maintain an effective profit contribution through value analysis and cost reduction techniques.
2. Obtain the best value in purchased materials at the lowest price, consistent with quality requirements.

Make a list to:

*   Focus on the buyer's intrinsic buying power—use leverage to improve your company's competitive market position.
*   Integrate commodity productivity projects with new product development projects.
*   Identify product cost reductions with engineering.
*   Provide cost data to engineering on future pricing trends.
*   Conduct minority/small business program.
*   Performance-related strategies:
    Control department expenses
    Measure purchasing productivity and interpret results
    Upgrade product quality through quality and reliability efforts
*   Prioritize the above by importance.
*   Execute effectively!

Standardization and Substitution

A "standard" is set up as a rule to measure quantity, weight, extent, value, or quality. Much has been done by agencies and societies such as ASA, ASTM, SAE, NEMA, NAPM, and ASME to promote standards. Truth is everyone wants everyone else to standardize, but not necessarily themselves. The National Bureau of Standards (NBS) controls quality of the world's largest consumer, the U.S. Government. They act as advisor to industry, coordinating standards on a national basis. The NBS issues a Directory of Standardization that includes organizations that promote standards.

Standardization is an excellent way to control material costs, by the reduction of the number of different items bought. If two will do the job of three, inventory control is simplified, obsolescence is reduced, and the administrative costs of purchasing, receiving, stores, and the like also decrease.

Standardization is relatively simple. It's a matter of having technical people determine if some lesser-used items can be eliminated. For example, a distributor stocks 10 different bolts. One of them is bought in lots of 50 per year, whereas others are bought in 10,000 piece lots. The 50 could be replaced by other bolts, even if at a cost penalty. It would pay to eliminate the 10th bolt and inventory 9 items.

A way to facilitate multiple, or "pooled" buying, is through the use of available standard items. A generic pharmaceutical can be much more economical than a brand name. So, an item meeting a contracting standard can be bought from many sources. Through such standards, volumes can be pooled that result not only in reduced prices, but also in lower inventories and faster deliveries. A larger volume gives better standing with the suppliers as purchases are more desirable. Standardization opportunities are found in almost all types of purchases.

Benefits of standardization and simplification are that fewer items need to be stocked. Storage space is lessened and record keeping is reduced. Obsolescence and longer shelf-life often are experienced. Standardization results from reducing the number of suppliers also.

Simplification

Simplification is the selection of the most readily available parts or materials and eliminating all unnecessary features or costs. This is a by-product of competitive ingenuity with the goal to reduce the excessive variety of manufactured and purchased items, first by determining which of these are important, and then by concentrating purchasing and production on these items only. Buyers, by pushing simplification along with standardization, can obtain better value because the supplier's price reflects (or should) their savings.

Reliability and faster availability, coupled with better job scheduling, all make the materials flow job controllable. Better service on delivery and repairs is the rule, since fewer items are inventoried and less likely to become obsolete. Lower operating costs, better maintained equipment, and less downtime are the result. The purchasing function itself may be simplified to streamline inquiry and purchase order forms and the like.

Value and Engineering Analysis

As a buying technique, value analysis (VA), sometimes called engineering analysis (EA), is a tremendous tool for the professional buyer. Value analysis is a systematic study applied to *any* item used, the goal being to maintain *adequate* quality but at a lower cost. Whether it is called purchase analysis, economic value analysis (EVA), purchased material cost reduction, value control, value engineering, or simply cost and engineering analysis, it has a general theme— to save money. Most purchasing people prefer the value analysis title.

Value analysis is a proven cost reduction technique used by competent industrial buyers and engineers. There are also times when construction contract buyers can apply it to advantage. VA is not simply a "study of value" to achieve lower costs, and so prices paid. Nor is it solely cost reduction. In a strict sense, it is an organized approach to study value and cost relationships, wherein the objective is to improve buying performance. Team meetings will enhance the number of good ideas, but VA can be practiced by the one-person department.

Suppliers play an important role in cost reduction since they furnish data and innovative ideas on which results depend. At a minimum, you should make use of suppliers' know-how and suggestions. Persevere, and give credit to others who may help you. A salesperson giving assistance in VA projects should be given increased buyer respect and opportunity to sell. The buyer interested in value analysis will rightly be open to sellers' suggestions.

A formal VA study takes an item and first determines what it does in terms of two words—a verb and a noun. For instance, pencils make (verb) marks (noun). Then other ways of doing the same job are considered. All ideas are written, perhaps in a brainstorming session, to allow free thought association and to get a fresh approach. VA doesn't simply question cost, it looks at the item's function, what has to be done, and puts a price on it. The biggest savings result from a change in design specification. It isn't a question of *what is the item worth,* but of *what the item's function is worth.* VA is a supplement to cost reduction and good buying, not a substitute for them.

VA/VE is an organized study of function and cost. The objective is to find workable alternatives at a lessor cost without reducing value. It is a dynamic program to reduce costs in an effort to increase profits in a disciplined technological manner. It isn't a crash cost-reduction effort based on criticism of existing designs or systems.

When asked, design engineers respond that supplier performance is most important to them. They want and expect technical assistance, and after-sale service. Holding competitive pricing after an item is incorporated in the design is also of significant importance. Failure to do this is a reason stressed by engineers for mistrusting supplier offerings.

The six steps of value analysis are:

- Step one is to identify the basic function of the item under scrutiny, preferably with just two words. For example, a pencil "makes marks."

- Step two involves a speculative or brainstorm approach. All ideas that would do the same function of "making marks" would be listed.

- Step three is to analyze those alternatives. Some people call this "blast and refine" before analyzing associated costs and performance.

- Step four is to study other ways to provide the same function, but at *lower cost.* Rank the alternatives from lowest to highest cost. Test one or two proposals.

- Step five is to implement the new design, method, manufacturing process, packaging, or shipment method. Then follow through.
- Step six is to report results on the project to management.

The transition from study (step 4) to implementation (step 5) is usually the most difficult in practice.

Key elements of a successful approach to VA are: wide scope of information collected, costs are well identified, and functions are defined and evaluated effectively. These elements must be augmented with support from others in the company. PMs should set an example. Buyers judge the importance of the savings effort by the amount of effort, involvement, and support of top management, and the PM, give the program. People need encouragement. Clipping an ad or idea with a personalized "Sally, could this help on our product?" can help.

Here's a typical VA checklist that has proved useful. You might prepare one for your specific use:

1. What is the material used?
2. Is the shape mandatory?
3. How does it work?
4. Does its use contribute to value?
5. Is strength critical?
6. What process is used in construction?
7. What is the primary function?
8. What else will do the same job?
9. Can a standard part be used?
10. Can a less expensive part work?
11. Are all machined surfaces necessary?
12. Can tolerances be loosened?
13. Can the design be changed to simplify?
14. What type maintenance is needed?
15. Are special tools needed?
16. Can it be easily packaged?

The above list can be much longer, but is typical of how buyers can create a checklist for their own company's use.

Overcoming Resistance to Change

Pitfalls are commonly expressed as: "You can't do that in this company," "We tried it before," "Why change now, it's working," and so on. Unfortunately, almost no important value change or savings is accepted quickly, and it takes time and effort to put into effect. Buyers *must expect initial resistance to change* they present! An example of this resistance is the case history of a small shaft plug. Used as a centering device, it has absolutely no function after the shaft is balanced. A buyer came up with a good cost reduction, substituting molded nylon in place of a machined metal plug. Before it could be approved, the sales department was asked to evaluate it. The immediate reaction was, "It won't sell—plastics are too cheap." To get around this objection, the plug was covered with aluminum paint and driven into place in the shaft. The salesman, looking at the two models, one with the silver and one with the white head, promptly said, "There! That's what we want right there—that one." Upon closer examination, becoming suspicious he asked, "Did you trick me?" However, the item was now approved. But at a small extra cost, the plug was made of gray plastic so that it looked like metal because of an old belief that plastics are inferior and can't be sold.

Some engineers believe that VA can easily be downgraded into cost reduction solely, and in turn leads to corruption of quality. One said, "No cost-cutter can take the basic function of the engineer to innovate." "Second-guessers" of engineering decisions are not popular.

Many people resent anyone outside their sphere telling them how they can do their job better. It is human nature to dislike one's own judgment being questioned. A design engineer was quoted, "These specialists who analyze a design for lower cost make a tremendous impression on money-minded management. The result of their work is easily understood by nontechnical sales and financial types who don't appreciate the vital technical contributions of the design engineers."

PMs should ask themselves if their department has some form of planned cost reduction, or VA. Do targets of savings to achieve exist and are they audited for accuracy? Are written procedures for reporting in existence? If a purchasing department doesn't do the above, how would the management know the buyers are getting the available cost improvements?

Many companies have shown 25% to 35% and more cost reductions resulting from formal value analysis/value engineering team efforts. Team meetings within larger operations will generate a substantial number of ideas for further evaluation. With representatives from product engineering, purchasing, service, and so on, this is similar to the quality circles approach. It is essential engineering plays a key role, so they don't have to be "sold" by nonengineering people. Engineers should make the technical decisions, as part of the team approach.

Here are some actual examples of good VA results; many savings are due to smart buying:

1. A company initially bought its oil in barrels. By buying in 10,000 gallon tank cars versus barrels received every few days, $15,000 annual savings quickly paid for a new tank in 3 months.

2. Red sheet rubber gasket material always had to be red; that is, until a buyer found out it cost extra to color it red. Now, black does the job at 12% less cost.

3. Yellow paint was bought at 15 cents per gallon lower in price, by changing from a 5-gallon pail to a 55-gallon drum. In addition, handling was quicker and more efficient.

These are very simple examples. However, we want to go a step further into in-depth analysis. Value analysis reverses the thought process to place the burden of proving why a constructive idea *cannot* be carried out with the person who wants to block it. For instance, while inspecting an air receiver tank, a buyer asked an engineer, "What are these two holes for?" The engineer said one opening was for the inlet for air, the other was an inspection opening required by the ASME code. The buyer retorted, "But couldn't you unscrew the inlet pipe and look in?" Upon reflection, the hole was eliminated, resulting in savings of over $10,000 annually for many years. Note that not one bit of *value* was removed from the product.

The following true incident illustrates receptivity of an idea and follow through. An engineer sat at a buyer's desk idly tossing a small carbon resistor. Each of his engines used 12 resistors costing $2.85 each. The buyer wondered what the resistors did, while the engineer got interested in their cost. The engineer was astounded to find that what he thought was a 25-cent item was costing almost $3. Resistors like this one were found all over the production floor. Workers tossed them playfully at each other.

When challenged, the supplier reduced its price for these resistors to $1.60 simply by the buyer's specification of the supplier's part number rather than buying to a special drawing. Now the buyer and engineer were working together. The engineer made a new sketch, and the buyer shopped with carbon-shaping manufacturers. They found resistors could be custom made for 9 cents each. Upon being appraised, the original supplier offered to buy them from the buyer's company. Until this time, no one had done their homework!

Persevere, and give credit to others who may help you. All of the previous examples were based on the senior author's experience with a multi-million dollar savings program. In his department, 60% of savings resulted from buyer action, 30% by product study and changes in specifications, and 10% by substitution of material. As this is just one department's experience, you will want to measure your own savings.

It is human nature to be somewhat complacent in the absence of competition, so why not create a cooperative competition? Baseball derives enthusiastic followers who get enjoyment from watching the long ball hit out of the park. In purchasing we surely don't create such thrills (maybe the opposite?) among others in making a good buy; yet buyers must get personal satisfaction from it to feel rewarded and effective. Some practitioners have tried to make the purchasing game more fun and rewarding. Giving out a few prizes can stir interest and create a good atmosphere. Use of a few incentives can make VA rewarding for the company and the individual practitioners alike.

Incentives make people feel important. Recognize and reward performance! Outstanding contributors can be singled out to receive certificates signed by the Director of Purchasing and the President of the company. Taking the buyer to lunch is always appreciated. However, there is some question about the merit of awards, as some PMs consider them gimmicks. Of course, there are differences in what motivates some people versus others. However, when rewards commend good performance, they are an effective acknowledgment of a job well done.

Use of the Learning Curve[2]

When a buyer has no competition, yet is buying a complex technological item, the learning curve (L/C)—called by some an "improvement curve"—may be the only technique available. The curve is a sophisticated mathematical form of price analysis that can be very useful to the buyer. It is based on the fact that the time required to do work will decrease each time it is done. Repetitive production uses a percentage less labor cost. This decrease will be smaller each time the quantity produced is doubled, and can be charted.

The need to determine the "right" price is always present. New, highly engineered products often are priced higher because costs are high; but when costs fall, the purchasing manager can't afford to let the initial high price stand. The learning curve, a challenging purchasing tool, is a special cost reduction and negotiation technique every purchasing manager and technical buyer should understand. When applied by the skillful negotiator, its success is not simply theoretical. Case studies show that the curve technique has enabled buyers to cut thousands of dollars from the cost of purchased materials.

How the Learning Curve Works

Complex operations become simpler with repetition. Recall the first time you built something, for example, window screens. The first one took all day, the second took half a day, and the third 2 hours. Why? Because the worker requires less time to analyze the job and his motions become more efficient. Short cuts are discovered and refinements made. Also, tooling is improved, newer and faster equipment may be used, waste reduced, and fewer engineering changes are now needed. The result is that costs go down.

The L/C results from plotting straight lines on a log–log graph of the supplier's

---

[2]Victor H. Pooler, "How to Use the Learning Curve," *Purchasing Magazine* July 17, 1961, and refined since.

actual cost experience that will enable future costs to be predicted—as will be explained. The learning curve is a line on a graph that shows two things:

1. That the time to do work will decrease each time it's done, and
2. The amount of decrease will be less each time a unit is produced.

The L/C has been used in negotiations, pricing, and forecasting direct labor hours for new products. It is an accepted tool in industries including aircraft, electronics, appliances, and shipbuilding. It is widely used by the Air Force and the Navy for weapons acquisition.

Each time the total quantity of units produced is doubled, the cumulative average hours required to produce the new total quantity is a percentage of the original average. There are reasons for this. As quantity increases, the worker needs less time to analyze the job before starting and the operator's physical motions become more efficient. There is improvement in operational sequences, machine feeds, and so on. Better equipment may be used: tooling is improved; rejections and rework decreases. Management controls get better and there is less waste. Fewer engineering changes are needed and costs go down.

During World War II the Air Force commissioned the Stanford Research Institute to make a statistical study of direct labor input of military aircraft. A series of L/C's resulted and paved the way for its use in industry. An exact curve never occurs when production records are graphed. The aircraft industry's rate of learning, between doubled quantities, averages about 80% of previous time required. Amazingly, to build the 1000th B29 bomber took only 3% of the time used to produce the first plane!

Aircraft production is ideal for L/C use because 75% of the cost is in assembly labor where much learning can occur. In machinery manufacturing, however, where assembly time might be 25% and machining 75%, learning is much less a factor, so a 90% or 95% curve would be more applicable.

A horizontal 100% leaning curve would mean no learning is possible; this might apply only to an automated "man-less" factory. A 50% L/C means that when the production quantity is doubled, the second half is produced at no cost, which is also an impossible condition. The useful range of learning curves lies between the area of 70% and 95%.

For most applications, the curve for machining and assembly work will be around 95% for complex machining. For detail fabrication and assembly, it would be in the 70% to 80% range.

During negotiation the buyer should urge the supplier to plot its own curve. It is difficult to refute an effective presentation. Defensive data needed to refute the L/C case for lower prices must be presented. So, data for a cost/price analysis may do the job anyway.

For easy reference, a simplified chart is useful. Figure 13-2 depicts a 90% curve drawn on regular graph paper as a hyperbola, a difficult curve to work

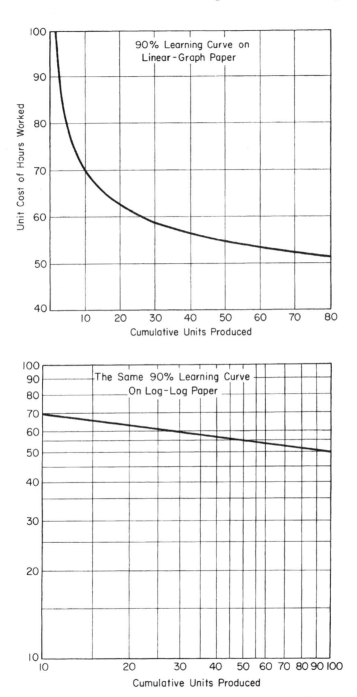

Figure 13-2 Learning curve graph to log–log straight line.

with. By putting the identical data onto log–log paper the same 90% curve becomes a straight line, as seen in the bottom graph, which is both easy to draw and easy to read.

Figure 13-3 will show how one works. This 90% curve was developed in the following manner:

1. Plot point A on the graph for known quantity versus price.

2. Double the original quantity and plot point B versus 90 (or other) percent of original price. Draw a line through A and B.

3. Compare the expected price for any quantity following the example below.

Two hundred units were bought at $30 each. How much should be paid for a quantity of 400 units? Again, plot A and B (step 2 above). Draw a line through A and B at 600 total quantity (200 original plus 400 new order). Trace vertically to L/C line, and read $25 at C by following the dotted line. Total cumulative average price is 600 × 25 = $15,000. Old order cost was 200 × 30 = $6,000. So, the new order value should be $15,000 minus $6,000 = $9,000. The new unit price is $9,000 divided by 400 = $22.50 each. This would be $18 on an 80% curve.

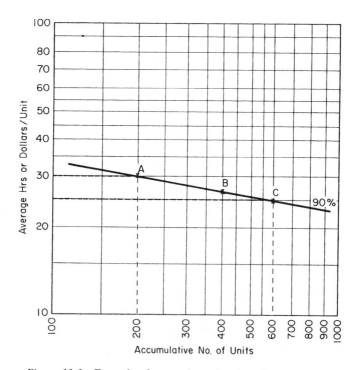

Figure 13-3 Example of computing prices by a learning curve.

The L/C is used by buyers as a negotiation tool, and to predict future costs. Give thought to a learning curve under any of the following conditions:

1. The product manufactured is a special, nonstandard, and made to your design and specification.
2. Proprietary factors limit competition for a complex technological item, wherein the L/C may be your only technique available.
3. Quantity is large enough to allow "learning" to occur.
4. Direct labor costs are high compared to material costs.

The curve's importance lies in its ability to reduce costs and as an incentive for producers to cut costs. One president confronted with facts said, "you've got me. If I denied the savings were there I'd be admitting we couldn't improve our operations one bit. I know better." So, the curve is a way to apply economic pressure to reduce costs; it is a means of checking the reasonableness of suppliers' quotations, and can serve to step up negotiations and thereby arrive at the correct price.

Defensive suppliers have said, "Sure our labor hours go down, but look at the 50% of materials we buy over which we have no control." This is answered by an analysis of price as we reviewed earlier under price/cost analysis.

Plotting of new price proposals will show any discrepancy in pricing trends. For example, if future costs don't allow for learning, the buyer can introduce a factor for it. To overcome a supplier's reticence to accept a L/C, the buyer can offer a later upward price revision if reduced costs aren't evident. This helps allay the supplier's fear that his costs might be higher later.

Pitfalls to avoid are:

- Don't apply the L/C to an estimated price, thereby magnifying errors in the original estimate.
- Don't apply the curve to standard items as if the first article purchased was the first produced.
- Avoid applying the wrong percentage curve, or using 80% for the sake of simplicity.
- Caution! Sometimes graphing supplier quantity discounts might indicate a more generous learning than yours, so in such a case, don't use it!

Remember, while the L/C uses a statistical and highly technical analysis, it is an estimate of costs. Actual costs can be known only after the production takes place. Yet, as a negotiation technique that leads to a mutually agreeable price it can be most effective, especially if buyers involve the supplier in plotting their own data and lead them through a trial exercise. When tactfully done with honest intent, this can help to build a superior supplier partnership. By cooperating, suppliers are able to make manufacturing cost savings that might not otherwise have been attempted. The L/C is an attack device when the price is high. But if it doesn't truly apply, don't use it.

Not only does the curve help buyers understand suppliers' sophisticated pricing methods better, but it also encourages suppliers to volunteer information about them. A negotiating session, which often results in changing a supplier's prices, can prove advantageous to both parties. The seller gets a chance to hold on to business he might otherwise lose. And the buyer receives a fair price, and discovers ways to make savings in manufacturing costs that might not otherwise have been attempted. In one case a supplier that was unable to save much on labor costs became convinced, after studying the learning curve that the price it paid for a purchased component was too high. The result was a 35% reduction passed on to the buyer from a subcontractor, making the business safe from competition.

Suppliers play an important role since they must supply data on which results depend. Invite key suppliers to a series of meetings whereby competitive components or items are scrutinized, looking for cost reduction or quality improvements. Search for more joint design effort opportunities. Competition can be healthy!

Leasing Versus Buying

Leasing is a form of acquisition without ownership. The concept of leasing goes back many years and probably started with land and buildings. For many years, industrial equipment and plant machinery, trucks and cars, as well as office equipment, furniture, and the like, have been available on a rental basis. How a lease works is not always understood by those buyers who may have had little or no exposure to leasing.

Is it better to lease or to buy? There is no pat answer to that question. The buyer must study the cost versus the benefits of both and decide. The "break-even" point is a financial calculation which occurs when *total* leasing costs are equal to *total* costs of outright ownership. That depends on the cost of the equipment and the monthly lease fees, life span for equipment—which depends on the usage, and what the equipment will be worth at the expiration of the lease. Other factors include use of money (are there more valuable uses?), services required, and so on.

Some of the specific benefits of leasing are:

- Cash is conserved.
- Leasing overcomes a budget restriction, as 100% financing is available.
- It is often simpler than borrowing money.
- Other credit options are unaffected, and remain open.
- Leasing eliminates the need for partial down payment.

- It removes the risks of ownership.
- It provides a hedge against obsolescence of high-technology equipment.
- Fixed payment allows accurate budgeting.
- As a sales vehicle that enlarges the potential market for the seller, leasing provides economies of scale (as lessor buys larger volume at better discounts).
- Leasing sometimes provides tax advantages, though this should be carefully analyzed by your tax people to determine applicability of your circumstances.

An effective sales pitch is, "Profits don't come from owning, but from *using*!" The lease concept means that a buyer pays for use of equipment while it is being used, rather than paying for it outright at the time it is installed or acquired. Payment terms are highly flexible and negotiable. For example, a farmer paying for leased land might pay after the crop is harvested!

A major legal distinction is that when a company buys, it owns. When the buyer leases, the company does not take title, but does control the item, and uses it as it sees fit. Upon deciding to discontinue use of owned equipment, the owning company sells to get whatever residual value is still there. With a lease, the item is turned back to the lessor.

Popular today are leases for new and used computer equipment. Furthermore, aircraft companies have at least 50% of their aircraft on lease, while much of the nation's railway cars are similarly covered by such arrangements. Other major areas where leasing has become popular include automobiles, telephone equipment, large volume furnishings for hotels/motels, commercial buildings, medical equipment, and office equipment.

Methods of Acquisition

A lease is a contract between an owner (lessor) and the user (lessee) that enables the lessor to grant permission for use to the lessee usually for a set monthly fee. Two general types of leases are available: (1) a capital lease and (2) an operating (or true) lease.

A capital lease transfers ownership to another party, usually by the lessor, and is actually a time payment purchase, as equipment must be capitalized. On the other hand, with the operating lease, the lessee *rents*, and ownership does not pass to the lessee after the end of the lease. It allows tax benefits of the lease.

The lessee or customer commonly makes payments of a fixed monthly fee for a period of time (usually less than the asset's economic life). The payments must cover the cost of depreciation or use of the equipment during the lease term. When the term is over, the equipment is returned to the lessor, although arrangements can be made for the lessee to buy the used equipment for its residual value, that is, what has not yet been paid off, to amortize it.

Let's look at a leasing example. Leasing is one way to have use of something tangible that can be used to produce profit. Let's take the simple case where a car costs $20,000. Assuming there is no trade in, the options are:

1. Pay for it in cash and own it.
2. Finance it through one of the dealership's financing arrangements.
3. Finance it through a bank, and own the car.
4. Lease it from an independent lessor.

Buyers are usually completely familiar with the outright buy option. Over the long haul, buying outright will generally cost less than leasing. But, there are other considerations we'll now trace for a lease. If the car had been bought outright, the total proceeds after disposal will usually be a net economic plus versus the alternative to lease the car. Then, why lease? It's convenient, as there is no risk in selling an old asset, or haggling over its value.

Also, let's not lose sight of the fact that leasing keeps assets off the books! This means a company's ROI is improved. Below is the formula to compute the dollar amount to be financed. As seen, it can be tricky to estimate the value of the equipment 3 to 5 years in the future.

$$\text{Equipment Value} - \text{Residual Value} = \text{Equity to be financed!}$$

Other Leasing Considerations: Beware

Make sure how the value of the car (or other asset) is determined when the lease is signed, because that value is used to compute the payments. Also be advised that a lessor may arrange for a car from out of town that may make it difficult for the driver to get warranty service. As an example, most leases limit driving mileage to 15,000 miles, after which "so many cents per mile" will be charged for overusage. And with early termination, a buyout always brings a penalty cost.

The leasing company typically charges a financing rate roughly equal to that charged by a bank for a purchase transaction. But, since the leasing company pays a lesser amount to an underlying financing institution, their profit can come out of that difference. But, that's not all! The key lies in the fact that all leases are for a value somewhat less than their true value. This leaves a "residual" value after the lease has expired. This allows the lessor to sell that residual value to another investor who wants depreciation (or may in turn sell to other corporations who use depreciation). In our example, the residual could be $4,000.

For our example, to lease, the buyer pays $430/month for 48 months. An alternative use for the buyer's money is to invest it at a minimum of 5%, which would amount to $25,000 over the 4-year lease period. The economics of your company's financial position will be part of the rationale of whether or not to lease.

Tax Advantages

There are possible tax advantages from leasing. As an example, a company buys a bulldozer for $35,000. Financially, the company's books show the depreciation for 5 years on the straight line method. The more a company can increase depreciation expense, the less they pay to the IRS (assuming they have been fortunate enough to generate the revenue to owe taxes!).

A sublease allows transfer of the asset to another party, usually by the lessor. From the simple car lease involving two parties can come three- or four-party leases. The five-party lease is an expansion on the concept, where an investor steps in to purchase the residual value and gets depreciation tax advantages that either he can use or resell the benefit to someone who can. The five-party lease is said to be the key secret behind the leasing industry. The participants are: (1) the bank that loans to lessor, (2) the lessor who makes interest income on the investment and sells the residual value, (3) the customer, or user, (4) the manufacturer who sells the equipment, and (5) the investor who wants the depreciation break, or will resell.

Experts say a sound strategy is to invest in things that appreciate in value, and lease those things that depreciate. If the item requires some maintenance, often the lessor will want to insure it. But many larger companies want to "self-insure," so this can be arranged, and the costs removed from the lease. Users of an item have a responsibility to return the item in a condition expected from "reasonable wear and tear." Obviously, this leaves some room for judgment.

Leases can be highly complex. Buyers don't have to be financial experts, as they can always rely on the support and expertise of the company's finance function to provide analysis as required. The best advice is to consult your company experts when in doubt as to the relative merits of lease versus buy.

Tracking Cost Savings Results

Most departments have found it convenient to keep simple savings records—perhaps a simple box chart showing contributor's name, dollars saved, percent savings (based on purchases), and how accomplished. Occasionally there should be an audit of the recorded savings to ensure the integrity of the process.

Some suggested categories on how savings were achieved might be:

1. Change of supplier
2. Renegotiation of present source
3. Suggested engineering and/or material changes
4. Combined quantity buys
5. Miscellaneous or special (Spell out, such as learning curve, standardization, and others.)

The above should cover most areas of savings. No savings under perhaps $50 should be reported to conserve time and recording expense. In any event, use of some form of savings report is always productive.

Buyers are important players who have key roles in cost reduction programs. But, *how do you define a savings*? Although savings is traditionally defined as dollars paid below a previously paid price, experienced buyers have learned that with higher inflation, cost avoidance can be more important, though obviously not as important as actually reducing the costs below the previous level.

Obviously no ironclad rules exist for savings reports. Some disagreement over what should be reported is probably inevitable. From experience, following are some of the most common questions that buyers ask about savings programs, along with suggested answers to each:

1. On savings for specific projects, are savings measured from projected costs as originally budgeted? Answer: Could be, but most managers would accept a saving only when it is an actual reduction from a previously paid price.

2. On repetitive production runs, do savings count on the first invoice only, on all usage from then (obviously impractical), or is there a time limit? Answer: Savings should be reported only once, but on an annual basis.

3. Does elimination of "excess quality" qualify? An example would be substituting a shorter-life bearing for one that will outwear other parts of the machine. Answer: Yes, if the price reduction takes place, and quality is still suitable for the intended purpose. This is often a possibility where designs are ultraconservative and may be wasteful.

4. How about a voluntary price reduction? Answer: Absolutely not! This is one area where a buyer can take advantage of the system and fake a good job. The key is, did the buyer take the initiative? If a fine line, give credit.

5. How about elimination of secondary costs brought about by a higher price paid? Answer: Certainly, but the savings will be computed by deducting the extra price paid to accomplish the savings.

6. Are quantity discounts considered savings? Answer: Not on their own, but if a buyer changes the pattern of buying to take advantage of them, it is a valid saving. The key is, did the buyer do something different to effect the change? In this case, be certain the costs of carrying a higher quantity of inventory do not negate the savings.

Summarizing, savings dollar reports show the results of important buying activities. They encourage the buyer to act and they assure management support.

For purchasing to truly assert itself as a profit-productive function, such reports are vital. They are useful in awarding and encouraging all contributors.

Simple, straightforward reporting is an aid to any cost improvement plan. A monthly report should be issued by each buyer and sent through channels, to the PM and to the division manager or president. The report gives credit to individuals and keeps others informed of progress by projecting annual savings. A quarterly progress report may be of value as well. Remember: accounting details are not nearly so important as buyer awareness there is management support for savings, as these savings have an impact on company profitability.

14

Legal Issues in Buying

Purchasing's heritage lies in the Law of Agency, and purchasing alone has the formal authority to commit the corporation to expenditures. In view of this reality, purchasing is seen as independent and legally derived—not organizationally based. In this chapter we will look at the various aspects of law that apply to the buying job, in the context of both domestic and international buying. We will also look at many of the specific contractual clauses that should be considered for inclusion in purchase documents.

Current contract law derives from English common law, which is a body of documented case precedents. To create a contract, there must be an offer (to provide or do something) and an acceptance (signed acknowledgment to the purchase order), plus consideration (which is normally the payment). The purchase order becomes a binding contract upon acceptance or shipment of the goods.

A contract is simply a listing of promises made by the buyer and seller. A valid contract is made between capable parties with their mutual consent. Contract law is basically the same around the globe, in the sense that handshakes may still work, but in business and internationally, it's necessary to follow through with proper written documentation.

Satisfaction of the contract comes from performance. Nonperformance includes defective goods, rejection, and possibly damages. A party not complying with the contract commits a breach of contract.

Key Elements of Every Contract

For a contract to be valid, it will contain these key elements:

1. *Manifestation of intent*, which means both parties must agree to perform in some way.

2. *Consideration*, which is the price the buyer pays for what the supplier ships or does.

3. *Capacity to act*, which is to say, the parties must have the authority to commit their respective companies.

4. *Reality of intent*, which has to do with issues of mistakes or, as an example, use of duress when making contract.

5. *Legality of purpose*, which means that what is in the contract is not involved with crimes, torts, or violation of licensing statutes.

6. *Compliance with statute of frauds*, which protects a person from false testimony.

The buyer must be sure *who has ownership* and *who has authority to make agreements!* Because the buyer's job has legal accountability under the Law of Agency, wherein he or she has the authority to commit his or her employer through delegated signing authority, buyers are warned not to sign over their commitment authority limits.

Uniform Commercial Code

As we begin to look at the various laws and business issues that relate to buying, we will start with those that pertain primarily to domestic purchasing. This discussion will be followed by a review of the antitrust and other laws that govern international business arrangements.

The Federal government has authority to regulate business activity as stated in Article 1, Section 8 of the U.S. Constitution. Congress is empowered "to regulate Commerce with foreign nations, among several States, and the Indian Tribes." Within the U.S., the buyer has the Uniform Commercial Code (UCC) as the legal standard.

The UCC is a set of commercial laws that prescribe legal guidelines and limits for business transactions. Considered the most important regulation for U.S. commerce, the code attempts to systematize procedures and simplify confusing, complex, and often contradictory rules derived from common law and statutes from various states. The UCC consists of 10 articles covering Terms of Purchase, Letters of Credit, warehouse receipts, warranties, and other key areas. The UCC is a living document that is continually being interpreted by the courts to adapt to the practices of business today. Let's look at some of the more important clauses under the UCC.

"Boilerplate" is the term for a great deal of repetitive wording on inquiries, purchase orders, and follow-up requests. Certain clauses are used over and over. They can be standardized and brought into play as needed. The savings in typing is significant and the wording will be exactly as desired. Much typing and time to phrase the clauses is eliminated. A number of boilerplate clauses follow.

Warranties

What is the manufacturer's policy on liability protection to the buyer? It pays to be specific about supplier warranties. There are four types: express and implied warranties of merchantability, implied warranty of fitness for a particular purpose, and implied warranty of title. Warranties pass from the manufacturer through middlemen to the end-user.

Express warranties are in writing and state what the product will (or won't) do. For example, a battery will last 3 years under normal service.

Without anything in writing, the UCC (Section 2, Part 3) provides minimum requirements in an implied warranty. The buyer has a right to expect the goods to be merchantable, to "pass without objection in the trade under the contract description," and "fit for ordinary purposes for which such goods are used." If the buyer refuses to disclose to the seller how the item is used, that can lead to a later dispute.

When a seller makes a warranty orally and the confirming agreement between buyer and seller does not include this warranty, a problem may arise about whether the express warranty became part of the contract. Under the UCC, as part of the Law of Sales, the parole evidence rule states, "Oral or extrinsic evidence is not admissible to add to, alter, or vary the terms of a written contract."

Warranty clauses are most important when dealing with third-party arrangements. The UCC states that express warranties are "any description of the goods, which is made part of the basis of the bargain."

Warranties are negotiable! A warranty is a promise by the seller to the buyer that the goods purchased are of a quality conforming to certain standards. An express (written) warranty defines the extent of coverage and is created in three ways:

1. By "affirmation of fact or promise made by the seller,"
2. By description of the goods, and
3. By "sample or model"

In all three cases the promise, description, or sample must become "part of the basis for the bargain".[1] A *materials warranty clause* is mandatory for your protection! This is especially important when dealing with three-party arrangements. Spell out the obligations for warranties, repairs, etc. in the contract, using language something like this:

> "Seller shall be responsible for warranties of merchantability and fitness for a particular purpose and assures the products are safe to use.". (Buyer should spell out any special features, etc.)

---

[1] "Purchasing and the Law of Contracts," in McGraw-Hill's *Purchasing Handbook,* 4th ed., pp. 4–21.

"This warranty shall cover the first 12 months of use, or 18 months after purchase (or whatever). In the event of failure, the cost of replacement parts and labor will be reimbursed to the buyer by the seller. Items that fail under warranty shall be returned to the factory at the buyer's expense. Seller may choose to replace defective item(s) with a new replacement." (Again these issues are specific to the item.)

Epidemic Failure Clause

Epidemic failure can be defined in terms of failure occurring in "X" percent or more of total sales of the product to consumers within "Y" months of the date of the supplier's manufacture of them. You can negotiate the numbers! As an example, let's assume that "X" is negotiated at 3% and "Y" at 18 months. In this case, you can detail how the seller will repay you for excessive defects by using a clause such as this:

"An epidemic failure means a defect in materials or workmanship of a specific type that occurs or recurs in any part, component, accessory, or item of equipment of a product and that impairs the function, operation, or safety of such product: provided such failure occurs or recurs in three percent (3%) or more of the total sales of the products to consumers within eighteen (18) months from the date of manufacture.

"If such an 'epidemic failure,' Seller shall remedy such excessive defects more than the three percent [3%] in one of the following ways to be selected by Seller at its option: (1) Repair such units, (2) Replace such units, (3) Credit Purchaser units at Purchaser's unit price stated on the purchase order, or (4) Pay Purchaser for its reasonable expenses including labor, materials, and the usual transport allowances in correcting the units.

There is a chance the buyer can't get monies due from the supplier because of a lack of funds. In such case, the buyer may choose to insist on an insurance policy in his or her favor, provided and paid for by the seller.

Liability Insurance

The distributor buyer should be sure the manufacturer has adequate insurance to cover his product liability. One way to do this is to contractually indicate in the purchase order that the manufacturer is to furnish a Certificate of Insurance covering a specified insured dollar amount. While 98% of manufacturers will already have this coverage, it's the others that can cause a problem!

Force Majeure

A *Force Majeure* clause protects the seller, limiting his liability from "Acts of God." In stating the circumstances of a Force Majeure, the buyer should stipulate something along the lines of the following in the contract:

"Seller is responsible to notify Purchaser within seven (7) working days of such a happening, in writing, and Seller will make every reasonable effort to resolve the Force Majeure occurrence as soon as possible. Reportable occurrences would include (1) Acts of God; (2) civil uprising or war; (3) acts of the Government in either its sovereign or contractual capacity; (4) extreme weather conditions, fires, or floods; (5) epidemics or quarantine restrictions; (6) strikes; and (7) freight embargoes."

"Should the Seller be unable to fulfill the contract after a one month period, the purchaser shall have the right to terminate the purchase order, with its only liability being to pay Seller for products received by Purchaser."

Contract Cancellation or Termination

Spell out under what conditions either party can withdraw from the purchase. A *cancellation clause* should spell out under what conditions either party can withdraw from the purchase.

A *termination for convenience clause* is difficult to get seller's acceptance, but it can be done. An example of such a clause would be as follows:

"The Buyer may terminate this order for convenience. In the event of such termination, Buyer will reimburse Seller for all expenses incurred or committed up to the date of receipt of notice of termination."

A *termination for default clause* example is shown below:

"In the event Seller fails to properly fulfill any of the terms of this order, or if seller files a petition for bankruptcy, reorganization, assignment for benefit of creditors, or similar proceedings, Buyer may, by written notice to Seller, without prejudice to any other rights or remedies that Buyer may have, terminate further performance by Seller. In the event of such termination, Buyer may complete performance of this purchase order by such means as Buyer selects, and Seller shall be responsible for any additional costs incurred by Buyer in doing so."

This Default Compensation clause holds the supplier liable for procurement costs incurred by the buyer should the supplier default his contract.

Rejection of Goods

An indemnification clause can be controversial, and difficult to get supplier approval for, as its purpose is full protection of the buyer, which implies risk to the seller. Use this clause to protect yourself in the event of rejection of merchandise.

There are two areas to cover here. The first is personal or property damage, and the second is patent, copyright infraction, or trade secret theft. The latter area looms even larger in offshore buying, where the exact origin of a product may be less clear than in domestic buying. Buyers want the supplier's assurance that they, the customer, are held harmless from suits for both above areas. Include and use as much of the clause as possible to protect the buyer if the product or merchandise fails.

"Seller covenants and agrees at all times to indemnify, hold harmless (including, but not limited to, the payment of all reasonable expenses and satisfaction of all judgments) and defend Purchaser, its agents, and their respective directors, officers, employees, successors, and assigns against any and all claims for loss, damage or injury, suits or actions brought against Purchaser or such other parties by or on account of any third person, persons or entities, on account of any personal injuries received or sustained by such person or damage to tangible property, other than the product, caused by or growing out of any defects of the products supplied by Seller to Purchaser.

"Seller's obligations hereunder are conditioned upon Purchaser promptly notifying Seller of all such claims, demands, or legal proceedings. Seller shall have the right to control, manage, litigate, or compromise any such claim, suit or demand; and Purchaser shall provide such information and assistance in the defense as Seller may reasonable request. Purchaser agrees that it shall not compromise or settle any claim or case without the prior written approval of Seller.

"The indemnification shall not apply in event of misapplication of the product or improper installation, or Purchaser's negligence in handling or modification without Seller's written consent, that is the cause of any injury to persons or damage to property. Except for the foregoing, Seller will defend any suit and hold Purchaser and its partners harmless against any claim, demand, cost, or loss arising from a suit or proceeding brought against Purchaser or its customers based on the claim that any product or part thereof furnished hereunder constitutes an infringement of any patent, copyright, or trade secret of the United States, if notified and given authority, information, and assistance for the settlement or defense of the same that, other than for the assistance of Purchaser employees, shall be at Seller's expense; and Seller shall pay all damages and costs awarded therein against Purchaser."

Patents, Proprietary Information, and Disclosure

A *patent, or proprietary protection clause,* should be used if appropriate. This type of protection clause can be included as the last paragraph of the indemnification clauses, but also may be used alone.

In the case of most purchases, this clause is intended to protect the buyer should the item be patented by another party. The liability for using or reselling an item made by someone without a valid patent, without knowledge or intention on the part of the buyer, is great. So, a precautionary protective clause should be in the terms and conditions whereby the seller agrees to assume full responsibility. Such a clause could look something like this:

> "Seller warrants that his product(s) are of his own design and manufacture, and any use of others' patents or proprietary design has been cleared properly."

Sales of counterfeit trademark goods may be illegal in the U.S. The liability for the buyer reselling an item made by someone without a valid patent, with or without knowledge or intention on the part of the buyer, is great. A precautionary protective clause should be part of the terms and conditions getting the seller to assume full responsibility.

The warranty against patent infringement is deemed to be one of the *warranties of title*. But, when the seller is making something conforming to what is specified by the buyer, the liability could be the buyer's. This clause can be included as the last paragraph of the indemnification clauses, but it also can stand alone.

Buyers routinely sending out for quotations may have to provide new innovative designs or know-how. Notify the supplier about limitations to the use of this data by using a protection clause.

> "The *Confidential Disclosure* of . . . (info disclosed) shall only be used for the purpose of . . . (manufacture, assembly, etc.)"

Simply giving technical information without such a statement puts the data in the public domain.

Some lawyers have pointed out that Americans freely give or make available their information to the world when buyers make price inquiries of suppliers. In sending quote requests, the buyer has to be careful to send proprietary data fully protected. If the patent is not protected in the foreign country, it can be copied and made. A distinction is drawn for proprietary protection of data of a technical or business nature, which are classified as "trade secrets" or "confidential." These may be unpatentable, so by use of the following clause, the buyer shows data are submitted with restrictive provisions and establishes a proprietary or confidential relationship. Getting a signature of acknowledgement is more binding.

> "(Date)
>
> "To Chris Michaelson (person receiving disclosure);
>
> The *Confidential Disclosure* of Pooler & Associates' (your company) computer related idea (. . . spell out the type of information disclosed) to me on this date, shall only be used for the purpose of quoting (or assembly, evaluating manufacture costs, etc.). The purpose for disclosure is to determine if this product has economic feasibility.
> I agree to use this information mindful of Pooler & Associates' (your company) patent pending application.
>
> _____
> Chris Michaelson (Signature of reviewer)"

Other Suggested Purchase Order Clauses

Following are some boilerplate clauses that won't all be used for every purchase. Instead, these are representative examples offered to buyers who should adapt them to the specifics of each negotiation and specifics of the buy.

Many problems that arise when sourcing come mainly from improperly documented buying agreements. Some of the following instruction clauses should be added to the standard clauses used on the back of the purchase order form. Spell them out specifically for major buys. The individual buying company is responsible for its own proper wording, based on its buyers' negotiations with suppliers.

1. An *Entire Agreement* clause prevents a seller from later defending his mistake by saying essentially "Your letter, or quality people told me to do it differently." The purpose is to strengthen written agreements:

    "This agreement shall solely control the term of Purchase and Sale of the products/services hereunder. Any contrary, different or added terms in any purchase order, contract, sales acknowledgment, or other documentation of either party shall have no effect and this agreement shall override any such documentation. This agreement may not be changed or modified except by written notice signed by both parties."

2. *Assignment of Agreement.* Buyers may want to prohibit assignment of the agreement or subcontracting to another party without the buyer's approval. To ensure you know who is doing the work, use the clause:

    "This agreement may not be assigned to any other party, nor any interest transferred without the written consent of the other party. Furnishing of any products (other than component and replacement parts) shall not be subcontracted by Seller without the prior written consent of Purchaser."

3. *Repairs, Service Parts, and Replacement* clause, spells out obligations on repairs and parts into the contract. This is especially important when dealing with third-party arrangements. The buyer's interest here lies in any surprise changes in the design of items purchased. Also, some suppliers may find it convenient to drop a product and not provide for replacement components later. Insert:

    "During life of this agreement, Seller agrees to provide Purchaser a complete description of any changes in form, fit, or function of component parts or accessories of products purchased. Seller agrees to furnish all component specifications, drawings, and installation instructions for parts sufficient for service and installation.

    Seller agrees to make available for replacement purposes for those products sold, functional fabricated or purchased replacement parts (or acceptable substitutes) ten (10) years after date of last unit of production by Seller of (name key parts here)."

This bears repeating! These clauses are representative examples only and suggested as a training aid. The buying company is responsible for its own proper wording, based on negotiations with the supplier and the specifics of the goods bought.

Socioeconomic and Environmental Laws

There are other socioeconomic and environmental laws that can have implications for the buyer. Although these were touched on in Chapter 1, it is worthwhile to highlight the more important ones here.

Public Law 95-507 mandates goals for minority purchases. It requires any prime contractor receiving government contracts over $1 million to establish minority sourcing programs. The Defense Department itself has set percentage minority participation goals for its defense procurements, and these in some cases allow premium prices to be paid to meet the legislation's objectives.

Other examples of legislative regulations include:

- The Toxic Substance Control Act of 1977, which addresses disposal of hazardous substances—supervised by the Office of Hazardous Materials Transportation, Department of Transportation

- Radioactive materials and reactors—controlled by the Nuclear Regulatory Commission

- Radiation producing products, such as TV receivers, microwave ovens, x-ray machines, and laser products—covered by the Radiation Control for Health and Safety Act of 1968

- Narcotics and Drug control—under the Department of Justice

- Consumer products—must comply with the Consumer Product Safety Act as well as the Flammable Fabrics Act

- Household appliances—must comply with the Energy Policy and Conservation Act

Anti-Trust Laws

Let's look at some of the more pertinent laws in effect in the United States as they relate to the job of buying. The antitrust laws that are of concern are:

1. The Sherman Act
2. The Clayton Act, with its famous amendment known as the Robinson–Patman Act
3. The Federal Trade Commission Acts

Of these, the buyer's main concern lies with the Clayton Act and the Robinson–Patman Act, which address pricing situations that could be considered "restraint of trade."

The Sherman Act, passed in 1890, made *illegal* certain contracts and conspiracies in restraint of trade.

Section 2 of The Clayton Act forbids price discrimination between different buyers "where the effect of such discrimination may be substantially to lessen competition or tend to create a monopoly in any line of commerce." Section 3 forbids tying-in arrangements wherein the buyers must buy something they may not want in order to get what is wanted.

The Robinson–Patman Act redefined the above Section 2 in 1936. This Act prohibits a buyer from knowingly inducing and buying at discriminatory lower prices than other competitive buyers. This is to ensure equality of treatment to all buyers by a seller. Buyers can be in violation of this act should they induce the seller to lower the price by giving false competitive price information. For example, assume you were to say, "I can get it for $2 from Jones" when you're really paying $2.50. That's illegal! You can say you don't like the price, say it's too high, but you can't induce a lower price by falsely naming prices lower than you know exist.

Although domestically, buyers can be in violation of Robinson–Patman by giving false competitive price information, these antitrust laws don't apply overseas. Reciprocity, wherein "If you buy my wine, I'll buy your flour" is illegal in the United States. However, it is a common and legally acceptable type of business arrangement overseas.

The *Federal Trade Commission Act*, passed in 1914, created the Federal Trade Commission to prevent unfair methods of competition. *The Trade Act Of 1974* amended Title VII of the Tariff Act of 1930, and prevents foreigners selling at prices much lower in the U.S. than at home, an activity commonly known as "dumping." *Antidumping legislation* may be invoked when a foreign product is sold in the U.S. at a price lower than its cost. The Act provides for additional *countervailing duties* when foreign goods are dumped in the U.S. market.

Two sections of this Act apply specifically to this issue of dumping.

Section 201 provides relief from injury caused or threatened by unfairly priced imports, though it is noted that to date, only about 12 of 60 cases have resulted in successful relief.

Section 301 empowers the President to "take all appropriate and feasible action . . . to enforce the rights of the United States under any trade agreement . . . to counter any foreign trade practice that is unjustifiable, unreasonable, or discriminatory and burdens or restricts U.S. commerce."

Most new buyers have heard of the Buy America Act, and believe it to be an important law. The fact is that the Buy America Act of 1933 is practically a nonissue to many commercial buyers. It was passed to provide preference to U.S. suppliers when the Federal Government made purchases, but provisions of this Act were weakened by the Trade Agreement Act of 1979, and the Defense Acquisition Circular No. 76-25 in 1980. The Buy America Act still can apply where national security is at stake. For government procurement and purchasing by government contractors, it places significant restrictions on buying other than U.S. produced items.

Many states have enacted legislation for some type of American preference policy. However, Buy America is not a factor in most commercial buying decisions.

The preceding is by no means a comprehensive listing of all the laws applying to primarily domestic purchasing, but are the most important ones.

Now let's turn to the areas at issue as they relate to international buying.

United Nations Convention

"If it doesn't work, we'll sue 'em!" is sometimes the U.S. buyer's trained reaction. But, internationally, that's not easy. Global buying was intended to have come under the "United Nations Convention on Contracts for the International Sale of Goods." Known simply as the 1980 Convention (CISG), it contains 101 articles, covering formation of contracts, as well as the rights, debts, and remedies.

About 60 nations have ratified CISG, including the U.S., whose Congress passed it in 1986, making it effective in 1988. Essentially, the CISG makes it easier for the seller to enforce verbal agreements or phone conversations. In fact, terms appear to be more favorable to the seller in some respects, so "buyer beware!"

If your contract is with a supplier whose country also has approved, the new terms apply unless you specifically state *CISG does not apply*. Make sure you understand the implications of the CISG before you sign up to these provisions.

Geneva Agreement on Tariffs and Trade

In lieu of a code, international trade is being conducted through bilateral and multilateral trade agreements and under the General Agreement on Tariffs and Trade. The GATT agreement created in 1948 provides for periodic negotiations to reduce tariffs, settle disputes, and discuss ways to promote "free trade."

Through eight "rounds" of follow-up meetings (e.g., the Kennedy Round in 1984 featured such players as President Reagan, Premier Nakasone, and Prime Minister Thatcher), and the Uruguay Round concluded in 1995, tariffs on industrial goods have been negotiated down to the 2% to 6% range on average.

Global Trade Barriers

Boycotts

Some groups may call for boycotts of goods from countries based on an underlying social, political, or economic motivation. Boycotts, while not common, could be a problem for the buyer. Should a buyer honor a boycott, such an action is subject to punishment. A buyer not only should not make any agreement involving any boycott, but is obliged by law to report such attempts to the US government. Run to an attorney on this issue!

Cartels and Closed Countries

Cartels present buyers with an unfair pricing situation. They exist when companies that produce the same or similar products plan together to control their market share and prices. *By U.S. law such action is illegal!* OPEC is perhaps the most famous cartel, which was successful in controlling the price of petroleum at one time.

Next in order of potentially serious impediments to trade are "closed countries." Certain foreign governments play the protectionist game to close their borders to any import except those they absolutely want. Some newer industrialized nations ban foreign firms from making investments or acquiring control of native companies. This situation is constantly changing.

Legal issues arise from many commercial situations and they can't all be anticipated. But, with the preceding key reviewed legalities in mind, you as a buyer don't need to be a lawyer or be overly concerned with such matters. If situations arise, it is timely to seek legal help.

As explained in Chapter 1, countertrade is any transaction involving exchange of goods or services for something of equal value. Sometimes cash is used to compensate for value differences. It is an arrangement where there have been few problems, but this could raise antitrust implications. For example, if a buyer was trying to fulfill the countertrade terms, and he or she pressured suppliers to buy certain items along the lines of, "I won't buy from you unless you buy this, so we can compete abroad," this could be a questionable practice.

Counterfeiting and Piracy of Property

Agreements that protect ownership are: the Paris Convention for Patents, the Universal Copyright Convention, the Berne Convention for Copyrights, and the Madrid Agreement on Trademarks. Primary patent and copyright protection is under the World Intellectual Property Organization.

Gray market goods are authentic items brought into the country by unauthorized or unlicensed distributors. Although Customs doesn't sometimes appear to be overly attentive to the gray market, some companies are being damaged as their sales are diluted due to gray market activities. Electronic goods have been especially hard hit.

New technological developments speed around the world in months. Today, a company brings out a new product and it is copied in a matter of a few months, or even weeks. A few years ago, a company had up to 3 years when it could recover much of its research and development costs. Today, the speed with which piracy of design is occurring has begun to discourage some large research and development efforts.

An anticounterfeiting code has been in existence to be reviewed by GATT since 1970. Some headway is being made, but getting a consensus remains difficult. The GATT Round in Uruguay in 1986 took up the issue, but it was still under discussion in 1995. During 1996 there have been agreements to stop the activity, but rumors persist of continued violations.

The ITC decides proprietary rights and whether copyrights are violated. It decides injury to a U.S. company from foreign unfair trade practices. It does not determine *if* it occurs.

How can designs be protected if the American company is owned by foreign interests? This is an important question, as certain foreign governments feel their citizens have a right to use whatever information is available. They go out of their way to protect that right. Moderates believing the rest of the world denies free trade fear trade reprisals would undermine the world economy, so they advocate a cautious approach to solving some of these proprietary legal issues.

Appeals in U.S. patent-infringement suits go to the Court of Appeals for the Federal Circuit (CAFC). Of course, foreign companies have no monopoly on such disputes. Recent Kodak use of Polaroid's film is an example, where in 1990 the courts ruled Kodak had to pay damages.

Import Customs Laws and Regulations

Regardless of laws—international or otherwise—that may be considered applicable to disputes between foreign nationals, when buyers import into the U.S., they and their company are bound by all applicable U.S. laws and Customs regulations relating to such imports. You need to understand the essence of import regulations themselves.

Import duties for contractor type products are down to around 2% to 6%. For Most Favored Nations (MFNs), many duties have been lowered or eliminated.

When buying internationally, it's a good idea to contractually state in the purchase order that the party signing for the foreign seller must be a company officer, and has the authority to contract for the seller. This is recommended as foreigners often aren't delegated such authority. When buying globally, the same legal issues pertain as with domestic buying, but the scope of law expands to other areas such as Customs duties, embargoes, import licenses, etc.

Unfair Pricing and Protectionism

Organized labor is a major force trying to protect its jobs. Charges have been made of unfair trade practices in the shoe and textile industries, copper fabricators and miners, and others. There has been, and remains some, pressure in Congress to block Japanese products in retaliation for our inability to break into some Japanese markets.

It's not solely the Japanese whose business practices raise legal issues. When companies can't resolve their complaints about unfair pricing, they have some relief under various trade acts.

Antidumping Duties

As previously defined, selling products at prices less than their fair market value is termed "dumping." Although we commented briefly on the laws relating to antidumping in the earlier discussion of antitrust laws, let's look in more detail at the subject as it relates to the penalties involved for noncompliance.

Title VII of the Tariff Act of 1930, and as amended by the Trade Act of 1974, provides for added duties when foreign goods are dumped in the U.S. market. An antidumping duty may be assessed for imports sold to American buyers at prices less than their fair market value. As an example, a duty fine as high as 213% was put on imported Swedish bearings, as it was found that nine foreign bearing makers were selling at prices about one-third of those in their home countries. The response of the offenders was to simply reduce the shipments from their home plants, diverting through third parties in other countries who ultimately shipped the bearings to the States. Shipments from Sweden dropped almost 20% in 1989, while shipments were increased as high as 543% from Austria, Spain, and Argentina.[2] Then bearing shipments increased from plants in Spain, Poland, Mexico, Turkey, South Korea, and Hong Kong that don't make any bearings. They got away with it, as it is difficult to prove.

The U.S. Department of Commerce (DOC) rules on dumping, and makes the price ruling based upon complaints presented. It is difficult to get the DOC to make a dumping ruling because getting good data is not easy. To improve the chances for success of a filed complaint, critics want this authority transferred to the U.S. Trade Representative.

Action against dumping is controversial, as seen by the recent try to impose a 35% penalty on Canadian housing shake shingles. A problem of using duties to protect American industry is that there is always a tradeoff penalty paid by the American consumer. In this case, a tariff was imposed that would have eliminated $350 million of Canadian lumber exports to the U.S. Four thousand Canadian jobs would have been eliminated. While highly unpopular in Canada,

---

[2]"Cat and mouse game," *Forbes*, May 28, 1990, p. 48.

it was considered by some Americans as an acceptable way to react to severe hardship suffered by American labor. This action generated Canadian debate on punitive countermeasures.

The final solution to the conflict was a 15% surtax that was imposed on Canadian lumber dealers by the Canadian government to prevent higher proposed U.S. tariffs. Though praised as a compromise, this action meant a 15% increase in cost to U.S. consumers.

Government subsidies can take the form of duty rebates, lower sales taxes, income tax concessions, transportation taxes, cash rebates, and lower interest rates on loans. A spate of retaliatory tariffs hopefully will be avoided. Foreign companies, as well as American, are often given government incentives and subsidies to export. Procedure to answer a complaint is to call for an investigation by the U.S. Trade Representative; staffed with about 130 people, the office of the Trade Representative takes up cases involving U.S. companies claiming they can't get into a foreign market.

Value Added Taxes are used by governments in various ways. Certainly as a way to raise money, they often influence trade by enhancing or discouraging it. Taxes are another tactic used for protectionism. Some 50 countries have a Value Added Tax (VAT). This VAT is widely used in Europe.

The U.S. has long complained about these discriminatory type taxes. For example, the VAT is not imposed on goods Europe ships into the U.S., while American goods are subject to it when going into Europe. Thus this tax discourages American exports.

Canada has a business-transfer tax that is similar to a VAT though it shouldn't affect their cost of products. The Goods and Services Tax (GST) is 7% of value that was imposed in 1991 to replace an older manufacturers' tax. The GST differs from a retail sales tax in that the tax is paid as value is added. As an example, an aluminum sheet is sold for $10 to a stamping plant that pays 70 cents of taxes at that time. The stamping plant sells to a fabricator and collects a 7% tax of $3.50. When the stamping company pays its tax, it gets to deduct the tax it has already paid (70 cents) to the aluminum mill. Each firm in turn does the same accounting until the consumer pays his 7% on the retail price. The Canadian Government claims that consumers will pay no more, though the government collects its taxes faster. The level of taxation is of major importance in the business environment.

Countervailing Duties

Countervailing Duties are the internationally approved way under GATT to prevent unfairly priced products being sold at excessively low prices. Higher tariffs and surcharge taxes are permissible when there is a balance-of-payments problem.

Countervailing Duties may be levied against any foreign government that permits or causes an unfair trade advantage within the U.S. Many governments have been accused of violating U.S. trade laws by subsidizing their industries to gain an unfair advantage. As an example of how this works, let's say the Greek government gives a 2% rebate to encourage export of a certain product. Spain does not. If Spain or the U.S. company complains, U.S. Customs might add a 2% countervailing duty to buys from Greece, to level the market.

A well known complaint is the U.S. charge that government subsidies granted European farmers prevent U.S. agriculture produce sales. Many European companies are government owned, so some people believe the U.S. government should become a participant in their problems.

When Title Passes

A key to solving disputes is answering the questions, "Who has ownership of the goods," and "When do I take legal possession?" The clauses that follow are vital to the prevention of disputes and useful when one occurs.

The Chamber of Commerce has standardized and modernized 14 International Commercial Terms that are known as INCOTERMS. Buyers sometimes misuse such terms, because of confusion concerning their use and meaning.

The basic function of an INCOTERM is to call for the preferred method of shipment. It also spells out clearly the division of responsibilities and obligations between buyer and seller. The goods are legally delivered by seller to buyer at a point spelled out in the specific FOB within the INCOTERM. Figure 14-1 summarizes responsibilities based on identifying the transfer point for possession of goods. An INCOTERM determines who will pay the costs, and who assumes the risks.

International Commercial Terms

Purchase orders may contain an INCOTERM clause such as the following:

> "This contract will be governed by the provisions of INCOTERMS. In case of dispute, the published reference by the ICC, specifying 'What the buyer and seller are responsible for' will apply".

In case of dispute, the buyer has a published reference, specifying "What the buyer and seller are responsible for."[3]

Lacking mention to the contrary, a purchase order is treated as a shipping point contract, with risk on the buyer when the seller has delivered the goods to

---

[3]ICC's "INCOTERMS" booklet, ICC Publishing, 156 Fifth Avenue, Suite 820, New York, NY 10010. (212) 206-1150

B = BUYER RESPONSIBILITY
S = SELLER RESPONSIBILITY

INCOTERM	BASIC RESPONSIBILITIES	LOADS INLAND VEHICLE	SELECT & LOAD SHIP SHIPPING DOCUMENTS	PAYS FREIGHT	OBTAINS INSURANCE	ASSUMES RISK DURING TRANSIT	PAYS DUTY
EX WORKS	ORIGIN SPECIFIED AS TO PLANT SHIPPING DOCK.	B	B	B	B	B	B
FOR/FOT	SELLER ARRANGES RAIL CARRIER. OBTAINS BILL OF LADING.	S	—	B	B	B	B
FAS VESSEL FOREIGN PORT	SAME AS FOB EXCEPT BUYER PAYS FOR LIFTING.	S	B	B	B	B	B
FOB VESSEL	SELLER ARRANGES INLAND SHIPPING TO SHIP DOCK.	S	S	B	B	B	B
C & F	SELLER'S PRICE INCLUDES TRANSPORTATION.	S	S	S	B	B	B
C I F	SAME AS C & F AND ALSO INCLUDES INSURANCE.	S	S	S	S	B	B
EX SHIP	SELLER TO IMPORT SHIP LOADING.	S	S	S	S	B	B
EX QUAY (DOCK)	SELLER PAYS TO IMPORT CUSTOMS.	S	S	S	S	S	S
FOB DELIVERED	SELLER PAYS ALL COST.	S	S	S	S	S	S

MAXIMUM BUYER ← RESPONSIBILITY → MAXIMUM SELLER

Figure 14-1 INCOTERMS define buyer and seller responsibilities.

the carrier. Usually at the point of ownership exchange, buyers will take possession. They assume the responsibility and risks for further transport and costs.

A distinction is made between who has possession and is controlling the shipment and who bears the risk and responsibility to settle problems occurring during shipment. The buyer has to be wary, as under some terms, this risk has already passed to you though the seller has paid for and is controlling the shipment.

Seldom will buyers choose maximum responsibility using *Ex Works*. Firms using this term, such as banana plantations, have strong skills, and want to control everything. Most buys will gravitate toward the middle, C&F, CIF, or Ex Ship. The 14 full INCOTERMS are reviewed in Chapter 17.

Battle of the Forms

Daily throughout the U.S. and the rest of the world, thousands of purchase orders are prepared with carefully time-developed terms & conditions (T&Cs) of purchase. Methodically, supplying companies acknowledge these customer orders on *their* forms with conditions of sale. Buyers mailing their POs often ignore the supplier's terms, just as the supplier does. Should major difficulty arise, each party falls back on its terms and somehow reaches a settlement. Without the buyer's T&Cs it would be difficult to build a logical negotiating argument, much less a legal case. The implication is clear: use care in developing the provisions, terms, and conditions of your purchase! To do otherwise is to invite a dispute.

Dispute Settlements

An aspect of the buying job is that buyers have to settle conflicts and disputes. Since the buyer must often question many aspects of a purchase, the buyer is in "conflict between two worlds"—that of the company he or she represents and that of the supplying interests.

There is no substitute for trust and a willingness to negotiate to clear any disputed commercial transaction. When all else fails, the last resort is to go to court. But in a sense, that's tantamount to an admission of failure, as the relationship may be irreparably damaged. Lawsuits often leave parties unable or unwilling to do business again as resentment is too deep.

Most commercial disputes that arise are settled amicably. The best inducement for settlement is the understanding that the seller wants another sale, and the buyer likes or needs the materials being purchased. Despite the utmost care in preparing the purchase order, the chance of an occasional sticky dispute is always present.

Settling consequential damages resulting from product failure is difficult. As an example of consequential damage, consider a situation where a a fuse blows and a factory shuts down for the day, sending 100 people home. An overzealous buyer might try to collect for the lost wages, but in most cases this will be unsuccessful, as the damage is "consequential."

It's possible to contract for consequential damages by negotiation and stating it is covered in your purchase order. However, there will invariably be heavy costs charged into the pricing by the seller looking to cover the added risk—and that will discourage most buyers trying for it.

Title to company items passes without a document, just as when you shop for groceries. You don't have to prove ownership when buying contractor and industrial items. Yet, in case of dispute, or mixup and losses during shipment, it is the issue of *ownership* that determines who must act and who must pay the cost.

Generally, in a conflict the following typically hold true:

1. Typewritten insertions in context take precedence over preprinted (or "boilerplate") items.

2. Handwritten insertions take precedence over typed or preprinted.

3. Spelled out numbers typically take precedence over the Arabic numerals.

4. Conflicts favor the first stipulation in order of presentation.

5. Ambiguities are often interpreted against the party who inserted the language that is the source of the ambiguity.

Disputes start with a conflict between two parties. The settlement steps arranged in increasing complexity are: (1) problem solving, (2) mediation, (3) arbitration, and (4) litigation. Perhaps buyer and seller, by using problem solving techniques, will reach a settlement. This is the preferred resolution.

If buyers focus objectively on the need of a resolution, and do not use a "We" versus "They" approach, most disputes can be settled amicably. Failing this, the next level of settlement is pursued. Although there is a tendency in our litigious society to pursue a legal approach too quickly, it should be remembered that court action is too uncertain and certainly too complex and costly to be the course of first action. In any event, it's just as certain that both parties, assuming integrity, want to solve any dispute. But, what if you can't find a way to settle? Submitting an unsolvable dispute to binding arbitration is one alternative.

Alternative Dispute Resolution

Increasingly, resolutions have taken place through "alternative dispute resolution" or ADR, which consists of arbitration and/or mediation. What's the difference? While mediation implies a "counseling" role for the mediator wherein decisions are reached by consensus, arbitration is generally backed by laws in the U.S. and abroad. In binding arbitration, the arbitrator—the neutral third party—listens to both sides' "best case" arguments and renders a decision.

A major advantage of the arbitration process is the shorter time between filing and a decision from a court action. Also, hearsay testimony is permitted. The procedures followed usually will be prescribed by the American Arbitration Association or the International Chamber of Commerce. Inclusion of a purchase order clause providing for use of either of the two organizations commits the two disputing parties to use this method to secure a neutral judgment. So, use of a standard Arbitration clause in the contract gains advance agreement of the parties to arbitrate as part of their contractual understanding. A buyer may never invoke the clause, but should the need arise, it commits the two parties to a practical way to a neutral judgment. If the buyer fails to enter the clause on his purchase document, arbitration will still be possible if both parties agree.

The American Arbitration Association (AAA) suggests the following clause be inserted into the purchase order:

> "Any controversy or claim arising out of or relating to this contract, or the breach thereof, shall be settled by arbitration in accordance with the Rules of the American Arbitration Association, and judgment upon the award rendered by the Arbitrator(s) may be entered in any Court having jurisdiction thereof."

The arbitrator acts as a type of judge, making a decision that is based only on the evidence that has been given. Judgments are given in a short written form, but they are not published. An arbitrator can be challenged before a final decision is reached and the AAA will determine whether to disqualify. After a decision is rendered, and in the event it is inconsistent with the parties' negotiated rights or the law, an appeal can be made to the court.

The other option is the International Chamber of Commerce's (ICC) Court of Arbitration. Their wide contacts within many nations make them preferable for offshore squabbles. If you wish to use the ICC, insert a clause as follows:

> "All disputes arising in connection with the present contract shall be finally settled under the Rules of Conciliation and Arbitration of the International Chamber of Commerce by one or more arbitrators appointed in accordance with the Rules."

After 30 days the order becomes final. If a party wants to litigate before a judge or jury, a complaint must be filed during the 30 days. The arbitration proceedings are admissible as evidence in a trial. The court may enforce the ADR decision or render its own.

Remember that when buyers give power to a third party to solve their dispute through binding arbitration, an appeal from the award or decision is not expected. It's to prevent recurring quarrels over the same incident and the use of lawyers, but symptomatic of our legal system, lawyers are often willing to make any challenge.

Mediation

As implied earlier, mediation differs from arbitration, as the third party doesn't have authority to settle, but merely aids in clarifying issues. Mediators have the right and responsibility to suggest compromises or solutions. Mediators are neutral third parties that act as moderators between the disputants. They try to cause the two parties to discuss and focus on the disagreement, and to assist the parties settle their own grievances. Local agencies sponsored by local or state governments usually provide mediation service free of charge.

Mediators are most desirable for small family businesses or an intracompany dispute where the parties must keep working together. Again, this is the preferable course as lawsuits often leave parties unable or unwilling to do business again as deep resentment continues.

How would you, as a buyer, solve this bid scenario? A few years ago, a New York discount house placed an afternoon newspaper ad featuring portable TV sets at $89.50 each. Unfortunately, the printer goofed, and the price was listed as $8.95 in the advertisement. This was a well publicized situation that resulted in a rush of thousands who showed up demanding a set at the quoted price. Ultimately, the police had to come and close the store. To quiet the customers, the manager agreed to let all sets go at the low price as a matter of good public relations. However, he stressed that legally they did not have to sell on the basis of an obvious error.

The American Arbitration Association had a similar situation to resolve—though caused not by a typographical error, but a mathematical miscalculation. The question came down to "Can one party *bind another to the terms of a contract that they know is erroneously stated?*"

In this case, the contracting parties were a general building contractor and a plumbing subcontractor. In preparation for bidding on the construction of a commercial building, the general contractor had shown the architect's plans to several plumbing firms. He asked how much each would charge to handle all the plumbing and air conditioning work.

Material costs were fairly uniform in the area. All plumbing contractors were subject to the same union contracts, so it was expected the bids would be quite close. They all were, except for that of one company, whose bid was remarkably low.

The general contractor was experienced enough to know this low bid was based on miscalculation. More than that, he knew exactly where the error was, but decided to accept the bid and proceed on that basis. The low bid seemed to be a blessing to the general contractor who wanted to lower his own bid to the real estate syndicate that was putting up the structure.

On the strength of the unusually low price for plumbing, the general contractor entered a low bid of his own and nailed down the job. Shortly after the project got under way, however, the plumbing subcontractor discovered the error. Promptly, they got the general contractor on the phone. "Look," he said, "We just spotted a mistake on our work sheets. We forgot to include the extension of air-conditioning ducts into a wing of the building that was not part of the original plans. We will have to charge more for that."

The general contractor expressed sympathy, but offered no relief. "That's tough on you," he said, "but a contract is a contract. If I gave you more, it would come out of my pocket. I've already bid on the basis of your estimate. Now you're stuck with it." The general contractor reminded the plumbing contractor that the contract contained a damages clause that would be invoked if the work wasn't done according to the specifications, and on time. Both parties needed a quick decision. This contract also had an arbitration clause, and the plumbing contractor promptly invoked it.

During arbitration, arguments and evidence for the case were aired. The general contractor's lawyer stated, "Neither the law nor an arbitration hearing should be available to any businessman for the purpose of escaping contractual obligations that may prove to be onerous. They may have shown bad judgment in bidding low. That's too bad for them. But, my client acted on the basis of his belief, and the plumbing supply house should be held to it."

"This is not a case of an improvident contract" replied the attorney for the plumber. "This is just a matter of an obvious mistake in arithmetic, and, furthermore, it is a mistake that the general contractor must have known about when he accepted the bid so hastily."

Now, put yourself into the role of the arbitrator who must render the award. Would you return a decision for the general contractor or for the plumbing subcontractor? Generally a supplier will not be held to an erroneous quotation especially if he advised the contractor in time to alter his bid.

Foreign Corrupt Practices Act

The 1977 *Foreign Corrupt Practices Act* raised ethical issues for Americans involved in international business dealings, as it declared it a crime for American business executives to pay for favors or otherwise offer bribery to foreign government officials. Corporations face fines up to $1 million and individuals $10,000— and the employer cannot indemnify the individual. Penalties for the individual can also include a jail term of up to 5 years, so take note! An example of a potential buying problem is if a foreign official offers to arrange for purchases through his connections. Your challenge is to discern whether you are running into unnecessary government bureaucracy or whether their law mandates the administrative delay.

This law came on the heels of the Watergate scandal. About 400 corporations, including 117 of the top 500, were found to have paid out hundreds of millions of dollars for these nefarious services. The Security and Exchange Commission described it as a national crisis. Money was used to influence foreigners who had discretionary authority to assist the company to get or maintain business. The new law did not prevent payments of lesser figures to get someone to perform normal duties at a clerical or lower administrative level. In 1988, the Senate relaxed on this issue, stating that U.S. business personnel could pay "if payments were legal in a foreign country where they were made to expedite routing government action."[4]

Consider some real-life situations: You can't move your shipment from a port, and it seems a gift might ease its release. When does a gift become a bribe? Is it any different if it's in an Italian or a Korean port? In either event, make sure any service given is legitimate and not part of the official duties of the official offering the service. This is a sensitive area because people-to-people contacts are there, providing potential for illegal payments.

Examples have been cited by Americans, who, upon completing a deal, were told what gift would be proper to celebrate the occasion. Bribery is not a crime in many developing countries. In fact, gift giving is often part of their heritage— and is in no way considered a bribe.

Summary: The Buyer and Legal Issues

As we close out this chapter, let's consider the following scenario about "the angry supplier," which will bring out some legal issues that should interest most buyers:

Ross Dielectric, Inc., a major supplier to distributor buyer Justin Meyer, produces resins, laminates, and plastic coatings. They have developed a problem in keeping different products from contamination by product carryover materials during processing stages. Storage prior to final packing and shipping was a contributing cause. In time, expensive handling, cleaning, and inspection instructions have mushroomed into a major cost factor. Jim Maheu was charged with improving the system as a formal cost reduction project.

In his previous job with a small plastics company, Jim had used the Poulin Machine Works for fabrication of some custom-made process equipment. He thought of calling in Poulin's sales engineer for a review of the problem. After a long and detailed discussion, Poulin's sales engineer took the general specifications with him, promising a fast answer.

Sure enough, the next week, the sales engineer returned with sketches of a novel tote box and conveyor system that completely protected the material during critical process steps. It also delivered the material through processing to packing in a closed system, and provided for automatic clearing of the boxes after use.

Pleased with the concept, Jim transposed the specification in detail onto his drawings and assigned new drawing numbers. He then sent these drawings with requisitions to buy to the purchasing department. Purchasing in turn sent requests to four firms, including Poulin Machine Works.

When Poulin's sales manager Richard Brown got the request for quotes, he

---

[4]*New York Times*, 3/16/88, p. D7.

made a get-acquainted visit to meet Ross Dielectric's purchasing manager, Mel Edwards. Richard learned their sketches had been sent to competitors for quote, and promptly blew his top. Returning to his office, Richard dispatched the following letter to Ross Dielectric's general manager:

> Dear Sir:
>
> On May 1, 1997, we submitted in good faith sketches of a tote-box handling system to Ross Dielectric Company. It now appears that our designs have been reproduced onto Ross Dielectric drawings. Further, it appears that competitive quotations have been sought from suppliers other than Poulin.
>
> We should like to point out that this system is a proprietary design, and was submitted for your review with no authority to reproduce it, or have it reproduced. Unless your action of duplicating drawings and soliciting quotations from others thereto is rescinded at once, we shall have no alternative but to commence appropriate legal action to protect our interest.
>
> Sincerely,
>
> Richard Brown
> Sales Manager
> Poulin Machine Works

How would you as buyer handle this problem? For further consideration, how would you answer the following questions:

1. What is the legal significance, as you see it, of Poulin's letter?

2. What was purchasing's responsibility to check or establish the identity or origin of the drawings developed?

3. Even though the system was not patented and Poulin did not specifically state that they were not to be reproduced, what are the business ethics involved?

4. If you are purchasing manager Mel Edwards, what would you do?

    a. Do you give the order to Poulin without competition?

    b. Do you give Poulin a special price consideration in the bid evaluation?

    c. Do you take exception to Poulin's letter and attitude?

    d. *Get creative—there may be more than one solution!*

Actually, as with most "case studies" there is no single right or wrong answer to these questions, as we would need to know more of the specifics to reach a universally accepted conclusion. But what is clear is that some sort of mutually satisfying resolution should be attempted as a first action. Both parties have too much to lose by achieving anything less.

Volumes could be written (and have been!) on legal issues. Our intention here is not to duplicate that effort, but instead to highlight the more important issues that affect the buyer in both the domestic and the international business arenas.

The preceding review provided in this chapter covers the issues of most likely impact—but the buyer and purchasing management must become cognizant of those issues specific to the circumstances of their business situations.

15

Buying for Service-Type Companies, and MRO

Purchasing of services has become more important as about 70% of the United States' Gross Domestic Product is for services, while only about 20% covers manufacturing. Furthermore, service-type jobs account for about 80% of new jobs per the Commerce Department. As such, service-type buying has become more important and demanding with unique challenges. An example would be the purchasing organization for hospitals, which can be complex, often having many ancillary functions; purchasing may be charged with inventory control and management of stores, central processing and printing, laundry, cafeteria, maintenance, medical supplies, and distribution.

The number and type of service purchasing examples is both vast and diverse, and includes entities such as school districts, hospitals, Health Maintenance Organizations (HMOs), banks, utilities, computer training companies, advertising agencies, travel reservation agencies, hotels, car rentals, food processing and dispensers, cable networks, security personnel, and the like. In these cases, buying is similar in its process to industrial purchase of maintenance, repair, and operating (MRO) supplies. Many purchases are contracted time and effort (labor) that does not produce a physical end-product. Of course, many buys are for combinations of goods and services.

In many of these cases, the purchases are for either a person's or company's time, not always a physical item. And, of course, service buys often do include labor, parts, and materials used.

Service contracts are often negotiated after bids or quotes are taken. That's because the proposals often provide ideas and suggestions not previously considered. When buying services, the statement of work to be performed is akin to the specification. The request for bids or prices, supplier sourcing, and all other buying functions are identical.

Terms of payment should be discussed early, for many smaller companies expect advances as they have little capital on which to operate.

Purchasing is known to have plenty of help in some of these types of companies. Acquisition of property, capital equipment, utilities, insurance, and travel are sometimes assigned to nonbuying people who may have suitable experience and backgrounds for such special assignments. Purchasing is mostly charged to buy office supplies, MRO items, and resale items. There often isn't need of inventory control of raw materials, or in-process goods. However, stocking and distribution requirements planning (DRP) and materials requirement planning (MRP) can be adopted depending on the organization. Certainly inventory is of universal concern.

Buying is universal. Because much of the technical buying outlook in this book is applicable to industrial buyers does not mean that different types of buying jobs are less important. Moreover, many buyers and purchasing managers who have changed jobs know the buying process is similar. Much of what has been detailed in this book with respect to negotiation, cost reduction techniques, conflict solving situations, and the like is equally pertinent to the service-type buying jobs. Another good example is managing inventory. While most service buyers may have no interest in Material Requirement Planning (MRP), the Re-Order-Point (ROP) inventory control using the ABC system and Economic Order Quantity (EOQ) is ideal for service type buying and MRO items.

Distribution Buying

Several approaches are used to enhance the multilocated distributor business. Though the smaller distributor/warehouse buying operation doesn't want or need to be as elaborate as the more complex larger operations, the principles remain the same.

Large distributors have several branches in multiple locations to better serve customers. Distributors, aware of industrial buyers shopping their various branches, call it "branch shopping." That's because industrial buyers have learned that service provided, stock carried, and prices could vary with different branches of the same distributor, and often may search out this information, as sellers must often price to suit the individual marketplace. In similar fashion, the distributor/ contractor buyer should shop among industrial sellers.

As part of their educational program, the American Supply Education Foundation, Inc., Chicago, IL, published *Purchasing: Balancing Price and Value* in 1987. This book is directed toward the specific needs of distributor buyers.

Because of the major impact of materials and components cost, the wholesaler/ distributor wants alert, aggressive, and intelligent purchasing personnel who practice modern techniques of buying. Purchasing has become recognized today as an important economic factor in the business. Central inventory makes central buying easier. A distributor could segregate items to be centrally bought, and leave specials, or smaller volume items, to each branch. This is similar to multi-plant buying by major manufacturers.

Buying for a distributor or contractor has distinctive challenges. It is not always easy to exert any leverage when buying components and parts from a manufacturer whose line the distributorship sells. Other than this, the authors' seminars for distributors confirmed that most buys were similar to industrial MRO type buying. Buying is generic with universal principles.

A materials budget is commonly used for major projects. It may be broken down into monthly increments covering the project span, or for one year. Such a budget is usually estimated based on expected performance; and construction contractors may have separate budgets for each of their major projects. In contrast, government and college or university purchasing departments usually operate under definite, inflexible limitations on expenditures. Some flexibility may, however, be provided by authorizing purchasing to forward-buy up to a certain percentage of the total value. In effect, this sets up a revolving fund to take advantage of fluctuating price situations.

Merchandise Buying

Buyers of merchandise for resale have the same buying functions, but the added tasks of marketing. The image of the products bought can dramatically affect their salability. The markets are highly seasonal, so buys are often made of a supplier's productive output capacity. For example, while buyers may not know the exact new styles for clothing, they must secure capacity to cut and sew in advance. So, they contract for longer term commitments that are flexible to meet their customer demands.

Those who have studied this field tell us that the buying responsibilities are again essentially identical, the exception being the added tasks of advertising and promotion sales. And buying cooperatives are often used. The same issue with respect to the optimal number of sources is faced. If many suppliers are used, there isn't as much leverage to negotiate, while if only a few, they may lose out on the latest fashion or innovations. So either two or three major suppliers will usually be used.

Ways to measure buyer performance differ in that the number of complaints and returns are most important. Also, if many alterations, refinishing, or excessive costs occur, these are all reflections of the buyer's decisions. While there appears to be no purchasing association for this type of buying, there is a National Retail Merchants Association (NRMA) that provides guidance on good business practices.

Hospitals and Health Maintenance Organizations

With fast rising health care costs, the importance of purchasing in the medical field is evident. Insurance companies and companies that pay for their employees' health insurance have been putting pressure on the providers to cap their costs. In turn, this impacts on the buying job and must lead to more sophisticated buying practices, including use of centralized buying to produce better results.

The American Society for Hospital Materials Management represents buying interests in this field. The technical demands of buying pharmaceuticals, laboratory supplies, and equipment all require greater technical skills just as in industry. Group buying agreements are often used by hospitals. There are hospital shared services that provide approved price lists.

Schools and Educational Buying

As in the case for health care, educational expenses have risen faster than the general economic growth. Cooperative buying has been one way for educational institutions to buy better. The National Association of Educational Buyers (NAEB) set up the Educational and Institutional Cooperative Service some years ago. This group sets up contracts for furniture and other items.

Government Procurement and Military Buying

State and local government buyers are represented by the National Institute of Government Purchasing (NIGP). Also, the National Association of State Purchasing Officials (NASPO) is active. Both strongly support training activities. A difficulty in studying government buying activities is that they often report to individuals with titles other than purchasing, such as commissioners, etc.

The Department of Defense (DOD) is the source of the majority of the Federal Government's expenditures. The Office of Federal Procurement Policy (OFPP) has exhaustive regulations covering all the award activities, from determining the requirement through to completion. The purchasing contracting officer (PCO) handles the pre-award activities, and the administrative contracting officer (ACO) administers the contract after it's let.

The Armed Services Procurement Act (ASPA) has been amended with the Defense Acquisition Regulation (DAR), and the Federal Acquisition Regulation (FAR). This activity is too complex and detailed to attempt any detailed description. Suffice it to say that, as in other cases reviewed, purchasing principles are essentially the same.

In summary, because the purchasing is for nonprofit organizations does not mean reducing costs is not a top priority. The significant point is that buyers for *any* type organization should be able to apply many purchasing techniques reviewed in this chapter and throughout the book.

Co-op and Consortium Buying

Many times we're dealing with a cooperative company (co-op), and don't know it. As companies get larger, co-ops present one way for the smaller business to survive. "Hundreds of independent druggists buy their pharmaceutical and other supplies through business co-ops, allowing them to compete with mass merchandisers. More than 20,000 independent hardware stores and home repair centers take advantage of joint purchasing, joint advertising, and assurance of quality products through membership in 10 retailer-owned wholesale co-ops."[1] Co-ops give buyers greater choice of supply by not having suppliers dominating one-sided negotiations.

What about the smaller single-location distributor? Enterprising buyers sometimes act as a central clearing house. Following the example of some school districts and area hospitals, the distributor buyer can often get improved deals by adding to his or her volume. For example, by phoning a half dozen users of valves in the region, a buyer was able to place a truckload order. He or she gets 500, and has 50 or so shipped to the other buyers' locations. Or, the seller may drop ship individually at the agreed price.

By cooperatively pooling their buying volume with several other smaller users, considerable savings result. This type of pooling makes the order quantity large enough to run economically. The major problem is finding other buyers who have data readily available when contacted, so that quick decisions can be reached.

Consortium Purchasing

Some companies participate in the consortium arena as a purchasing group. Consortiums are envisioned as part of strategic supply chain management. They are an outgrowth of the success of co-op buying that is widely used by schools, hospitals, and local government purchasers. Over 100 group purchasing arrangements are claimed to have been formed in the pharmaceutical and medical areas alone.

Consortiums are organized differently than co-ops which often have competitors as members who use staff for administrative service. Co-op members pay dues, and suppliers pay fees. In contrast, a consortium is a formal corporation whose members may be large business firms from different industries. Members preferably hire a third party to negotiate. Usually a membership fee or percent of savings supports the administrative costs.

Proponents say the grouping of several companies' buys allows suppliers to gain added sales volume allowing quality improvements. A study by the NAPM's CAPS reports savings in the range of 5% to 15%.[2] Consortiums exist for business travel that include many major U.S. companies. The participants pay a fee that supports the independent operation which represents more than a billion dollars in air-travel expenditures.

Questions about possible antitrust violations bother some people, as collusion that affects prices is as illegal under Robinson–Patman Act among buyers as among

---

[1]"Co-op Buying Gives Consumers, Small Business More Dollar Power," *Syracuse Herald Journal,* March 14, 1988, p. D 14.

[2]*Purchasing Today,* May, 1996, p. 34.

suppliers. In 1994, the Department of Justice and Federal Trade Commission set out a position about joint purchasing among health-care providers. It condemned price fixing, while supporting legitimate joint purchasing, saying, "An agreement among purchasers that simply fixes the price that each purchaser will pay or offer to pay for a product or service is not a legitimate joint purchasing arrangement and is a *per se* antitrust violation. Legitimate joint purchasing arrangements provide some integration of purchasing functions to achieve efficiencies."[3]

The Antitrust Division of the U.S. Department of Justice has developed a standard known as the "35-20" rule. This means that if its purchases account for less than 35% of the total sales of the seller's product or service for that good or service, and the cost of individual goods is less than 20% of the user's final product price, there should be no concern regarding antitrust. There is ambiguity on this point as some lawyers believe the buying consortium members should compete with each other, and the purchases must account for less than 20% of the revenues of each of the members of the purchasing group. Like any new arrangement, legal challenges will sort this out. In the meantime, legal scrutiny of this issue will be essential.

Other mitigating circumstances were if the buyers didn't get all of his purchases of any item from a particular supplier, or an independent agent negotiates for the users, and all communications are confidential. Again, the justice department is attentive to significant discounts and whether they're available to others.

Inherently, consortium buying requires teamplay to make decisions and concessions. The buyers naturally have to have some commonality of what they buy.

Buying for Major Projects

Equipment Purchases and Disposal

There will be increased influences from others outside purchasing for this type of buying. The buyer should still be a party to finalize the pricing and delivery issues.

Disposal of obsolete equipment is complex. Perhaps, a machine can be traded in for newer models. Or, can the machine be used by another plant location?

Construction Contracting

When companies build costly new buildings, they often depend on specialists to lead in the coordination. When it comes to equipping and arranging the plant layouts many engineers are involved. Increasingly buyers who have gained experience on other projects are placed in charge of the coordination role. Major projects will be coordinated by a team put together to follow it to completion. Usually,

---

[3]"The Consortium: Basic Antitrust Principles," *Purchasing Today,* May, 1996, p. 18.

however, a clerk-of-the-works will track most details. This should be welcomed by most buyers.

Recycling and Trash Removal

These are some of the ancillary functions sometimes given to purchasing. Trash disposal today is a high-cost item. Recycling efforts mandated by regulations make it quite demanding. For example, batteries can't simply be tossed out, nor can oil. Asbestos and other hazardous materials can't be put out with the rubbish. Sorting, special handling, and care in disposal all come into play.

Use of Bids

Bids imply that formal price quotes are to be solicited. This is a good tactic when there is a large project or contracting job to let. By getting bids, often more favorable pricing will be offered. Competitive bid solicitation is a formalized way buyers can decide from whom they will buy. The idea is to document what is wanted, so sellers can give buyers facts to analyze the proposal.

What type of bid should the buyer choose—formal or informal? Use formal for projects, or work that is by specialized craftsmen and not easily cost targeted in advance. Usually many of the suppliers are local and known to the buyer. Are the bids open to all? Sealed?

Most bids are "closed," wherein the buyer has the option of reserving the opening and studying the bids in private, and deciding not to reveal competitive prices. "Open" means the suppliers are invited to share in the data—most commonly used when buying construction or other capital type projects.

The solicitation package must include as many as possible of the terms and conditions, and other data that will be contained in the contract. Also the buyer should give an explanation to the prospective supplier about the information needed to allow evaluation of the bid or offer. Do you intend to negotiate with the suppliers, or will you take the best offer the first time with no second chances to bid again?

In case of contracts for construction, bid guarantees, performance, and payment bonds should be required. A bid guarantee provides the buyer the assurance that the bidder will not withdraw the bid, and will execute a written contract and furnish such bonds as required. A performance bond assures that the contract performance will be met, including all terms and conditions that are spelled out in the contract. A payment bond secures the payment to all persons supplying labor and material in the execution of the work provided in the contract.

If special items will be part of the bid, address these in the invitation. Examples might be requiring a certificate of licensing within the state, amount of insurance covering the supplier's liability, tooling, fixtures or dies, hourly rates charged, or any special arrangements needed.

Systems Contracts for MRO Supplies

Although most MRO items may be bought using the same processes as for other buys, there are some additional steps that can be taken to address the high administrative costs of these types of buys. "Systems contracting" can be used for repetitive, low-cost/high-variety maintenance, repair, and operating type buys. Under this scenario, requirements are negotiated based on a "catalogue" of items, and the catalogue is made a part of the contract. Administrative costs are greatly reduced. Under such an arrangement, using departments can release requirement "calls" for whatever is needed by telephone or short release form.

The consolidated invoice is mailed monthly to the buyer for review and approval. Simplified methods of releasing "calls" act to reduce the need for longer formal purchase orders. Using systems contracts, the buyer determines source and price, while the user releases only what is needed, and states when it is required.

The benefits of systems contracting can be summarized as follows:

1. Designated users can deal directly with suppliers (while the buyer controls conditions of purchase).

2. The supplier keeps records of usage, with invoices providing a check on this.

3. The supplier maintains inventory stock, thereby permitting 24-hour delivery requests supportive of just-in-time (JIT) needs.

Though the benefits are significant, a possible systems contracting pitfall is having a "locked-in," single source of supply. There must be periodic reevaluation of performance to ensure competitive performance. But beyond this, there is the additional concern over other suppliers attempting to replace the supplier who is "in." The buyer has to find a way to keep these situations from deteriorating.

Program Evaluation and Review Technique

Program Evaluation and Review Technique (commonly referred to as PERT) has been credited with speeding the planning of the Navy's Polaris weapons system. PERT is credited with improving management control, the handling of resources, decision making, and implementation. It has proved especially useful as the most widely used system for managing contract project work.

Although the technique has been in existence for a number of years, PERT remains a dynamic charting method to follow design projects of technological complexity through the various stages of activity. An excellent application is using it when constructing a building, or a complex assembly line. When PERT forecasted events are combined with program budgets, and tied in with costs, it's known as PERT/COST. Both time and costs are shown to occur along the time path.

PERT is a systematic approach that is event oriented. Designed to control the sequence of project events, the program will determine the progress, completion time of each activity, and the final conclusion. It has been most useful in military projects and research and development activities, especially during the planning stages.

Figure 15-1 shows a 10-month PERT/COST project chart from product planning through engineering until finally shipped. The "critical path" is defined as the route of those events that take the longest time to complete. If the course of the critical path requires more time than is allowed to complete the entire program, the PERT graph will show the event, process, or supplier that is going to cause the delay. With this information, expediting can take place *before* trouble occurs. In ways, PERT charting resembles a production control chart, and is visually recognizable, which is superior to a presentation of pure statistical data.

Special expediting, overtime, or extra labor can then be applied to avoid troublesome logjams. If management takes action to shorten the time required

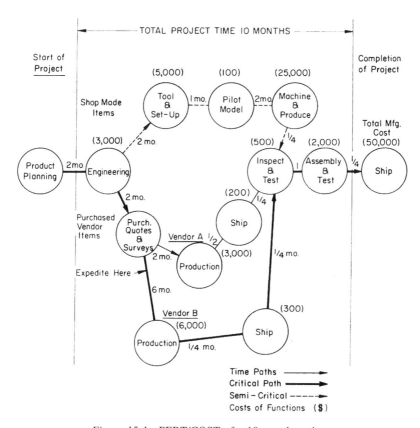

Figure 15-1 PERT/COST of a 10-month project.

to complete the critical path, then another path or paths may become critical. These alternate networks may be recognized as "semicritical" paths. Some paths in the network may be completed, so management may borrow manpower temporarily and shift it to break bottlenecks without endangering the overall project timing.

A formula for determining the time that an event will be completed is shown below:

$$\text{Estimated time to complete} = \frac{T_o + 4T_1 + T_p}{6}$$

Where:

T_o = optimistic time
T_1 = most likely time
T_p = pessimistic time

If you analyze the formula, you will quickly learn that the idea is to weight times to counter the perceived tendency of most engineers to underestimate the time needed for a job. Using colored celluloid overlays, complicated and intricate activities occurring at the same time can be grasped quickly. This type of chart can be highly effective for visual transparency or PC-based presentations. The system may be carried out manually, but is most effective when developed on a computer.

Instant Cash and the Procurement Credit Card

Some companies use a one-page simple purchase order form that has a blank check (with low dollar limit) attached to the bottom. Sometimes called an "instant cash PO," this procedure is used for routine, low-value repetitive purchases. No back orders are allowed, which is an incentive to the seller to complete your order before those not similarly tied to the check. The seller makes the shipment and fills out and cashes the buyer's draft check.

Some buyers consider this a radical approach, but it can be a great help in simplifying buying of repetitive low cost items. This is useful if a distributor sends a pick-up driver across town. Under this scenario, there is no need for invoices to be sent for later payment.

Some finance people decry this practice, yet it can be successfully implemented with known local suppliers where there is a limit to the check's value. Needless to say, any supplier abusing the system loses any future business. Still, the recent development of the use of the procurement card appears to some a more readily acceptable way for acquisition of low-cost items.

The Procurement Card

This method of payment is familiar to most business people, as they use credit cards for their personal buys. When the procurement-card system is used by a company, users are given their own cards. The cards can be branded with the company's name—prominently displayed.

A benefit resulting from use of the card is that the card effectively "outsources" much of the clerical workload! Accounts payable is relieved of the need to make many separate, small value payments, while the buyer receives detailed reports to use in supplier selection. Cards can also be used for expense tracking.

Rather than simply using a local bank card, selection of a procurement card should be carefully shopped, as there are significant differences among the alternatives. Some capture sales tax data, while others provide minority/1099 supplier tracking and reporting. Some cards give access to item detail such as description, quantity, unit size, and any discounts you have arranged with your suppliers, while others provide less detail.

When might use of the procurement card be unwise? There are some problems with the procedure; users report some managers get a card and allow others to sign for them, thereby creating a signature authorization control problem. Rules spell out limitations to each cardholder on the allowable dollar value, what can be acquired, and the suppliers that may be used. Other issues that complicate its use: (1) only authorized people are given the privilege of the card's use, and (2) the card must be turned in if a job change makes it no longer needed, or the employee is terminated or resigns.

Procurement card use is a recent development in which little trouble or fraud has been experienced. Lost cards have been reported, but are primarily the bank's responsibility. Some companies continue to study, but are skeptical—as they were of the Instant Cash PO mentioned earlier.

"Smart Cards"

This type of card is used where cash purchases for low-value buys are possible. During 1996, VISA introduced "Visa Cash" at the Olympics in Atlanta. However, this type of card is already used by many college bookstores which allow plastic to replace coinage. The University of Michigan's Ann Arbor campus uses a MasterCard/First America smart card for its bookstore, restaurants, as well as about 50 local retail outlets such as laundries, photocopies, and so on. And, commercial companies such as Kinko's have their own cards which the customer replenishes as the funds are used.

The "smart card" looks like other credit cards, but holds a miniature electronic memory chip that can store and retrieve a variety of data. Cash-chip machines are fed dollars and transfer money from a bank account using an ATM card. As funds are used, the balance is displayed.

The smart card is like cash. Anyone having it can spend it, so beware: you lose leverage in negotiating cash reimbursement settlements as with any purchase already paid for—just as with cash! Further, care must be taken not to lose the card based on the same fact—again, it is the equivalent of cash.

Since many smaller suppliers have to be capable to accept smart cards, they are not yet practical for widespread commercial use. This is expected to change as buyers learn of the benefits and encourage sellers to subscribe.

16

Improving Management of the Purchasing Job

Many management books contain lots of ideas to consider. This chapter draws upon those management principles that have proven highly useful when applied on-the-job to purchasing and supply situations.

Not every buyer is a paragon of virtue, and may not do everything right. But, one thing is certain, "No buyer is completely worthless. He can always be used as a horrible example." And, of course, "Old buyers never die, they just go bye-bye." (Remember, a sense of humor is needed for creativity and problem-solving.) Purchasing departments throughout the country have personnel who are not properly motivated and have low morale. Simply paying buyers a fair salary, giving them an office, and telling them what to do does not ensure positive effort or results. Seldom can initiative, enthusiasm, or loyalty be bought. Buyers show up every day, do their work, and return home. They may not be unhappy with their jobs, but at the same time they may not feel a part of their company. They continue because they have to support themselves and their family, and they haven't any better idea how to do it.

How much better these people would do if they not only *had* to do a good job, but also *wanted* to do it! Like managers in other professions, the purchasing manager (PM) is told he must "understand" those he supervises, "communicate" with them, and "motivate" them—in short, persuade them that the company's need for improved productivity and profitability is compatible with their private needs, hopes, and ambitions.

How can a mere PM use the accumulated knowledge of the social scientist to improve his job effectiveness when the human mind continues to baffle the most learned psychologists? Certainly, there is a danger in amateur psychology, but we can stick to intuitive feelings of how to deal with other people and concentrate on simple, basic principles and their use in job situations. People want to get into the act! Poor job performance is often more due to lack of involvement than to laziness or incompetence. Buyers who are allowed as much influence as possible on the decisions that affect them can be motivated to find solutions, while those who feel no need to act will ultimately become ineffective.

Following World War I, business became preoccupied with people's motivation, guidance, and relationships. Perhaps today the pendulum has swung too far away from sensitivity to people as companies continue to downsize their operations. But managements should still bear in mind what the pioneers of scientific management learned about dealing principally with *people*. After all, management is responsible for organizing elements of money, materials, equipment, processes, and people to serve the best economic interests of the company.

Application of Management Principles to Purchasing

Too often in practice the conventional wisdom exists that without management action, the employees would be passive or even hostile to the company's interest. The underlying assumption, therefore, is that people by their very nature prefer to work as little as they can, resist change, lack real ambition, dislike responsibility, and want to be told what to do. Moreover, by this way of thinking, they are seldom very intelligent and often quite gullible. So, they must be controlled by a system of rewards for good and punishments for bad performance—in effect the "carrot and the stick" approach.

Interestingly, when asked to identify what they thought their employees wanted from them, a group of managers came up with the following rank order listing to the left as shown below:

What Managers Thought	What Employees Wanted
1. Good wages	1. Full appreciation of work done
2. Job security	2. Feeling of being "in" on things
3. Promotion and growth in company	3. Sympathetic help on personal problems
4. Good working conditions	4. Job security
5. Interesting work	5. Good wages
6. Personal loyalty to workers	6. Interesting work
7. Tactful discipline	7. Promotion and growth in company
8. Full appreciation of work done	8. Personal loyalty to workers
9. Sympathetic help on personal problems	9. Good working conditions
10. Feeling of being "in" on things	10. Tactful discipline

Several surveys of PMs gave similar results. However, if buyers were under-paid, a good bet is that wages wouldn't appear in fifth place. This study tells the PM that some non-cost incentives are worth trying, as indicated by the personal wants of the employees.

The PM may find a guide to understanding of human needs in the "hierarchy of values" arranged as a ladder by A. H. Maslow. Though developed decades ago, this work is seminal. At the bottom are the physiological needs: to stay alive, to be fed, followed by the need for sexual gratification and personal security. Social needs, such as a sense of belonging and being part of the group are next on the ladder, followed by the ego needs for self-confidence, achievement, status, and recognition. Finally at the top of the ladder is the need for self-fulfillment or self-development and a sense of realizing one's full potential.

Herbert Van Schaack, professor of psychology at New York State University College in Oswego, says, "The further a person is from achieving adequacy, the more distorted his perception, the more forced his behavior." He went on to conclude that the PM should develop an understanding of the behavior of people. Unless a manager can decide *why* a buyer acts the way he does, they can never hope to predict behavior . . . "A person's needs are the mainspring of his perception; they are the fuel that gives direction and force to behavior."

So, to deal effectively with buyers, for example, the manager's role should be one of "helping others achieve a sense of adequacy." For managers to reach their goals, it's essential that the buyers' goals are compatible with their own. Consideration for their ego needs and their desire for self-realization can pay real dividends.

The human is often termed a "wanting animal." As soon as one need is fulfilled, another takes its place. In short, few of us are ever fully satisfied. However, when channeled properly, this can have a favorable result, as those who have the most needs are usually the "doers" who accomplish things. If the PM realizes this, it will make the job of managing much easier.

Remember that as any one need is threatened, people will revert to the "lower" level. For example, a buyer is achieving a salary that lets her fulfill most of her economic needs. She is a part of a good purchasing team, earning a fair living and contributing to the company. Yet, on occasion she may feel entitled to a bit more status, expressed by a need for recognition and achievement. Now, as downsizing threatens to eliminate one-third the buying jobs, the buyer becomes defensive, apprehensive, and reactive. Reverting to the level of needing continuing income to keep her present standard of living, a pronounced change in attitude and work performance occurs until management reassurance is provided.

Some managers are overly authoritative and do not delegate anything. Others may let everyone else do the job. In between is the manager flexible enough to change style with the need. He or she can be authoritative, democratic, or participative, according to their subordinates' needs and the requirements of the situation.

On-the-job experience has taught that when a change in attitude and job performance had to be made, confusion often led those involved to accept that change. A college professor discussing management-directed change once said that, "Out of chaos comes great flexibility." On the surface, that sounds like a foolish assertion. But, when we observe difficult problems, we find it's often true.

An experience comes to mind about a plant PM who was adamant to drop a certain motor supplier at the urging of his boss, the plant general manager. The CPO knew it was an impossibility, for other locations had to use this supplier as their only source for highly special products. The CPO decided that the best way to solve this was by agreeing completely. In a large meeting he instructed this PM to notify the supplier. In the room were other personnel who immediately objected, pointing out they would be out of production. Chaos erupted! Ultimately, chaos yielded way to flexibility with the final result that the supplier remained on the approved supplier list.

Theory "X," "Y," and "Z"

Douglas McGregor is credited with the definition of management philosophies in two broad categories, termed Theory X and Theory Y.

Briefly, Theory X has been based on two models: the military and the Catholic church, both of which have performed well for the purposes intended. Theory X can be "hard" or "soft." If the manager is easy going, reluctant to apply proper control, this is seen as soft X management style. It is often viewed as an abdication of management that people take advantage of, which provides validation to the hard-X advocates who maintain that people must be controlled by threat or punishment. But in an affluent business society the threat is lost when it is relatively easy to get a new job. Though lately some of that threat has returned, the wise management will understand that people will not stand for tactics they dislike if they perceive that they don't have to.

Examples of Theory X are the "bull in the china shop" manager, or polite boss who tells everyone exactly what, when, and how to do things. His way is the only way.

Theory Y assumes that people are *not* resistant to the interest of the company; rather, all people, depending on individual capacity, can assume responsibility and are ready *to motivate themselves* toward the good of the company. In such a scenario, management can't control this intangible process of self-motivation, but must make it possible for employees to realize their fullest potential. That is, management must so organize its conditions and methods of operation that employees can achieve their own goals—which is best accomplished when each person controls his efforts toward company goals. Most people will do what is right when they know those goals, and understand the problems involved in achieving them, so if management can make clear the existence of mutual objectives, they will naturally provide the needed support and encouragement. Management is not abdicating its responsibilities, but substituting this emphasis on common objectives for workable teamplay to achieve good results.

Apply Sound Theory to Purchasing

So, what does all this theory mean to a PM? Simply that, if PMs put their energy into a supportive role, the buyers will realize purchasing's profit role as championed throughout this book, and they will perform accordingly. The more complex the task, the better the possible end results. Each person should be contributing fully as best he or she can, without constant supervision.

Let's further explore Theory Y, as compared with Theory X, using a simple buying situation. Theory X advocates would say that the PM must direct and control his people; so the buyer is told to reduce the price of a special valve by getting the supplier to agree to a lower price. The buyer negotiates persistently and gets the lower price, but the supplier cuts his costs by using a cheaper gasket and eventually valve leaks are reported in the buyer's end product.

Now let's apply Theory Y to the same situation. In contrast, the PM points out the need to reduce the cost of the valve, explaining why it is essential to do so. The PM doesn't tell how it must be done, but she may suggest several ideas: material substitution, analysis of the supplier's cost, or possibly a new offshore source. In short, she leaves it to the buyer to find the solution. Several avenues may be explored, and the final result may be completely unexpected. The supplier may have a different line of valves that can provide even greater savings. So, both parties benefit. It's a "win–win" situation.

While the above is a simple situation, no single manager can know how best to achieve the lowest cost for the thousands of items bought. Exaggeration or not, Theory Y points the way toward a high form of supportive management that helps build and maintain personal worth and importance.

In short, friction exists wherever people interrelate. Sound human relations is another tool of purchasing as with any other management specialty. Neither CPOs or buyers can overlook its importance.

Effective Communications, Both External and Internal

It isn't necessary to sell any progressive manager on the need for better communications. It has always been business' biggest headache to overcome. Many studies and surveys have documented that faulty communication is often behind poor employee attitudes. When something goes wrong down the line, it is often because someone didn't get the word about what was expected.

Vigorous leadership is not possible without effective communication. No plan can be carried out if the originator is unable to communicate it to others. Communication is a two-way street. Repeated studies have shown that the PM follows the pattern of how a typical executive communicates in an average day. On this basis, in an average hour, a PM spends about 5½ minutes writing, 9½ minutes reading, 18 minutes talking, and 21 minutes listening. At a salary of $45,000 (or more) per year the PM's talking costs about $800 per month. The price of talking isn't cheap.

The PM is paid for listening about $925 per month, so hopefully that is a value-added activity. Being receptive and asking questions pays well. In any given day, the PM and most buyers communicate with salespeople, managers, engineers, and others in the company and the suppliers. But this doesn't mean that good communication takes place.

By nature, the span of human attention is very short, lasting only a few seconds at a time. During about 10 minutes of conversation a person is usually able to grasp the precise meaning of about 600 to 900 words. But our thinking speed far exceeds our listening rate, so while we're waiting for the speaker to catch up, our attention may wander. The speaker watches for this and may repeat statements several times to regain our attention to get the message across. We must listen and watch too if what is said should be of interest to us. Voice, gestures, posture, and facial expression all may provide clues to a person's true thinking and intentions. Or, they may be used deliberately to deceive us. The glib, fast-talking sales veteran as well as the inarticulate but determined engineer are characters familiar to every PM.

If you had to give up all the qualities of a manager save one, what might that be? In our worst nightmares, we can conceive of some managers who were feared—even hated—egocentric, dull, dishonest, or noteworthy for some other unfavorable trait. Yet can we conceive of any true leader without the ability to communicate? Doubtful! All business transactions come down to how well the individuals understand each other.

Effective managers know that you often talk *through* people, not *at* them. The idea is that a manager often tells something to a person knowing they'll tell it to others—so the message is broadcast! In expressing your thoughts to a person, that individual in turn multiplies the message many times over. The buyer must communicate well with quality, engineering, manufacturing, finance, and others, to involve them. Likewise, the purchasing professional must communicate clearly with suppliers.

Tact is an indispensable lubricant of business relationships. The word *tact* is from the latin, *tactus*, or to touch. But touch goes two ways! Some people "rub people the wrong way," and lose the support of those they need to get the job done. Communication is more than just speaking, listening, or writing; for example, we communicate when we tap someone on the shoulder, slap them on the back, or when we shake the hand of a visiting salesperson. We gesture with the head, point the finger, nod at someone, or shrug a shoulder, smile, frown, wink an eye, or simply raise the tone of voice.

Demonstrating how use of identical words can have totally different meanings is a dialogue between a PM and a buyer. Try reading the following dialogue in two different tones, first with a *praising* attitude that is cheerful and pleased with the effort. Then repeat the words with a condescending manner, displeased and *derisive* of the job done.

Dialogue	First way (Praising)	Second way (Scolding)
	Attitude and tone of voice	
Buyer: What's up, boss?	Confident	Fearful
PM: Take a look at work Danielle did. That's a savings report.	Proudly emphasize "That's."	Sneer, and question, emphasizing "report."
Buyer: Boss, you know the people I have. That's the kind of work they do.	With pride	Apologizing. What can you expect?
PM: Don't be modest. Surely you shared in this.	Complimenting to be sure buyer takes some credit	Sarcastic, so buyer doesn't get away with it
Buyer: I reviewed it, but I have to rely on Danielle. It's her work.	Modestly. You don't want to take glory away from her.	Duck the blame so Danielle's identified
PM: You're not going to get out of it that easily.	Jokingly, you know he's developed Danielle's capability.	Sarcastic. Don't let him get out of this
Buyer: If you insist, I guess I share in it.	Still modest, but ready to admit you're pretty good	Reluctantly yielding, so you won't be the target
PM: Can we expect continued work like this from Danielle?	Hopefully	Disgustedly gesture at report with contempt!
Buyer: We can. (Then adds) But she is being transferred.	First sentence is happy. Second is regretful.	First sentence is regretful. Second is happy
PM: I'll be sorry to see her go.	With regret	With relief and glee
Buyer: We're going to miss her.	Worried how will we replace her	Happily, no mess to fire her

In this example, notice how the two versions paint entirely different pictures of the situation. So too, our dialogs with supplier partners need to be carefully constructed. It is the ability to use intellect, words, and pictures that makes humans the dominant species. And, our ability to leave behind a trail of progress allows those who follow to learn from past mistakes. Although communication has seen significant advancement in effective use, it remains as always our major problem—the ability to let others know what we really think and mean.

What would the impact on history have been had Winston Churchill said, "Now I may be wrong about this, but it would be my suggestion that we fight them on the beaches. Hopefully, we might engage them in the fields and streets, should that be necessary. There is a high probability we may have to fight them even in our hills. While some of you may not agree entirely with me, if I have my way, we shall never surrender!" The positive power of words clearly conveyed cannot be overstated! Unfortunately, the same can be stated with respect to the negative repercussions from poor communications.

Language is often the first and most important barrier whether communicating with offshore or local suppliers. Offshore supplier personnel speak much less English than we Americans think. Because they nod and say, "yes," trying to be friendly, doesn't necessarily mean they always understand. So it takes extra care in communicating with offshore sources. The good news for Americans is that English is the language of international business in most areas of the globe.

Some buyers may dislike using clear, simple words and direct language. More likely, they lack the discipline of clear logic. Choice of words is important. It might be technically correct if a waiter asked if you would like "dead chicken fried," but, that wouldn't have the persuasive appeal of "southern fried chicken."

Let's look at another example of poor communications—when what was said was not what was understood. A PM called a meeting to stress the need for more aggressive buying. As he walked through the door, the sign, "PUSH" caught his attention. He opened the meeting saying that there was one quality more than any other that was needed to get ahead in this department; and "it's inscribed on the door to this meeting room." Straining their necks, the buyers saw the word "PULL."

A little pull surely helps since someone above you must recommend you, and someone who has faith in you promotes you. However, it's just as true that some "push" needs to come from those with whom you work, and those who report to you. "Push–pull" actually needn't be in opposite directions. If one person pushes on the door while someone pulls from the other side, opening the door is much easier.

Productive Work Habits

Nothing is so useless as doing with great efficiency what should not be done at all. Another consultant termed the number one problem of industry as "energetic stupidity"—eagerly spending time, effort, and money on doing things that shouldn't have been started in the first place.

What are some buying situations that cause unnecessary work? How about reading materials that have no bearing on the job, a failure to organize work, taking too long to respond to a letter, sending long memos when a quick phone call might suffice, spending too much time on pleasantries during sales visits, and processing paperwork such as in-coming requisitions not properly completed. Also included are reading letters only to place them into a pile until later when they must be reread to refresh your memory before acting, telling too many jokes or stories, or simply taking too much time for personal conversation.

Working on everything in sight may achieve little. No artist can paint everything he or she sees. The picture has to be focused. No contractor can build a building everywhere; he limits the plot of ground, as the architect limits the style. The mathematician can't solve all equations, and the buyer can't make every buy.

Productivity is a matter of quality, not quantity. Before jury duty a PM was hard pressed to keep up. During the 2 weeks he spent on jury duty, the manager had only about 2 hours per day in the office. Buyers were told they could have about 5 minutes to talk about any urgent problems. The result was the buyers solved most of their own problems.

Management, like any productive work performed, must add value beyond its cost. "Try, try again, and if you don't succeed, try again," often should be reworded, "Try, try again, and if you don't succeed, then quit." Persevering in the face of all obstacles has helped solve many a problem that may seem unsolvable. On the other hand, there are many people who keep plugging away, when it would have been far smarter if they gracefully quit and moved on to other tasks worthy of effort.

How many purchasing people work endlessly in routine that produces little results? How many buyers spend a great deal of time on quotations and sales interviews that will bear no fruit? Worse yet, working to the wrong goals is like the floundering swimmer who when rescued was found to be paddling toward the open sea.

Need to Support Education and Buyer Development

One path to purchasing success—whether it be professional, technical, or managerial—is through education. PMs need to learn useful tools: as the mechanic uses a wrench to help tighten a bolt, the manager uses ideas that enable him or her to better grasp complex situations. In short, to be a good purchasing manager one must possess a broad scope of business acumen and human understanding—which comes from education and experience.

There are many sources of education available to would-be purchasing professionals, and these are not restricted simply to college courses. In part, self-development may be a major factor to an expanded global outlook. Training should be customized as much as possible. The purchasing manager should recognize and reward good performance. When you don't offer the fullness of the prize, you can't demand the person pay the price to achieve it.

What about on-the-job efforts to help development of the buyers? On-the-job experience is hard to surpass. A company can hire a specialized instructor to develop a seminar directed toward its own needs. This in-house solution is often an effective alternative based on cost to otherwise send three or four participants to another seminar site. Also, many companies run their own programs aimed at expanding the knowledge of the department. In such a case, the agenda can be highly flexible to suit the participants and the specific needs of the company. Subject matter may include methods of inspection, purchase specifications, value analysis of specific products, relationships with other departments, and responsibility and authority discussions—and may include speakers from other departments.

Experience shows that the well-educated group develops a remarkably self-dedicated approach to problem-solving and appropriate action. This follows the belief that people *will* do the right thing when they are allowed to come up with their own solutions. The opportunity to discuss the difficult buying situations faced by others lends conviction as to their own handling of the same difficulties.

Purchasing education originally was undertaken by National Association of Purchasing Management (NAPM) practitioners to newcomers. Now, activities are driven by academics who have unleashed abundant new energy and sophistication to the field. Today, there are many educational opportunities, including NAPM-sponsored meetings, conferences, and seminars. Management classes are given by the American Management Association, NAPM, and The World Trade Institute. During 1997, week-long programs are scheduled by such noted universities as Michigan State, Arizona State, UCLA, and Florida State. A result is an explosion of terms and ideas, which can only support the profession over the long run.

The *International Journal of Purchasing and Materials Management* provides a forum for newer professional thinking that is published quarterly by subscription. NAPM also provides InfoEdge, which is a monthly "publication of job-related tools for purchasing and supply management professionals." Available by subscription, each 16-page issue is devoted to a single topic with emphasis on different subjects.

There are so many avenues to pursue a person can research this for himself. There's always a good selection of appropriate books and trade magazines that provide thought-provoking information.

Pursue Buyer Development Programs

Professional development efforts are ongoing worldwide to take advantage of educational opportunities to become truly professional. Most developed countries have organizations devoted to professional purchasing and supply management. Truly, purchasing is one of the oldest arts known, and therein may lie one of the professional's chief headaches. Everyone thinks he knows how to buy.

Excellent PM skills are similar to general management skills. While the company can provide opportunities to learn, it is the buyers themselves, supported by management, who must assume responsibility for their own development. Good buyers will develop with proper guidance. The best of them—with the proper motivation—will move upward and eventually become purchasing managers and CPOs, or perhaps go into other key management jobs.

Certified Purchasing Manager Program

Ever since 1974, the NAPM has bestowed the Certified Purchasing Managers (C.P.M.) certificate to those passing and meeting their requirements. Computerized tests are given in about 300 locations worldwide. This program has been an unqualified success. As of 1996, over 26,000 purchasing professionals have earned the C.P.M. designation, of which 18,000 remain current.[1] Requirements for the C.P.M. are you must earn a total of 35 points, and pass four modules in the areas of: (1) purchasing, (2) administration, (3) supply, and (4) current issues. Points are earned by attending sanctioned meetings, seminars, or courses. You must hold a 4-year degree and have 3 years of purchasing or supply management experience, or, in the absence of a college degree, at least 5 years of such experience.

Potential candidates may get a C.P.M. Study Guide which includes a diagnostic list to help identify areas for study. Further information can be gained by contacting the nearest National Association of Purchasing Management chapter in the phone directory, or by writing to NAPM, Tempe, AZ 85285.

Accredited Purchasing Practitioner Program

During 1996, the NAPM implemented a program and examination process for Accredited Purchasing Practitioner (A.P.P.) candidates. By June, they reported over 2,100 A.P.P.s were accredited. This program is aimed to serve entry-level buyers, and those who have procurement responsibilities though outside their company's purchasing department. The accreditation may interest business owners who buy, and others who want to gain purchasing expertise, yet are not ready to aspire to the full C.P.M. status. The attainment of the A.P.P. can be applied toward achieving C.P.M. status later.

Requirements for A.P.P. accreditation are that you must pass Modules 1 and 4 of the C.P.M. exam, have an associate's degree and one year of work experience, or in the absence of a degree, 2 years of work experience that includes work related to purchasing and supply management. Consistent with NAPM's overall charter, the goal is to increase participation and encourage professionalism within the purchasing and supply community.

Contact with foreign buyers can be made through the International Federation of Purchasing and Material Management (IFPMM), of which NAPM is an affiliated member. IFPMM identifies specific members offering assistance in most coun-

---

[1]*Purchasing Today,* NAPM, Tempe, AZ, February, 1996, p. 47.

tries. They also provide excellent international meetings and seminars held in major cities using expert translators. Write IFPMM—International Management Institute, PO Box CH—5001 Aarau, Switzerland. Tel: (064) 247131, Telex 981293.

In addition to the above, there are a number of other certifications in the supply field, some of which include:

- The American Production and Inventory Control Society (APICS) awards the "Certified in Production and Inventory Management" credential. Those passing their series of tests may use their CPIM designation after their name.

- The American Society for Quality Control (ASQC) grants a CQE (Certified Quality Engineer) and a CQT (Certified Quality Technician) or CRE (Certified Reliability Engineer).

- The National Association of Educational Buyers (NAEB) is aggressively active in promoting professional activities.

Use of Job Descriptions and a Purchasing Manual

Managers have often found it much easier to break jobs down into parts to be done by different people than getting people to understand their role in the big picture. Position or job descriptions are tools that help both old and new personnel understand their role and perform it more effectively. They serve as guides, indicating the job's main activities, its responsibilities, and its relationships with other jobs or departmental functions.

Job descriptions are popular with management, and most agree people need to know what their job is. However, the PM cannot simply hand one to a new buyer and expect performance to improve automatically. A key element in development of a job description is the inclusion of ideas from persons who are doing the job. They should construct the first draft. The process can go smoothly by taking these steps:

1. Explain the nature and purpose of a job description. Emphasize that it is a description, not a performance measurement.

2. Prepare some sort of an outline or checklist indicating what goes into a job description and in what form. Go over it carefully with the individual concerned.

3. Review the first draft thoroughly with the employee, pointing out with patience and tact the corrections or improvements that should be made.

4. When the job description is finally completed, review it thoroughly with the employee to ensure a mutual clarity of understanding.

In the Appendix are three job descriptions that have been used in purchasing organizations: one for a purchasing manager, another for a buyer, and the third for a purchasing engineer. These will serve as examples to the purchasing practitioner in constructing similar documents consistent with the situational needs of the company.

A job description should not be interpreted as if it limits one's responsibility. No job can be covered completely on paper. Moreover, most jobs change—with time and with the incumbents. As long as these limitations are recognized, however, the usefulness of having superior and subordinate sit down together and establish the responsibility and authority to be assigned to a job cannot be overemphasized.

Job Descriptions are a way of bringing clarity and structure to the purchasing job—and structure is certainly a concept consistent with management. Another tool available to bring structure is the Purchasing Manual. Properly constructed and maintained, the Purchasing Manual becomes the guiding document for policy and procedural reference.

Certainly, as a strategic management initiative, creation and maintenance of a Purchasing Manual is an important undertaking for the professional purchasing department. As a reminder, the steps involved in creating a manual are outlined in chapter 4, page 63.

17

Transportation Strategies to Reduce Logistics Costs

Transportation costs become a major factor as part of the overall purchase transaction. Since deregulation of the transportation industry, shipping costs have had more impact on total purchase costs than in the past.

Today, just-in-time (JIT) delivery advocates favor shipping more frequently to keep inventory to a minimum. This has to be balanced carefully with higher cost of acquisition, effect on material purchase price, and transportation costs.

Because of the major impact of transportation on materials and components purchased, companies want alert, aggressive, and intelligent transportation personnel who practice modern physical distribution. Traffic, in the past often perceived by its own management as more of a clerical function, has become recognized today as an important economic factor in the business.

Since deregulation of the transportation industry, transportation's impact may range between 11% and 19% compared to about 5% of total purchase costs just a few years ago. The impact is far greater, and much too important to ignore! Transportation costs are part of the buyer's overall purchase transaction. Yet, transportation knowledge is sometimes a weak area for purchasing personnel.

Buyers should learn of the many actions possible to get the best transportation service at the least expense. A buyer is able to negotiate advantageous contract terms, especially when there exists a steady or large volume to be transported. Transportation, like any other commodity purchased, is negotiable. Discounts are widely available in this competitive area.

Buyers have told how they've been annoyed when someone in the traffic operation tried to back charge for routings that were more expensive than the "cheapest way." Some buyers decry the few transportation specialists who are so wrapped up in the details of freight that they miss the big picture. Although there is perhaps some truth in that, it is also true that transportation costs are a significant cost item that must be managed carefully.

Whether buyers know it, or even admit it, they often need help. Buyers need to know delivery, documentation, and transportation cost, to compute total landed costs. In some cases, they don't have this information, and perhaps they don't know how to get it. But the specialist does, or can learn more quickly, because it's their profession.

Developments with a Profound Impact on Transport

A number of developments in recent years have had a profound impact on the transportation industry. These include:

1. Computing technology evolution—which has dramatically increased the amount and availability of information.
2. Container revolution—economic advantage and ease of handling, stack loading internationally. Domestically, trailer, and container-on-flatcar moves, and the double stack are gaining favor.
3. The process of deregulation leading to a free market—allowing for negotiated rates.
4. Advanced warehousing and inventory handling processes.

A few years back, technical experts handled transportation in the back room. Today, however, based on the above major developments, the emergence of physical distribution has helped bring about an expanded outlook.

Surveys among purchasing managers (PMs) indicate about 75% of the information buyers obtain on new products comes directly from salesmen. Where do buyers get input on transportation? In most cases, today, the answer is an independent transportation or traffic representative. This may be a single individual or a department, depending on the size of the operation. The function may report to purchasing or it may be entirely independent in terms of reporting relationship. Regardless, purchasing and traffic must work closely together to optimize operation in this vital area.

Buyers should include traffic in their purchasing planning process to influence and control shipments better. There are tradeoffs between the various modes of transportation available. Speed of delivery certainly relates to higher cost in most cases. Figure 17-1 depicts how a transportation decision involves balancing speed of shipment versus cost for a multimodal shipment. Other tradeoffs relate to the use of light packaging for lower cost versus the higher cost of heavier packaging and risk of damage.

During the 1970s, government regulation was seen as stifling efficiency but this is no longer true. In the early 1980s, the Interstate Commerce Commission's role of protecting carriers, ruling on tariff violations and other "economic abuses" was reduced. This freed carriers to compete in a more open market. Since 1978, many regulations have been relaxed or eliminated. The ICC has the responsibility to regulate interstate commerce carriage contracts.

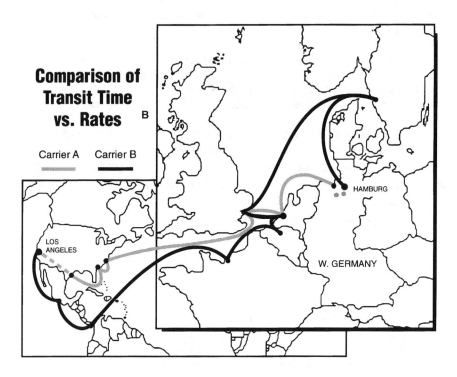

Carrier	Routing	Transit Time	Freight Charges
Carrier A	Rail from Los Angeles to Houston, thence by ship to Bremerhaven. Truck from Bremerhaven to Hamburg.	31 days	$1,891.00
Carrier B	All-water; by ship from Los Angeles to Hamburg via Panama.	26 days	$2,225.00

Figure 17-1 illustrates the trade-off of rates for transit time by comparing two carriers' actual sailing schedules and published tariff rates. The freight charges shown are for a hypothetical shipment of 1 x 40' container of food-processing machinery, measuring 20 cubic meters, from Los Angeles to Hamburg.

Reprinted with permission of *Traffic Management Magazine*.

Figure 17-1 Chart depicting time versus cost for shipments.

Laws, rules, and regulations about contract carriage are in the ICC regulations within Title 49, CODE OF FEDERAL REGULATIONS (Parts 1000 to end). These regulations specify obligations of the carrier, shipper, and receiver. They cover routing permits, contract filing, and other services.

Many shipments are interstate or intrastate movements in nature. State economic regulators vary from those with none (such as Florida and New Jersey) to those considered tighter than the ICC before 1980 (for example, Ohio and Georgia).

Significant Buying Issues

A strong program of transportation/traffic management complements the overall purchasing strategy, and addresses general purchasing concerns relating to cost, quality, and schedule performance. As such, some of the objectives of a good transportation/traffic program will include the following measures or activities:

1. Secure cost/benefits of consolidating inbound shipments from a number of suppliers in certain locations.

2. Eliminate cost of transportation errors, such as freight miscalculations or simple overcharging.

3. Reduce costs of customer dissatisfaction resulting from slow or late deliveries.

4. Evaluate costs versus benefits of changing product packaging or shipment unitization procedures.

5. Reduce the total logistics costs in buying materials and components.

Carrier financial instability is always of concern. Are their finances, that is, debt, cash flow, and capital strong enough to ensure long-term survival? Motor carrier operating ratios are one index of financial health. A carrier consistently above 100 is not covering operating costs.

Motor carriage is the most popular mode for domestic transport. In choosing a trucking company, consider how many break-bulk (sorting) terminals your shipment will pass through. Availability of a shipper's terminals to sort and consolidate is a major consideration. Break-bulk terminals sort and group shipments, according to ultimate destination. Usually located in strategic hub cities, shippers can tie in with other connecting carriers. Fewer "breaks" means faster transit and less damage.

General freight carriers haul a variety of commodities, differing in size, weight, and bulk. They combine different classifications of freight into truckloads, to reduce line haul costs. Motor carriers provide a wide variety of services. Specialized freight carriers usually carry only one, perhaps two, types of commodities. For example, a tank truck can normally not carry both food and nonfood cargoes.

Carriers can track the location of shipments quite readily when computers are used to expedite freight handling, and some in-transit information through satellite trucking and communication with individual units. You can take advantage of the transportation industries' free floppy disks for service, rate, and other information. Disks are available upon request from many truckers. Their EDI systems can give you rates, manifests, rated shipping orders, shipment location, and detailed shipping reports.

Freight Consolidation

Smaller volume users may have trouble getting a less-than-truckload (LTL) shipment moved promptly. LTL rates are always higher per hundred weight (cwt) than full truck or bulk rates. You can make your shipment more attractive, however, by consolidating shipments of a variety of items into a single LTL shipment, and pay a lower price per cwt. However, packing is simpler when shipments contain only one kind of package. Another idea is to arrange for suppliers to ship only on a certain day, for example Friday. So, creating a full load gains a transport rate.

Through a freight forwarder or consolidator, your shipment might be combined with other firms to get lower rates. For new importers, there is a tendency to rely on the foreign manufacturer or his foreign freight forwarder to get the product out of the foreign country. By training and experience, buyers know that in the U.S. manufacturers typically handle all aspects of the transportation task, so why not the same when we source offshore? Often the buyer is dealing with a new foreign exporting company. Neither may have the experience to make transportation work smoothly. In such a case, it can be dangerous to allow a little known seller to handle shipping arrangements. The offshore supplier may use a "buddy" who charges excessively. Reportedly, some foreigners with a cozy relationship can rebate part of their charge to those who hire them. Customs vary among different regions of the world and further, among individuals, so relying on the foreign supplier to monitor your costs and interests could be a costly bad judgment call.

When buying transportation services, these are major issues of concern to the buyer:

- Equipment availability and suitability—Does the carrier have enough of the right equipment to do your job? Is it in good repair?
- Time in transit
- Control of shipment—Does the carrier know where your shipment is, so they can track and advise you of progress?
- Prompt proof-of-delivery
- Inconsistent services, such as poor shipment tracing—Can you get reports on damage? What damage ratios does the carrier have? Are they computerized?

- Timely settlement process for loss damage claims
- Clear rates and charges, and minimal instances of overcharges

The buyer should specify how goods are to be packed and labeled. Dented, marred, or rusty products can hurt visual appearance, influence sales, and lead to customer rejection. Shrink packaging used along with moisture-absorbent silica gel absorb small amounts of moisture that could otherwise damage items such as motors and machinery. "See through" shrink wrap is an excellent way to prevent load shifting, and also makes it more difficult to steal. Crates and skids allow forklifts to move easily. Also, they keep the cargo off the floor, above small puddles. Unitizing the pallet load by strapping or banding keeps it compact and tight.

Cautionary labels for hazardous materials depend on your items. They require universal symbols adapted by the Inter-Governmental Maritime Consultive Organization.

Modes of Transport

Transportation may be by land, air, and sea, and sometimes is a multimodal combination of these. For small packages, United Parcel Service (UPS) gives fast dependable service. They have specific size limitations of 108 inches, derived by adding the longest length of the carton to the smallest girth measurement around it. The maximum weight taken is 70 pounds per carton.

When maximum speed is needed, have the item shipped by Air. Some of the advantages are:

- This mode is much faster than by land.
- Insurance is less expensive.
- Cost of warehousing is generally lower.
- Packing needs are less.
- Damage is minimized.
- Loss by theft is reduced. (However, major thefts have occurred at airports in specific cases where freight has not been moved promptly.)
- Transferral to truckers is easy.
- Purchase lead-time is reduced.
- Small-item inventory costs are reduced, as less lead-time is needed to acquire the item.

While passenger airlines, cargo plane operators, and air freight forwarders publish rates, remember that most volume shipment rates may still be negotiable. Air freight service is routinely provided by carriers who handle up to 50, 70, or

150 pound maximum weight packages. Shipments under 1,500 lbs now can move economically by air, while heavier shipments of 2,000 lbs or more usually require special arrangements.

In selecting an air freight forwarder, the buyer has a number of choices available, including:

1. Air Parcel Post (Express mail for 2 lb envelopes for next day delivery)
2. Direct airline
   a. Door-to-door by such carriers as American Airlines
   b. Counter-to-counter, such as American, Delta, USAIR, United, and others
3. Overnight Express (Federal Express, UPS, Burlington Air Express, and Airborne Express) that offer:
   a. Overnight freight service with a 100 to 150 lb per carton limit
   b. Overnight Envelope Service—generally up to 2 lbs
   c. Air service for second business day delivery, with possible next morning delivery in major markets, with some weight restrictions.
4. Air freight forwarders and others that use the lift of scheduled passenger carriers. They often provide lower cost "time definite" delivery for 2- to 5-day transit, to support just-in-time needs.
5. Charter airlines

When shipping by air, breaking the shipment down into smaller (50 lb) cartons sometimes allows speedier handling. However, some carriers charge more for multiple piece shipments. Packages weighing 100 lbs have lower rates than those weighing 250 lbs, which are more difficult to handle. Also, some carriers have different "cube" rules. For example, "166 cubic inches are equal to a pound of chargeable weight." Some aircraft operators will waive these cube rules, so you should check the specific services and rates available before specifying packaging.

In addition to air, there are also the other available modes on land and sea. With respect to the former, the Motor Carrier Act of 1980 brought about a high degree of deregulation to truckers. Also, the 1980 Staggers Rail Act is credited with creating more competition by reviving the railroad system. These deregulatory acts gave shippers and carriers freedom to negotiate contracts without heavy-handed government interference. So remember, transportation, as any commodity, *can be negotiated!*

Whether air, land, or sea is selected for a given shipment will depend on a variety of factors to be considered by the buyer. These factors pertain not only to the item being shipped, but also to the attributes relevant to the available modes of shipment. Factors to be considered by the buyer will include:

- Date needed
- Rates, cost of shipping
- Cost of insurance
- Cubic size and weight of shipment
- Value of products
- Discharge and destination point
- Possibility of deterioration
- Susceptibility to shipping damage
- Handling requirements during shipment
- Possibilities of theft
- Use of containers, type: 20, 40, or 45 ft, standard or high cube, insulated, refrigerated, controlled atmosphere, etc.
- Paperwork required

How many of the above *can* you influence? How many *do* you?

Transportation Contract Contents

Interstate motor carrier contracts are regulated by the Interstate Commerce Commission. While contracts are no longer filed with the ICC, they must be in writing, and conform with rules governing contracts. If not, the contract can be declared invalid, and higher price class rates apply (even retroactively).

The ICC's role of protecting carriers and ruling on tariff proposals has been reduced drastically. With deregulation, more general contracts can now be made. Instead of one specific haul agreement, a contract can call for various items to be hauled within the United States, at an agreed rate, such as $3.00/mile hauled. As each shipment is ready, the shipper is advised to make a pick-up.

There are now four key freight characteristics used to set classification (reduced from 15 before deregulation). They are:

1. Density (weight per cubic foot)
2. Stowability
3. Ease or difficulty of handling
4. Liability (including value per pound, susceptibility to theft, damage, perishability, propensity to damage other commodities with which it is transported, and propensity for spontaneous combustion or explosion)[1]

---

[1]R. Bohman, "Characteristics that Determine Freight Classification Ratings," *Traffic Management,* May, 1989, p. 25.

The above first item, density, has been evolving as the major characteristic in classifications.

Common carriers are readily available. They may operate over regular or irregular routes. Most less than truckload (LTL) carriers operate regular schedules, while truckload carriers schedule to meet your specific needs. They consolidate and distribute shipments at terminals within their system.

Negotiation of point-to-point LTL rates, along with discounts ranging from 20% to 50%, are possible.[2] These early successes were confirmed by a trucking survey that indicated that "three out of four discounts gotten by buyers are in the 30 to 50 percent range." Most discounts for domestic carriers were in the 10% to 50% range, and 10% were higher than 50%. Without doubt, if a current survey were conducted these discounts would be even greater now!

From a transportation buyer's perspective, the following issues should be considered when drafting a transportation agreement:

- Determine your company's risks and exposures.
- Determine carrier's liability (common?, $/pound?, or other?).
- Consider escape clauses with minimum notice times.
- Are the provisions (such as "most favored rates") enforceable?
- Choose proper insurance coverage (after analysis of premium and loss statistics).
- Choose a venue to settle disputes.
- Become aware of available carrier resources.

The contract for transportation is similar in structure to other buying agreements. Here are some key clauses to use:

- Scope of the Work clause
- Dispute clause
- Replacement of Prior Agreements clause
- "Most Favored Shipper" clause
- Force Majeure clause

Scope of the Work clause is an exacting section that must explicitly specify the work required and by whom. Spell out any special handling instructions or expected perils.

The Dispute clause is similar to the arbitration clause reviewed in Chapter 14. Replacement of Prior Agreements clause means that this new contract replaces any older or prior agreement.

---

[2]*Purchasing Magazine,* April 23, 1987, p. 56.

Most Favored Shipper clause is similar to Most Favored Buyer clauses inserted in purchase orders by buyers. The essence is that the shipper agrees to extend any lower rate given anyone else for comparable volume and commodity. Lower rates extended to one shipper must be given to another with similar volume to eliminate shipper discrimination. Also, providing equipment or free loading or unloading to another shipper means these concessions must be given to the most favored shipper also.

The Force Majeure clause is well known to buyers as the "Act of God" clause. It provides for temporary relief from contractual terms should events occur beyond the control of the parties—such as a work stoppage, highway accident, or storm damage to goods in transit.

Ocean Carriage Contracts

The Shipping Act of 1916 set conference regulations enforced by the Federal Maritime Commission (FMC). With passage of the Shipping Act of 1984, a U.S. shipper can now enter into long-term contracts with ocean carriers. The shipper has an option to move cargo under the regular liner rates or negotiate service contracts.

The Ocean Bill of Lading formerly covered each shipment as a single-haul agreement. Buyers can now commit their total volume, and negotiate lower fixed rates in broader ocean carrier contracts (in exchange for "take or pay" provisions). Today, more contracts are signed through negotiation of rates with ocean carriers than by acceptance of published rates.

Service contracts require that the shipper commits to provide a minimum quantity of cargo over a fixed time period. The carrier commits to a certain rate schedule, and defines the assured space, time in transit, port rotation, or similar service features.

Deregulation has forced carriers to be more attuned to customers' needs. While deregulation made special agreements possible, they still must be filed with the Federal Maritime Commission. Because a contract filed with the commission cannot be amended, you must use specific terms that are well thought through, covering such issues as length of agreement, the exact transport work to be performed, the amount and terms of payment, and performance shortfall penalties.

There are three types of ocean carrier: (1) conference carrier, (2) independent steamship line, and (3) "tramp," or special charter service.

1. An ocean conference carrier is a member of a legal association of carriers joined to set common freight rates and shipping schedules. By signing a contract with the conference, lower rates are available. Rates are equal on all vessels in the conference. Buyers regularly contracting get good service. The conference operates on a nonprofit basis for the benefit of its carrier members.

2. Independent steamship lines quote rates individually and may be lower by as much as 10%, but it's necessary to take into account:

- Space is allocated based on availability.
- All ports may not be covered.
- Changes in destination may occur.

3. Tramp vessels usually carry only bulk cargo and have irregular sailing schedules. Charter rates vary widely.

A conference carrier must stop at each scheduled port. Most regular trade lanes (U.S.–Japan, U.S.–Australia, U.S.–Hong Kong, U.S.–Northern Europe) have regular conference schedules. A nonconference carrier may skip and land at an alternative port, depending on the volume of business and trade available.

Shipping by ocean carriage enjoys the advantage of being the most economical method of transportation, especially for bulky products. To select a carrier, you can look in the daily "shipcards" section of the *Journal of Commerce Shipper's Digest*. Find ship schedules of types of carriers going to your destination port for the month of your shipment.

Although ocean carriage is usually the lowest cost option for large products, there are some disadvantages that need to be recognized. These include:

- Length of transport time
- Goods are more susceptible to deterioration because of long transit time and exposure to salt air and water, as well as ship motions
- Exposure to theft in dock areas
- Occasional longshoremen strikes can tie up goods. Sometimes several U.S. ports will be struck simultaneously in a labor dispute. Usually foreign ports are struck singly, and alternates can be used
- Congested ports (including airports) often cause slow unloading
- Handling at ports can produce damages

Containers

Ocean shipments often use containers that are packed at the factory, and sealed to prevent pilferage and contamination. Within the last 20 years, use of containers has become the prime method for international ocean and air shipment. Containerization on water allows the use of fast modern container ships that use deck-stack loading. Containers come in various sizes, materials, and construction. The FEU (*F*orty-foot *E*quivalent *U*nit) is the most common size in use. It is equal to 2 TEUs (*T*wenty-foot *E*quivalent *U*nits), the original standard.

Containers are often truck bodies, lifted off their wheels and placed on the vessel. Getting a new set of wheels at the import terminal eases inland shipment. For rail shipment, this is known as a COFC (container on flat car) shipment. The term "fishyback" was sometimes used to describe this type of ocean shipment.

"House-to-house container" means the goods are placed in the container at the factory before going out for shipment, and the goods are delivered in the receiving country at the consignee's door. Most containers are steamship company owned and a rental fee is not charged. If a rental is used, and the container is unused on its return trip, then the container rental company increases their container use fee. Containers for rent can be found in the telephone Yellow Pages.

Special containers may have air conditioning equipment when the shipment warrants its use. They reduce product damage due to excessive moisture. If the product can shift inside, the container should be internally braced.

Trailer-on-flat-car (TOFC, formerly called "piggy-back"), is when the motor carrier puts a container or truck chassis on a flatcar for rail transport. Upon arriving at a rail yard, a driver attaches the truck cab to the trailer and takes the shipment directly to its final destination.

Insurance

Insurance is sometimes difficult to buy at any price. Because the rates have escalated, some truckers have failed to keep up with adequate insurance. So, the buyer has to be on guard and *be certain that insurance exists.*

Insurance rates depend on many factors. Value of cargo is computed by its cost plus 10% for contingencies. Rates vary according to product, destination, shipping method, volume, and contractual relationships. If you have a large volume of goods, it may make sense to buy your own insurance. Only the end-user or buyer knows exactly what's best required.

Global buyers should put into their purchase order (and Letter of Credit) that *either a policy or a Certificate of Insurance* is required as part of the documentation. This ensures insurance is in force, or relieves the buyer of responsibility to pay.

Of paramount concern are exclusion clauses defining limitations of coverage. Examples are: nuclear exclusion, wars (war risk policy is special), strikes, riot and civil commotions, delay clause, nationalized insurance restrictions, "all-risk"—Definition of Risk, and the Explosion clause. Insurance is a complex area; buyers should seek help when delving into insurance matters.

Proper planning for loss prevention is the best insurance! Are special risks covered where required? Is insurance coverage in effect throughout the journey? Make sure you have enough.

Cost Analysis of Motor Carriage Transportation

Costs relating to transportation services can be broken down into four general groupings:

1. *Cost/mile of moving materials or goods.* Usually this is the hourly cost of vehicle operation divided by the number of miles traveled in one hour. Costs include labor, tolls, vehicle depreciation, and fuel consumed.

Also included are costs related to maintenance, wear on tires, and taxes. The total cost is usually standardized for terminal-to-terminal travel.

2. *Costs of billing.* These are the costs to set charges, correctly rate and bill, and collect undercharges.

3. *Terminal costs.* Costs that result from picking up goods from various customers, and moving for consolidation, etc. Upon delivering, there is a reverse cycle of distributing. Such costs include forklift handling, etc., and is heavily labor intensive.

4. *Carrier Overhead Costs.* Like any business, this item includes cost of management, overhead, and those costs not directly connected to individual shipments. Included are costs for vehicle registration fees, insurance, and depreciation of the buildings.

As in any buy, the detailed information known by the buyer is invaluable in seeking better carrier rates. Item 4, overhead cost, is an area that many truckers will remove rather than lose the business. So, this is the first area to negotiate!

Knowledgeable buyers select preferred routings that are often a compromise between speed and expense. Backhauls are often the secret to a carrier's profits, so if a buyer can help secure a full round trip, this is an excellent method to achieve cost reductions.

Negotiating Rates with Deregulated Carriers

To reduce shipping costs, two questions need to be answered:

1. What is the classification of the parts to be transported?
2. What is the frequency of shipment?

To answer the first question, analyze the parts just as is done in classifying items in inventory, that is, into A, B, and C groupings. A would be the high-cost items, while medium- and low-cost items would be designated as B and C items, respectively. In answer to the second question, many companies will take deliveries of low-value C items three or four times per year, while A items will be purchased as needed. It is the B items that will require careful analysis.

The next step is to negotiate for a better deal. This type of negotiation is basically no different from buying goods or services. But, before attempting negotiation, give thought to proper shipper classification and terminology. The standards are described in the National Motor Freight Classification (NMFC) and the New England's Coordinated Freight Classification (CFC).

The NMFC and the CFC contain descriptions for all commodities that move by motor carrier. The description of the item shipped can affect the rate, depending on the type of material the product is made of, such as aluminum, plastic, or sheet steel, and also whether it is assembled or knocked down, folded as nested, packaged in crates, in packages or on skids. The following items can also affect costs:

- The density (weight/cubic foot), or length of the item
- Whether it's new, used, reconditioned, or scrap
- A liquid or solid
- Finished or rough form
- Hazardous, dangerous, or "reportable" as such

The proper description for your item will determine a specific NMFC number assigned to it, and a "class" that correlates to the economic value. For example, umbrellas (folded) in boxes are NMFC #188000, sub 1, and are rated class 100. Umbrellas (other than folded) are NMFC #18800, sub 2, and are assigned class 400. These designations indicate that open umbrellas will cost about four times more than folded ones to transport by truck.

There is no substitute for studying these classifications carefully. An occasional review by experts to determine the best classification for your items could pay off. Remember, the objective is to achieve the lowest total cost without sacrificing service.

Trends in domestic transportation costs are published by *Traffic Management* magazine. A "Logistics Cost Index" tracks 2 years of historical data. The base is computed equal to 100 as of 1985. Forecasts are made for various methods of shipping, such as truckload, LTL, rail, and air cargo, projecting cost levels ahead the next four quarters. Also, warehousing and total inventory carrying costs are tracked. This is an excellent reference comparison with your own experiences.

INCOTERMS

An "FOB" term, included in the purchase order, spells out the division of responsibilities for transportation and passage of title. The goods are deemed to be delivered by seller to buyer at a point spelled out in the specific term.

Based on identifying the transfer point for possession of goods, the term determines who will pay the costs and who assumes the risks. It is called "INCOTERMS" (a contraction for International Commercial Terms) and spells out "What the buyer must do" and "What the seller must do." INCOTERMS are detailed in Chapter 14 as a dispute settlement instrument. Lacking mention to the contrary, a PO is assumed to be a "shipping point contract." That means you, as the buyer, are responsible when the seller has delivered the goods to the carrier.

Let's review your options. The first four of these eight possession terms, listed below, are shipping point terms:

- *Ex-Works* means possession changes along with title at the seller's shipping dock, ready to ship but not yet loaded. The buyer may be responsible for loading, and is always responsible for transportation and insurance (plus duty and customs clearance if an import). This is a contract with minimal risk to the seller. This term should be used only by those buyers who have strong transportation specialist support, and have a reason to control the entire shipment. Otherwise, it should be avoided.

- *FOR/FOT* ("Free on Rail" or "Truck") refers to a railway wagon, and is intended solely for goods transported by rail. Title passes to the buyer when the goods have been delivered to the rail carrier.

- *FAS (Free Alongside Ship) to Named Port of Shipment.* Under this scenario, the seller provides transportation for the goods to the point of departure alongside the ship. The buyer has the responsibility to get ocean freight space, and marine and war risk insurance rests with the buyer.

- *FOB (Free on Board) to Named Point of Shipment.* In this case, the price quoted applies only to an inland shipping point. The seller arranges for loading of goods on, or in, railway cars, trucks, barges, or aircraft, etc. The buyer will pay for all transportation costs, and assumes responsibility to make any claim. This is the most commonly used term.

The following four are the "destination point" terms:

- *C&F (Cost & Freight) to Named Port of Destination.* This is a shipping point contract though the seller pays the charges. Title and risk of loss passes to the buyer when goods are delivered to the carrier.

- *CIF (Cost, Insurance, and Freight) to Named Port of Destination.* This is the same as C&F above, but the seller also arranges and pays for insurance.

- *Ex-Ship to Named Port of Destination.* This is an arrival contract, wherein title to the goods changes when they pass over the ship's rails at the U.S. port of entry.

- *Ex-Quay to Named Port of Import.* As with the item above, this is an arrival contract. The seller's price normally includes costs for the goods plus all other costs to place the goods on the quay (or dock), at the port of destination.

The above eight, the most common INCOTERMS in use today, were adopted in 1953. The following two terms were added in 1967 as goods moved increasingly across national borders:

- *DAF (Delivered at Frontier) to Named Place of Entry at Frontier* implies delivery to the border of the destination country of import, by either rail or truck. For the U.S. buyer, this applies only for shipments from Canada or Mexico.

- *DDP (Delivered Duty Paid) to Named Place of Destination in the Country of Importation.* This includes any mode of transport. Total landed costs to the buyer's destination, including duty, are paid by the seller.

With increased use of air transport, the following term was added in 1976.

- *DAP (FOB Delivery at Airport) from Named Airport of Departure.* The buyer uses this term solely for air shipments. In this case, the seller pays all costs to the departure airport, and the buyer assumes possession at the import airport.

As Customs adopts its new computerized systems, still being installed, three more systems have been added that are expected to gradually replace C&F and CIF since they will get higher priority:

- *FRC (Free Carrier From Named Point).* of a cargo terminal located at a seaport or inland.
- *DCP (Destination Carriage Paid).* This is for land transport, but does include inland waterways. Seller pays freight to destination, but risks of loss are the buyers.
- *CIP (Carriage and Insurance Paid)* to named port of destination. Same as above DCP, but also includes insurance. It is similar to CIF.

These are the latest modern revisions, adaptable to multimodal forms of transportation. Stick with the proper terminology on the purchase order. Spell out easily misunderstood terms. These 14 INCOTERMS are preventive aids for buyers should disputes arise.

Getting the Best Air Fares for Travelers

Although we don't generally think of purchasing as being in the job of people moving, the fact is that often the travel function is a part of the job.

This is a highly specialized area for pricing study and one in which whole books have been written. Many price arrangements are available, but not widely broadcast. We will not attempt to provide detail in this area, but will touch on a couple of tips for managing air travel costs.

First, it must be recognized that the airlines are an extremely competitive industry where pricing schedules are changing constantly. The complexities are such that when you phone for reservations, it's necessary to know what to ask for. As an example, there may be a special low fare from New York to St. Louis.

A person flying from Boston to St. Louis may find that if he bought two separate tickets—one round trip Boston to New York, and the other, New York to St. Louis—a lower fare overall results. Another trick has been to buy a ticket to a city with a low fare that may stop at the airport the passenger wants to reach. By getting off early, and not using the full trip, money is saved. Such practices are being resisted by the airlines.

Super-saver fares, senior citizen discounts, limited travel during certain days, 30 day advance notice, etc., are all a part of the deregulated, competitive and confusing rate structure. Most disconcerting is that many advertised fares are for only a few seats on each aircraft, so they are difficult to get and often entail severe time travel restrictions. To minimize costs, business people have to keep to a schedule and not travel at the airlines' convenience—unless there are no other options. It may pay you to negotiate with a local travel agency who will search for the lowest fares, in a rapidly changing marketplace.

The best deals can be made by buyers using an agency-supplied computer. Under such an arrangement, the agency, in return for the business, rebates back to the company a percentage of its commissions, which tend to average 10% for air travel and hotel reservations and 5% for car rentals. Buying this service in-house can return between 3% and 6% of airfare costs.[3]

Claim Settlements and Adjustments

Claims can be controversial and so take much time and expense to settle. The first step is to find out who should file the claim. That is when you fall back on the INCOTERMS, or FOB point, in the contract. The shipping point used settles many a controversy about shipments as explained in Chapter 14. While it may appear easier to make it the shipper's problem, often the buyer will need to replace the goods, and must act at once. Take an example where a shipment is four cases short. You must reorder, and pay for the goods again. Meantime a claim is placed on the carrier.

Claims fall into categories known as (a) known loss, (b) concealed loss, (c) known damage, (d) concealed damage, and (e) loss or damage due to delay.

"Known loss" refers to damage that renders the goods worthless. It is the simplest claim to settle. Known damage is noticed and acknowledged by the carrier when delivered. Such information should be noted on the receipt for goods before signing for receipt. The receiver must legally receive the goods, but this does not prevent a legitimate claim against the carrier for restitution.

A "concealed loss" means one not apparent when delivered, but discovered later. The item appears to be in good order and receipt is given. Perhaps the material doesn't agree with the quantity, implying an error in loading, or someone

---

[3]*Purchasing Today,* February, 1996, p. 43.

has stolen part of the contents. Because the carrier did not have the opportunity to inspect and acknowledge, this is a tougher claim to clear.

The Bill-of-Lading (B/L) is the legal contract between shipper and carrier, serving as a receipt for goods, evidence of title to goods, and sometimes is used as a packing list. On it are stated the description of items shipped, routing, and rates that are applicable. This document is used to determine the freight charges. When signed upon receipt, it an important document in settling loss and damage claims.

A "clean" B/L, when signed by the carrier, acknowledges possession of goods in good condition. An "unclean" or "foul" bill means that the goods are damaged, or packaging is broken. Any defect is noted by inserted writing by the carrier, such as "damaged boxes." Carriers may reject shipments that do not meet packaging requirements.

A straight bill provides for delivery only to the named party. A "To Order" bill does not name the receiver specifically at the time it's issued. It is a negotiable instrument that is delivered to anyone endorsed on the bill. The bill protects the shipper dollarwise by declaring exact payment charges. When signed upon receipt, the B/L is important for supporting loss and damage claims. Exceptions noted on the delivery receipt make claims easier to pursue.

Losses or damage due to delay in-transit are determined by comparing the actual time versus normal length of time in transit. The carrier has to deliver within a "reasonable time." If the carrier can be shown to be negligent, a claim can be made. However, unless a statement is made on the B/L about the urgency of delivery, such a claim is almost impossible to collect.

Many carriers for rail and motor carriage state that any claims must be filed within 15 days of delivery. This is not legally so, since the 9-month rule applies. All claims must be filed in writing within the proper time limit, that is within 9 months from date of delivery, or, in case of loss, after reasonable time for delivery has elapsed. Standard legal forms are available for claims submission.

Set a minimum claim to file, such as $100, as it's not worth going after less. Claims can be taken to the Transportation Arbitration Board, made up of shippers, carriers, and attorneys. Any final recourse against a carrier for not settling our claim can be taken only by court action.

Audits of Freight Bills

Those who audit freight bills paid know that savings almost always can be achieved. Often human error will cause overcharges. Five types of clerical errors can cause an over-or-under charge claim. These errors are found in (1) rate, (2) weight, (3) commodity description, (4) tariff interpretation, and (5) company identified as payer of freight charges.

Audits verify the classification used, weights billed, and extensions of total dollars. They process overcharge claims, and settle all losses and damage occurring during transit. Buyers have three years to audit the freight bills.

Although purchasing or traffic management can perform this audit, it may be preferable to employ outside specialists who perform such audits on a contingency fee basis. Since their fees are typically based on a portion of the savings they find, this approach is a good one—as you pay only when overcharges are found, so there is a built-in budget to do the audit!

18

Measurements of Purchasing Performance

Simply put, during this working day, over $16 billion will be spent by purchasing people in the U.S. But how well will that money be spent? That's what productivity improvement and measurement are really all about!

Most professional purchasing departments try to measure their results in some way. Attempts at measuring purchasing effectiveness have been extremely varied, but usually limited in scope—somewhat like checking the oil with a car's dipstick, and declaring the engine is in excellent shape.

Why bother with measurements? Quantifiable measurements such as cost reductions *can* be evaluated, yet experienced managers and buyers know they can't measure everything. Certainly not all the procedures to be described in this chapter will be presented with the idea that they will be immediately applicable. Rather, they show the diversity and possibilities in this field of measurement. The professional CPO must continue the quest for better ways to measure based on the specifics of his or her particular business.

As a practical reality, purchasing managers (PMs) frequently find themselves trying to justify their department to a management that judges purchasing solely by financial statistics relating to salaries and costs, or to a production-minded management that is interested primarily in a steady flow of critical material with minimal investment in carrying an inventory.

Because the validity of the chosen yardsticks is critical, it is sound practice to get management input as to the key elements to be measured. One way to do this is to set our goals and ask management to look them over. However, judging purchasing performance is difficult for most managements. There is need for a more objective measurement procedure than that which was illustrated in an AMA study that polled presidents and CEOs about their thoughts on purchasing performance. This study revealed that:

- 70% of 201 surveyed said they rely on audits, an accounting technique that ensures honesty and procedural accuracy, but not too much beyond that.
- 24% said they judged purchasing by percent savings (fair enough—that's a start!).
- 23% judged by comparing prices paid against "standard cost," a technique controlled by someone's estimate of future cost.
- 19% reported they looked at the department's operating budget.
- 13% said they judged by gauging the timeliness and accuracy of information submitted on markets and prices.

It should be noted in the above analysis that the percentages add to greater than 100% based on the fact that many respondents provided more than one response.

One president said he plotted the number of orders each buyer placed and the number of dollars each spent. He defined the resulting curve as "the performance norm for the department, and each buyer can be checked against this norm." Imagine that! The next time you buy a double order of widgets using a single purchase order, be sure to ask for a doubling of your salary based on the concurrent doubling of your productivity!

This sort of management ignorance is reminiscent of a true life story at the ballpark where 11-year-old Steven excitedly exclaimed, "Dad, Look! The first baseman has the ball hidden in his glove!" Let's set this up: the home team was leading 2 to 1, but the opponents had the bases loaded with two out in the top of the ninth inning, and the home team—which couldn't buy a hit late in the game—had to get out of this inning. Their first baseman strode nonchalantly over to talk to the pitcher with the ball hidden in his glove. Returning, he stood close to first base, and when the runner took a lead, he promptly tagged the runner to make the final out.

The first baseman held up the ball, and shouted to the startled base umpire who looked over to first to see the runner safely back on the bag. The umpire signaled with both hands outstretched—"safe." The first baseman argued and pleaded, and many first base fans knew he was dead right; but the truth was that the umpire's eyes were similar to some management's—the "action" was on home plate where the batter stood ready to swing at the next pitch.

Buyers are sometimes in the position of that first baseman. They make a solid contribution, and look to the chief executive for acknowledgment, while the focus may be on perhaps sales or engineering. However, buyers are still in the ball game—and need to be sure their results are noticed.

Expressing frustration, some CEOs make comments about their viewpoint on purchasing performance. "Sometimes I get the feeling that we are 'too soft' on our suppliers. I believe my purchasing department knows its stuff; but how can I really measure purchasing performance?" Such comments confirm a sense of measurement uncertainty among top management.

Management is not interested, as a first focus, in optimizing purchasing per se, but they are (or should be) interested in purchasing's contributions to the company's business strategies. In short, efforts to show the effect of performance on such key goals as return-on-investment and profit contribution should be appreciated.

Measurements that will satisfy everyone may not exist. The reality is that many opinions or judgments exist about performance—and though these opinions can be influenced by measurements—to a large degree these quantitative measurements are colored by the interrelationships that purchasing has with other functions.

When financial controllers think of purchasing, they relate to areas that affect them. Engineering, not interested in the controller's concerns, cares about those areas that relate to its design responsibility. Differing opinions exist within any company about what constitutes good job performance. In considering overall purchasing performance, it makes sense to look at it through the eyes of those other functions to which purchasing relates. All eyes may be on Purchasing and Supply Management, but *what* they see may differ greatly.

How well purchasing performs relating to others will determine how these others will rate purchasing. And that's not theory—it's reality! The sum total of those opinions is purchasing's "image"—which too often is negative. Why? Because purchasing cuts across so many major functions, truly spectacular results may not occur at any single juncture. Often the only news top management hears is negative. If something goes wrong such as the production line is short of material, orders aren't processed quickly, or cooperation is lacking—then it is only natural that there is a complaint. Fortunate indeed (and rarer still) is the purchasing person whose management understands that this is the nature of the job!

It only makes sense that any function responsible for spending well over 50% of the sales dollar is going to be subjected to the accounting or managerial eye. The CPO must be prepared with some kind of a yardstick that will help pinpoint weak and strong points. A review of current measurement practices is helpful.

The important implication from this chapter is the varying validity of the yardsticks reviewed. This chapter has been arranged to review historically the efforts to improve measurements on-the-job. We must somehow tell management what to measure, or do it ourselves anyway! The gap between existing measurement theory and the practical knowledge of the buying professional needs to be bridged.

Managers wanting to develop their own system may find these steps can be useful in designing a measurement system:

- Define the area of purchasing activity to be evaluated.
- Select the measurable factors in each area (parameters) that the manager believes are indicators of the quality of productivity performance.
- Arrange the parameters mentioned above in order of importance.

- Assign a weight factor to each category.
- Periodically review the above and update, as necessary.

As a generalization, experts in the profession can use three specific measures to determine if a professional department exists. In chart form, these measurements and range of values are as follows:

Criterion	Measurement Standard	Measurement Desired
1. Purchasing savings effectiveness	$\dfrac{\text{Total annual savings}}{\text{Annual purchases}}$	About 2% (below previous pricing)
2. Procurement planning: commodities planned as % of major items	Number of plans per buyer	6 to 12/buyer (~70% of volume)
3. Purchasing efficiency	$\dfrac{\text{Prices paid}}{\text{Market prices}}$	Percent below market versus base period
	$\dfrac{\text{Total buying costs}}{\text{Annual purchases}}$	0.8% to 1.0%
	$\dfrac{\text{Purchasing employees}}{\text{Company employees}}$	0.7 to 0.9%

The purchasing manager's ability to produce evidence of measurements of the above three activities indicates the first signs of a professional purchasing approach. But what if you have no standard from which to measure? During the 1986 CNN TV broadcast covering the Statute of Liberty's anniversary, a Navy historian said the definition of a "tall ship" was one that could not go under the Brooklyn Bridge. This was an example of a new standard created by comparison— in the absence of an agreed upon standard, we create one. However, before you start from scratch, you will want to review some measurement systems that have been used successfully.

Smaller companies do not want or need elaborate statistical measurement systems. But there should exist some standard of performance to gauge how well the buying is being done.

Various Kinds of Measurements Used

The purchasing department budget is an accounting and administrative control over the cost of operating the department. Too often it is used as a measurement. Improvement comes from simply cutting costs. The big item of cost in operating a purchasing department is salaries and wages, such that when employee benefits are included, they may run well over 80% of the total cost. When you add the cost of communications, telephone, and faxing, and printing and stationery, you account for the bulk of the costs. While this measure of cost control is universally used, it is also the least indicative of the kind of purchasing job being done in terms of productive results in spending efficiency. Costs alone cannot measure the quality of material purchased, reliability of sources, services rendered, and suggestions to reduce costs, to name a few.

Internal Audit

Auditing is another form of measurement that should be used. It's defined by auditors as "the measurement of job performance and the clerical comparison to what it should be." Few auditors, however, know how to determine the best job that can be done. Audits are most effective in reviewing documentary controls. For example, were purchases properly authorized, did buyers adhere to their dollar commitment limits, and is the purchasing process verifiable based on records kept?

A good internal audit is vital to ensure management that purchasing is performing properly. The Institute of Internal Auditors issued "Internal Audit and Control of the Purchasing Department," a publication that defined auditing as "a type of control which functions by measuring and evaluating the effectiveness of other types of control." A prime requisite for success is a sympathetic understanding between the purchasing group and the internal audit group.

The art of purchasing is often an enigma to the auditor. By traditional audit methods, a relatively poor purchasing department might be rated higher than an aggressive one. That is because the aggressive department goes out of its way to negotiate price and contribute to profit, but might make more slips in the paperwork functions. A buying department can go through the motions of buying, expediting, and keep excellent records, yet not take advantage of profit opportunities within its grasp.

Here are a few specific points that might be included in any checklist of internal audit requirements for purchasing:

1. Are company goals known? Does purchasing have its own goals and strategies that support them?

2. Is there an awareness of buying value, making use of proven buying techniques such as cost and value analysis?

3. Are reports on savings made, and are they audited? Are these reports sent to top management?

4. Are buyers acquainted with TQM, ISO9000, SPC, and similar quality concepts?

5. Are buyers alert to new product availability? Is there evidence of an ongoing search for global supply?

6. Are buyers familiar with, and using, sound negotiation techniques? Were they fruitful? Were negotiations conducted on an ethical and honorable basis?

7. Are salespeople interviewed with reasonable promptness?

8. Is correspondence handled promptly and price quotations held in confidence?

9. Do buyers explain to suppliers the end-use and function of what they are supplying?

10. Is there evidence of the modern purchasing job? Though posted slogans and other displays may be external trappings, they nonetheless are usually indicative of a culture where employee development is fostered.

Internal audit is another means whereby the need for specific corrective action is made clear by isolating and examining the department's procedures. An audit should not be solely a fault-finding session. Recommendations for improvement will grow naturally out of the process of scrutiny.

There is good reason for purchasing and internal audit to be allies. They both seek control and understanding of a profit-making function that is difficult to measure, yet too important to ignore. Auditors are in a position to suggest to top management that buyers need authority to control the flow of money. Giving leverage to buyers in dealing with suppliers does pay dividends. Most managers who have had a first-class audit are unanimous in saying, "It helps!"

Management by Objectives

Purchasing managers sometimes forget that managing by objectives (MBO) is still a highly useful and workable form of measurement. Supervisors should sit down with their subordinates and arrive at an agreement—the job to be done, and the rating system for merit pay. Use of MBOs can be both a means of improving performance and an aid to measurements.

What can be learned from experience of others? Reducing MBOs to a simple piece of paper, a discussion of the purchasing manager and buyer is held. Written key goals, and a means to find out how well the job is done, are basic. An MBO program doesn't have to be complex to be effective, but must state results expected of the person being measured. Let's consider four steps of a simplified MBO process that can assist the PM:

1. Accurately describe job outputs—the key desired results.

2. Set goals for each buyer that tie-in to company strategies as part of a corporate planning and control system.

3. Agree on goals jointly—buyer and manager. Commit to writing so there is joint responsibility for success.

4. Set standards for measurement and checkpoints along the way.

For MBOs to impact company performance the goals should be verifiable, weighted, and part of a network—in short, a *system* of measurement. Use measurements that can be quantified. As an example, an acceptable objective would be "$100,000 will be saved in 1998," while a poor, unacceptable version is "I'll save money on purchases this year."

Rewarding good performance is a key to successfully managing buying. But how do we know whom to reward? In short, who are the effective performers in the department? And which suppliers have performed best to meet the company's needs?

We may want to track and report on some of the following:

- Strategic plan—company's objectives with emphasis on purchasing integration and contribution

- Annual plan—departmental budget, material costing, standard cost price forecasting for production materials

- Individual objectives—MBOs, quarterly and year-end reports

- Superior and subordinate agreement scoring values, and pay for performance

Measurement of these factors, allowing feedback about performance, is an integral part of the buying process itself!

Indicators of Purchasing Efficiency

It is difficult, if not impossible, to try to evaluate all purchasing departments on the same basis. There are simply too many variants. One department checks invoices, another handles freight bills, and the like; another in the identical industry may do none of these things. There are, however, year-to-year variations *within a specific purchasing department* that provide interesting and useful data. They can be used as indicators of purchasing efficiency which, for simplicity, we shall call IPEs.

The PM can use these IPEs to make graphs, display data, and satisfy others that the department is performing properly. It is not difficult to gather this information. At a minimum, a PM should know most of the following IPEs. To be meaningful, data on about a 5-year period should be kept, as shown in Table 18-1.

The factors listed in the table are a starting point only; the manager may add or delete factors based on his or her own requirements. In this example, note the rising volume of purchases (No. 1), and at the same time note the ratio of purchasing people to total employees (No. 5) is decreasing. Would this be an indicator of purchasing efficiency?

An excellent indicator is the percent of savings (No. 9), but this should be

Table 18-1   Data chart on indicators of purchasing efficiency

No.	Factor		Year			
		1	2	3	4	5
1.	$ Purchases Per year (millions)	12.4	16.6	20.4	16.8	18.0
2.	$ Sales per year (millions)	24.3	33.0	41.5	33.6	35.7
3.	$\frac{\$ \text{Purchases}}{\$ \text{sales}}$ (%)	51.0	50.2	49.0	50.0	50.5
4.	No. of purchase orders	24,909	25,530	25,655	26,230	26,000
5.	$\frac{\text{Purchasing employees}}{\text{Total employees}}$	$\frac{1}{124}$	$\frac{1}{122}$	$\frac{1}{126}$	$\frac{1}{131}$	$\frac{1}{146}$
6.	$ Cost of purchasing dept.	120,000	140,000	153,500	150,000	152,000
7.	$ Cost per purchase order	4.83	5,59	5.97	5.73	5.85
8.	$ Saved per year	125,200	127,000	321,000	353,000	295,000
9.	$\frac{\$ \text{Saved}}{\$ \text{Purchases}}$ (%)	1.01	0.77	1.58	2.10	1.64
10.	Purchased Material Price Index (CMB) (Base = 100)	50.1	51.2	55.3	58.1	61.0

seen in the light of market conditions, CMB (No. 10). Softened markets could improve percentage savings and vice versa.

A number of graphs have been taken from the statistics, as it is much easier to see trends when they are graphically depicted. For example, as seen in Figure 18-1, graph No. 1 shows that when the volume of sales and purchases dropped in the fourth year, purchasing personnel were reduced. Increased productivity by the purchasing personnel could be used as an argument to obtain pay increases for the more effective buyers.

Graph No. 2 shows that the company purchase price index (CMB) advanced, showing higher prices are being paid, despite an increase in purchasing savings. The inevitable question is "Why?" The alert purchasing manager seeing this relationship will investigate and be able to point out to management that the prices paid would have been even higher if savings had not been effected. This fact is readily seen when in the fifth year savings fell off sharply and the index shot upward.

There is no way of predicting how any given company's statistics would chart or what indicators or questions would be evident. However, no one would know more about the statistical measurements of the purchasing operation than the company purchasing manager. The proper interpretation and use of these statistics

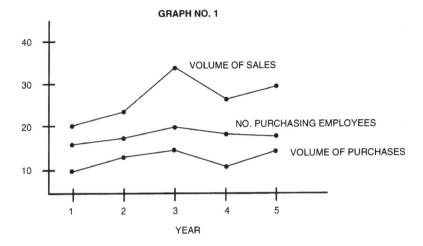

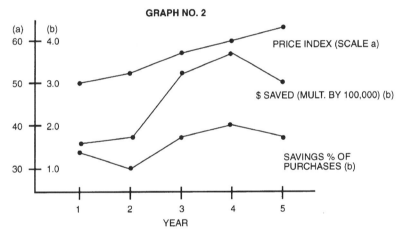

Figure 18-1 Plotting indicators of purchasing efficiency (IPE).

are a measure of managerial capability. In the process of keeping these IPEs, various aspects of good or poor performance will become evident, so changes can be made. The efficiency of a purchasing operation cannot be measured in terms of such data alone. Quality of material bought, reliability of sources, service rendered, and suggestions for reducing costs are some other considerations.

While other buyer attributes such as personality, integrity, and intelligence are extremely important, they cannot be charted, as they are subjective personality traits that even the trained psychologist finds difficult to measure effectively. We are interested in the *results* of these traits that can be measured using available statistical data.

Such charts help to show whether the department is maintaining a reasonable level of performance. It's important to differentiate between workload and job effectiveness. "Workload" refers to the quantity rather than the quality of work. It is possible to have extremely efficient buying with light workloads yet have far too many employees. That's why the term "indicators" is preferred over "measurement." An analysis may prove that the question raised by an IPE is fully justified.

When the last out of the world series is made, each player's batting average will be recorded for all to see. It's either a badge of pride or embarrassment. Surprisingly, the difference between the league-leading hitter and an average professional ballplayer is relatively small. Take a player sporting a .310 batting average compared to the average of .250. So, that player gets only one hit every 20 times at bat more than most others; yet, his salary is about four times that of the others. The difference in ability of the professional buyer and an average one is likewise small, though it's not common practice to compensate in a manner similar to that used in baseball! Is this because of the difficulty of judging the score on good buying?

Benchmarking

The desire to evaluate has led the NAPM to promote benchmarking as a purchasing performance measurement. Tests have been developed to enable the users to find ways to improve their performance. A benchmark is defined as a standard or point of reference in measuring or judging quality or value.

Measurements are possible on the following types of activities:

- Internal processes, performance and people
- Competitive activities, within a company's industry or business
- Functional activities
- Noncompetitive activities, outside a company's industry

The attempt is to assess current performance and find new ways to improve processes. Specific goals should be set to make improvements.

The NAPM's Center for Advanced Purchasing Studies (CAPS) has collected nonpricing practices and methods. Collecting price information itself is both difficult and fraught with negative legal repercussions. CAPS Benchmarking reports are available on some industries such as aerospace/defense, food, and government buying—and these are available at no charge to NAPM members.

NAPM defines three phases in the benchmarking process, and these are outlined below:

In PHASE I, the usual way to begin is to have a benchmarking team that decides what to benchmark. The team collects and analyzes the data, and evaluates a way to monitor processes on a continual basis. The team also gathers purchasing performance benchmarking reports from selected companies.

PHASE II consists of identifying the "best-in-class," by selecting organizations that most closely parallel your type of purchasing operation, or are at least reasonably compatible. For example, a bank's purchasing management will want to compare other banks' practices.

PHASE III are optional visits to best practices sites. Each participant can judge how best to use the reports within his company. Among benefits reported is the ability to take process improvement action.

Individual items benchmarked by NAPM include many ratios and workload measurement IPEs. Newer additions include the percent of purchases received by minority or female companies, the percent of purchases actually made by the purchasing department, and others too numerous to list.

Information gained from benchmarking allows comparisons of results of an individual company to an industry standard. Groupings have been made of television, semiconductor, goods/services, and petroleum companies. An estimate is that most companies will be included in 30 groups. Data submitted are treated confidentially and individual companies are not identified.

The NAPM encourages use of benchmarking, and it has become a common and accepted practice. The authors recall the failure of past NAPM attempts to measure any department versus others back in the 1930s; it simply didn't prove workable because of the diverse scope of jobs performed. Perhaps computer capabilities and better organized effort makes benchmarking work. It is doubtful the final answer to the measurement challenge has been found.

The TREND Measurement System

To sort out the measurement confusion, the TREND concept was created and first published in 1966. That's significant, as TREND has withstood the test of time, and it's as valid today as when introduced. It is available today as a NAPM video program.[1]

"Total Recognition of Environmental and Numerical Development," or TREND, evolved from earlier development of Indicators of Purchasing Performance, or IPEs. It is a strategic approach to measurements and similar to the way JIT philosophy applies to inventory. The TREND philosophy may be summarized as follows:

1. Purchasing can and should be measured.
2. Comparison with another purchasing operation can be helpful if it's possible to benchmark with success.

---

[1]"Measuring Purchasing Efficiency/Trend" (PAL 33 Video for Company Training), NAPM, Tempe, AZ, 1986.

3. The trend of performance today with respect to past performance is the best measure.
4. Measurements should be made in three basic areas: Conceptual, Behavioral, and Resultant.
5. Measurements should be in quantitative terms that are easily recognized by management.
6. Accomplishments should be reported in terms of their total effect on the business.

The point to recall is that most numerical measurements are partially indicative of the job being done. The three distinct steps for measurement are shown in Figure 18-2. All three steps have to be studied.

If the PM looks at these as three separate yet interdependent areas, it is clear, it's not enough to analyze results only. It doesn't show *how* improvement can be made.

Step 1 is, in effect, "How well has the PM achieved an understanding of efficient purchasing with the buyers, and how well have they studied what makes buyers want to buy well?"

Next the PMs see, in Step 2, what their buyers *do!* Is it what they say they'll do, and the manager believes they should?

Finally, the PM, like all managers, is interested in Step 3—Results. So he or she tries to measure the end product of performance.

If Step 3 end results are not what we'd like, it can be changed by feedback to steps 1 and 2. For example, if savings are too low, and it's known that buyers don't know or use cost and value analysis, then a buyer development program might be implemented. Through a process of planning, acting, measuring and then feedback to repeat the three-step cycle, improvement should result.

No wonder there is confusion about measurements. Some say, "Measure by objectives," and another, "You must measure by results;" while still another says, "Modern purchasing techniques must do the job." Some managers, believing

1 CONCEPTUAL (OBJECT)	**2** BEHAVIORAL (HOW)	**3** RESULTANT (WHAT HAPPENED)
MEASURED BY OBJECTIVES	MEASURED BY METHODS I.E., VALUE ANALYSIS, COST ANALYSIS, LEARNING CURVE	MEASURED BY RESULTS
BUYER PERFORMANCE REVIEW DEPARTMENT OBJECTIVES INDIVIDUAL REVIEWS	INTERNAL AUDIT SYSTEMS ANALYSIS	STATISTICAL DATA, BUDGETS, (OPERATING & MATERIAL), SAVINGS, STANDARD COST, PRICE INDEX, PURCHASING PROFIT

Figure 18-2   Three-step TREND measurement system.

measurements are useless, say, "It's a matter of having good people, and they will provide the best results." But how do these people *know* they're getting results? Each is right, but only partially. Areas can always be found that are not being measured that may be just as important to the operation.

TREND, the three-step purchasing measurement system, shows that no universal yardstick will ever be the final answer; rather, many areas for improvement will present themselves. All have a positive or negative effect on purchasing performance. Emphasis on any one TREND step to the exclusion of the other two can only produce partial results.

Something is pushing the chief purchasing officer (CPO) to measure his operations. Using the trend concept, the CPO can segregate the functions of purchasing and supply management into the three schools of management. In chart form, Table 18-2 shows that the concept a person holds influences the behavior on the job, and so the all important results. *The basic purpose of any standard of measurement is to make an improvement; otherwise, it is wasted effort.* A performance standard must be high, but not so high that it is beyond reach. Patience is needed. There are to be expected delays between a change and its results.

By studying the department effort in its entirety, any deficiencies in the three steps that can be corrected *will affect the overall department in some manner.* When the concept or understanding of the buying job's global role is clarified, the results will improve.

Use of Standard Cost as a Measurement

Sometimes "standard cost" is used as a measure of purchasing performance. The standard is set in advance of the year to be measured. Whether prices paid are higher or lower, purchasing is said to have done a good or poor job. Most PMs and buyers are familiar with how standards are set. In any case, if there is any question, it would be wise to go back and review Chapter 10 about how standards are set.

A detriment to the use of standard cost purchase variance (PV) as a true measurement of purchasing performance has largely been a lack of understanding. Managements who know standard cost's usefulness to track their product costs don't always appreciate its potential significance as a purchasing performance measurement tool. Also, most purchasing managers can't explain how the data can be interpreted usefully. That failure to understand was dramatically proven when the CPO's new president phoned early in the year congratulating him about the large amount of positive purchase variance. That CEO saw positive PV as money not spent, and so in the profit column.

By midyear when PV became slightly negative, the congratulatory calls stopped as the final months produced no further positive variance. Though the material budget was right on target, this lack of comprehension had to be overcome if

Table 18-2   Management overview using the TREND concept

Concept	Behavior (how done)	Results
Change sourcing relationships	Use alternate vendor Change vendor Adjust volume among suppliers	
Change design or quality	Value analyze Use less expensive grade Substitute material or part Standardize Redesign Supplier certification	
Change way to buy	Negotiate concessions Forward buy Use long-term POs System contracting Make-vs.-buy Lease-vs.-own Subcontract Apply learning curve	(A) Less ultimate material cost
Change in delivery	Select proper INCOTERM Buy quantities—less freight cost Point-of-use Use own truck fleet Use rail vs. truck Different hauler Piggy-back	(B) Lower cost of acquisition/use (C) Higher profit and increased ROI
Volume buying	Buy larger quantity—discounts Consolidate needs Longer production runs Reduce set-up time/cost	
Change inventory policy	Lower or increase safety stock Negotiate shorter lead times Just-in-time Toss out obsolete stock Simplify paper methods Vendor stocking—outside Consignment in plant	

the purchasing chief was to stay employed. This section reveals actual charts used on-the-job, and is not a theoretical attempt at measurements.

We realize that younger buyers will perceive these percentages as exaggerated. They were used, however, when some prices rose 28% in 1982. Also, they remind us that today's inflation is historically low! Figure 18-3 shows the derivation of a new measurement system with three cases of price increases, each of which

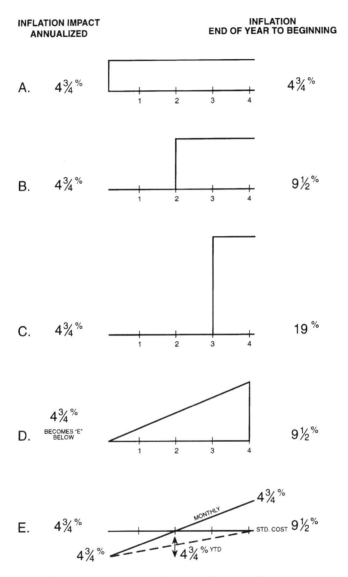

Figure 18-3 Derivation chart showing inflation's effect on purchases.

has an identical effect on a company's profitability. A at the top depicts an assumption that a price is expected to increase 4¾% the first day of the new year and stay steady throughout the year. In B, a 9½% increase will occur in July. In C the price will be unchanged until a 19% increase in the third quarter.

Knowledgeable managers know that when buying thousands of items price increases occur as purchase orders expire and the overall material costs will approximate a gradual inflation from zero to 9½% at year-end as shown in D. Note that each of these four cases depicts the same overall result on the material budget by year-end.

The above exercise teaches us that to achieve the expected budgeted expenditures on a monthly basis there must exist enough positive variance the first half of the year to balance the expected negative variance during the final half of the year. The monthly purchase variance (PV) should approach zero about mid-year. On an accumulative basis, PV starts at the same point on our chart as the first month's PV, but rises until it is at zero or the standard cost baseline as shown in E. Of course, real-life charts as documented each month won't always be as straight lined, but in practice they do track quite closely. The accumulative year-to-date PV provides a partial means to measure productivity in purchasing. PV's shortfall is twofold. First, it measures the combination of ability to control price rises, and the ability to foresee the same. A manager is not able to separate the two from the PV data. Secondly, the focus on price alone distracts from, and even contradicts, major cost improvement opportunities in acquisition. So, the use of PVs as a measurement has fallen into disfavor. We believe there is now potential to adapt PV as a step forward. Drawing on this background a measurement system evolved as described below.

How the Purchasing Dollar is Spent

Here is a measurement system to consider that has been successfully used for more than 15 years yet never before formally published. This might be the answer to your search for the epitome of evaluation.

Alexander Haig, while president of United Technologies, wrote a memo to all divisional heads to establish programs to improve productivity. He first commissioned someone to "Find out what it is!" That's consistent with reality, for purchasing productivity can be measured only after it has been specifically defined.

Productivity is a perplexing and abstract phenomenon on the economic scene. Little is truly understood about all its fundamental sources and interrelationships. And it must be measurable.

Purchasing must be an important contributor to the profitability and growth of the company through forward-looking procurement productivity programs that are proactive rather than reactive. Forward-looking procurement productivity programs help. Buyers must make things happen in "getting the most of every dollar you spend!"

Well over 90% of *Fortune's* top thousand corporations track labor efficiency and productivity. Only a few have documented a valid tracking system for measurement of how well their company spends its dollars. Here is one answer to the question of "What is productivity?"

Computing a Company's Productivity

How can we judge whether it's a buyer's or seller's market without understanding the difficulty of buying? How can a management determine its cost savings or price reductions are good? In inflationary times, the prices paid should never rise as fast as the inflation rate. When market prices fall, are buyers keeping ahead of the decline? If buyers can consistently control their actual prices paid, so they are lower than the market movement, these measurements give some indication of control of the buying activity.

If we look at the three cornerstones of evaluating savings, they can be identified as:

1. The *marketplace* in which the buyer operates—the external environment

2. *Documented savings* that are made

3. The *actual prices paid*, which is the net sum of all the extras as well as cost reductions

Understanding of these three areas gives us an insight not otherwise possible. There is a correlation between the marketplace in which the buyer buys, the savings made, and the actual prices paid. However, before proceeding, let's give thought to the derivation of standard cost purchase variance charts. It is from this background that this productivity measurement evolved as we changed emphasis to getting the most for every dollar spent.

Buyers, of course, are not in control of all marketplace events. However, they do have a say on prices paid and savings resulting from effective buying. Any measurement of materials price trends does not reflect only buying activity. Rather it shows a composite of all influences that affect prices paid—engineering, manufacturing, quality control, and of course purchasing negotiations.

If buyers are not paying some or all of the price increases announced, then the purchase variance would reflect that fact. Similarly, if the company marketbasket (CMB) index is going down, but the positive variance is not increasing, and the buyers make little or no savings, that could be an indication of poor performance. Perhaps greater savings should have been achieved as decreases available in the market were not taken by the buyer.

Prices rise usually as the result of capacity shortages or some condition causing insufficient supply. If the buyer's markets are advancing sharply and yet he or she has high savings, it is not enough to measure savings only. It could be argued that the buyer was busy getting deliveries because of extended lead-times. However, in truth, the extended lead-times are reflected in the market. Market prices do not normally advance as strongly when lead-times are shrinking.

The market can be defined by an index that is the composite of the supply situation indicating the difficulty of buying under the conditions at that time. There are economic and industry statistics that are published by many sources.

Among them are the Bureau of Labor's Producer Price Index (PPI), and Consumer Price Index (CPI). When converted to a company's index, CMB, as explained in Chapter 10, this gives a composite of marketplace price trends that affect your buying activities.

Some other useful information for forecasting the state of the economy are:

- Money Supply is designated as M-1. It represents the most liquid of currency, plus all checking accounts. It is announced each Thursday afternoon by the Federal Reserve System. Where money chases supply of goods and services, prices are affected by this factor. In turn, it affects over a longer range the interest rates for borrowing.

- Prime Rate is an economic barometer of the interest rate the major banks charge the largest borrowers, primarily major corporations for the use of borrowed money.

- Index of Leading Economic Indicators is compiled by the Department of Commerce at each month's end and considers new construction permits, wholesale orders, and new company formations, etc.

- Treasury Bills, yields of which are reported Monday night, set the rates of other short-term investments such as 6-month CDs and money-market funds.

- Unemployment Rate is another indicator of economic activity.

- Dow Jones Industrial Average is based on the prices of 30 blue-chip stocks. The composite index adds 15 utility and 20 transportation stocks.

The calculations used for purchasing productivity are based on: the rate of change of market prices, minus the rate of change of prices paid, divided by the base year's performance on the same attributes. The base year used is the previous completed year that is acceptably accurate.

Mathematically, then, purchasing's productivity (relative to the base year) can be expressed by the formula:

$$((C - A) + 100)_i / ((C - A) + 100)_{i-1}$$

where   C = Company index (CMB) forecast,
        A = Actual rate of change of prices paid,
        and i = Current measurement year (i − i = previous, or base year).

On the left side of the chart shown in Figure 18-4 are plotted the PPI, CPI, and your company (CMB) index. [Remember, the company index is a weighting of the PPI for the items it buys.] The data shown were that actually reviewed by the company management on a monthly basis as the facts became known. So, there is a confidence in the base year data.

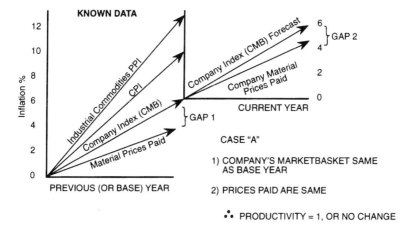

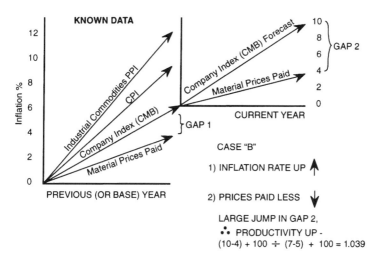

Figure 18-4 Productivity measurement for purchased materials.

To explain how it worked on-the-job, Case A shown at the top of the chart assumes that the company marketbasket (CMB) is predicted to be the same +6.0% as in the base year. On this expectation that inflation will continue the same as the year just completed, and the prices paid are at the same rate of change, the productivity = 1.00. That's derived from $((6 - 4.5) + 100) / ((6 - 4.5) + 100) = 1.00$. A productivity ratio of 1.00 is neutral. That is simple enough, but seldom is the new year exactly the same as last year.

Less than 1.00 is unfavorable, and that would cause questions regarding the trend. Let's consider a case not shown, where the marketbasket inflation of 6%

is expected to remain steady, but the prices paid will be +7% that are higher than the base year's 5%. In this case, the measurement is less than 1.00, computed as $((6 - 7) + 100) / ((6 - 5) + 100) = 0.98$ productivity indicator.

Above 1.00 is indicative of good performance depending on the magnitude of the number. Case B further assumes that last year's market index forecast was a 7% increase, while actual CMB prices paid rose 5%. Case B further assumes inflation will rise to +10% based on economist, management, and buyer judgment. That increase is programmed into the company's cost system, the percentage varying with different items bought. As the year unfolds, the actual prices paid are increased by +4%, for a larger "gap" than before. Here the productivity is up, computed as $((10 - 4) + 100) / ((7 - 5) + 100) = 1.039$. Before giving into the temptation to think this is too theoretical to be practical, realize that this case represents an actual performance by the senior author's department with the actual 1980 base with projection for 1981. Recall 1982 had the largest jump in industrial prices in many years, reaching up to +28%.

In practice a chart of 3 years plus the coming year for three indexes—PPI, CPI, and the CMB (company market basket)—were kept. As expected the CMB more closely tracked with the PPI than the CPI. There is no reason this measurement won't work in any year for any company.

The above can be simplified by showing only the CMB predictor, and plotting the monthly prices paid as the year unfolds.

Each year during meetings on materials cost impact on the products, transparency overheads were used that had moveable arrows. The CMB was in blue, and the price target estimate of prices to be paid was in red. As various estimates of inflation were discussed, the arrows could be moved to visualize the trends.

In practice, a company can plot its data monthly to not only follow the trend of prices paid compared to the expectations, but also to give a measurement of the effectiveness of the buying effort. The correlation of these three areas, and the experience gained from reviewing, give us an understanding not otherwise possible. To recap, these measurements are (1) the expected prices, (2) the actual prices paid, and (3) the "gap" or difference between the two, which is compared to the base year.

Reports to Management

A report to top management is an important business communication. Oral, important reports are often written to be effective with less chance of misinterpretation. The best report to management is one favorable to purchasing that is given by other departments. But, that won't happen too often. Many PMs find written reports invaluable to keep management apprised of purchasing's potential and accomplishments.

Poor reports or attempts to get unwarranted attention aren't well received. Some company cultures don't encourage reports while others view them favorably. PMs might consider why they should go to the trouble in the case of the former situation.

A good report should serve a threefold purpose: first, to convey facts to the person(s) responsible for acting on them; second, reports help management to judge how effectively a job is being done; third, reports assist PMs in doing their own job. If nothing else, the preparation helps to clarify their thinking, and forces them to analyze problems. Reports help develop and establish goals, review accomplishments, and sell ideas.

What should be reported? Put yourself in the top manager's shoes and look at the report as he or she might. Think of what management will find important, not necessarily what is easy and pleasant to report. Certainly of interest to most managements is information about any large increases or decreases in the price of major purchases that impact strongly on profit. News about savings made by purchasing action and teamplay are also encouraging, and should be reported as well.

Having each buyer give the PM a report, following a short outline, is a good start. This activity causes buyers to reflect on what they've done. If not much to write, perhaps this is a motivator to get going. This input, coupled with the PM's overview with organized headings will let the reader choose what is most interesting to him. Remember, when reading the sports page most of us pick out the headings to read about our interests.

Reports should be simple with a positive outlook, objective, and as interesting as possible. Timeliness is important. One or two pages should suffice. On occasion it may be appropriate to work it into the in-house computerized news or management information newsletter. Below is an outline of headings popular with several companies that have sound reporting procedures.

Report to: President, Vice President, Major Department Managers. Also Director, Managers, Buyers and select purchasing and supply personnel.

HIGHLIGHTS: [As an example]

1. Improved engineering service and liaison by assigning a buyer to the engineering area. Eliminates friction and speeds up placing of orders by 48 hours.

2. Savings of $180,000 made through application of learning curve to new order for heat exchangers.

A. Special Business Conditions

B. Lead-time and Deliveries

C. Prices and Trends

D. Strikes Affecting Production
E. Trouble Jobs
F. New Programs and Suggestions
G. Purchase Analysis Savings

The PM doesn't need a course in reporting. By consistent reporting the chance to call attention to a situation is available without making a federal case of it. As an example, consider a situation where the boss has not been actively supporting purchasing in its cost reduction program. It's better to report, as a reminder, the relevance of such a program to the company's overall profit performance. Clearly, this would be more favorably received than a claim that purchasing is not getting top management support.

Statistics Don't Lie . . . But!

A short armed fisherman is not as big a liar as a longer armed friend. Today, some might prefer a politically correct substitute for the word lie, such as "terminological inexactitude" or "disinformation." Be warned that this section is a tongue-in-cheek analysis, but is useful because the manner of presenting data does have an impact on our PM's audience.

Let's look at the department's 10 year performance for savings which is shown in Figure 18-5. Not too great, especially the first 5 years, so we'll show the 10-

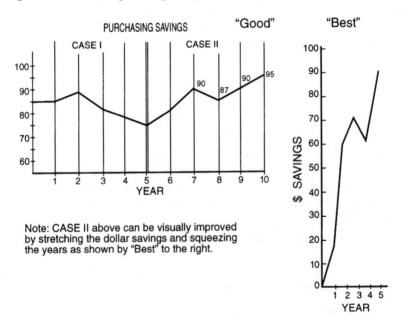

Note: CASE II above can be visually improved by stretching the dollar savings and squeezing the years as shown by "Best" to the right.

Figure 18-5 Charting purchasing savings.

year history to the buyers to motivate them to do better. However, for management, we'll show only the last 5 years because the slope of the line gives an image of success. We certainly don't want to bore them with old data—and of course, a 5-year window shows a steady gain in purchasing savings. Also, we know most of our management don't like lots of detail or statistics, so what could be simpler?

Of course, the majority of us do perform well, so there is no need to fake it. Take case II as an example. Here are displayed versions of identical data. "Good" shows savings rising. We can imagine that "Better" has much more magnitude, but, to really show a sharp increase, we can stretch the dollars and squeeze the years. "Best" does it best! And of course our data are accurate as can be.

Finally, since we happen to have other plants in our company, someone is always comparing "our plant to theirs." Because they're bigger, they usually show up more important than we do in everything. Purchasing savings is no exception, as shown in the top of the chart as A in Figure 18-6.

Comparing plant A ("Us") to plant B ("Them") unfortunately shows they're saving more money. Don't despair, as we won't use the traditional first example; instead, we'll use log–log graph paper—and while we still look smaller, our savings are growing faster, because it's true. But darn, we still look lots smaller! So, by creative statistical measurement theory and using modern visual techniques, we can index savings with the base year as 100. No one knows exactly how many dollars we are saving anyway. Really, they are proprietary and confidential data that shouldn't be flaunted, and may make others jealous, too. But now, focusing on our rate of growth for savings, we can take credit for our accomplishments as shown here in C. Surely good performance is readily depicted here. Note that at no time, in the above have we shown false data. And of course we never lied!

Charts and visuals can be highly useful with a bit of creativity and ingenuity. The intent is not to deceive, but to give thought to how to best depict measurements. Remember, "Statistics don't lie . . . but!"

In summary, purchasing can and should be measured to some degree of reasonableness. In our embryonic scientific space race to the moon, wasn't it wonderful we had the Russians as a benchmark? Without them, how would we have known whether we were leading or lagging? The trend of recent performance compared with past performance is the best benchmark. Measurements should be simple and quantifiable.

At the Hayden Planetarium, a guide explained that for centuries the astronomers made little headway in understanding the universe, with its planets moving in odd gyrations until they finally accepted the fact the earth is not the center of our solar system. So, buyers must see themselves as part of the whole company, contributing to its cost effectiveness and profitability. And through sensible measurements we gain a better understanding of purchasing and supply management.

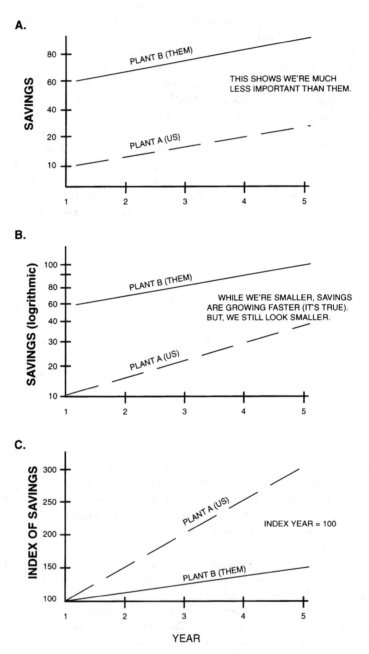

Figure 18-6 Comparison of two purchasing operations, "Us versus Them."

19

A Look into the Future

We began this book with the observation that purchasing is indeed an unusual job—operating at "the vital intersection between buyer and seller where supply and demand forces meet." As we move into the next century, this will remain as true as ever. Purchasing will remain an exciting and challenging profession that will continue to evolve.

Though forecasting the future can be dangerous—as the reader will enjoy the benefit of hindsight in reading this years from now—it is still worthwhile to speculate as to where the profession is headed. The extent to which our speculation has some basis in accuracy is the extent to which those who subscribe to the forecast can improve their competitive advantage in the marketplace.

First, it is reasonable to believe that professional purchasing managers and buyers will keep advancing along *managerial* lines. The clerical role has been diminishing, a trend promoted by computers and the automation of many of the administrative processes required in purchasing.

Advances in data processing and computer technology—both software and hardware—have provided significant productivity tools for the profession. Automated buying by electronic blanket orders has eliminated much routine paperwork. Moreover, MRP and MRP II and EDI are becoming commonplace as these systems' productivity enhancements have become widely known and documented. These trends will continue. Increased automation has had, and will continue to have, the positive effect of freeing up purchasing managers (PMs) and buyers to do more important work managing the buying function and controlling the supply of materials in its broadest sense.

Like all attempts to predict future events, time has proven that the future always brings surprises. As one example—and not intended to be a critical one—the rosy scenario for Europe's cohesiveness has not totally emerged as foreseen in the book *Megatrends 2000*. However, one trend that purchasing people can confirm is that a global economy is here to stay. And, that fast-changing global economy needs decision makers in the area of purchasing and supply management. There will continue to be a need to analyze and investigate global supplier capabilities, and evolve strategic business alliances with world-class supplier partners.

As always, changing economic political situations will bring changes in the various marketplaces. And as always, supply solutions will have to be found. Notwithstanding the importance of a global view, dependency on local suppliers will continue as well, even as marketing of larger companies becomes centralized. Just-in-time (JIT) initiatives will foster this bonding. Purchasing people will still visit suppliers' facilities and meet with their management. Coordination is a trait inherent in the purchasing and supply management process; it will always be required in the buyer–seller relationship, and good communication will always require dedicated effort.

While change is constant though erratic, new concepts and methods will keep evolving with time, while the fundamentals and principles remain steadfast. Day-to-day operations and techniques may change, and be totally automated and staffed by specialists with titles still unknown. Some people predict "purchasing" will become known as "supply management." Regardless, the fundamentals in the buyer–seller relationship will prevail, so the job of *Purchasing and Supply Management* will inherit many of the goals and techniques reviewed in this book—well into the 21st century and beyond.

The Realities of a Global Economy

Some people feel the U.S. is still not faring well in today's world economy. Unions fear Mexican low cost labor! But if cheap labor was the reason for economic success, our major threat would be Bangladesh. Protectionism and free trade are the two extremes. These conflicting forces must be somehow balanced to achieve the adopted slogan, "fair trade."

That sounds great, but how is it done? Should the U.S. adopt a comprehensive trade policy? Proponents of such a policy point to the need to create and protect jobs. Advocates have called for a Department of International Trade at cabinet level to put real teeth into enforcement. But the imposition of a trade policy brings additional questions:

1. Can we distinguish between products made abroad by U.S. owned or joint ventures and domestically produced goods, but owned by foreign companies?
2. Should we try to discourage offshore countries from owning U.S. plants here?
3. Does it matter who provides work for American workers?

Holding back repressive protectionist measures have been those moderates who fear trade reprisals that will undermine the world economy. While most trade experts believe in tearing down trading barriers, no international free trade umbrella of law or rules exist. Some believe it is folly for the U.S. always to continue to champion the free trade philosophy that other nations sometimes exploit.

There are also some people who believe the United States imports too much. The flood of imports has hurt many American companies and eliminated jobs. However, in the long term it may stimulate America's competitive instincts. The pendulum swings. The 1990s have seen a global reawakening of American ingenuity and resourcefulness. America's factories have cut costs, modernized, reduced work forces, and capped pay increases. As a result, many of these same companies today are in a better position to compete in world markets.

Significant Trends

An era of cost, time, and quality competition with lower inflation is already here! And certain other trends have been evolving over recent years, which will demand purchasing's attention through the balance of this century and into the next. Among the most significant trends, which will impact the Purchasing and Supply Management job, are:

- Countertrade in purchasing is becoming a necessity in conducting global business.

- There is ongoing redeployment of capital and human resources.

- Continuous company reorganization/reengineering is resulting in fewer people, with a new philosophy of work scope flexibility.

- There is increasing use of global partnerships and alliances which will require a truly strategic purchasing orientation.

- Increasing global competition is pushing large organizations to look increasingly at increasing profit potential through more effective purchasing—specifically with respect to the pooling of purchases for negotiation leverage.

- As mentioned earlier, the growth of data processing technology continues; and the Internet offers the potential to become a significant medium of future buyer/seller interaction!

- Emergence of trade agreements such as NAFTA and "EC92" are changing the competitive equation by dropping trade barriers within those economic regions.

- The emergence of multinational global manufacturing corporations is placing greater importance on global supply management to optimize efficiency and competitiveness.

- There is an ever-increasing need for cost control to achieve product price leadership.

- Future shortages of materials will become an increasing area of focus as shorter manufacturing cycles are experienced—coupled with the need for lower inventories.

- Energy availability and cost, as in the past, will be a major factor in determine the balance of economic power not only for individual companies, but for entire countries.

Purchasing's role will continually shift as supply and demand forces change. Scarcity of materials will cycle again. As in the past, higher prices will be needed at times to reduce consumption as the world's resources are being devoured. And, inflation won't always stay as low as we'd like, so the buyer will need to stay knowledgeable about global supply!

Becoming a globally oriented purchasing supply expert offers the purchasing manager a direct shot at joining the company's top planning councils. The opportunity to overview the global economy and understand the financial implications is important. Within their own companies, buyers are exposed to every other department to some degree. In fact, buyers work with different people with varying temperaments both *within and outside* their companies. Daily, potential disputes and supply problems provide a challenge.

As companies rise to the challenge to better compete and sell abroad, quality of product, manufacturing, cost to make versus buy, and purchasing and supply management must be focal points of corporate strategy. Those companies that can deliver a product *anywhere* at the lowest possible cost will survive and grow, as others fall aside. Coping within an era of economic supply assurance requires an expanded purchasing outlook. How well economic supply assurance is accomplished will determine how American companies will survive in the marketplace.

Global buying requires a forward look. Purchasing must *foresee* and anticipate the shortages of supply materials and items. Economic power must be used to contract for and ensure supply first, seeking and finding new sources on a global basis. This need to look ahead, to plan and to manage, will continually engage purchasing and supply management.

Fortunately, the buyer is used to dealing in the future. He or she negotiates not for today, but for the circumstance that will exist when goods are delivered tomorrow. Buyers must be planners to be effective and successful. On the job daily, the buyer is future-oriented—today! It remains for buyers to broaden their vision, capability, and experience to cope with—or better yet, *master*—the challenges ahead.

The key to purchasing's future lies in creation of the future purchasing role to be played within the individual company. As much as we might not want to admit it, the fact is that top management is not interested in the optimization or the professionalization of purchasing as a primary focus! Facing that reality, we come to grips with the fact that top management is looking for you to contribute to the key business strategies and objectives—profits and growth, or such others as are pertinent to the overall business.

We conclude with the prediction that purchasing's star will be higher in the business firmament tomorrow than today! Whether you and I rise with it depends primarily on us and the role we choose to play. The opportunity is ours.

As we move into the next century, let's consider the importance of creating a vision and perspective for future action! In Chapter 1, we began with the analogy of the Apollo spaceship rocketing into the heavens and looking back at the Earth from a perspective never before seen. Remember that when our astronauts reached the moon, through TV's eye we shared the experience of looking back to see an "Earthrise." What a vision!

As we redefine purchasing in today's complex and dynamic global environment, we will need to proceed with flexibility and creativity—and vision! The purchasing manager must create the vision—for as the future of our vital function is conceived, so shall it be destined!

Appendix

This section contains three generic job descriptions: (1) Manager of Purchasing, (2) Buyer, and (3) Purchasing Engineer.

Manager of Purchasing

General Function

1. Reports to the Director of Purchasing. Handles special assignments as requested by the Director. Supports company policies and Director's philosophy of purchasing.

2. Reports on developments and offers advice on management matters; helps the Director weigh facts to reach decisions.

3. Directly supervises an Assistant Purchasing Manager, three Senior Buyers, five Buyers, Engineering Research, Engineering Liaison and Buying; Byproducts specialist, and clerical help.

4. Responsible for volume of purchases of about $50 million of production material annually. Responsible for raw material, nonferrous and steel, all castings, and other mechanical items. Creates at all times a purchasing image of service to the company. As a representative of the company to the supplier salesman, the manager should convey the image of buying quality products that make up the company's fine products. May often influence a future customer because of extensive acquaintance with supplier personnel.

5. Acts as Small Business Liaison Officer, and handles Environmental and Hazardous Materials, and other regulatory requirements by alerting proper company personnel.

Specific Duties

About 25 specific listings detailing responsibilities and tasks that are to be performed. For example, (1) Responsible for hiring and developing the buyer staff. (2) Supports a system of supplier rating and reports to management.

[There is no need to detail these, but indicate the scope of activities included in the job.]

Buyer

General Function

Performs buying assignments of a complex nature requiring experience in corporate purchasing policy and procedure.

Specific Duties

1. Searches continuously for improved and/or less costly materials and supplies within the classifications assigned to him/her.
2. Receives requisitions for materials and checks promptly for conformance to policies and requirements and, if necessary, checks back with department issuing requisition to get the best overall results.
3. Responsible for selecting sources of supply as follows:
    *   Through shopping for new items to be purchased.
    *   Through maintenance of information of suppliers stock lists, catalogues, price sheets, and discounts (in files, or preferably on a PC).
    *   Maintain information of prices, special agreements, and purchase order contracts.
    *   Closely tracks trade papers, catalogues, and other sources of information to be aware of new sources.
    *   Completes each requisition carefully by selecting the best source of supply, setting the price, terms, and other information needed.
    *   Interviews suppliers' representatives promptly and courteously.
    *   Communicates tactfully with sources of supply or potential sources to overcome misunderstandings, complaints, and the like, or to get further data about purchased items.
    *   Ensures supplier quality; checks rejections and advises supplier of the reasons for rejection, seeking prompt corrective action.
    *   Advises in-house users or customers of any changes in product including pricing that might influence decisions.
    *   Performs miscellaneous assignments as required.

Purchasing Engineer

Immediate Supervisor: Director of Purchasing

General Function

1. Supplies profit center personnel with purchasing information to improve their profitability, on such as purchased material variance data, possible areas of savings, price trends, and important supplier data.
2. Supplies purchasing with profit center planning and project engineering data to gain lowest ultimate product cost.

Specific Duties

1. Conduct and follow-up worldwide source selection activities on all new product development programs.
   - Purchasing selection of supplier tooling to meet new products or quality specifications
   - Increasing supplier capacity to meet increased production requirements
   - Timely pilot parts to meet engineering test models
2. Develops new sources for existing or new components having limited sources of supply.
3. Serves as purchasing representative on wide range of engineering activities, such as standardization, value analysis, design reviews, and qualification boards.
4. Reviews and analyzes new engineering specifications. Provides suggestions for cost and quality improvement.
5. Assists in supplier review and approval of technical components. Analyzes supplier performance and initiates action to correct or improve quality, delivery, or price.
6. Resolves problems of a technical or quality nature with buyers and engineers or quality control representative.
7. Ensures coordination and integration of purchasing with engineering, manufacturing, quality, and others on vital technical information needs.
8. Assists all branch plants with new product introduction and items to be purchased and sourced.
9. Initiates and joins in providing technical assistance to buyers and engineers for the following programs to achieve the best possible values in purchased materials and components:

- Technical backup for supplier negotiations and source selection effort
- Make-versus-buy studies
- New product development teams
- All reviews of projects
- Procurement planning particularly where technical knowledge is needed
- Management staff meetings as required.
- Product change activity
- Value engineering studies and teams.
- Standardization efforts
- Single source elimination
- Specification analysis

10. Reviews engineering material cost estimates of purchased materials and components to ensure they are accurate and meet targeted goal when in production, and that consideration is given to availability of design parts, new materials, tooling, and equipment. Also considers supplier capability and capacity to provide needed materials or parts.

11. Performs miscellaneous duties as required.

Nature of the Job

Primary function is to promote early application of engineering department efforts toward qualification of components and materials in product designs to maximize the company's purchasing power. Job involves coordination of a large number of individual goals toward effective component specifications allowing lowest total cost of purchases. Plans of action must be initiated, alternates explored, and best course selected.

Contacts with Others

Regular contact with buyers, engineers, quality, and manufacturing engineers. Frequent contact with suppliers' technical and sales people. Occasional travel to key suppliers is expected. Persistent follow through is required. About 80% of the activities will be interrelated with others so good personal relationships are critical.

Supervision

Primarily an individual contributor

Desirable Background and Experience

A college technical education or equivalent is necessary. Experience related to company's products and design is important. Must be able to support and guide engineering decisions during product design and qualification. Should be analytical, and use selling techniques in achieving goals.

Performance Criteria

1. Savings and cost reductions resulting from position activities
2. Improvement in relations with own engineers/buyers and other technical people as well as supplier personnel (scale of 1 to 10)

Selected Bibliography

Ammer, Dean S. 1980. *Materials Management and Purchasing,* 4th ed., Richard D. Irwin, Inc., Homewood, IL.

Baker, R., Buddress, L., Kuehne R. 1992. *Policy and Procedures Manual for Purchasing and Materials Control,* 2nd ed., 350 pages.

Barlow, C. Wayne and Eisen, Glenn P. 1983. *Purchasing Negotiations,* CBI Publishing Co., Boston, MA.

Bierman, Edward J. 1988. *C.P.M. Study Guide,* National Association of Purchasing Management, Tempe, AZ.

Cavinato, J. L. 1984. *Purchasing and Materials Management,* West Publishing Co., St. Paul, MN 55164, 475 pages.

Dobler, D. Burt, and Lee, L. 1990. *Purchasing and Materials Management Texts and Cases,* 5th ed., McGraw-Hill, New York, 843 pages.

Doust, S. R. 1987. *Basics for buyers* (training manual), 261 pages.

Doust, S. R. 1987. *More Basics for Buyers,* 261 pages.

Fearon, H. E., Dobler, D. W., Killen, K. H. 1992. *Purchasing Handbook,* 5th ed., (Formerly *Aljian's Handbook*), McGraw-Hill, New York, 907 pages.

Heinritz, S., Farrell, P. V., Giunipero, L. C., Kolchin, M. G. 1991. *Purchasing Principles and Applications*, 8th ed., Prentice-Hall, Englewood Cliffs, NJ, 580 pages.

Leenders, M. R., and Fearon, H. E. 1993. *Purchasing and Materials Management*, 10th ed., 672 pages.

Magad, E. L., and Amos, J. M. 1989. *Total Materials Management*, Van Nostrand Reinhold, New York, 551 pages.

Monckza, R. M. and Giunipero, L. C. 1990. *Purchasing Internationally: Concepts and Principles.* Bookcrafters, Chelsea, MI.

Murray, John E. 1975. *Purchasing and the Law,* Purchasing Management Association of Pittsburgh, PA.

Pooler, V. H. 1991. *Global Purchasing: Reaching for the World,* Rutledge, Chapman & Hall, New York, 266 pages.

Pooler, V. H. 1987. *Purchasing: Balancing Price and Value,* American Supply Education Foundation, Inc., Chicago.

Pooler, V. H. 1985. Purchasing Management. Purchasing section in *Handbook for Professional Managers,* Lester R. Bittel and Jackson E. Ramsey (eds.), McGraw Hill, New York, pp. 1016–1025.

Pooler, V. H. and David J. 1981. Purchasing's Elusive Conceptual Home. NAPM's *Journal of Purchasing and Materials Management* (Summer issue), pp. 13–18.

Pooler, V. H. 1978. Movie *TREND: Measuring Purchasing Productivity.* 1987 Revised VHS editions. PAL 30. NAPM, New York.

Pooler, Victor H. and Robert Johnson. 1976. *Fundamentals of Effective Purchasing,* Program Instruction Course. Argyle, New York.

Pooler, V. H. 1973. Measuring the Purchasing Man: TREND. *Journal of Purchasing and Materials Management,* Vol. 9, No. 4, November, pp. 68–85.

Pooler, V. H. 1964. *The Purchasing Man and His Job,* American Management Association, New York.

Pooler, V. H. 1964. Developing the Negotiation Skills of the Buyer, American Management Association *AMA Bulletin #50.*

Pooler, V. H. 1966. TREND: Total Approach to Measuring Purchasing Performance. *Purchasing,* May, pp. 54–61.

Pooler, V. H. 1967. AMA Training recording and manual *Listen in on Purchasing,* American Management Association, New York.

Pooler, V. H. 1978. Purchasing Management. In *Encyclopedia of Professional Management,* Lester R. Bittel (ed.), McGraw-Hill, New York, pp. 1016–1025.

Pooler, V. H. 1970 & 1980. Contributor to: *AMA Management Handbook.* Also to McGraw-Hill's *Purchasing Handbook.*

Pooler, V. H. 1962. Can Vendors Really Be Rated? *Purchasing,* June 18.

Pooler, V. H. 1960. Can We Measure Purchasing Efficiency? *Purchasing,* January 18.

Pooler, V. H. 1961. How to Use the Learning Curve. *Purchasing,* July 17.

Pooler, V. H. 1962. Is Value Analysis a Fad? *Purchasing,* March 26.

Pooler, V. H. 1986. Ten Rules for Offshore Buys Will Help Get You Started. *Purchasing,* October, p. 62A21.

Pooler, V. H. 1987. How to Construct a Library of Valuable Information Sources. *Purchasing,* Feb. 26, p. 97.

Pooler, V. H. 1987. Understanding the Options When You Choose a Buying Channel. *Purchasing,* June 11, p. 130A35.

Pooler, V. H. 1987. More Options to Fill Out the Buying Channels Picture. *Purchasing,* Sept. 24, p. 98A16.

Pooler, V. H. 1988. Know the Laws of the Lands When You Start Global Sourcing. *Purchasing,* Jan. 28, p. 34B35.

Pooler, V. H. 1988. Standard Transportation Terms Are Recognized Worldwide. *Purchasing,* July 28, p. 121.

Pooler, V. H. 1988. Customs Brokers Take Big Load Off Importing Buyers' Shoulders. *Purchasing,* Nov. 10, p. 96C8.

Pooler, V. H. 1988. Don't Be Backward About Starting with a Forwarder. *Purchasing,* September, p. 96.

Pooler, V. H. 1989. Buyers Should Know How to Make Letters of Credit Work for Them. *Purchasing,* March 9, p. 93.

Pooler, V. H. 1989. You Can't Duck Documentation, So You'd Better Understand It. *Purchasing,* March 23, p. 129.

Pooler, V. H. 1989. Methods of Payment Deserve Close Look on Offshore Buys. *Purchasing,* May 4, p. 96B31

Pooler, V. H. 1989. You May Have to Put a Different Spin on Some of the Traditional Terms. *Purchasing,* July 20, p. P100A9.

Pooler, V. H. 1989. Stateside Buying Terms Can Be Adapted for Use Overseas. *Purchasing,* July 24, p. 100A9.

Pooler, V. H. 1990. Watertight Contracts Keep Offshore Buys from Harm. *Purchasing,* April 19, p. 134.

Pooler, V. H. 1990. Understanding Import Duties is First Step to the Best Deal. *Purchasing,* May 3, p. 84A12.

Ritterskamp, Jr., James J. 1987. *The Purchasing Manager's Desk Book of Purchasing Law.*

Ritterskamp, James J., Jr., Abbott, Forrest L., Ahrens, Bert C. 1961. *Purchasing for Educational Institutions,* Bureau of Publications, Teacher's College, Columbia University, New York.

Sherman, Stanley. 1985. *Government Procurement Management*, 2nd ed. Woodcrafters Publications. Gaithersburg, MD.

Zenz, Gary J. 1987. *Purchasing and Management of Materials,* 6th ed. John Wiley, New York.

The following can be ordered from the ICC Publishing Corp., 156 Fifth Avenue, Suite 820, New York, NY 10010. (212) 206-1150

ICC INCOTERMS: International Rules for the Interpretation of Trade Terms. 1986. ICC Services, Paris, 135 pages.

Rules for the ICC Court of Arbitration (rules and schedule of conciliation and costs). No. 291, 34 pages.

Introduction to ICC Rules on International Contracts. Points to be considered in negotiating international trade contracts.

Standard Forms for Issuing Documentary Credits. Uniform customs practice and banking information. Primarily of use in explaining use of documentary credits, No. 323. Some banks have this available free.

U.S. Government Printing Office

The following are for sale by the Supt. of Documents, U.S. Government Printing Office (GPO), Washington DC 20402:

Importing into the United States. Describes the customs organization and procedures to follow when importing goods into the U.S. It covers clearance, entry of goods, duty assessment, invoices, marking, special laws, and foreign trade zones. Customs publication No. 504 for sale by Department of the Treasury, Bureau of Customs, Washington DC 20229 and GPO.

Guide to the U.S. Generalized System of Preferences. 1988. Office of the President, U.S. Trade Representative, Washington DC GPO 271

Harmonized Tariff Schedules of the United States (HTSUSA). 19 (latest) (Loose-Leaf edition of U.S. Customs Regulations). Lists all articles imported into the U.S. Published by the U.S. International Trade Commission, Washington, DC 20436. It can be purchased from the Superintendent of Documents and can be found in most large public libraries.

Index

Biographies of the Authors

Victor H. Pooler

Victor H. Pooler, C.P.M., P.E., is President of Pooler & Associates 1986–1994, a New York consulting firm specializing in purchasing and materials management projects. Prior to forming his own company, Mr. Pooler was Director of Purchasing for the Carrier Division of United Technologies Corporation. He also served as an engineer and senior buyer with the Ingersoll–Rand Co. He has a BSME degree from the University of Maine and is a licensed Professional Engineer, and a lifetime Certified Purchasing Manager.

Mr. Pooler has written extensively in the areas of purchasing and supply management, value analysis and value engineering, and international buying, culminating in the publication of four books and more than sixty articles.

The recipient of the Shipman Gold Medal, the highest national honor in purchasing, Mr. Pooler held many National Association of Purchasing Management posts, including the National Professional Certification board chairman and national Vice President. He served as an adjunct professor at Syracuse University and its International Management School where he taught and lectured on procurement and materials management. The author writes from an industrial and commercial background, and also has wide experience with military type government contract buying.

He has conducted seminars for numerous corporations and lectured for universities, as well as having developed programs for:

World Trade Institute at the World Trade Center

National Association of Purchasing Management

American Management Association

The American Supply Education Foundation

Mr. Pooler has written training movies, tapes, and video programs for the NAPM and AMA. He has lectured extensively for many years. Travelling to over 30 countries, he has presented programs throughout Europe, Scandinavia, and India.

David J. Pooler

David J. Pooler is currently Vice President, Global Business Development for Tactech, Inc., a computer services firm based in Yorba Linda, CA. Prior to joining Tactech in 1996, Mr. Pooler held senior management positions within both Textron Marine and Land Systems and General Dynamics Corporation. Most recently with Textron, he was the Director of International Offset and Trade Development, where he was responsible for the negotiation and execution of the company's worldwide offset and countertrade obligations. He holds both B.S. in Business Administration and Masters of Business Administration degrees from the University of Maine.

Mr. Pooler's background with Textron was preceded by 15 years experience with General Dynamics in both international business development and purchasing capacities. His purchasing background is extensive, having conducted buying missions around the world, and coordinated purchasing activities across this diverse $10 billion corporation.

Beginning as a buyer of electronic components, Mr. Pooler ultimately achieved the position of Corporate Director of Procurement and Subcontracts for General Dynamics. In this capacity, he was responsible for worldwide purchases in excess of $5 billion annually, and coordinated the buying activities of 12 major manufacturing divisions.